Constructing a Religiously Ideal "Believer" and "Woman" in Islam

Palgrave Series in Islamic Theology, Law, and History

This ground-breaking series, edited by one of the most influential scholars of Islamic law, presents a cumulative and progressive set of original studies that substantially raise the bar for rigorous scholarship in the field of Islamic Studies. By relying on original sources and challenging common scholarly stereotypes and inherited wisdoms, the volumes of the series attest to the exacting and demanding methodological and pedagogical standards necessary for contemporary studies of Islam. These volumes are chosen not only for their disciplined methodology, exhaustive research, or academic authoritativeness, but also for their ability to make critical interventions in the process of understanding the world of Islam as it was, is, and is likely to become. They make central and even pivotal contributions to understanding the experience of the lived and living Islam, and the ways that this rich and creative Islamic tradition has been created and uncreated, or constructed, deconstructed, and reconstructed. In short, the volumes of this series are chosen for their great relevance to the many realities that shaped the ways that Muslims understand, represent, and practice their religion, and ultimately, to understanding the worlds that Muslims helped to shape, and in turn, the worlds that helped shaped Muslims.

Series Editor:

Khaled Abou El Fadl is the Omar and Azmeralda Alfi Distinguished Professor in Islamic Law at the UCLA School of Law, and Chair of the Islamic Studies Program at UCLA. Dr. Abou El Fadl received the University of Oslo Human Rights Award, the Leo and Lisl Eitinger Prize in 2007, and was named a Carnegie Scholar in Islamic Law in 2005. He is one of the world's leading authorities on Islamic law and Islam, and a prominent scholar in the field of human rights.

Titles:

Custom in Islamic Law and Legal Theory: The Development of the Concepts of 'Urf and 'Adah in the Islamic Legal Tradition
  Ayman Shabana
The Islamic Law of War: Justifications and Regulations
  Ahmed Al-Dawoody
Shi'i Jurisprudence and Constitution: Revolution in Iran
  Amirhassan Boozari
Constructing a Religiously Ideal "Believer" and "Woman" in Islam:
Neo-traditional Salafi and Progressive Muslims' Methods of Interpretation
  Adis Duderija

Constructing a Religiously Ideal "Believer" and "Woman" in Islam

Neo-traditional Salafi and Progressive Muslims' Methods of Interpretation

Adis Duderija

palgrave
macmillan

First published in 2011 by
PALGRAVE MACMILLAN®
in the United States—a division of St. Martin's Press LLC,
175 Fifth Avenue, New York, NY 10010.

Where this book is distributed in the UK, Europe and the rest of the world,
this is by Palgrave Macmillan, a division of Macmillan Publishers Limited,
registered in England, company number 785998, of Houndmills,
Basingstoke, Hampshire RG21 6XS.

Palgrave Macmillan is the global academic imprint of the above companies
and has companies and representatives throughout the world.

Palgrave® and Macmillan® are registered trademarks in the United States,
the United Kingdom, Europe and other countries.

ISBN: 978–0–230–12057–0

Library of Congress Cataloging-in-Publication Data

Duderija, Adis, 1977–
    Constructing a religiously ideal "believer" and "woman" in Islam :
    neo-traditional Salafi and progressive Muslims' methods of
    interpretation / Adis Duderija.
        p. cm.—(Palgrave series in islamic theology, law, and history)
        Includes bibliographical references.
        ISBN 978–0–230–12057–0
        1. Women in Islam. 2. Women (Islamic law) 3. Salafiyah. 4. Islamic
    modernism. I. Title.

BP173.4.D83 2011
297.082—dc22   2011012451

A catalogue record of the book is available from the British Library.

Design by Newgen Imaging Systems (P) Ltd., Chennai, India.

First edition: October 2011

10 9 8 7 6 5 4 3 2 1

Printed in the United States of America.

This book is dedicated to my young daughter Layla Duderija (b. February 16, 2008) and my even younger son Fahim Duderija (b. November 26, 2010) with the hope that they will grow up to be people committed to and contributing to the realization of the ideals of justice, equality, and libratory knowledge in a world where every human being can reach his or her full potential.

Contents

Series Editor Preface

There is a growing number of academic studies on contemporary Islamic thought published in the West each year. Yet despite the sharp increase in books that attempt to study the works of modern Muslim theologians and jurists, only a few of these studies manage to offer original insights on the normative assumptions and choices made by the internal participants to the current Muslim discourse. Fewer still are successful in analytically engaging the internal debates of contemporary Muslims on their own terms without projecting onto these debates assumptions and values that inevitably distort and even misrepresent them. It is the relative absence of sound and thorough scholarship in this critical and timely field that makes this book by Adis Duderija so compellingly necessary.

This book, which is the fourth in the Palgrave Series in Islamic Theology, Law, and History, is remarkable in its breadth and depth. The author takes on the formidable task of analyzing the thought of the most influential and important orientations in contemporary Islamic thought: what the author calls the neo-traditional and progressive orientations. The author focuses on a pivotal issue that oddly enough has received but scant attention in non-Muslim and Muslim scholarly analysis. In an admirably tight and rigorous exposition, the author investigates the methodologies deployed by the representative participants of each orientation in understanding, narrating, and representing the role and meaning of the Qur'anic text and traditions of the Prophet, his family, and companions. The author carefully and systematically unpacks the methodologies that define how various theological and legal thinkers relate to the Islamic tradition and its role and relationship to the contemporary realities and challenges of the world today. One of the truly valuable contributions of this book is the author's analysis of the epistemological, hermeneutical, and moral assumptions at the core and foundations of the methodologies employed by the proponents of each orientation. The author ably demonstrates the extent to which normative moral and epistemological assumptions dramatically influence the methodologies of each orientation and indeed, the very attitude and way that they understand, conceptualize, and construct the Islamic tradition and its normative role in the modern world. Perhaps the most original and profound contribution of this book is the author's eye-opening analysis of the ways that the two main orientations have contrasting conceptions or constructions of the prototypical Muslim believer and of the normative commitments expected or anticipated from such a believer. The author also convincingly demonstrates that the imagined and constructed conceptions of "the Muslim believer" have a direct effect upon the adoption of the normative assumptions at the heart of a particular orientation's methodology in dealing with and interacting with the text. Indeed, this is the first systematic study to explore the intricate and necessary relationship between the theological conception of the believer, as the prototype for the pious and orthodox Muslim, and the methodologies per which the religious text is understood and represented.

This book is a must-read for students of contemporary Muslim thought, and it is also a necessary study for readers interested in the future of Islamic movements, institutions, and the possibilities of reform. But beyond the field of Islamic Studies, all readers interested in questions of authenticity, legitimacy, and the construction of religious meaning in the modern world will find the contributions of this work invaluable for any comparative understanding of the role of religious texts in negotiating between, on the one hand, the normative impact of tradition and history, and on the other, the contingencies and imperatives of the present. As this book powerfully demonstrates, stereotypical generalizations about the avowed determinism of Islamic texts or the determinative role of revelation in Islam are to say the least deeply problematic. Like other religious traditions wrestling with the same issues, Muslims struggle to anchor themselves in a perceived orthodoxy and authenticity as they confront and negotiate the numerous challenges of modernity and post-modernity.

The Palgrave Series in Islamic Theology, Law, and History endeavors to publish works that make truly original and indispensable contributions to understanding the internal micro-discourses and debates taking place within the Islamic tradition. This new study by the gifted young scholar, Adis Duderija, substantially raises the bar for all future studies dealing with the issues of fundamentalism, traditionalism, reformism, and authenticity and progress in Muslim thought. One of the most insightful and even startling contributions of this book is that it analytically and rigorously interrogates the claims of various and disparate Muslim participants that their thought and methodology authentically represents the religious truth of Islam—the religious truth as embodied in the text of the Qur'an and the oral traditions of the Prophet Muhammad. Upon reading this book, no Muslim or non-Muslim researcher will be able to rest with the superficial assumption that either the traditionalists or reformers are more genuinely anchored in the textualist sources of Islam. In my opinion, what makes this book a necessary read for any Muslim or non-Muslim interested in the future of Islam and Muslims is that it convincingly demonstrates the pivotal importance of scrutinizing the interpretive and constructive methodologies of Muslims competing to represent Islamic authenticity. Employing a scholarly methodology that is uncompromising in its objectivity, detachment, and rigor, Adis Duderija demonstrates that there is a considerable gap between dogmatic perceptions of legitimacy and authenticity, and the extent to which the methodologies employed by neo-traditionalists and progressives actually reflect normativities inherent or necessary to the religious foundational texts of Islam. At the very least, anyone reading this book will be forced to seriously re-examine their understanding of the dynamics governing the relationship between critical conceptual categories such as orthodoxy, authenticity, tradition, and progress. The author of this book does not determine who authentically speaks for modern Islam. But he does invite Muslims and non-Muslims alike to a serious critical engagement with the value choices and coherence of various participants claiming to represent Islamic normativities in the world today.

Khaled Abou El Fadl
Los Angeles, California
April 2011

Acknowledgments

There are a number of people without whose consistent support this book would not have been possible. First of all, I would like to express my deep gratitude to my parents Zehra and Dervis Duderija and to my brother Ismar Duderija for all of the sacrifices they made to enable and assist me in my academic interests. I would also like to thank my lovely wife Sri Megawati for her unflinching support for my academic endeavors and her belief in me. My many thanks go to Professor Khaled Abou El Fadl who enthusiastically proposed and embraced the idea of this book. I would also like to acknowledge the financial contribution provided by the Centre for Muslim States and Societies (The University of Western Australia) and its founding director Professor Samina Yasmeen.

My thanks also go to my professor Samina Yasmeen for having confidence in me very early on in my aspirations to become an academic.

Introduction

Background to Study

This study identifies, compares, and contrasts the interpretational models governing Neo Traditional Salafi (NTS) and progressive Muslims' approaches (*manahij/manhaj*)[1] to conceptualizing and interpreting the Qur'an and Sunna and the assumptions that inform these *manahij*. The study also examines what the interpretational *implications* of these assumptions governing the NTS and progressive Muslims' *manahij* are in relation to their respective interpretations of what is believed to constitute a religiously ideal "Believer" and "Muslim Woman" concepts.

The broader contexts of this study are the contemporary intra-Muslim debates on the issues of religious authenticity, legitimacy, and the authority to speak for, and thus, define the very nature and future of Islam and the growing awareness of the contested nature of the Islamic tradition (*turath*).[2] These intra-traditional debates are fuelled by forces of modernization and globalization[3] and for Muslim minorities living in the West with social dynamics of belonging to a new immigrant minority religion.[4] The resultant democratization of religious knowledge and the fragmentation of religious authority has engendered a situation in which an increasing number of Muslims are participating in the debates on "normative" Islam.[5] By *normative* I mean an Islam based on the teachings of the Qur'an and Sunna however differently they might be conceptualized and interpreted and the discourses surrounding questions of the authoritative interpretation of them. The tragic events of 9/11 have further intensified these debates, resulting in strong polarizations of Muslim opinion often framed in terms of the divide between the "moderates" and "fundamentalists."[6] As a corollary, a plethora of communities of interpretation[7] and religious groups have emerged among contemporary Muslim groups all claiming authoritativeness.[8] This study discusses two of these two contemporary Muslim communities of interpretation termed here NTS and progressive Muslims. As such, the two communities of interpretation that are the focus of this study are not to be seen as somehow objectively detached from the debates on the questions of authenticity of the Islamic tradition, but each, in their own way, wish to influence, shape, and help define it. Furthermore, it is not the intention of this study to advocate for preferability or superiority of one interpretative approach over the other but to identify and compare the assumptions governing the respective *manahij* and explain why they emerge.

The above succinctly stated context, in turn, has set into motion complex processes of contestation over religious authority and legitimacy and the appeal of various "communities of interpretation" to a number of "normative Islams." In this regard the issue of scriptural interpretation and hermeneutics has taken center stage.[9] In this context two issues explored in this study have drawn a lot of scholarly and nonscholarly attention. The first being the question of what constitutes a religiously ideal "Muslim Woman" concept in relation to the role and the status of Muslim women in (Islamic/ Muslim) societies, and the second being the issue of what the fountainheads of Islamic teachings, the Qur'an and the Sunna, say about the religious status of the religious Other, especially those belonging to Christians and Jewish communities of faith. By religious or salvific status here is meant what the boundaries of the concept of belief (*'iman*) in Islamic theology are, and, in particular, whether or not adherents of other religions can be considered either as Muslims (*muslimun*) in an nonreified sense of those 'who assent to God' and/or believers (*mu'minun*), who thus attain salvation. This is what I refer to as a concept of what it means to be a "Believer."

The current literature recognizes that divergent scripture interpretational models have been employed to construct variant, competing, and, at times, mutually exclusive conceptualizations of both of these concepts.[10] However, there are no existing studies that aim to identify and examine which presuppositions governing different scripture interpretational models may be responsible for the construction of competing concepts of what constitutes a religiously ideal "Muslim Woman" as well as a "Believer." In this context, in relation to what here is termed a "Muslim Woman" concept, Sharify-Funk alerts us that "much of the literature on women and Islam— especially literature critiquing Islamic forms of patriarchy—maintains a curious silence on matters of hermeneutics, in favour of a predominantly structuralist account of social change and contestation."[11] This study aims to break this silence in relation to two contemporary Muslim communities of interpretation, namely NTS and progressive Muslims. As such the study aims to answer the following questions:

1. What type of a religiously ideal "Muslim Woman" concept is conceptualized and advocated as normative by NTS and progressive Muslims?

2. How do the proponents of NTS and progressive Muslims define the scope of a "Believer" from a normative vantage point?
3. Which scripture interpretational models of the primary sources of Islamic thought, the Qur'an and the Sunna, may explain the formation of these concepts, and on what hermeneutical, epistemological, and methodological interpretational assumptions do they rest?

On the Study's Methodology

In order to answer the above posed questions, my methodology is based upon several sub-methodologies. With respect to the chapters dealing with NTS thought directly, I investigate the literature written by NTS scholars such as hadith scholar N. Al-Albanee[12] (d.1999), the former Saudi Arabian Mufti A. Bin Baz (d.1999), some of their prominent students such as M. Al-Madkhalee and M ibn Uthaymeen (d.2001), and, to a lesser extent,[13] their Western followers, which include the personalities such as Jamal Zarabozo and Dr. Bilal Philips. The chapters on progressive Muslim thought draw upon the works of leading progressive Muslim thinkers such as Khaled Abou El Fadl, Omid Safi, Farid Esack, Ebrahim Moosa, Kecia Ali, Amina Wadud, and others.

In chapters dealing with the issue of comparing and contrasting the NTS and progressive Muslims *manahij*, their assumptions, and interpretational implications, the study's methodology is to identify a number of criteria that *usul-ul-fiqh* theory encompasses, including sciences pertaining to the nature of language, theology,[14] hermeneutics, epistemology, law, and ethics, and to analyze the differences between the two *manahij*. The assumptions of the NTS and progressive Muslims *manahij* relate to the following issues:

- the function and nature of language in the Qur'anic text and the nature of Revelation;
- the process of derivation of meaning of the Qur'anic text;
- the extent of the recognition (or otherwise) of the role of context in the shaping of the Qur'anic content;
- the role, legitimacy, and scope of reason in Qur'anic interpretation and the nature of ethical value in the Qur'an;
- the extent of the employment of a thematic, corroborative-inductive (or systematic) approach to the Qur'an's interpretation or lack thereof of (i.e., prevalence of what here is termed *textual segmentalism*);

- the scope of an ethico-religious and purposive, or aim-based approach (*qasd*) to Qur'anic interpretation; and
- the nature and the scope of the concept of Sunna and its interpretational implications.

Here I draw upon the insights of relevant non-Muslim and Muslim scholarship by discussing the works of Wael Hallaq and Bernard Weiss, as well as of Fazrul Rahman, Hashim Kamali, A. K. Soroush, Nasr Hamid Abu Zayd, Muhammad Arkoun, Abdullah Saeed, Sherman Abdul Hakim Jackson, and others.

With respect to the concept of a "Believer," I do not only investigate how the relevant Qur'an and hadith body of texts are interpreted by NTS and progressive Muslims as based on their respective *manahij*, but I also briefly examine the recent scholarship that studies the emergence and evolution of the Muslim Self in relation to that of the Religious Other and the importance of the historical context in the same. This is so because not only is every discourse/text embedded in its broader sociohistorical context but also because, according to this body of scholarship, this context had a very important role in the emergence and the evolution of the Muslim confessional identity.

Another aspect of my methodology relates to the analytical and theoretical tenability of the very notion of a religiously ideal "Muslim Woman" concept. There are two analytical and theoretical considerations here. First, what does *religiously ideal* mean and how analytically useful is this analytical category, and second, how theoretically tenable is it to talk about a "concept" of a "Muslim Woman"?

I borrow the (limited) usefulness of a "religiously ideal" as an analytical category from F. Hussein who, in her introduction to the book *Muslim Women,* which she edited, draws a distinction between the *ideal* and the *contextual* realities of Muslim women. The former is based on what she terms *Islamic* norms and *Islamic* history—referring to the period of Qur'anic revelation and the lifetime of the Prophet— and the latter on *Muslim* history—the period subsequent to that of Islamic history, culture, and tradition, which she considers to have fallen well short of embodying or reflecting the Islamic norms and Islamic history.[15]Such a clear and neat distinction is clearly problematic in a number of ways. First, it tends to deemphasize the subjective nature of all interpretation and is seemingly based on the assumption that there exists a single, valid interpretation of Islam/Qur'an/Sunna. Second, it tends to obscure and downplay the importance of the idea of socially, politically, or culturally hegemonic or marginalized interpretations of religious traditions as a result of an aspect of power associated inherently with the process of interpretation. However, it is useful in a sense that it does provide us with a heuristic device not to conflate certain interpretations of the Qur'an and Sunna as being "divine" or "final." Importantly, it also enables the interpretational endeavor of offering alternative yet "authentic" faith-based interpretations that can resist and counteract hegemonic ones.

As far as the analytical tenability of the concept of a "Muslim Woman" is concerned, here I refer to the work of Miriam Cooke, who considers that this neologism is useful in contemporary discussions on Muslim women because it "draws attention to the emergence of a new singular religious and gendered identification that overlays national, ethnic, cultural, historical, and even philosophical diversity" by a variety of actors be they Islamist men, non-Muslims, Orientalists, or non-Muslim or Muslim states wishing to decide on behalf of Muslim women what's right and what's wrong for them.[16] She further argues that the concept of a "Muslimwoman," as a marker of exclusively ascribed collective identity that dispenses with and wishes to erase Muslim woman's individual identity by fusing its gender and religion aspects, is a potent cultural standard for the *umma*, the collective Muslim society worldwide. Although the concept of Cooke's "Muslimwoman" is rejected by some Muslim women and accepted by others, importantly, Cooke maintains, it is strategically employed by those who accept it in order to subvert the hegemonic discourses that deploy it.[17]

One way in which the act of subversion of this ascribed identity of Cooke's 'Muslimwoman' is being formulated is by means of novel faith-based Islamic feminist hermeneutics whose task is to develop interpretations of the Qur'an and Sunna that not only expose the patriarchal nature of much of the inherited Islamic tradition, especially in the fields of Qur'anic exegesis and Islamic jurisprudence, but also to develop alternative women liberatory interpretations.[18]

The role and status of women in a Muslim society are often described and sanctioned in religious terms by means of directly ascribing the role and status of women in a Muslim society to the Qur'an and the early Islamic traditions (hadith).[19] Based on the above considerations outlined by Cooke and the focus of this study being on the assumptions governing different scripture interpretational models (*manahij*) of the Qur'an and the Sunna, the notion of constructing a normative, religiously ideal concept of a "Muslim Woman" in this study refers to the methods of interpretation (*manahij*) of the Qur'anic and Sunna-based bodies of knowledge—or in the parlance of Islamic legal theory, the relevant textual indicants (*'adilla/dalil*) found in these sources—employed by NTS and progressive Muslims to formulate such a concept.

On what criteria can such a religiously ideal concept of a "Muslim Woman" be based?

The relevant contemporary literature on the role and the status of women in Muslim societies suggests that these discussions have been mainly framed in relation to issues of female sexuality, spousal rights and obligations in marriage, and the segregation of sexes. In relation to the last criterion, the practices of seclusion of women and certain styles of dressing, with the emphasis on the veil in particular, are employed frequently when discussing the role and the status of women in "Islam."[20] Other criteria such as employment and education are also mentioned but fall outside the scope of this study.[21]

For example, Hussein maintains that social problems relating to the role of an adult female in a Muslim society center not only on the veil and a woman's role as a wife and mother, but also on issues of marriage ,divorce, virginity, and sexual chastity.[22] Stowasser similarly frames the issue of women's status in Islamic society in terms of the separation of "the female world" (the home) from "the male word" (public affairs) by means of secluding and barring women from it. On the other hand, F. Mernissi alongside F. Sabbah, F. Malti-Douglas, A. Barlas, and K. Ali emphasize that certain views on the nature of female and male sexuality play an important part in the manner in which the status and the role of female in a Muslim society is conceptualized. Following these insights the criteria upon which the concept of a religiously ideal "Muslim Woman" is constituted are:

a. the nature of the female (and by implication male) sexuality;
b. role and function of women in broader society/public sphere, especially the purpose and function of seclusion and veiling for women; and
c. spousal rights and obligations, especially the role of the wife in marriage.

Now we turn our attention to the methodology of the study with respect to defining Muslim groups or ways of being a Muslim.

The task is fraught with problems. Which criteria can effectively achieve this task?

The basic premise of this study is that an important factor in forming views on a particular question pertaining to any issue relating to the Islamic tradition are the differences in the assumptions—methodological, ontological, hermeneutical, and epistemological—used in conceptualizing and interpreting the Qur'an and the Sunna. This study is also premised on the notion that it is important to consider the relationship of these differences to the larger, cumulative, and contested intellectual tradition of conceptualization and interpretation of the two sources. Another consideration that this study takes into account in relation to the question of defining Muslim groups is, as Kurzman argues, that various "socioreligious interpretations" of the Islamic tradition "overlap and intertwine and should not be considered mutually exclusive or internally homogenous but as *heuristic devices* which provide insight into the history of Islamic discourse."[23] As such neither NTS nor progressive Muslims should be seen as *entirely* internally homogeneous groups or as rigid categories but that the concept of progressive Muslim or NTS thought should primarily be seen as a *heuristic tool* that may be used to define and delineate a particular type or way of being a Muslim. Since the focus of this study is primarily textual/interpretational in so far as it focuses on the study of texts, it conceptualizes, classifies, and refers to NTS and progressive Muslims primarily as "communities of interpretations" and aims to delineate their features, especially, but not only, in relation to the assumptions that govern their respective *usul-ul-fiqh manahij* but also with reference to the validity, or otherwise, of the various sciences underpinning the modern episteme in interpreting the Qur'an and the Sunna.

As it is widely held, the meaning of texts and its derivation is formed within the context of interpretative communities, which can be historical, sociological, or textual. What is common and thus gives rise to these communities is the fact that they "share certain epistemological assumptions, concerns and basic values." This, in turn, enables them to "share and objectify their own subjective experiences by sharing particular epistemological assumptions, linguistic practice and/or overlapping way of talking about meaning." Communities of interpretation, however, "do not necessarily agree on a whole host of determinations of meaning."[24] Resultantly, an individual scholar considered to be belonging to a certain community of interpretation need not necessarily self-identify with it as long as her *manhaj* assumptions are found to be in agreement it.[25] As a corollary, this study's heuristic regarding the question of "defining" groups and the related issue of "representativeness" is that it is the *manhaj* assumptions that serve as a ultimate criterion for these purposes. As such the study does not offer a fixed definition of NTS and progressive Muslims (if such a thing was possible in the first place). Instead, it identifies the delineating features of their respective interpretational assumptions that characterize their *manahij* in order to demarcate each interpretative community and distinguish it from another.

Before I provide the outline of the chapters that make up this study, the following section discusses some of them most important works that are closely related to it.

Review of Literature

I) *Works on women and gender Islam with special focus on those that discuss the issue in relation to methodologies of interpretation*
Today there exists a very sizeable amount of literature written on the issue of women and gender in Islam. Here I solely focus on works that discuss the issue from an Islamic feminist hermeneutics perspective. I define Islamic feminist hermeneutics as a body of scholarship that advocates for gender equality and women's legal rights from *within* the Islamic epistemic and methodological framework by systematically deriving and justifying these rights on the basis of a particular conceptualization and interpretation of the inherited Islamic tradition, especially its primary fountainheads, the Qur'an and Sunna.

This approach was ushered in earnest by the work of an African American Muslim convert by the name of Amina Wadud with her book *The Qur'an and Woman: Rereading the Sacred Text from a Woman's Perspective*, written in 1992.[26] In her preface to the book's 1999 edition, the author gives us an insight into the various methodological and hermeneutical principles and strategies she employed in the book in order to develop a female inclusive Qur'anic exegesis. These pertain to questions such as the nature of (Arabic) language, derivation of meaning, and philology. The first such principle she calls the "hermeneutics of tawhid," which emphasizes a "holistic" approach to the Qur'anic discourse based upon its textual "unity" in contrast to what she terms an "atomistic" approach, a term borrowed from a modernist Muslim scholar F. Rahman.[27] Making a systematic distinction between "fundamental" and "unchangeable" Qur'anic "universals" and "particulars" by means of its comprehensive contextualization so that each Qur'anic term can "be examined on the basis of its language act, syntactical structures, and textual context in order to more fully determine [its] parameters of meaning"[28] is another methodological tool employed in the work. Closely related to this is another hermeneutical strategy employed by Wadud, termed *textual development*. By textual development, Wadud wishes to alert the reader/interpreter to be sensitive to how the Qur'anic text establishes new moral, social, and political trajectories that go beyond the literal and concrete meaning and searches for the underlying rational (*ratio*), or what F. Rahman has termed the *élan*, or the spirit, of the Qur'an.[29]

The notion of new moral trajectories leads Wadud to take a hermeneutical recourse to ethical principles such as equity, justice, and human rights as being constitutive of the Qur'anic ethos as well as being its hermeneutically most powerful principles of interpretation. Another important hermeneutical strategy noted by Wadud is the notion of textual silences or ellipses in the Qur'an, which, although not articulated in it, can be deduced from the Qur'an's existing structural forms that primarily exist as grammatical constructs. Wadud, in this context, pays close attention to the gender-specific language of the Qur'an, especially the grammatical constructs of female and male noun forms the Qur'an employs and their hermeneutical implications. In particular, Wadud does not consider the Qur'anic Arabic to be a sacred language per se. Instead she forms the view that its main function is to ensure its comprehensibility and that the gendered nature of the Arabic language ought not to restrict the meaning of a divine revelation. Wadud also shows awareness of the importance of the interpreter/reader in the process of interpretation and incorporates it into her hermeneutical model by referring to it as the "prior text." She defines *prior text* as "a language and cultural context in which the text is read."[30] Furthermore, Wadud considers that gender-specific language, such as Arabic, is responsible for creating particular "prior texts" that affect the Qur'an's interpretation. Finally, she also makes an important distinction between textual relativism and legitimate contextual readings of the Qur'an by acknowledging that textual relativism is curbed by the process of "points of convergence in interpretation." She summarizes her hermeneutical method in relation to the analysis of each Qur'anic verse in the following manner:

> In its context; in the context of discussions on similar topics in the Qur'an; in the light of similar language and syntactical structures used elsewhere in the Qur'an; in the light of overriding Qur'anic principles; and within the context of the Qur'anic Weltanschauung , or world-view.[31]

As the title of her book suggests, the scope of Wadud's methodology of interpretation is restricted to that of the Qur'an and Qur'anic exegesis in particular and is not informed by considerations relating to Sunna or to that of Islamic legal theory. As such it can only offer a partial understanding of how normative Muslim woman constructs are formulated.

A more recent influential addition to Muslim Qur'anic hermeneutics committed to gender justice is A. Barlas's *Believing Women in Islam: Unreading Patriarchal Interpretations of the Qur'an*.[32] The book purports to restore what the author views as the Qur'anic basis of sexual equality in Islam by freeing the Qur'an from the patriarchal nature of its classical and some modern exegesis (or, as Barlas would argue, eisegesis). She does so systematically on both historical and hermeneutical grounds.

On historical grounds, Barlas argues that the strong association between patriarchy evident in the most classical commentaries of the Qur'anic exegesis and the Qur'an itself (in the eyes of those who find the Qur'an to be a patriarchal text) is a result of the manner in which Muslim history has unfolded. This process was "central in determining and defining religious epistemology and methodology, thus also how Muslims came to read the Qur'an"[33] in a patriarchal mode. Barlas argues that the most crucial aspect of this process was the nature of the classical legal theory and its methodology of making the Qur'an depended on and dislodging its hermeneutical privilege vis-à-vis its own exegesis by that of the concept of Sunna, which was later conceptually conflated with the canonical ahadith body of literature. This, in turn, resulted in restricting the scope of the Qur'an's "authentic" or authoritative exegesis as well as its epistemological, methodological, and hermeneutical sources and techniques. Consequently, a certain type of intertextual dynamics came into place that made the Qur'an and its interpretation heavily dependent upon the so-called four sources hierarchical theory of a medieval Muslim scholar Shafi'i (d.204 AH) whose epistemologically, methodologically, and epistemologically anchoring precept were the authentic ahadith with, as far as the status of women is concerned, largely legally/hermeneutically inconsequential variances between different schools of thought (*madhahib*). Hadith literature and, by extension, *hadith*-based or tainted Qur'anic exegesis contain strong misogynistic elements and are thus, according to Barlas, the main culprit, based on the above mentioned classical legal theory method championed by Shafi'i, as to why the Qur'an was interpreted in a patriarchal manner. This is not the entire story, however. Barlas argues further that extratextual sources, meaning primarily the political state, were also responsible for ensuring that the patriarchal readings of the Qur'an quashed any egalitarian readings that might have emerged. In this context she asserts that

> the conservatism of Muslim tradition, method, and memory, I have suggested, can be ascribed to a specific configuration of political and sexual power that privileged the state over civil society, men over women, conservatism over egalitarianism, and some texts and methodologies over others."[34]

Contrary to the views expressed by some Muslim and non-Muslim scholars, or (Neo)-Orientalists, who consider the Qur'an as irredeemably patriarchal and claim that the only avenue of Muslim women emancipation can come by means of an epistemological rupture with the premodern Islamic tradition, Barlas develops a systematic "anti-patriarchal Qur'anic hermeneutic of liberation" to argue that the Qur'an can be:

1. Read in a sexually egalitarian manner (in the sense that "the Qur'an considers sex as irrelevant to moral agency") and
2. Moreover, that it is antipatriarchal in nature.

To demonstrate this, Barlas first develops a comprehensive definition of patriarchy as "a continuum at one end of which are misrepresentations of God as Father, and of fathers as rulers over wives and children, and at the other hand, the notion of sexual differentiation that is used to privilege males while otherizing women."[35]

Barlas puts in place a number of perceptive theological and methodological precepts in order to demonstrate that the Qur'an is antipatriarchal. Central to this is a theological argument/postulate derived from the Qur'an that Barlas terms "God's self-disclosure" that encompasses principles of Divine Unity, Justice, and Incomparability/Unrepresentativeness as the hermeneutically privileged site from which to read the Qur'an's antipatriarchal nature. Here Barlas links ontology with hermeneutics to argue that the Qur'anic God as manifest in God's self-disclosure does not advocate any of the patriarchal dimensions as found in her definition. Moreover, on this account, Barlas argues that the Qur'an can be seen as antipatriarchal because it insists on God's sovereignty. In this context, she maintains that "not only does Islamic monotheism, properly understood, serve to liberate women from the tyranny of male rule, but, by privileging the rights of God, it dislocates rule by the father as well as theories of male sovereignty, which are at the roots of women's oppression."[36]

Another methodological principle employed by Barlas to read the Qur'an for "liberation" is her subscription to the view of the polysemic nature of the Qur'anic text, which she uses to argue that the Qur'an may be read in a number of different contextually legitimate ways, patriarchal *as well as* liberatory modes. Barlas also utilizes the intra-Qur'anic hermeneutical principle of reading for best meanings and textual holism to argue that the Qur'an cannot advocate *zulm* (injustice) against women as in the case of patriarchy. Another methodological principle she employs can be described as "comprehensive textualization," or a historical approach to Qur'anic interpretation. This comprehensive contextualization heuristic, which again can be traced to the works of F. Rahman,[37] consists of two elements, as identified by Barlas: reading behind the text, that is reconstructing the historical context from which the text emerged, and reading in front of the text, that is, re-contextualizing the text in light of present needs.[38]

Faced by the conundrum of the Qur'an's *own potential* responsibility for its misreading, in the postscript, Barlas develops a theory of textual responsibility underpinned by the abovementioned methodological and theological principles to argue that the Qur'an both anticipated its misreading and formulated a "hermeneutic" for its own proper reading (for best meaning and textual holism) and as such cannot be held responsible for the abuses of its signs.

Unlike Wadud, Barlas's hermeneutic does take into account the role of Sunna and hadith in gender justice sensitive Qur'anic hermeneutics. Unlike the vast majority of scholars writing on the issue of Sunna in Islamic legal theory, she does draw some important distinctions between the Sunna and hadith concepts and, more particularly, between Sunna of the Prophet and the Sunna of the Medinian community. However, her concept of Sunna is still epistemologically and methodologically dependent upon the hadith body of literature and conceptually divorced from the Qur'an. This has important implications insofar as it identifies misogynist elements of hadith with the Sunna that, in turn, based on the widely accepted classical legal theory maxim, discussed by Barlas in length, of the Qur'an's hermeneutical dependency on Sunna, infects Qur'anic *tafsir* with misogynistic elements. This study does make this very important epistemological and methodological distinction, which, as demonstrated in the fourth and the seventh chapters, has very important hermeneutical implications as to how normative concepts of a "Muslim Woman" and a "Believer" are formulated.

Another dimension that is lacking in Barlas's study is that it does not discuss the question of the nature of ethical value in the Qur'an and its ethicolegal philosophy. This is a significant omission because, as Abdullah Saeed has demonstrated,[39] any systematic hermeneutic needs to, at least partially, be anchored in certain ethical values or principles. Barlas does take hermeneutical recourse to the concept of God's justice as being one important facet of God's self-disclosure. However, the questions of the nature of God's justice and whether, from the Qur'anic perspective, it is to be understood in ethically objectivist or voluntarist terms are not addressed. In this context, Barlas just laments in the postscript[40] that Muslims, despite the Qur'an's emphasis on justice and its condemnation of *zulm*, have read the Qur'an in a way that has done *zulm* unto women. This discussion of the nature of ethical values and its hermeneutical importance in the NTS and progressive Muslims *manahij* will be discussed in more detail in the fourth (NTS) and sixth (progressive Muslims) chapters, respectively.

Lastly, Barlas's above mentioned historical description of why the Qur'an was read in patriarchal modes, although grounded in a large body of scholarly work of the highest caliber, is completely founded on the premise that the Islamic tradition was based on a written discourse or texts. As such, it misses an important dimension: that of orality and its function in religious discourses, and how orality shaped Islamic disciplines such as *tafsir*, law, and legal theory. Orality is just mentioned in reference to the distinction between the Qur'an as oral discourse based on divine revelation and that as text (*mushaf*) by primarily drawing on the scholarship of M. Arkoun.[41]

However, this distinction is not developed further or employed to argue for the importance of orality in Islamic tradition including hermeneutics, *tafsir,* and/or legal theory, something that this study does take into account.

Another important contribution on the issue under discussion from a hermeneutical perspective is the work of Khaled Abou El Fadl titled *Speaking in God's Name: Islamic Law, Authority and Women.* The author of the book is calling for the return to the archetype ethicomoral premises governing early traditional Islamic juristic practice and resistance to and the deconstruction of the dominant contemporary "Wahhabo-Salafi" authoritarian approaches toward interpreting God's signs/indicators (*'adillah/dalil*), especially in relation to the status and role of women in Islam and Islamic law. The overall theme of the book is a strong criticism of contemporary authoritarian, and what the book's author considers intellectually dishonest juristic practices that, according to him, have corrupted the integrity of Islamic legal heritage and that threaten to disintegrate and abandon the traditional premises on which the Islamic law was constructed.[42]

Having defined the nature of and critically analyzed primary textual sources of Islamic jurisprudence, El Fadl concludes that for numerous reasons (which will be discussed subsequently) a current authoritarian reading (vs. authoritative-deemed necessary for pragmatic reasons) of the sources of Islamic law is not warranted. To substantiate this claim El Fadl cites Qur'anic verses upholding the principle of God's Sovereignty and Omnipotence and the ontological relationship between The Creator and the created, namely that of the Lord and His vicegerent. In this context, he claims that due to this very hierarchy in the natural order, the human representatives of God on Earth can never self-identify themselves with God's intent or profess to have grasped His Knowledge beyond any shadow of doubt or ambiguity, a practice that has, in his opinion, become quite widespread among present-day authorities on religious issues. In contrast, the author asserts that the prevalent Wahhabo-Salafi "authoritarian hermeneutics," is oblivious to the intricate and subtle relationships existing between the author, text, and the reader regulating "the determinacy of meaning" of God's indicators, thus is guilty of equating the author's intent with that of the reader, thereby violating the principles inherent to the Qur'anic *Weltanschauung* and its ethicoreligious foundation.

El Fadl, on the other hand, proposes a more balanced approach when engaging in the task of interpreting texts such as the Qur'an in which neither the author's intent nor the language nor the reader have the upper hand in determining its meaning. It is the balance between these three, which upholds the "inherent ambiguity" embedded in the textual sources, thus acting as an antiauthoritarian interpretative measure. Thereby El Fadl advocates what Umero Eco has termed as "an open" (versus closed) interpretation that is capable of sustaining "multiple interpretative strategies."[43]

Another element in his conceptual framework aiming to analyze "the theory of authority within Islamic tradition and its misinterpretation/ misuse in contemporary setting" pertains to the notion of what El Fadl terms as "multiple authorship" and "authorial enterprise" considered to be inherent in hadith literature. The unsuitability of an authoritarian approach to ahadith interpretation, the author argues, does not only rest on the premises established by the traditional *ulum-ul-hadith* but also on the notion that sayings attributed to the Prophet are result of "what a number of Companions have seen/heard, recollected, selected, transmitted and authenticated in a non-objective medium" (multiple authorship). Thus, in each report a "personality of the transmitter is indelibly imprinted upon the report" (authorial enterprise).[44] In other words each hadith report is constitutive of multiple authorship and is a result of authorial enterprise to which the Prophet is to varying extents related. As such one can never attribute a particular hadith *completely* to the actual words of the Prophet himself. To disregard the importance of these principles and the sociohistorical circumstances in which the genesis of many Prophetic reports took place, without scrutinizing the validity and reliability of processes pertaining to mechanisms inherent in evolution, shaping and forming of ahadith literature and in addition to lack of moral insight to guide this process when interpreting the same, -the practice El Fadl accuses many contemporary *ulama,* especially those based in Saudi Arabia and their Western followers-, leads, in El Fadl's opinion, to a distorted picture of Prophetic message/intention, especially in relation to issue of the status and role of women in Islam.

Another way in which some present-day authorities on Islam assert their authoritarianism is, argues El Fadl, by adopting methodologies and principles that are selective or are guilty of suppression or nondisclosure of complete evidence, as well as basic underlying assumptions guiding their legal determinations, practices that clearly contradict practices of early Muslim jurists.

By ignoring and turning their backs to abovementioned antiauthoritarian measures, which are, in El Fadl 's view, at the heart of Islamic heritage, and by adopting an unjustified "paralysing dogmatism" reflected in an ahistorical and unethical interpretation and reading of ahadith literature, asserts El Fadl, are not only eroding the rich and complex intellectual legacy of Islamic jurisprudence but severely curtailing freedoms and rights of Muslim citizens in certain "Muslim countries," who in the vast majority of cases are women.

Perhaps the most alarming characteristic of contemporary practices of the Wahhabo-Salafi scholars, according to El Fadl, is the lack of their consideration to the moral and the ethics in Islam. El Fadl argues further that this "ugliness" and distorted picture of the Qur'anic God is particularly evident in *fatawas* (legal opinions) issued by them concerning women according to which women's mere presence in public spaces/forums is to be considered a moral threat to their male counterparts.

El Fadl's analytical conceptual framework is coherent and does tremendously well to expose the contemporary authoritarian, unethical approaches to interpretation of Islamic heritage, but it lacks, as he himself concedes, a systematic ethicomoral theory that would give more credence to his philosophy of reviving the concepts of Moral Beauty in Islam. Additionally, although putting in place important methodological mechanisms, such as the principles of authorial enterprise and multiple authorship discussed above, which can be very useful in the process of authenticating individual hadith, El Fadl still conceptually conflates hadith and Sunna concepts and therefore does not develop a systematic theory of divorcing the concept of Sunna from hadith, which is both epistemologically and methodologically independent of hadith.

II) *Discussions on the religious/salvific status of non-Muslims in Islam and the concept of religious pluralism in Islam with emphasis on methods of interpretation used in order to arrive at a certain interpretation.*

Over the last two decades in particular, a growing number of works on the issue of "religious pluralism in the Qur'an" have been written. However, very few discuss the concept of a "Believer" in the Qur'an in relation to the non-Muslim (in a reified, historical sense) Other, and fewer discuss the concept by linking it systematically to broader hermeneutical questions.

Here two existing works are related to the aims of this study will be discussed. The first one is F. Esack's *Qur'an, Libration and Pluralism: An Islamic Perspective of Interreligious Solidarity.* What concerns me in particular is the discussion on the nature and the method of his hermeneutic.

Esack is a prominent South African Muslim liberation theologian. In his abovementioned work Esack develops what he terms a "contextual hermeneutic of religious pluralism for liberation" that aims, among others things, to achieve a number of objectives. The most germane to this study are: a contribution to the idea of formulation and advancement of theological pluralism within Islam; to rethink the way the Qur'an defines a concept of a "Believer" (Self) and "non-Believer" (Other) as to be have room for the righteous and just Other.

The broader context informing his hermeneutic is the universal struggle for justice and religious pluralism and the necessity to "rethink and reshape the nature and the role of religion so that it facilitates such a struggle."[45] The methodology Esack adopts to achieve these aims is by examining primarily the Qur'anic terms *Muslim/Islam, mu'min/iman, din, kafir, ahl-kitab, wilayah,* and *mushrikun*[46] on a basis of a particular hermeneutic. The author also examines the views of several prominent and influential premodern and modern Islamic theologians in relation to the same. Here he argues that what he terms "Islamic conservatism" has "persistently narrowed the theological base for defining *iman, islam,* and widened the base for *kufr*" with the attendant result of gradual expanding of the categories of other so that fewer and fewer were seen as believers and more and more as *kafir* (unbelievers).[47] His view on hadith literature, when citing it, is not based upon a belief in its authenticity, but its reflection of "the presence of, and support for, the idea among earlier Muslims."[48] He does not draw any distinction between Sunna and hadith concepts.

What are the constitutive elements of Esack's hermeneutic? They include the theories of contemporary reading hermeneutics developed both by non-Muslim[49] and Muslim scholars (such as M. Arkoun and F. Rahman) that deal with the relationship between the author, reader and the text, and the conditions under which one understands the text; a thematic or holistic approach to the Qur'anic text as a unity and the belief in the necessity of contextualizing the Qur'an in relation to its revelatory background and its dialectical relationship with it as reflected in but going beyond traditional Qur'anic sciences such as abrogation (*naskh*) and *sabab al-nuzul* (occasion of/for revelation).

In a summary of the ideas that underpin his hermeneutic, he includes the belief that the act of reading is always tainted by personal experience and context, that meaning is always tentative and biased, produced, not extracted, and as a corollary, that no interpretation (of the Qur'anic text) is universal; the emphasis on orthopraxis as a means of arriving at orthodoxy; and the acceptance of the righteous and just religious Other as being intrinsic to the Qur'an if examined holistically and historically. More specific to his "contextual hermeneutic of religious pluralism for liberation," Esack develops three important "hermeneutical keys" that underpin the hermeneutic task and form the "keys to understanding." They are based on the abovementioned assumption that the process of meaning derivation is dynamic and is significantly affected by the reader/interpreter or a community of readers/interpreters and her/their "prior text." The first set of terms constituting the first key is the concept of *taqwa* (awareness of accountability to God) and *tawhid* (God's absolute unity implying an inherent dignity of all humanity). They are "theological glasses" with which to examine the Qur'an in general and, more specifically, the texts dealing with the religious "Other." Their hermeneutical function is to couple the notion of belief with that of social justice activism, the process of "walking the walk" not just "talking the talk." In particular, they act as an aspiration to be acquired "beyond the immediate task of interpretation," thus establishing the abovementioned symbiotic relationship between orthopraxy and orthodoxy. Second, they force an interpreter to be introspective and engaged in social and self-transformation alongside principles of justice, freedom, honesty, and integrity. Importantly, they are also meant to prevent the "activist as an interpreter" "from becoming a mirror image of the very tyrant being fought."[50] Third, they are an insurance policy against monopolization of meaning/interpretation and the notion of a final or absolute meaning or interpretation. As such these principles are seen as both a "necessary components of pre-understanding" as well as hermeneutical principals.

Since the human mediation of the divine revelation is fundamental to the hermeneutical task, Esack includes an additional hermeneutical key that he terms "the location of interpretative community" at the level of humanity and the inherent dignity of each human being as a carrier of God's spirit. He considers the *humanum*, grounded in tawhid, as a criterion for truth. He is quick to add that he is not advocating an *autonomous humanum* as an absolute criterion "but one drawing its sustenance from tawhid."[51] Here and in other place where Esack mentions ethical values and principles, he seems to identify with the position, although does not discuss, of ethical objectivism and (partial) rationalism that has been a minority view in Islamic theology. Another hermeneutical key identified by Esack relates to the positioning of the interpreter in relation to the text prior to the act of reading/interpretation. In the context of Esack's "hermeneutic of religious pluralism for liberation," this means interpreting from the vantage point of solidarity with the disempowered and marginalized in accordance with what he considers to be the Qur'an's own self-positioning.

Lastly, the methods and the ethos that are responsible for producing and shaping a contextually dependent meaning are to be founded on the principals of *'adl/qist* (equity/justice) and jihad (defined as a praxis mirroring these principals).

In addition to the above, Esack incorporates lexicography and philology in his interpretative method.

While this study also employs the above defined hermeneutical principles, it differs in its approach from that of Esack (and all other scholars whose works have been reviewed in this section) but insisting on the separation of Sunna and its epistemological and methodological or hermeneutical dependence on hadith and emphasizes its hermeneutically symbiotic relationship with that of a particular Qur'anic hermeneutic. It also discuses theories of the nature of language and how this affects the process of inter-pretation that also is not present in Esack's work. Additionally, this study examines the issue of the Qur'an's ethical philosophy and how it affects the process of interpretation that cannot be found in any of the reviewed works. Moreover , unlike Esack's work, it also juxtaposes and explains how two different *manahij*, namely NTS and progressive Muslims, in relation to the question of the religious status of the Other are employed to inter-preted the relevant Qur'an and hadith "adillah" in order to construct two different concepts of a "Believer." Esack's work lacks this dimension too.

Muhammmad Shahrur's *The Qur'an, Morality and Critical Reason: The Essential Muhammad Shahrur* is another important work that is closely related to the current study. Although the author's emphasis is epistemo-logical rather then hermeneutical in so far as its principal aim, according to the author himself, is to go "beyond the epistemology of traditional Islamic scholarship,"[52] it contains a number of novel hermeneutico-philosophical and linguistic principles, especially in relation to the nature and the scope of the concept of Sunna and its relationship to the Qur'an[53] and hadith body of texts that require our attention. Importantly, it employs these in order to arrive at novel understandings of, among other things, the con-cepts of *al-islam* and *al-iman*, which are directly relevant to our study. Again, as in the case of discussing Esack's work, my focus in this chapter is to briefly analyze Shahrur's broader epistemological and methodologi-cal principles. How these, in turn, are employed to formulate his views on the concepts *al-islam* and *al-iman* will be the subject matter of Chapter Seven.

The first epistemological (and ontological) tool that characterizes Shahrur's *manhaj* is the argument, reminiscent of that of Muhammad Iqbal,[54] that the contemporary epoch, which commenced with the death of Prophet Muhammad, "no longer requires God's prophets and messen-gers because human beings have matured to such an extent that they can, without direct interventions from God, confidently explore the laws of the universe."[55] This, in turn, continues Shahrur, enables the humankind to be sovereign legislators in their societies. Shahrur insists that the Qur'an in form of Al-Kitab, as the ultimate expression and the seal of the first epoch, ought to be understood in the light of *contemporary* knowledge. Acknowledging that he is radically departing from the existing traditional methodologies and scholarly disciplines, Shahrur proposes a new ways of conceptualizing and interpreting Al-Kitab (and the Sunna and hadith) based on both linguistic and philosophical-hermeneutical principles. Here I will primarily focus on the hermeneutical-philosophical due to the nature of this study but will start with the brief summary of the linguistic principles.

Some of the Shahrur's most important linguistic tools include the notion of the complete meaningfulness of the Al-Kitab's text, which is contrary to that of the Islamic tradition that maintains that some parts of the Al-Kitab are beyond human comprehension; the argument of the utmost perfection with which the Al-Kitab's structure, composition, and meaning is defined and employed; the premise that every single word in Al-Kitab deliberately has its own specific function and meaning. This implies that no Qur'anically employed word can be considered as an exact synonym of another; the idea that the explicit meaning of the word can be derived from its implicit meaning that, in turn, is derived from the composition and the grammatical structure of a certain piece of text; and the notion that Al-Kitab has nothing redundant nor superfluous in it. As a result of this Shahrur considers words such as *al-islam* and *al-iman* not to be synonymous or interchangeable, in actual fact, as will be shown in Chapter Seven, he argues that they signify two different types of faith both of which are acceptable in the eyes of God.

One of the hermeneutical principles Shahrur's subscribes to pertains to the area of reading hermeneutics and determinacy of meaning. Although, in principal, believing in the discoverability of author's intent, Shahrur considers that the human knowledge of divine texts is partial and limited and that the text can be interpreted in a number of different ways. Echoing Abu Zayd, who makes a hermeneutical distinction between the fixed nature of the text and the dynamic nature of its meaning,[56] Shahrur forms the view that although the text of the Qur'an is unchanging its content "moves." This quality of the Al-Kitab he terms *al-tashabuh* or "assimilitability." Shahrur considers that this provides the Al-Kitab with flexibility of the meaning/interpretation that is inherent in it and is a core element of the urreligion of monotheism, the *hanifiya*. Like Esack, Shharur also points out that this hermeneutic does not necessarily lead to ethical and moral relativism but instead provides a divinely set boundary with its upper and lower most limits within which Al-Kitab's flexibility operates. The flexibility in interpretation, on the other hand, is crucial for the Al-Kitab's responsiveness to the changes in historical contexts and social realities of its readers/interpreters. Furthermore, Al-Kitab, insists Shahrur, ought not be read in isolation from social reality and must ever be alert to different historical contexts of its readers as it was the case with its first audience of the community of Prophet Muhammad. Shahrur, therefore, like other here reviewed authors, subscribes to the polysemous nature of the Qur'anic text and its historicity without denying al-Kitab's divine origin and nature.

Shahrur's most important philosophical principle with which he approaches and interprets the Al-Kitab is his tripartite concept of existence according to which its three constitutive elements "being" (existence) and "progressing" (time) are inextricably linked to that of "becoming" (transformation). With this model, Shahrur challenges and wishes to free the Islamic tradition from its traditionally embedded regressive view of the nature of history and time that found its expression in the form of salafism or the idea of following in the footsteps of the *salaf-us-salih*, the righteous predecessors usually understood to be the first three generations of Muslims.[57] By advocating the inevitability of "progress" until the Last Hour, Shahrur argues the following:

> To sum up, "progressing" or time cannot be removed from human existence, "being" can ontologically not *not* exist, and becoming is historical change (al-sayruriyya al-ta'rikhiyya) which human beings-in exercising their free will, either accelerate or slow down but can never stop.[58]

Based on this tripartite philosophical model Shahrur argues that humanity, in terms of its beliefs, has gone through a process of transformation (becoming) from the belief in "personified, concrete godhead to belief in an abstract, invisible God."[59] Shahrur considers the Islamic credo of "there is no god but God" to be the most advanced and most abstract form of belief that can be shared by everyone. It is this belief that Shahrur terms *al-islam*. What pertains to the evolutionary nature of beliefs also is valid for ethics and morality and legislation.

Importantly, Shahrur's work is also a novel attempt to define the nature and the scope of the concept of Sunna in relation to that of the Qur'an and hadith body of texts.

As explained in more detail in the second chapter, the Islamic tradition has developed a theory of Qur'an's reliance on Sunna, i.e., the Prophet's example, which over time found its expression primarily in form of "authentic" hadith or reports about actions and utterances of the Prophet—for the purposes of clarification and elaboration of Qur'an's theological, exegetical, legal as well as ethicomoral principles bringing Sunna to a quasi-ontologically equal status with that of the Qur'an and privileging it hermeneutically over everything else, including that of the reason or, at times, even other Qur'anic evidence. Shahrur laments this development and aims "to show that the sunna of the Prophet is culturally and historically conditioned and that it lacks the universality of Allah's book."[60] By making a distinction between the prophetic (*nubuwwa*) and messenger (*risala*) aspects of Muhammad's divine mission, he argues that the former deals with the universalist dimension of the divine message as embodied in the Al-Kitab that he restricts to eschatological and purely theological issues that are ambiguous and transcend this objective reality. The former is concerned solely with definite, unambiguous, and objective reality that is subject to human faculties and senses. He argues that Muhammad's mission as concretely manifested in his life and example (i.e., his Sunna) consisted of both of these elements. Applying his tripartite model above Shahrur argues that only the Qur'an possess the ontological quality of "being in and for it self" and not the Sunna that he defines as Prophet's own human-bound, non-absolute *ijtihad*/interpretation/understanding of the Al-Kitab. After critiquing the traditional hadith-dependent concept of Sunna,[61] Shahrur argues for a specific and circumstantial nature of the concept of Sunna of the Prophet based on five principals including: i) the idea that Prophet's decisions were conditioned by his historical context; ii) his *ijtihads* in restricting the allowed did not need divine revelation; iii) his restrictions of the "unrestricted permissions"(*halal mutlaq*) were subject to constant corrections as a result in change in circumstances in his own life; iv) his *ijtihads* , unlike revelations, were not infallible; and v) his *ijtihads* regardless if they are of prophetic or nonprophetic nature do not constitute Islamic legislation.[62]

In concluding his section on Sunna, he asserts the following:

> We have demonstrated that is it necessary to place sunna into the epis-temological, cultural and political context of seventh century Arabia. We showed that we, living in the twenty-first century, must be critical of the sunna's contingent and context-bound nature as well as of formulations and definitions of sunna that Islamic fiqh invented during the seventh to the ninth centuries.[63]

Although Shahrur makes a number of important and novel distinctions between Sunna and hadith, he still considers hadith to be its only vehicle of transmission. Additionally, despite the fact that Shahrur's work also deals indirectly with the concept of who is a "Believer" from a normative vantage point and discusses the issue of women in Islamic law, his work, just like none of the other studies discussed so far does not aims to do so in systematically comparative and juxtapositional manner. Also his work neglects a number of other *usul-ul-fiqh* related issues that feature in this study such as the discussion on the nature of Qur'anic ethics and moral philosophy or that of the *maqasid* or the purposive nature of Islamic law.

One extant work that is comparative in its focus approximating in this respect the current study is another work by El Fadl titled *The Great Theft: Wrestling Islam from the Extremists*. This book in essence aims to shed light on how one can delineate between the belief and the practices of what the author terms the Muslim "moderates" and "puritans" on a range of issues concerning, *inter alia*, the nature of law and morality, approaches to his-tory and modernity, interaction with non-Muslims and salvation, and the nature and role of women in Islam. Although the subject matter of this book mirrors and overlaps to some extent with that of this study it does not include a systematic discussion of issues from a *usul-ul fiqh*/reading hermeneutics vantage point as it is primarily written for a nonacademic audience. The author is well aware of their importance but considers them to be outside the scope and the purpose of the book. In this context, he asserts,

> The meaning of religious texts are heavily affected by the moral and ethical predispositions and commitments made by the readers of those texts, but they are also affected by the technical tools that people use to understand the text. But this is not the place to get into the heuristic devices of puritans and moderates and the methods they use to unpack the meanings and implications of texts."[64]

I attempt this in this study in relation to the concept of a religiously ideal "Muslim Woman" and "Believer" concepts from the perspective of NTS and progressive Muslim *manahij*.

The next section provides a brief outline of the book's chapters.

Outline of Chapters

The first chapter presents, in broad terms, a genealogy of the still ongoing debates over the relative status and authenticity of various sources of legal authority in the Islamic tradition. It starts with an explanation of the historical background and the evolution behind two major approaches to the Islamic tradition, namely the *madhhab*- and the *ahl-hadith* based, and highlights the differences and commonalities between them. It discusses the concept of *salafism* in order to show the centrality of this concept in relation to how the Islamic tradition is conceptualized and interpreted. Finally, it briefly situates the NTS and progressive Muslim communities of interpretation against this historical background.

In the second chapter, a discussion on the main representatives of NTS community of interpretation is presented and placed in relation to several issues that formed the subject matter of the previous chapter, including the historical context behind the emergence of the premodern *ahl hadith* and *ahl-ra'y/madhhab* schools of thought; NTS's understanding of the concept of salafism; NTS's ideas in relation to what constitutes legitimate knowledge (*'ilm*) and its sources; NTS's concept of the nature and the scope of the concept of Sunna; and the NTS's own self-description of their *manhaj*.

The third chapter is divided into two sections. The first part identifies the assumptions informing the premodern embedded *manahij* with respect to the Qur'an and presents a critical analysis of the interpretational implications of these assumptions. The second section examines the interpretational assumptions behind the NTS Sunna *manhaj* and their interpretational implications. As far as the assumptions of premodern *usul-ul-fiqh manhaj* are concerned, I rely upon the scholarship that primarily was addressing the madhhab-based scholarship since many are shared between the NTS and madhhab-based *manahij*.[65]

My task in the fourth chapter is to explain how the NTS *manhaj* may be responsible for the formation of the views of NTS scholars pertaining to the issue of what constitutes a religiously ideal "Believer" (Part One) and "Muslim Woman" (Part Two) concepts. In order to do so, I will present relevant Qur'an-*hadith* textual indicants employed by NTS scholars and analyze which aspects of their NTS *manhaj* inform their opinions on these two concepts.

The fifth chapter consists of four sections. In the first part the aim is to present a discussion on some defining themes underpinning progressive Muslim worldview. The second and the third sections historically contextualize and place progressive Muslim thought in relation to their intellectual predecessors coming from both the non-Muslim majority and Muslim majority worlds. The last part outlines progressive Muslim approach to conceptualizing and engaging with the Islamic tradition and the concept of modernity/modern episteme.

Analogous to what was outlined in the third chapter about the NTS *manhaj*, the aim of the sixth chapter is to discuss the delineating features of progressive Muslims *manhaj* and its interpretational implications.

The final, seventh chapter aims to explain how the progressive Muslims' *manhaj* may be responsible for engendering progressive Muslims' concepts of a religiously ideal "Believer" and "Muslim Woman." It uses the same methodology as the one adopted in the fourth chapter. Progressive Muslims' views on the issue of what constitutes a religiously ideal "Believer" concept are presented first (Part One). Subsequent to that the progressive Muslims stance on the religiously ideal "Muslim Woman" concept (Part Two) will be offered.

In the concluding section the study's theoretical underpinnings, its methodology, aims and findings are summarized. In particular, the study's importance is framed with respect to the broader discourses and issues surrounding the Muslim communities especially the contemporary intra-Muslim debates and contestations between "conservative" and "modernist" currents over religious legitimacy.

Chapter 1

Genealogy of Debates on the Relative Status and the Authenticity of the Various Sources of Legal Authority in the Sunni Islamic Tradition

This chapter presents, in broad terms, a genealogy of the still ongoing debates over the relative status and authenticity of various sources of legal authority in the Islamic tradition. It starts with an explanation of the historical background and the evolution behind two major approaches to the Islamic tradition, namely *madhhab*-based and *ahl-hadith* based, and highlights the differences and commonalities between them. It then discusses the concept of *Salafism* in order to show the centrality of this concept in relation to how the Islamic tradition is conceptualized and interpreted. Finally, it situates the NTS and progressive Muslim communities of interpretation against this historical background.

1.1 Introduction

The word *tradition or heritage (turath)* in classical Sunni Islamic thought is usually linked to concepts such as continuity, stability, authenticity, and authority. It literally means "handing over" of Islamic practices and beliefs.[1] In its broader sense, *turath* can be characterized as a fluid, dynamic, and cumulative religiohistoric construct with a central intellectual core, primarily the Qur'an and Sunna, and a number of later developed doctrines derived from its core pertaining to philosophy, theology, ethics, jurisprudence, legal theory, and mysticism, as well as certain sociological and political attitudes and notions.[2] Again, it is helpful to highlight at this juncture that the concept of *turath* is a contested terrain and that various Islamic groups from the past and the present, including the two communities of interpretation this study focuses on, conceptualize differently, rejecting or accepting certain aspects of the cumulative tradition as belonging to it or not. Since the focus of the study is on issues pertaining to the origins and the development of the Islamic tradition with respect to the relative status and authenticity of various sources of legal authority in the Islamic tradition, which form the subject matter of Islamic legal theory (*usul-ul fiqh*), I use the word Islamic tradition in this more specific sense. Kamali defines *usul-ul-fiqh* as a science "concerned with the sources of [Islamic] law, their order of priority, and methods by which legal rules may be deduced from the source materials of Shari'ah [Islamic law].[3] Ahmed offers a somewhat more elaborate definition of *usul-ul-fiqh* as consisting of three components: 1) a theory of practical legal determinations (*ahkam*), which are considered the fruits of legal thinking; 2) the sources of the law, both textual and extratextual; 3) and the principles of legal reasoning that link the sources of the law to practical legal determinations.[4]

According to the classical majority doctrine, apart from the Qur'an and Sunna, the other sources of the Islamic tradition include those that are deductively derived from them, namely the consensus of Muslim scholars (*ijma'*) and that of *qiyas* (analogical reasoning). In addition to these, most of the Islamic schools of thought (*madhahib*) from the fourth century onwards in their overall legal hermeneutic also came to recognize, to varying extents, nontextual sources of law such as *istislah* (public interest), *istidlal* (inference), and certain reason—derived principles commonly referred to as aims of the law (*maqasid al-shari'ah*) that, inter alia, include the protection of life, religion, property, and others.[5]

The Qur'an and Sunna, as primary sources of the Islamic *tradition*, are uniformly recognized by Muslims as the ultimate points of Islamic reference and the most authoritative sources of the Islamic tradition.[6] Even a cursory examination of the Islamic intellectual tradition testifies to the centrality of the concepts of Qur'an and Sunna in all its aspects. In the past as well as in the present, a variety of interpretive communities across the Muslim ideological divide have formulated both their creeds (*aqidah*) and interpretive approaches (*manahij*) on the basis of these sources. Often these groups would invoke a formula of "going back to the Qur'an and Sunna," which throughout the Muslim historical experience, up to and including the present times, has served as an ideological battleground in terms of whose understanding, definition, nature, and scope of these (textual) sources is the most representative of God's Intent/Will and the Prophet's embodiment, clarification, and elaboration of it. Moreover, often this slogan is used to "provide doctrinal, ideological, or geo-political theme used by peripheral Muslim groups against a central power."[7] In addition, these two sources "are used episodically in discourses of various kinds—political, legal, social, and others—in order to align the efforts and discourses made by the exegete into a pre-established corpus of truth."[8] In other words the meaning and the interpretation of these two fountainheads of the Islamic tradition have always been and continue to be contested among various Muslim groups.

The concept of what today is considered as mainstream Sunni Islamic tradition, as a doctrine and practice in its broadest sense, developed largely as a result of numerous ideological battlegrounds and the sectarian developments, some of which led to civil wars that emerged immediately after the Prophet's death.[9] Investigation of these developments, in accordance with the abovementioned specific aims of the chapter, is necessary in order to paint a clear(er) picture of the nature of the Islamic tradition and the factors that shaped the debates behind its various conceptualizations and interpretations. This is what follows below.

1.2   The Premodern Period: From the Time of the Prophet up to the Eighteenth Century

While the Prophet Muhammad was still alive, the Muslim community had access to not only the conveyer of the Qur'anic Revelation but its embodiment, elaboration, and clarification in the *persona* and the character of the Prophet Muhammad himself. With his death, however, Revelation ceased and the Muslim community no longer had the opportunity to inquire about and consult the Messenger of God about the meaning and significance of the revealed verses. His most notable Companions took over this task with the view of holding close to and preserving the teachings of the Qur'an and the Sunna. However, as Muslim history amply testifies, they were not able to prevent partisan tensions and schisms from surfacing within the nascent Muslim community even before the Prophet's funeral rites had been finalized.[10]

A number of factors contributed to the early development of schisms in the Muslim community. The two that are of direct concern to us in relation to the interpretation of the Islamic tradition, the legitimate sources of its legal authority and the relative status of those sources, can be traced to the very nature of the Qur'anic revelation and the Prophet's embodiment of it and the fascinating speed at which the Arab Muslims conquered vast geographical regions. In relation to the first point, it can be argued that apart from evoking the importance of certain ethicoreligious principals, such as God consciousness (*taqwa*), accountability (*hisab*) for one's deeds at the Day of Judgement/Accountability (*jawm ul-qiyamah/hisab*), and the fraternity of believers (*mu'minun*), the Muslim community could neither find specific guidance in the Qur'an nor in the Prophet's legacy[11] on a plethora of important theological, political, or legal issues. For example, these included the question of free will (*qadar*), the scope and nature of belief (*iman*) and unbelief (*kufr*), the relationship between the role of reason and revelation in formulating law, the nature of Prophetic religious and political authority, etc. All of these caused major divisions among the nascent Muslim community. As a result, a large number of sects rapidly emerged forming distinct and often conflicting views on the abovementioned issues (and others).[12]

The second reason, which synergized the first, was the speed at which the Muslim empire became established. In a matter of three generations after the Prophet's death, the Muslim community grew into one of a Muslim empire conquering lands from central Asia to Spain.[13] Arab Muslim conquerors formed a minority in these lands and absorbed an increasing number of converts from various ethnicities, cultures, and religions who had no historical or emotional connection with or knowledge of the early Muslim community of the Prophet Muhammad. Upon the realization of this situation, a view among the mainly Arab Muslims of the established stock soon became so widespread that the expanding Muslim empire would become organically detached from the teachings of the Qur'an and the Sunna unless there was a systematic attempt to preserve them. According to the traditional Sunni accounts, very early on these circumstances prompted the early Caliphs Abu Bakr (d.12 A.H.) and Uthman (d.35 A.H.) to initiate a process of "canonization" of existing Qur'anic manuscripts and compile them into one book (*mushaf*). This task was largely achieved during the reign of the third caliph Uthman. A related concern was to preserve the memory and the legacy of Prophet Muhammad (i.e., Sunna) with the hope of unifying the various Muslim sects and preserving the integrity of the nascent Muslim community.[14] During the first three centuries, the concept of Sunna was understood as a general, not systematically defined, behavioral practice of the early Muslim community predominantly formulated, preserved, and transmitted either orally or *in actu* independent of its any written recording.[15] Guraya, for example, argued that the concept of Sunna, as understood during this period, meant a concept based on "recognized Islamic religious norms and accepted standards of conduct derived from the religious and ethical principles introduced by the Prophet.[16] I refer to this as a non-*hadith* dependent concept of Sunna.

However, just before the end of the first century of the Islamic calendar, an initiative toward a systematic documentation of the events surrounding the Prophet's life, known as *talab al-ilm* phenomenon[17] in a written form of traditions (*ahadith/sg.hadith*) began to take place. One reason for the documentation and collection of the material on the Prophet's life was to utilize this body of knowledge for the purposes of law explication to meet the legal, religious, political, and social needs of the ever expanding Muslim Empire. Additionally, a change in political leadership and the subsequent rise of the Abbasid dynasty (132 A.H.) was another factor. The Abbasids appropriated the caliphate from the Umayyads on the basis of claiming to be the legitimate custodians of the Prophet's Sunna, whose religious importance was being increasingly recognized by the Muslim masses by tracing their lineage to his uncle's cousin Abbas, so as to justify and legitimize their political power. This state of affairs created an ever greater impetus for a more systematic searching for and collection of Sunna, and especially in its written form of *hadith*.[18] This gave rise to the sciences of hadith (*ulum-ul-hadith*). These included branches of knowledge pertaining to the collection, assessment, and evaluation of ahadith based upon certain methodological principles and mechanisms designed to ensure their authenticity. I refer to this broader process as traditionalization of the Islamic thought and the "hadithification" of Sunna. In a broader sense, this process refers to those social, political, and jurisprudential mechanisms that throughout the latter half of the first and the entire second and third centuries Hijri contributed to:

-the continued growth and proliferation of hadith;
-the increased perceived importance given to hadith at the cost of non-hadith dependent concept of Sunna;
-the absorption of practically and verbally based Sunna into hadith;
-the increased application of hadith in Qur'an and Sunna sciences, such as *usul-ud-din, tafsir, usul-ul-fiqh, usul-as-Sunna;* and
-the development of hierarchical, legal, and hermeneutical models that were entirely textually based (i.e., based on Qur'an and hadith) and the marginalization of nontextually based epistemological and methodological tools of Sunna (and Qur'an), such as notion of *ra'y* (reason-based opinion) or that of Sunna (and the Qur'an) being conceptually coterminous with certain ethical values or principles such as justice or righteous conduct.

By "hadithtification" of Sunna, I mean that the written hadith body of knowledge became Sunna's only vehicle of transmission/embodiment and the hadith-dependent methodology of derivation of Sunna.

As a result of these processes, a shift in understanding of boundaries of legitimate religious knowledge and its sources (*'ilm*) took place. For example, prior to the abovementioned process of traditionalization of the Islamic thought reason (*'aql*) and ra'y were considered as constitutive of the concept of *'ilm* (legitimate religious knowledge) and were essentially seen as legitimate, pragmatic tools in extrapolating law. Thus, they had a positive connotation to them.[19] Subsequent to the traditionalization of Islamic thought, the legitimacy and scope of *'aql* and ra'y gradually started declining, leading to their eventual exclusion from *'ilm*. The only traces of reason as a source of legal authority were to be found in *qiyas*.[20]

At the beginning of the second century, Hijri hadith collections were considered by some section of the Muslim community to be a truer reflection of the Prophet's legacy (Sunna) than that of other methodologies used by other groups whose concept of Sunna was, epistemologically and methodologically independent of hadith. By the second half of the second century the former were named *ashab al-hadith* or *ahl-hadith* and the latter *ahl-ra'y*.[21] *Ahl-hadith* school of thought considered hadith as being the sole and the complete depository of Sunna and the only vehicle of its perpetuation. This hadith-based approach to Sunna came into being out of opposition to the *ahl-ra'y* concept of the nature and the scope of the Sunna (and by extension to that of the Qur'an itself) and the role of *ra'y* or reason-based opinion in interpreting the Islamic tradition.[22] The *ahl-hadith* insisted that all law had to be traced back to the Qur'anic text and hadith-based Sunna and that *ra'y* was to be considered either an illegitimate methodological tool in derivation of law[23] or that its use had to be constrained to those cases in which Qur'an and hadith texts offered no insight at all.[24] In Melchert's opinion, *ahl-hadith* considered the Qur'an and the "authentic" hadith as the only religiously legitimate basis of Islamic law and theology. They preferred to resort to weak (*da'if*) hadith over principles generally deduced from the Qur'an or through analogical reasoning.[25] According to the *ahl-hadith* proponents, there was no difference between a hadith and a law expert. As such, the proponents of the *ahl-hadith manhaj* dealt with juridical problems by exclusively referring to and reciting relevant hadith reports. In ninth century Baghdad, the *ahl-hadith* group was associated with the followers of the eponyms of the Hanbali *madhhab* Ahmed ibn Hanbal (d.241 A.H.). On the other hand, the *ahl-ra'y*, or in the words of Melchert the "semi-rationalists," considered jurisprudence as a separate field from hadith sciences, employing the rational techniques of scholastic theologians (*ahl-kalam*) to justify the accepted theological tenants. This school of thought was primarily associated with the emerging Maliki and Shafi'i schools of thought of the second Hijri century.[26] The two designations *ahl-ra'y and ahl-hadith*, thus, can be considered to have "originally referred to branches of legists occupied with the investigation of Islamic law: the former were concerned with the study of transmitted sources (i.e. hadith) and the later with the practical aspects of the law."[27]

As the influence of hadith-based Sunna gained more credence in the second and third century Hijri, the *ahl-ra'y*, which at this point in time crystallized into several regional and subsequently personal schools of thought (*madhahib*),[28] took certain steps to accommodate and award more legitimacy to the mushrooming body of texts based on the hadith-based notion of the nature and the scope of the concept of Sunna in their overall Qur'an-Sunna hermeneutic. Thus, a process of synchronism and cross-pollination between *ahl-ra'y*, the precursor of the *madhahib* and *ahl-hadith* methodologies, took place, resulting in the formation of what are today the four extant Sunni schools of thought (*madhahib*).[29] The formed Maliki, Hanafi, and Shafi'i *madhahib* were generally considered closer to the *ahl ra'y* model of interpretation of the Qur'an and the Sunna for the purposes of legal derivation. The Hanbali *madhhab* is generally regarded as the successor of the *ahl-hadith* approach.[30] However, the concept of the nature of Sunna according to the *madhahib* was still independent of hadith both epistemologically and methodologically. This hadith-independent concept of Sunna was also evident in the writings of the eight century *madhhab* scholars from Iraq such as Abu Yusuf (d. 182/798) who referred to it as *al-Sunna al-mahfuza al-ma'rufa* , the well established Sunna, or that of the Medinian scholar Malik ibn Anas (d. 178/ 795), who referred to it primarily as *Sunna madiya l'amal*.[31]

However, Brown writes the *madhahib* "had given assent in theory to the importance of hadith while resisting its thorough application," thus creating a tension between *ahl-hadith*'s definition of Sunna and "the actual doctrine of the madhhab."[32] The consolidating *ahl-hadith* movement increasingly questioned the already systematically constructed Qur'an-Sunna hermeneutical doctrine of the *madhahib* as not being based on true Sunna.[33] This opened the doors for the argument of *ihya al-Sunna*, the revivification of and the return to Prophetic Sunna. This was to be achieved by insisting that only an unflinching adherence to the body of "authentic hadith," as defined by *ahl-hadith manhaj*, constitutes *ihya al-Sunna*. Thus, the main purpose behind the call for *ihya al-Sunna* was to undermine the *madhhab*-based approach to conceptualizing and interpreting the Islamic tradition, especially their concept of the nature and the scope of the concept of Sunna.

At this juncture a few words about another approach to the Islamic tradition, that of *ahl-kalam*, are in order. The *ahl-kalam*, are usually given the epithet in Western Islamic scholarship as the first Muslim "rationalists" who subscribed to the principals of ethical objectivism in understanding the nature of Qur'anic ethical philosophy with their emphasis on God's Unity, Transcendence, and Justice and against the anthropomorphic tendencies present in *ahl-hadith* theology. This school of thought emerging in the eight century also emphasized the importance of reason and free will in theology and the formulation and explication of Islamic law. The *ahl-kalam* rejected the hadith body of literature in principal and the sciences underpinning its body of knowledge as being capable of retrieving or authenticating Sunna. They did not, however, reject the notion of the Prophet's authority/Sunna per se. It is important to note that *ahl-kalam*'s view on the nature of knowledge (epistemology) and theology greatly influenced legal jurists belonging to a particular *madhab* (and to a much lesser extent that of *ahl-hadith*), especially in relation to how they authenticated the hadith body of knowledge as shall be noted below.[34]

As a summary to the above, we can deduce that one point of contention between the *madhhab*- and *ahl-hadith*-based approaches to conceptualization and interpretation of the Islamic tradition is the difference in which these two schools of thought approached the question of the nature and the scope of the concept of Sunna.

Another point of difference between the *madhhab*-based approach to the Islamic tradition and that of ahl-*hadith manhaj* is the role and the function of external authority in the explication of the Islamic Law. To understand this point, we need to briefly describe the nature of classical Islamic law. In essence Islamic law can be characterized as being an accretive,[35] ascriptive,[36] and socially constructed[37] discourse embedded in the larger oral-based framework that privileges "authoritative parlance,"[38] to use Souaiaia's phrase, of certain individuals (such as the Prophet Muhammad, Caliphs ,founders of the *madhahib*, etc.) considered to be authoritative by the Muslim community.[39] In other words authority in Islamic law is first and foremost epistemic in nature.[40] As a result of the (legal) reasoning (*ijtihad*) of authoritative individuals over time, accumulation of legal precedents took place and became considered as binding by the Muslim community, because these were seen to be in accordance with the teachings of the Qur'an and the Sunna. This, in turn, gave rise to the concept of *taqlid*. In his discussion of this principle and its function in Islamic jurisprudence, Jackson argues that *taqlid* is not so much related to the notion of it precluding novel interpretations, as it is commonly held, but rather as a means of validating jurist's legal interpretation "retrojectively," i.e., by searching back to the interpretation with an established source of authority. Furthermore, Hallaq considers that *taqlid* not only functioned as an effective means of legal change but even more so than *ijtihad* itself, because, unlike *ijtihad*, *taqlid*-based interpretations were seen to be loyal to and continuous with the ongoing tradition.[41] *Taqlid* is, therefore, to be seen as a hermeneutical mechanism whereby rather than abandoning existing legal theory rules in favour of new interpretations of the relevant textual indicants found in the Qur'an and hadith without precedent; a jurist develops new interpretations within the framework of the established *madhhab*-based hermeneutic. Hallaq forms a similar view by seeing *taqlid* as a reasoned defense of a particular legal doctrine based on a *madhhab*'s overall methodology and hermeneutic.[42] This allegiance to the *madhhab*-based legal theory hermeneutic by the means of *taqlid* was derived from the consensus of scholars belonging to a particular *madhhab*.[43]This legal mechanism's primary purpose was to ensure that the legal opinion of a jurist is able to gain wide(r) acceptance by embedding it into the "sacred past." For the *madhhab*-based approach, this consensus of *madhhab* scholars is the ultimate criterion in determining the compliance or otherwise of a particular legal principle[44] with the Qur'an and the Sunna and not the hadith as in the case of the *ahl-hadith manhaj*. Therefore, the majority of *fuqaha*, belonging to one of the *madhahib*, especially those of lower status, rather than opting for acceptance of a hadith unknown to previous authorities belonging to the same *madhhab*, were faithful and obedient (*muqallid*) to their own school's hermeneutic.[45] It is important to keep in mind that each *madhhab* did have scholars who were associated with it and specialized in hadith sciences, but the predominant *madhhab* view was a result of the overall *madhhab* legal hermeneutic.[46]

The *ahl-hadith manhaj* rejects the broader, hierarchical hermeneutic upon which the practice of *taqlid* is based. The proponents of the *ahl-hadith manhaj* argue instead for an unmediated return to the Qur'an and Sunna in the form of Qur'an and hadith-based texts. *Taqlid*, according to the *ahl-hadith approach*, is an innovation, *bida'ah*, and a deviation from Sunna.[47]Instead, the *ahl-hadith* consider that the uncontested adherence to hadith, as the sole vehicle for the perpetuation and depository of Sunna, termed *ittiba'*, is the only way of remaining truthful to the Prophet's Sunna. Furthermore, the *Ahl-hadith* also aimed to minimize the hermeneutical leverage of nontextual-based sources of the Islamic tradition such as preference (*istihsan*), analogy (*qiyas*), speculation (*nazar*), the writings of ancient philosophers, or the views of scholastic theologians of later times.[48]

This situation led to constant debates between these two opposing camps. These internal skirmishes between the *ahl-hadith* and the *madhahib manahij* are well depicted by A. Islahi, a contemporary Muslim scholar who offers a useful description of the protagonists of these two camps and their respective methodologies in relation to the question of employing and authenticating/criticizing hadith body of knowledge. In Islahi's book, the *ahl-hadith* are characterized as being completely concerned with the collections of *all* kinds of hadith, including those that are rare or based on just a single (*gharib*) narrator. They are accused of not paying much attention to the text, meaning, or the spirit of the theme of ahadith but instead are said to concentrate on raising objections and criticizing legal theorists and constantly accusing them of opposing the Sunna. The *madhhab*-based legal theorists, on the other hand, are described as not paying much attention to hadith of *any* kind and that they use them only if ahadith agree with their own prior views or convictions. We are also told that the *ahl-hadith* adherents also criticize the *madhhab*-based legal theorists for their carelessness with quoting the sayings of the Prophet Muhammad and for readily accepting only the sayings of their own imams.[49]

Differences between the *madhhab* and *ahl-hadith* based approaches to the Islamic tradition are also evident in their respective conceptualizing and interpreting of the Qur'an and Qur'an-based sciences (i.e., 'ulum-ul Qur'an) and the role of *ra'y* in them. As a direct consequence of the above described *ahl-hadith* conflation of hadith and Sunna bodies of knowledge, the Qur'anic sciences pertaining to chronology, modes, and occasions of revelation, the Qur'an's collection and transmission, the formal presentation of the Qur'an's definite recension, prosody and textual units, exegesis, and historical notations are all epistemologically constrained by the body of knowledge that underpins traditional hadith-based sciences, the 'ulum-ul hadith.[50] For example, the *ahl-hadith* based Qur'anic exegesis (*tafsir*) is characterised by an unflinching epistemological addiction to hadith-based and hadith-constrained bodies of knowledge and is known as *tafsir-bi-l-ma'thur* or the traditionalist, hadith-based exegesis. This *tafsir bi-l-ma'thur* is just one of many *tafsir* categories that exist in the broader Islamic tradition.Others include theological, literary-rhetorical, mystical, *ra'y*, literary-philological, shi'a, esoteric, or juristic exegesis.[51] Although there were traditionalist *mufassirun* (exegetes) within each *madhhab*, the *madhhab*-based *tafsir manhaj* included other approaches too and allowed more scope for *ra'y* in it.[52]

Another important distinction between the two approaches to the Islamic tradition concerns the evaluation of hadith's authenticity and validity. A hadith consists of two parts: an *isnad,* which is the name of the people involved in its transmission, usually going back to the Prophet, and the text (*matn*) itself.

The assessment and evaluation of the authenticity and validity of particular hadith has been approached via two general avenues. One method was developed by the specialists in hadith's authenticity/criticism, transmission, compilation, and classification, namely the *muhadithun*, who are largely associated with the *ahl-hadith school* of thought. These *muhadithun* have predominantly focused on assessing hadith authenticity and reliability by probing their *isnad* (chain of transmission), which, in essence, largely amounts to concerning oneself with the reliability of the *rijal* that is those individuals who feature in the *isnad*. To a lesser extent they also examined hadith's *matn*.[53] Based on this approach hadith's overall authenticity/ reliability was evaluated and their subsequent classification ranging from "sound" (*sahih*) to "weak" (*da'if*) was developed. The main problem with this approach is not only the paucity of material from the first century of Islamic thought that fuels the ongoing debates among Muslim and non-Muslim scholars alike on the historical authenticity of the *isnad* as a means of establishing hadith authenticity[54] but also the subjective nature of the criteria used in hadith evaluation[55] and lack of standardization of terminology in classical *ulum ul-ḥadith* sciences.[56]

Another approach to evaluating hadith was from a purely epistemological vantage point associated with the *madhhab* approach. This practice was adopted by Islamic legal scholars (*usuliyyun*) as part of their overall approach to conceptualizing the Islamic Law as, to borrow Zysow terminology, "the economy of certainty."[57] This method focused first and foremost on developing criteria relating to the quantitative transmission of knowledge based on probability. Questions such as at what point in time and at what evidentiary level would human faculty of reason "accept" transmitted knowledge as either inducing certainty (*yaqin*), thus yielding immediate knowledge (*daruri*) or amounting to less than that(*zann/probable* and acquired knowledge) were decisive[58]. Classification of hadith according to this technique ranged from isolated (*ahad*) hadith that yielded *zann* knowledge only to that of *mutawatir,* or successive hadith, that, according to the majority of *usuliyyun*, reached *daruri* knowledge.[59] The problem with this method in relation to Sunna is that only very few hadith, not amounting to more then a dozen,[60] or according to some none,[61] can be considered to have fulfilled the criteria of *mutawatir* level of transmission. In this context the debate between the *madhhab*-based and *ahl-hadith* approaches concerns primarily the validity of *ahad hadith* as authentic sources of valid norms in areas of law and beliefs. The latter consider the *ahad* hadith to be authentic sources of valid norms and the former do not.[62]

In summary, we can conclude that the nature of the concept of the Islamic tradition in relation to the question of the relative status and the authenticity of various sources of its legal authority, especially the nature and the scope of the concept of Sunna and its relationship with the hadith and Qur'an, has always been contested. Over time this led to the emergence of *madhhab*-and *ahl-hadith*-based approaches. The two approaches differed in relation to both epistemological and methodological underpinnings of the Islamic tradition and the interpretation of its legal sources. They especially differed on the issue of the nature and the scope of the concept of Sunna, and as a corollary, the authenticity of hadith as a source of legal authority.

In order to have a more complete understanding of the nature of the Islamic tradition and the *madhhab-* and *ahl-hadith-*approaches to it, we need to have an understanding of importance of the concept of the "sacred past" mentioned above in the context of discussing *taqlid* and the accretive nature of Islamic law. The notion of the "sacred past" in the Islamic tradition has found its expression in the notion of Salafism to which I turn my attention now.

The concept of Salafism refers to not only to the notion of how the Islamic tradition is to be conceptualized and interpreted but also concerns the questions of reading of history and the nature of time. In Islamic jurisprudence the phrase *as-salaf as-salih* has different meanings as "every group has defined salaf according to its own orientation and school." According to one definition the term *as-salaf as-salih* refers to the "early Mujahid scholars of the Schools" (*madhahib*) who are accepted and imitated, such as, depending upon the *madhhab*, Abu Hanifa and his companions Abu Yusuf and Al-Shaybani (Hanafi *madhhab*) or Imam Ahmed ibn Hanbal (Hanbali *madhhab*), the Companions of the Prophet and the *tabi'in* (Successors)." The second definition found in the Shafi'i *madhhab* defines *as-salaf as-salih* as those who came first in the history of the Muslim community (*awa'il hadhihi al-umma*). According to another definition *as-salaf as-salih* refers to the Companions, the Successors, and the immediate followers of the Successors who are encompassed by the hadith of the Prophet: "The best of the community is my century, then the one that follows it, then the one that follows that."[63] According to Imam al-Suyuti (d.911/1505), one of the most prolific premodern Sunni Muslim writers,[64] the era of the *as-salaf as-salih* is a time spanning approximately up to 220 years Hijri before "innovations appeared en masse, the *Mutazilah* let their tongues loose, the philosophers raised their heads, the people of knowledge were put on trial for saying that the Qur'an was created, and the state of affairs changed radically." Another definition of the *as-salaf as-salih* defines the concept as those who lived before the year 400 Hijri and the *khalaf* as the subsequent generations of Muslims.[65] Therefore, given the various definitions of *as-salaf as-salih*, generations and who belongs to them, the concept of Salafism is not precisely defined in the Islamic tradition.[66]

Salafism, as an Islamic precept, seems to have been developed in the late second century Hijri. As a concept the genesis of the Salafi mindset is best understood in the light of the political and theological schisms that took place in the Muslim community in the first century Hijri alluded to above.[67] At that time, the concept of Salafism was used as an anchoring point for various ideologically competing groups who were all eager to show that their views, unlike those of others, were consistent with those figures who were held in high esteem during the inception of the Muslim community. This is, for example, evident in the use of word *as-salaf as-salih* in treaties attributed to Hasan al-Basri's (d. 110/ 728) to support the doctrine of free will to which he, unlike his interlocutors, considered as being a doctrine espoused by the *as-salaf as-salih*.[68] This quest for religious legitimacy by linking one's theological, political, or legal views to that of the *as-salaf as-salih* would, thus, imbibe these factions with the sense of normativeness, credibility, and authoritativeness. The same holds true for the contemporary usages of Salafism, including the two communities of interpretation under examination here.[69]

From a historical point of view, the earliest usage of the terms *as-salaf as-salih* is therefore to be understood as a particular outlook of the post–*as-salaf as-salih* generations of Muslims on the early historical events that took place after the Prophet's death regarding the issues considered unresolved in the Qur'an and Sunna, as well as the means of getting to terms with the abovementioned political and doctrinal schisms that plagued the nascent Muslims community. This salafi doctrine proved particularly important for the formation of what now is largely considered "mainstream" Sunnism, at times referred to as *Ahl-Sunna wa Jama'ah* (The People of Sunna and Muslim Majority Community) in the fourth century. Its significance was in its function of serving as a political mechanism that purported to cleanse all of the Companions[70] of the Prophet Muhammad of any partaking in or responsibility for the ensuing conflicts and violence between various Muslim factions that threatened to disintegrate the very social fabric of the nascent Muslim community.[71] As a corollary, the salafi worldview can also be conceptualized in the idea of the "emulation-worthiness" of the first century religious and political authorities who were perceived as having remained faithful to the teachings of the Qur'an and the example of the Prophet (i.e., Sunna) in relation to *'aqidah* (beliefs), *manhaj,* and *'ibadah* (worship) in contrast to those who deviated from them. Moreover, toward the end of the second Islamic century this *salafi*-embedded worldview started to shape the epistemological boundaries of the Islamic thought soon becoming a norm for reasons outlined above in relation to the increased importance of Sunna and its documentation and the sociopolitically chaotic nature of early Islam. This is evident, for example, from the fact that the founders or initiators of the various Islamic sciences sought the ideas and the views among the *as-salaf as-salih* as intellectual antecedents in order to bestow legitimacy to their respective disciplines.[72]In this context, Goldziher asserts that

> as such the imitation of the *salaf,* the pious ancestors who formed their
> habits under the eyes and on the example of the prophet, became the ideal

of pious Muslims. Gradually Salafi, i.e. the one who imitates his ancestors, becomes the supreme title of praise in pious society.[73]

The concept of *Salafism* as "an invariable element within the Islamic conscience," to borrow Chaumont's phrase,[74] has also formed the conceptual foundation for the adoption of the *madhahb*- and *ahl-hadith*-based approaches to the Islamic tradition. The former, termed "genuine traditionalism" by Chaumont,[75] attempts "to neutralise the evolutionary effects linked with the tension between an ideal past and a present always on this side of the ideal past" and the latter, termed by Chaumont *salafiyya*,[76] ancient and modern, which

> continually endeavours to update the changes—conceived as necessary alterations in relation to deviations and innovations (*bid'ah*)—believed to be necessary in view of restoration in all respects of the ideal past (more or less freely defined in relation to demands of each particular period) of the *salaf*.[77]

As such these two approaches constantly challenged and continue to challenge each other to the present times competing for "authenticity"(*asala*) as evident in the contemporary debates between the so-called "*khalaf*" or *madhhab*-based scholars and that of the "*salaf*" or the *ahl-hadith*-based scholars.[78]

The concept of Salafism in premodern Islamic thought is also embedded in a particular understanding of time and history and their relation to the present (and future). This notion is derived from a reading of few *ahad* ahadith going back to the Prophet Muhammad in which he reportedly asserted that the best people were his generation and then the next and then the following and so on and that there was no year or day except that which followed was worse than it.[79] According to this understanding:

> It was the Sunna, rather than the Kur'an, which instituted one of the most characteristic traits of the Islamic vision of history by imposing the idea a priori that this history was said to have been inevitably followed by a period of relaxation of standards, deviation and finally of division.[80]
> Moreover, according to this salafi mindset,
> time is not conceived as in itself the medium and instrument of change, but rather as reappearance, re-enactment, after a period of abeyance, degradation, descent into superstition and irrationalism; in other words a combination of typology and the historicism of modernity.[81]

This Salafi-embedded worldview evident in both the *madhhab*- and *ahl-hadith*-based thought, therefore, sees the past to provide all the answers and constantly imposes itself upon the present. In other words, the authenticity of Muslim identity can only be established by returning to a fixed point in historical time, that of the Prophet and the early Muslim community. Consequently, the concept of traditional "authenticity" (*asala*) is solely conceptualized in terms of "contingent linking of both past and future by the ontological void of today."[82]

From the above discussion on Salafism, we can conclude that the concept refers to several interrelated phenomena. First, it signifies a particular methodology of interpreting the Islamic tradition as a way of distinguishing it from other approaches considered not to be based on the (supposedly) *as-salaf as-salih manhaj*. Second, it is a political doctrine purporting to bestow an amnesty on all of the Companions of the Prophet in the midst of sociopolitical chaos that characterized early Islam. Finally, it denotes an approach to conceptualizing the Islamic tradition premised on a presupposition of a regressive view of the nature of history and time.

1.3 The Modern Period—Eighteenth Century C.E. to the Present

During the modern period, here defined as spanning from the eighteenth century C.E. to that of the present, we see a continuation of the historical debates sketched above on the relative status of various sources of legal authority in the Islamic tradition, including the issues of the authority of Sunna, the authenticity of hadith and its criticism, and their relationship to the Qur'an.[83] These debates, and the broad sociopolitical context in which they emerged, can be understood in relation to a number of revivalist premodernist and modernist movements emerging in the eighteenth century to the present.

As mentioned above the calls for the return to and the revivification (*ihya*) of the unadulterated Qur'an and Sunna teachings based on *ahl-hadith manhaj* and in the spirit of the doctrine of Salafism have been a constant feature of the Islamic intellectual tradition from its very early days. The first three to four centuries of Islamic thought were characterized by intellectual creativity and dynamism. At the end of the fifth century of the Islamic calendar (end of twelfth century C.E.) with the establishment and subsequent flourishing of four of the surviving Sunni *madhahib*, a large degree of Qur'an-Sunna "hermeneutical stability" in the area of theology and jurisprudence/law derivation was reached. Thus, at this time, by a large measure, the contours of Islamic thought, the thinkable and the unthinkable within it, to borrow Arkoun's phrase, were established.[84] In addition, during this time, through a process of consolidation and systematization, the four Sunni schools of thought were embedded in the major centers of the Muslim Empire.[85] The established Sunni Islamic centers of learning, the *madaris*, were divided along the same lines as the *madhahib* and were responsible for the production of the highest calibre scholars, primarily theologians and jurists, thus ensuring the perpetuation of the tradition. The *madhahib*-based system of Islamic learning, with the support of the political establishment, was to dominate the Muslim intellectual discourses for the next six centuries, thus up to the modern period.[86] On the other hand, the interpretational inflexibility of "juristic empiricism," as embodied by groups such as the Zahiris or the Hashwiyya, who attempted to remain faithful to the *ahl-hadith manhaj*, resulted in their eventual extinction around the same time.[87] However, certain doctrinal and methodological tendencies present in the later Hanbali *madhhab*, as embodied in some of the writings of Ibn Taymiyyah (d.728/1328) and more so his student Ibn Jawziyyah (d.751/1350), rebelled against the *taqlid*-based hermeneutic of the *madhahib* reviving the *ihya us-Sunna* principle by largely adopting the *ahl-hadith manhaj* and their "juristic empiricism."[88] These tendencies for the reform of the *madhhab*-based legal and social institutions were further reinforced by Western political and military hegemony. In this context the central issue was the reexamination of the dominant *madhhab*-based religious authority hermeneutic and, in particular, the nature of Prophetic authority and, as a corollary, that of hadith authenticity and criticism.[89] From the eighteenth century C.E. onwards, the writings of these scholars formed and still form a foundation for a number of salafi *ahl-hadith manhaj* revivalist movements, which I will discuss below.

The loss of creative thinking embedded in popular forms of Sufism and the stultifying fixity and finality of the *madhahib* that characterized much of the medieval Muslim scholarship, spurred in the eighteenth and the nineteenth centuries a number of what Rahman terms *premodernist revivalist* schools of thought. These movements included, for example, the Wahhabis in the Arabian Peninsular, the Sanusiyya in North Africa, Fulanis in West Africa, and the eighteenth century *Ahl-i-Hadith* reform movement in India. On the basis of the *ahl-hadith manhaj*, these movements *radically* questioned the perceived degrading beliefs and religious practices manifesting themselves in popular religion, such as the practice of doing petitionary prayers (*du'as*) next to the tombs of saints or the practices of visiting their graves (*ziyarah*), which in the meantime had become integral parts of the cumulative tradition. These premodern revivalist schools of thought shared a number of common characteristics such as a desire to reverse what they considered to be a sociomoral decadence of the Muslim society, to shed Islam of the superstitions inculcated by popular forms of Sufism and to remove a predeterministic outlook that permeated popular religious culture. In the spirit and the letter of the *ahl-hadith manhaj,* these movements demanded adherence and the access to the interpretation of Qur'an and hadith texts without any intermediaries.[90] Furthermore, they emphasized the absolute authority to the supposed consensus of the *salaf* (*ijma' as-salaf as-salih*) on all doctrinal and methodological issues. Moreover, they shunned the institution of *taqlid,* which formed the backbone of the traditional *madhahib* hermeneutic, and asked for the reinstitution of *ijtihad,* or interpretation, based on direct access to the Qur'an and hadith body of texts. They also aimed to revive the hadith sciences as practiced by hadith scholars in the Arabian Hijaz with the emphasis on the early sources of hadith, thus bypassing the later compilations. In doing so they wished to assert their independence from the classical *madhhab*-based approach to hadith. Their aim was to study hadith with increased vigour and stringency. Unlike the *madhhab* approach, the hadith revivalist reformers upheld the supremacy of hadith in theory as well as in practice. Few of these movements were willing to achieve these goals by engaging in armed struggle if necessary. However, the most influential revivalist hadith-based movement, the *Ahl-i-Hadith* movement in India that went on to influence revivalist movements in the Middle East in the nineteenth and twentieth centuries, headed by Shah Walli Allah, (d.1176/1762) was politically quietest in nature.[91]

These premodern revivalist movements were, apart from the abovementioned *Ahl-i-Hadith,* largely antiintellectual, especially the Wahhabi form, a movement to which I will turn my attention in more detail below. The scope and the content of their *ijtihad* were narrow and inconsequential since it was limited to the *ahl-hadith's* methodology described above.[92] The *ijtihad* largely pertained to issues of ritual practice such as the correct performance of certain elements of the daily obligatory prayers (*salat*) or theology (such as the nature of God's attributes).[93] While the premodernist revivalist groups were a great liberating force in terms of their rejection of human authority as being final and absolute (as the presumed delineating feature of the *madhahib taqlid* doctrines) and their insistence on *ijtihad,* their antiintellectualism represented a considerable retrogression and intellectual starvation when compared to the *madhhab*-based Islamic tradition and its *madrassa*-based educational system.[94] By remaining faithful to a decontextualized reading of the hadith considered authentic by early *muhaddithun,* such as M. Al-Bukhari (d. 256 / 870) and Muslim ibn al-Hajjaj (d. 261/ 875) and by rejecting subsequent doctrinal accretions, the premodern revivalist movements believed that *only* their *manhaj* embodied and revived the authentic Sunna.[95]

A number of *revivalist-modernist movements* emerged from some of these premodernist groups. One of the most significant and influential of these was the *classical modernist* movement whose origins go back to the late nineteenth century.[96] The broader context behind the beginnings of this movement includes the prevalent perception among the contemporary Muslims of the civilizational waning of the Muslim world coupled with that of the rise of the colonial rule stemming from the West over much of the Muslim world, the subsequent critical evaluation of all aspects of the Islamic tradition at the hands of the Christian missionary and administatory apparatus and the conflation of the process of modernization with that of Westernization.[97]

This encounter of Muslims with colonial powers importantly synergised and propelled the modernists' project in earnest which, among others, involved the revival of rational elements of the *turath* such as the *kalam* science.[98] The creed's major proponents were authorities such as Muhammad 'Abduh (d. 1322/1905), Jamal Al-Afghani (d. 1314/1897), Sir Sayyid Ahmed Khan (d. 1314/1898), and Rashid Rida (d. 1353/ 1935).[99] At this period of time, the Arabo-Islamic civilisation, especially in Turkey, Egypt, and India, came under the growing intellectual and cultural influence of the colonialists. Remaining faithful to the salafi mindset these *classical modernists,* also known *as salafiyya,* reclaimed the conviction of the earlier Salafi and *ahl-hadith* oriented ideologies of being able to retrieve the "pure" teachings of the Qur'an and Sunna as exemplified by the Prophet and his rightly guided Companions by means of revivification of the "true" Qur'an and Sunna teachings (*ihya al-qur'an wa- s-sunna*). The proponents of the movement argued that their forerunners and contemporaries had become disengaged from the emerging global modernity only because they forgot, rather than adhered to, the always already modern early traditions of Islam.[100] This revivalism was largely to be achieved through the exercise of *ijtihad,* the rejection of *taqlid* and by means of a hadith-based reform.[101] Therefore *classical modernists'* reforms were inspired both by hadith-based reformism of the premodern revivalist movements described above as well as by their contact with the colonial powers. Thus, the primary motivations behind their impetus for reform were the desire to free the Muslim countries from the shackles of colonization and to curb the prevalent religious practices alluded to above that were deemed "un-Islamic."[102] Additionally, these *classical modernists* saw it as their task to reconcile the Islamic faith with modern values such as constitutionalism, nationalism, freedom of religious interpretation, modern-style education, women's rights, scientific education, and cultural revival to name but a few. *Classical modernists* built on the ideas of the premodern revivalist groups mentioned above in order to achieve these goals.[103] Like their salafi *ahl-hadith* revivalist predecessors, the *classical modernists'* worldview was built on a romanticized and utopian view of the past.[104] However, it largely rejected a priori adherence to the long-established juristic heritage and legal hermeneutic of the *madhahib* by engaging in the practice of *talfiq* or cross-*madhhab* legal hermeneutic, thus "deconstructing traditional notions of established authority within Islam."[105] Methodologically, the *classical modernist* approach differed significantly from that of the premodernist revivalist *ahl-hadith*-based *manhaj*.[106] The scope and the content of their *ijtihad* were much broader than that of the premodernist revivalist.[107] Their interpretation emphasized the importance of the Qur'anic scripture and what Rahman terms the broader "historical Sunna" in contradiction to *ahl-hadith's* hadith-based Sunna (i.e., Sunna embodied in the early hadith books). This is, for example, evident in the opinion of Rida, one of its main proponents, who considered Sunna *'amaliyya,* or practiced-based Sunna, as the only source of Sunna.[108] There was little reliance on hadith literature in their overall methodology.[109] Moreover, *classical modernists* were willing to question the judgments of the ancient *muhadithun*, most of which were accepted by the premodern *ahl-hadith*. They also argued for a more rigorous and renewed application of the classical system of hadith criticism without rejecting it *in toto.*[110] Thus, they had a more critical approach to hadith that, however, still operated within the classical hadith sciences. This approach is perhaps best illustrated by the works of hadith scholars such as J. Al-Qasimi's (1866–1914 CE) *Qawa'id al-tahdith min funun mustalah al-hadith (The Principles of Regeneration from the Technical Science of Hadith Study),*[111] T. Al-Jaza'iri's (d. 1337/1919) *Tawjih al-nazar ila usul al-athar(Examining the Principles of Transmitted Reports),*[112] or more recently the works of the Al-Ghumari brothers, Ahmed (d. 1379/1960), 'Abdallah (d. 1413/1993), and 'Abd Al-Hayy(d.1415/1995).[113]Their works emphasize the need for the fresh application of hadith sciences based on what they consider to be a considerable room for maneuver within this system without offering an alternative to the classical system to hadith criticism. Furthermore, *classical modernists*, unlike their premodernist revivalist predecessors, neither isolated themselves from nor were reluctant to engage with modernity. As such they were not inherently anti-Western.[114] Rather, they attempted to reconcile the realities of modernity and the era of postcolonially emerging Arab nationalism with the Islamic tradition itself by "reading the values of modernism into the original sources of Islam."[115] Kurzman gives several examples of this double translation such as that of translating the traditional Islamic concept of justice into the modern concept of law and juridical system and the process of translating the modern concepts of citizenship and rights with the traditional Islamic concept of equality. As such, *classical modernists* were engaged in a process of double translation, namely, that of translating modern values into Islamic terms and the Islamic values into modern terms. By engaging in this type of reform, *classical modernist* thought created a number of positive links between key Western institutions such as democracy, science, women's education, and the Islamic tradition.[116] However, this approach "attempted to espouse cultural and institutional modernity by seeking a synthesis between these concepts and Islam, but doing so without rethinking the traditional Islamic theocentric worldview."[117] In other words classical modern thought still aimed to maintain the traditional conception of reality based on religious truths that ought not to be changed and in whose light modernity was to adjust.[118] M. Al-Jabiri makes a similar assertion by stating that the *classical modernists* attempted

> [t]o formulate an ideal vision of the tradition within the framework of the Arabo-Islamic history but to tailor the future of the Arab societies according to the Western-European model. However, these attempts repeatedly failed and became useless because this form of compromise obstructed functionality of history and real process of development.[119]

One of the main reasons why *classical modernism* failed to capture the hearts and minds of the wider masses was the perceived lack of legitimacy of their ideas in the eyes of many traditionally minded scholars and masses. *Classical modernists'* ideas were primarily restricted to individual scholars, did not trigger large sociopolitical movements and did not have large numbers of followers. The colonial experience that Muslim societies were subjected to resulted in many perceiving Western civilization as the very anathema of the Islamic tradition. As such any reforms of the tradition that brought the Islamic tradition closer to that of the imperialist West were considered illegitimate. Additionally, the lack of a *systematic, post-traditionally* embedded epistemology, methodology, and theological-philosophy on the basis of which the Islamic tradition could be reinterpreted and reformed in a holistic rather than selective fashion was also a contributing factor for the failure of the classical modernist project.[120] Some fragments and elaboration of their thought, however, survive to present times as evident for example in the writings of Shaikh M. Al-Ghazalli, (1917–1996 CE) or Y. Al-Qaradawi (1926–) who were/are prominent advocates of moderate Islamic revivalism.[121] Because of their relative methodological affinity with the *classical modernists* (in contrast to that of *ahl-hadith* revivalist movements) we will briefly discuss them here. In his book *Al-Sunna al-nabawiyya bayna ahl al-fiqh wa ahl-hadith* (*The Sunna of the Prophet between the Legists and the Traditionalists*)[122] Al-Ghazalli contributes to the ongoing debates on the issues of Prophetic authority, hadith criticism and their authenticity and their status in relation to the Qur'an. He essentially upholds the classical approach to hadith criticism but with the emphasis on *matn* criticism not just *isnad*. Additionally, like Rida, one of the eponyms of the classical modernist *salafiyya*, he objects to rationally or theologically incompatible hadith or those which are in conflict with the above alluded broader aims of the Islamic law (*maqasid al-shari'ah*). He does so on the basis of a hermeneutical method which privileges a Qur'an-based interpretation of hadith as well as on the basis of Hanafi and Maliki Sunna *manahij*.[123] In writing the book Al-Ghazalli wished to criticize what he considered the fanaticism and the extremes of modern *ahl-hadith*, (associated with that day Wahhabism) and their *manhaj* considering them remnants of *"Beduin legal thought."*[124] Recently published Y. Qaradawi's book *Approaching the Sunna: Comprehension & Controversy* [125] is basically a continuation of this trend. In it the author is concerned to outline general characteristics and principles of Sunna for its better understanding and application as a method that will guard people who uphold the Sunna against three evils, namely that of the "distortion of the extremists," the deviation of the falsifiers, and the "interpretation of the ignorant."[126] In doing so, Qaradawi's concept of Sunna and the *manhaj* adopted for its criticism in terms of its authenticity and status as a source of law in relation to the Qur'an and hadith remain completely within the classical Islamic sciences. For example, elements of Qaradawi's *manhaj* emphasize the priority of interpreting hadith in the light of the Qur'an, take recourse to methods such as reconciliation of hadith (overgiving of preference), recommend a thematic, holistic treatment of hadith, make distinctions between figurative and literal, and call for the importance of recognizing the causes and objectives of hadith for their better understanding. Sunna is neither epistemologically nor conceptually divorced from the hadith, and the assumptions governing the classical *ulum ul hadith* sciences are not even addressed, let alone questioned.[127] All of the methods employed by Qaradawi were in one form or another already adopted by the *classical modernists*.

In the early twentieth century another modern approach to Prophetic authority emerged in the Punjab region self-designated as *Ahl-i-Qur'an*. The movement was an extreme counterreaction to and a dissident faction of the earlier *Ahl-i-Hadith* movement in India discussed above. It is associated with the works of scholars such as Ahmad Din Amritsari (d. 1348/1930) and later on Ghulam Ahmad Parvez (d. 1405/1985). This group contended that the *only* pure and uncontaminated Islam can be found in the Qur'an. Furthermore, the *Ahl-i-Qur'an* considered the *only* source of Islamic teachings that provides an authentic and reliable basis for religious practices and beliefs. As a corollary, they were at pains to prove that all the basic tenants of Islamic teachings could be derived from the Qur'an alone. They completely discarded hadith as a reliable and authentic source of Prophetic authority. They also rejected the institution of *taqlid.*[128] Some contemporary movements such as the *Ahl Al Qur'an* movement based in Egypt can be considered as an ideational outgrowth of this earlier movement. [129]

In the first half of the twentieth century the *classical modernist* approach to interpretation of the Islamic tradition took a conservative turn in the Middle East, the Indo-Pakistani subcontinent, and Indonesia providing an ideological springboard for political Islamism in the second part of the century.[130] Abu Rabi'i refers to them as neotraditionalists and defines the emergence of neo-traditional thought as a result of a modern confrontation between Islamic religious tradition and mentality and Western worldview that, as a result of this confrontation, was compelled to "forge an intellectual and political synthesis in order to respond to the challenges of Western modernity."[131] It included personalities such as Hasan al Banna (d.1368/1949), the founder of the Muslim Brotherhood of Egypt, the Pakistani Maulana Abu 'l-A'la Maududi (d.1399/1979), Sayyid Qutb (d. 1385/1966), and Muhammad Qutb (1919–). *Neotraditionalists* were primarily a form of an organized sociopolitical movement and were strongly influenced by *classical modernists.* They were in fact in part an acceptance of and a reaction to them. They emphasized a holistic nature of Islam as a way of life. Their scope of *ijtihad* was broader than that of the *premodern revivalists* but was primarily restricted to issues of denouncing practices such as the modern banking system based on interest, unveiling of women, and family planning. They also considered intellectualism as dangerous. *Neotraditionalists* insisted on distinguishing Islam from the West and considered *classical modernists* as too Western. Methodologically, they did not accept the method and the spirit of the *classical modernists* but exhibited a strong link with the *premodern revivalist* movement of the eighteenth century, particularly Wahhabism in their emphasis on the importance of following the *as-salaf,* the rejection of Sufism and *taqlid.* Apart from their broader *ijtihad* they differed from Wahhabism in their more critical attitude toward hadith literature.[132]

Wahhabi thought originated in the deserts of Saudi Arabia in the middle of the eighteenth century and was founded by Muhammad ibn Abd ul Wahahab (d.1207/1792). Abd ul Wahhab came from a family of Hanbali scholars. He, however, had no extensive religious training himself. Wahhabism was considered by contemporary Muslim, Sunni, and Shi'i scholars alike as very much an aberration of and an anomaly to mainstream Sunnism.[133] Wahhabism remained largely on the margins of the Islamic tradition until the 1970s when it started to aggressively spread with the help of Saudi petrodollars. The adherents of Wahhabism staunchly follow the *ahl-hadith* approach to the Islamic tradition and strongly reject any rationalist, intellectual, or mystic influences in it. By subscribing to "juristic empiricism' described above Wahhabi thought attempted to interpret the Divine law without any degree of contextualization or from a historical perspective. Rejecting *taqlid*, it proclaimed "the diacritical and indeterminate hermeneutic of classical jurisprudential tradition as corruptions of purity of Islamic faith and law."[134] Its entire rationale is to demolish the classical *madhhab*-based structures of law, theology, mysticism, and religious practice. Wahhabi thought is also characterized by a complete disregard for universalistic moral values and appreciation for ethics found in the classical writings on Islamic theology and law.[135] It mainly concerns itself with the issue of correct belief (*'aqidah*) as based on the principal of *tawhid* (God's Unity and Transcendence), against *shirk* (associating partners with God), and the concept of *bid'ah* (innovation) or deviation from Prophet's Sunna. This thought is best represented in Abd ul Wahhab's book *Kitab al-Tawhid*.[136] The book is nothing more than an amalgamation of Qur'anic verses and hadith used eclectically, ahistorically, and decontextually. In it Abd ul Wahhab condemns all those Muslims not subscribing to his ideas as guilty of *shirk* because they violate one component of principle of *tawhid*, namely that of *tawhid al-'ibada* (direct worship to God alone). In his view those Muslims who resort to religious practices such as petitionary prayer (*du'a*) in which a mention of the Prophet Muhammad or other saintly personalities from Muslim history is made to help in mundane or spiritual matters; those seeking *shafa'ah* (intersession) of prophets or saints; the practice of seeking of their blessings (*tabarruk*) at their tombs or similar become guilty of *shirk*.

Over the last two to three decades, the complex dynamics between social, political, and economic factors in Muslim majority countries, especially those in which premodern revivalist movements flourished, such as Saudi Arabia, has resulted in the merging of Wahhabism and neotraditionalism, especially the *Ahl-i-Hadith* movement from India,[137] and formulation of a new hybrid model that inherited both the Salafi worldview and *ahl-hadith manhaj*.[138] Roy refers to this complex intellectual matrix as neofundamentalism.[139] While Roy's neofundamentalist thought includes schools of thought such as the former Muslim Brotherhood, *Tablighi Jama'at*, the Taliban in Afghanistan, the *Ahl-i-Hadith* in Pakistan, as well as the Saudi Wahhabis and their Western sympathizers, this study will aim to shed light and discuss primarily those belonging to the Saudi Wahhabi school of thought and their Western counterparts here referred to as Neotraditional Salafism (NTSm).

Importantly, over the last fifteen years or so a strong countercurrent to NTS emerged, which, unlike secular or liberal approaches[140] to the Islamic tradition, not only takes the classical *madhhab*-based approach to the tradition very seriously but employs (post)modern methods of reading history and sacred texts in order to conceptualize and interpret the Islamic tradition. We refer to it here as progressive Muslim approach. A detailed discussion of progressive Muslim though is presented in the sixth chapter.

1.4   Conclusion

The nature of Islamic tradition and its sources have from its very genesis been contested and subject to intense intra-Muslim debates. In particular the nature and the authenticity of Prophetic authority(Sunna) and its relationship with the hadith and Qur'an bodies of knowledge has engendered a number of approaches to the conceptualization and interpretation of the Islamic tradition. This chapter outlined the broad contours of the historical background behind the debates surrounding the status and the authenticity of the various sources of its legal authority with a particular emphasis on the *madhhab* and *ahl-hadith*-based *manahij*. It also historically situated the NTS and progressive Muslim thought in relation to how they conceptualize and interpret *turath*. The following chapter will situate the NTS school of thought in relation to the history of the debates on the status and the authenticity of the various sources of its legal authority to give us a better insight into their own *manhaj* and conceptualization of the concept of an Islamic tradition.

Chapter 2

Neotraditional Salafism: Its Main Proponents and Its *Manhaj*

This chapter presents a discussion on the main representatives of NTS school of thought and situates Neotraditional Salafism (NTSm) in relation to several issues that formed the subject matter of the previous chapter, including the historical context behind the emergence of the premodern *ahl hadith* and *ahl-ra'y/madhhab* schools of thought; NTS understanding of the concept of Salafism; NTS ideas in relation to what constitutes legitimate knowledge (*'ilm*) and its sources; NTS concept of the nature and scope of the concept of Sunna and the NTS's own self-description of their *manhaj*. In this chapter, I will argue that the NTS approach to, and the interpretation of, the Islamic tradition is based upon the Salafi-revivalist premodern *ahl-hadith manhaj*.

Before I start my discussion, a note on the employment of term "Neotraditional Salafism" is in order. I have opted for this phrase to highlight several points discussed in the previous and present chapter that apply to its Qur'an-Sunna interpretational methodology and its approach to the overall Islamic tradition. Salafism–because of its worldview—is framed within the larger umbrella concept of Salafism. "Traditional" is linked to its premise of assigning the highest epistemological value to "traditions" (i.e., ahadith) in its Qur'an-Sunna hermeneutic. The prefix "Neo-" refers to the fact that it is a contemporary phenomenon. This is not to suggest that NTS have somehow managed to evade or exist in isolation from modernity but that in terms of their *manhaj*, i.e., the epistemologies and the methodologies employed in interpreting the Qur'an and the Sunna, they are a continuation of the premodern ahl-hadith *manhaj*.Thus, the prexif "Neo." An alternative term Neo-Ahl-Hadithism could also be used. The reason for the employment of the term "Neotraditional Salafism" rather than Neo-

Ahl-Hadithism is because the literature written by scholars who subscribe to this approach to interpret the Qur'an and Sunna use the term Salafism more frequently than the term Ahl-Hadith when self-defining.[1]

2.1 The Main Representatives and Proponents of Neotraditional Salafism

NTSm is a contemporary "community of interpretation." As outlined in the introduction among the most influential exponents of NTSm, among others, are contemporary Middle Eastern Muslim scholars N. Al-Albanee (d. 1999),[2] A.Bin Baz (d. 1999),[3] M. Al-Uthaymeen (d. 2001),[4] and H. Al- Madhkhalee (b. 1931–).[5] In the Western context, the NTS scholars include personalities such as Jamal Zarabozo[6] and Dr. Bilal Philips.[7]

Although the majority of NTS proponents are of Saudi Arabian background or have studied and/or taught in the Saudi Kingdom, the proponents of NTSm are well entrenched in many parts of the Muslim clerical establishment.[8]

In my survey of the NTS literature, I will consult primarily some of the representative works of the Saudi Arabian scholars, and to a lesser extent, their students and followers in the West.

Although the Saudi Arabian NTS scholars write exclusively in Arabic their Western colleagues write in English. The influence of the Saudi Arabian scholars is felt not only across the Middle East but also North Africa, the Indo-Pakistani Subcontinent,[9] and, due to easier and faster communications, in major Muslim communities living in the West where their ideological sympathizers have established their own publishing houses and Web sites. This is where the works of the Saudi Arabian NTS scholars are translated into English.The publishing houses, among others, include T.R.O.I.D. and *Tarbiyyah* Publications in Toronto; *Invitation to Islam* and *Al-Khilafat Publications* in London; and *Salafi Publications* and *Maktabah Darussalaam* in Birmingham. Among numerous Web sites are http://www.salafipublications.com, www.tarbiyyahbookstore.com, http//:www.qss.org, http://al-Sunna.com; http://www.salaf.com, and http://www.fatwa-online.com/. Also individual scholar's Web sites such as www.binbaz.org.sa, www.rabee.net, and www.ibnothaimeen.com have been set up by the proponents of NTSm in the West.[10] A number of these NTS websites are located and hosted in some Western universities such as the Universities of Southern California[11] and Houston[12] in the United States. A number of associations which endorse NTSm in the West include societies such as *The Qur'an and Sunna Society of North America*,[13] *The Qur'an and Sunna Society of Canada*,[14] and the *Jam'iyat Ihyaa Minhaj Al Sunna* in Britain.[15]

2.2   Preliminary Remarks Regarding the Methodology Adopted in the Writings of NTS Scholars

Before I examine some of the main ideas in the writings of NTS scholars from the perspective of our discussion in the previous chapter, a few preliminary remarks regarding the methodology employed in their works are in order. This is so because having noted the general characteristics of the NTS *manhaj,* we can make a better sense of the manner in which they construct and justify their arguments as presented in the subsequent sections of this chapter. In the ensuing part of this chapter, I shall examine their *manhaj* in more detail.

First, the writings of NTS scholars are in essence amalgamations of (parts) of Qur'anic verses and ahadith used atomistically and eclectically. There is little or no analysis or attempts to provide a coherent context/narrative of whatever is being discussed. Second, NTS scholars do not ground their methodology in any theory of interpretation/hermeneutics. Third, as shall become clear in the subsequent parts of this chapter, the proponents of NTS thought rely on works of selected authorities in the inherited Islamic tradition who, in their view, have remained faithful to the *ahl-hadith manhaj* as rudimentary commentary to the Qur'anic verses and the hadith cited. These usually include traditionalists/*muhadithun* or scholars belonging to the Hanbali school of thought such as Ibn Hanbal (d. 241 A.H.), Ibn Qutibah (d.276 A.H.),At-Tamimi (d.354 A.H.), Ar-Ramhurmuzi (d.360 A.H), An-Nisaburi (d.405 A.H.), Ibn Taymiyya (d. 728 A.H.), Ibn Al-Qayyim (d. 751 A.H.), Ibn Kathir (d.744 A.H.), and Abdul al Wahhab (d.1207 A.H.) and exclude, for example, many prominent jurists from the Hanafi, Maliki, and Shafi'i schools of thought.[16]

An excellent example representative of this methodology is the book by a Saudi scholar Al-Haadaadee[17] titled *The Book of Forty Hadeeth Regarding the Madhhab of the Salaf*[18] in which the author states that he had selected forty-seven "authentic" hadith as a means of clarifying important fundamentals connected to the salafi *manhaj.*[19] In other words the selected hadith themselves are constitutive of the actual methodology. The book itself is structured in such a manner that each "chapter" is given a heading followed by a hadith or a group of ahadith (supposedly) reflecting the theme of the heading and where the hadith is found.Sometimes a footnote is inserted to add some additional information as a means of clarifying terms or phrases or in form of some extratextual material on the topic with reference to one of ahl-hadith/NTS scholars. Below is a reproduction of two of these chapters:

Chapter/Heading: *The Nobility of the People of Hadith*

Hadith: On the authority of Al-Mugheerah bin Shu'bah, may Allah be pleased with him, that Allah's Messenger (saw) said:

> There will not cease to remain a Group from my nation manifest/victorious until the command of Allah comes, whilst they are still manifest/victorious.
>   Narrated by Al-Bukhaaree (Saheeh Al-Bukhaaree 6/2667 No.6881)

Commentary: The majority of people of knowledge have declared that this manifest/victorious group are Ahlul-hadith. (Refer to the book *'Ahlul-hadeeth At-taa'ifatul –Mansoorah, Shyakh Rabee' bin Haadee Al-Madkhalee*.)

Heading/Chapter: *Not Everyone Who Displays Aid for the Religion Is Accepted as Truly Aiding Until It Is Known that He Is A Person of Sunna*

Hadith: On the Authority of Abu Hurayrah, may Allah be please with him that on the Day of Khaybar Allah's messenger (saw) commanded Bilaal to call the people with:

> Indeed no souls shall enter paradise except a Muslim soul. And verily Allaah may give aid to this Religion by a way of a wicked man.
>   Narrated by Al-Bukhaaree (Saheeh,1/50 No.100) and
>   Muslim (Saheeh, 4/2058 No.13)

End of reproduced section.

This type of reasoning and argument presentation needs to be kept in mind throughout the discussion in this chapter.

2.3 NTSm in Relation to the Genealogy of the Debates on the Relative Status and the Authenticity of the Various Sources of Legal Authority in the Islamic Tradition

This segment of the chapter examines the NTS thought with respect to the historical context behind the emergence of the premodern *ahl hadith* and *ahl-ra'yl madhhab* schools of thought.

I first turn my attention to the relationship between NTSm and the *premodern ahl-hadith* school of thought. NTS scholars consider themselves to be the inheritors of the premodern ahl-hadith because of their view that this school of thought is the only sect whose *manhaj* has remained true to the Qur'an and Sunna. For example, Al-Atharee in his book "*Clarification that the Ahlul-Hadeeth Are the Saved Sect and Victorious Group*," is of the view that the "truth is found in the creed of the Ahlul-Hadith."[20] He praises the efforts of individuals who made long journeys in search of even only one narration collecting and authenticating hadith and criticizes the adherents of *ahl-ra'y* for their reliance on opinion instead of hadith. In this context, he asserts the following:

> Then he [individual collecting hadith] would not cease to be in pursuit of narrations and in the quest for it until they understood its authentic from its inauthentic; and its abrogating from its abrogated, and they knew who opposed it in exchange for opinion from the Scholars of fiqh.[21] [sic]

Another indication that the NTS scholars associate themselves with the premodern *ahl-hadith* school of thought and oppose the *ahl-ra'y* is Al-Atharee's assertion that the Ahl-Hadith of today "take the Religion from the Book [The Qur'an] and the Sunna" thereby inheriting harmony and unity whereas people of "innovations and desires" took "the Religion from the intellects and opinions" and as a result have inherited separation and differing (*ikhtilaf*).[22] Here Al-Atharee clearly refers to the prominent use of reason (*'aql*) and reason-based opinion (*ra'y*) that were featured in the *ahl-ra'y* Qur'an-Sunna *manhaj*.

Similarly, the Syrian scholar Jameel Zaynoo (1930–), who for many years taught in Dar-ul-Hadith al-Khairiyah in Mecca, in his book *The Methodology of the Saved Sect* (*Minhaj al-Firqat un-Najiyah*) forms the view that the premodern ahl-hadith are the Saved Sect. He bases his argument in the form of a hadith found in the early classical hadith collection by Muslims in which the Prophet of Islam is reported to have said that a group from his Ummah would not cease to manifest upon the truth. Zaynoo identifies the premodern *ahl-hadith* as being that group.[23]

NTS scholars also define themselves in relation to the early schisms that beset the nascent Muslim community and in this context clearly identify themselves with the premodern ahl-hadith group. Discussing the question of who the ahl-hadith are, Al-Atharee writes:

> So they are the ones who lie waiting to ambush every sect that opposes the Islamic manhaj, such as the Jahmiyyah, the Mu'tazilah, the Khawaarij,

the Rawaafid, The Murji'ah, the Qadariiyyah and everyone else who strays from Allah and follows his desires, in every time and place.[24]

Based on the above it can be concluded that the NTS scholars are, in fact, the contemporary version of the premodern ahl-hadith, something that they themselves willingly and approvingly accept.

Apart from their identification with the premodern ahl-hadith school of thought NTS scholars frequently ascribe to themselves the epithet "salafi" and consider that their *manhaj* is in complete accordance with the concept of Salafism and with the practice of following in the footsteps of the *as-salaf as-salih*.[25] For example, Bin Baz asserts in his booklet *A Statement and Clarification of Al-Salafiyyah: Concepts an Principals* that the concept of Salafism is based upon some "general and intellectual principles" "derived from the Qur'an, Sunna and Consensus (*ijma'*) which govern the method of acquiring din and understanding the Qur'an and Sunah according to the principles agreed upon by the righteous predecessors (salaf)." Furthermore, he considers those who abide by these principles as being on the way of Salafis and thus qualifying to belong to the mainstream Muslim community (*Ahl-Sunna wa'l Jama'ah*).[26] Similarly, Al-Albanee in his book *The Principals of the Salafee Methodology: An Islamic Manual for Reform* quotes the hadith according to which the first generation of Muslims is the best, followed by the next, and so on to argue the first three generations are/were the *as-salaf as-salih* and that all Muslims must take them as an example. Those who do, argues Al-Albanee further, are the Saved Sect.[27]

However, certain understandings of the concept of Salafism are specific to the NTS thought. One important aspect of this NTS conceptualization of Salafism for the purposes of this study is the notion that Salafism is to be viewed primarily as manifesting itself in the belief that the historical legacy of the Prophet's embodiment of the Qur'an, as it was understood by the most eminent authorities belonging to the first three generations of Muslims (i.e., the *as-salaf as-salih as-salih*) is normative, static, and universalistic in nature (in terms of methodology/*manhaj* and the creed/*aqidah*). One of the main proponents of NTS thought Al-Uthaymeen in the context of discussing the historical emergence behind the label "as-salaf as-salihiyyah," why and when it arose and its importance as a method to "distinguish those upon the truth from those upon the falsehood" asserts the following:

> As-salaf as-salihiyyah is distinguished from the various Islamic factions due to their ascription to what guarantees for them the correct and true Islam, which is adhered to what the Messenger and his Companions were upon, as occurs in the authentic Hadiths.[28] [sic]

And

> As-salaf as-salihfiyyah are not a group or a party but those who follow [the] Prophet's and Companions' aqidah, manhaj and 'ibadaah.[29]

Similarly, Al-Atharee links *only* the *ahl-hadith/ahl-athar*[30] group with those who have remained on the path of the *salaf*.[31]

With their conflation of the concept of Sunna with that of *sahih* hadith as defined by the early classical hadith scholars such as Bukhari(d.256 A.H.) and Muslim (d. 261) and alongside their belief in exclusively following in the footsteps of *as salaf*, it is imperative for the NTS scholars to uphold the doctrine of the uprightness and cleansing of all of the Companions of the Prophet because of their crucial position in the chains of transmission in the hadith literature and thus in safeguarding a very important component of the knowledge of the Islamic tradition itself. Al-Madkhalee in his book *The Methodology of Ahlus-Sunna Wal Jamaa'ah: On Criticizing Individuals, Books and Groups* forms exactly this view by asserting:

> Ahlus-Sunna wal-Jamaa'ah are well aware of their [Companions'] position and status, and they guard it with the strictest form of guarding. And they forbid others from speaking vainly about what occurred of dispute between 'Alee and Mu'aawiyyah and those who supported them from the rest of the Companions. Rather, they assert for them the reward that is given to the mujahids. And they ruled that all those who spoke about them—or even about one of them—were upon deviance, misguidance and heresy.[32]

He forms this view on the basis of a single hadith found in Bukhari's and Muslim's hadith collections in which the Prophet is reported to have ordered people not to revile his Companions because of their many virtues.[33]

Thus, NTS scholars embrace the concept of Salafism in two ways. First, they do so in its particular NTS version by linking the *manhaj* of *as-salaf as-salih to* that of the premodern ahl-hadith *manhaj*. Second, by subscribing to the doctrine of the righteousness and unblemishness of *all* of the Companions of the Prophet in relation to the early civil wars that beleaguered the nascent Muslim community.

Another way of situating the contemporary NTS thought in relation to the debates on the relative status of sources of legal authority in the Islamic tradition is by examining their ideas in relation to what constitutes legitimate knowledge (*'ilm*) and its sources. In the previous chapter, we discussed the gradual shift in the concept of *'ilm* with the onset of what we referred to as the forces of traditionalization of Islamic thought and the hadithification of Sunna that simultaneously epistemologically, methodologically, and hermeneutically marginalized reason and reason-based theories of interpretation in legal theory and promoted the view of founding and restricting the concept of *'ilm* to the Qur'an and hadith texts only. This concept of *'ilm* is evident in the thinking of Al-Uthaymeen in his book *A Reply to the Doubts of the Qutubiyyah Concerning Ascription to Sunna and Salafiyyah*. There he argues that the legitimate religious knowledge and its sources are restricted to the following: the Qur'an, the premodern sciences governing the process of its explication and interpretation, the "authentic" hadith, and the consensus (ijma') of Muslim scholars who have remained faithful to the Ahl/Ashab-ul-Hadith *manhaj*.[34] Similarly, Al-Albanee restricts the definition of *'ilm*, apart from the Qur'an, only to hadith and calls for the legal process to be purged of reason and replaced entirely by hadith.[35] He refers to this jurisprudence as *fiqh al-hadith*.[36] Bin Baz in his booklet titled *The Obligation of Acting upon the Sunna of the Messenger and The Unbelief of Those Who Reject It* echoes these views by quoting the words of Al-Bayhaqi, a famous Sunni hadith expert (d. 384 A.H.), who in turn quotes Sufyan Al-Thawri[37] as having said that "the whole of knowledge is knowledge of the narrations (i.e., hadith)."[38] According to this view, the science of jurisprudence (*fiqh*) is synonymous with and therefore restricted to that of hadith.[39] Al-Albanee forms this view when relying on the opinion of Ahmad bin Hanbal, who is reported to have said that the opinions of the major *madhhab* scholars were simply opinions and that the evidence was only found in the narrations (athar/hadith).[40]

The view that *'ilm* is entirely textually based is also expressed by Al-Madkhalee who quotes several authorities from the past[41] stating, "The religion of the prophet Muhammad is the narrations," "the knowledge that is followed is that what contains *'qalaa haddathana*[42] and everything else is whispers from the Shaytaan," and "the knowledge is what contains *'qalaa haddathana'* and everything else is error and darkness."[43]

Likewise, Al-Madkhalee restricts *'ilm* to textual sources only. This is evident in his argument against the types of *qiyas* employed by the "People of Rhetoric" (*ahl-kalam*)—whose fundamentals of Religion are said to be derived through the reasoning (*qiyas*) of the intellect—and the *fuqaha* belonging to the *madhahib*—who are said to be in large part also depending on *qiyas* for religious legislation. Furthermore, he states that the contours of *'ilm* according to ahl-hadith are confined to "the texts and the narrations of the Companions on all events in their basic and implied or deeper[44] meaning.[45]

In their opposition to the *ahl-kalam*, the NTS scholars also consider "philosophy" to be outside the scope of *'ilm*. For example, this view is represented by the assertion of Al-Albanee, who in the context of discussing how one is to obtain certain knowledge repeats on several occasions that "Islam is free from philosophy."[46]

NTS scholars, on the other hand, like the premodern ahl-hadith, believe in the normative value of *ahad* hadith as sources of *'ilm* in all spheres of the Islamic tradition.[47] Thus, ahad hadith constitute *'ilm* upon which it is obligatory to act.[48] For example, the following excerpt from Zarabozo's book *The Methodology of the Saved Sect* suggests this:

> In the history of Islam, there developed this concept that matters of faith, as opposed to matters of law, have to be based on "definitive" evidence and some categories of hadith do not meet this requirement. This led to a rejection of certain authentic hadith of the Prophet (peace and blessings of Allah be upon him). Ibn Abdul-Wahhaab opposed this approach, relying on the example set by the earliest scholars, and affirmed that all authenticated hadith of the Prophet (peace and blessings of Allah be upon him) must be believed in regardless of the topic.[49]

Here Zarabozo links the NTS *manhaj* clearly with that of Abd ul Wahhab to claim that *ahad* hadith are to be considered as having a normative value both in *'aqidah* and *fiqh*, unlike, for example, in the Hanafi *madhhab* where they do not. The prominence of Abu ul Wahhab's ideas and *manhaj* on the NTS will be demonstrated again below. Moreover, Al-Albanee considers that the distinction between *ahad* and *mutawatir* hadith as developed by *usuliyyun*, i.e., the legal theorists, is artificial and not part of the *salaf manhaj*.[50]

Another vista though which we can glean the limits of *'ilm* according to the NTS school of thought is Al-Madkhalee's discussion on the censuring of books written by well-known classical and contemporary non-NTS Muslim Sufi and/or *madhhab*-based scholars. In this list of books of "innovation and misguidance," he includes, among others, Abu Talib al-Makki's[51] *Qut al-Qulub* (Nourishment of Hearts), *Ihya Ulum ud-Din* of Abu Hamid Al-Ghazalli, *Al-Fusus al-Hikam* of Ibn 'Arabi, or the books by the prominent contemporary Muslim scholars Y. Qaradawi (Qatar) and S. Al-Buti (Syria).[52]

In summary, the NTS school of thought considers that the legitimate sources of *'ilm* are restricted exclusively to the Qur'an and hadith texts and that any use of reason can only be at best derivative.

I turn my attention now to discussing the NTS concept of Sunna. The concept of Sunna according to the NTS school of thought is defined by the *muhadithun* (and some of the *fuqaha*) as those statements (*qawl*), actions (*fi'l*), and tacit approvals (*taqrir*) found in the authentic hadith collections. For example, Al-Albanee defines Sunna as a statement (*qawl*), action (*fi'l*) and tacit approval (*taqrir*) of the Prophet Muhammad that has reached us in form of authentic ahadith as defined by using the methods of classical *ulum-ul hadith* sciences.[53] Likewise, Bin Baz in his discussion on the meaning of the concept of Sunna writes that the Sunna is "whatever is authentically narrated from Allah's Messenger."[54] M. Al-Azami's, another prominent NTS scholar, definition of hadith is identical to that of Bin Baz and Al-Albanee.[55] We are also told that Sunna cannot be known through *qiyas* and that its concept consists only in "attesting the athar without asking how and why."[56]

One important determinant of the concept of Sunna in NTS thought is their assertion that the *ahl-hadith* are the sole and true followers of the *as-salaf as-salih*'s understanding of the scope and the nature of the concept of Sunna because of their adherence to the "authentic" hadith. A contemporary NTS scholar Al-Madkhalee expresses this line of thought in a following manner:

> Then verily the one who studies the condition of the previous and subsequent ones [generations of Muslims] who are affiliated to the Ummah of Muhammad and studies their methodology, their beliefs and conceptions, doing so with justness, understanding and without bias, will find that the Ahl-ul-Hadith are the sternest of the people following, obeying and associating themselves to that which the Prophet Muhammad came to them with, by the way of the Book (i.e. the Qur'an) and the Sunna, in their beliefs ('aqidah), in their various acts of worship, in their dealings, in their da'wa, in their deriving of rulings and in their establishing of proofs.[57]

Sahih hadith and the nature and the scope of the concept of Sunna are, thus, used interchangeably in NTS thought. This argument is represented by Al-Atharee with the following statement:

> It will not be hidden from one who knows the Book that the usage of the term Ahlus-Sunna is not correct to be used for any of the current sects, except for the Ahlul-Hadeeth, because the hadeeth and the Sunna have come from the Prophet.[58]

Al Atharee similarly argues that the *ahl-hadith* are the defenders of Sunna as based on their *manhaj*.[59] To argue for this type of understanding of the nature and the scope of the concept of Sunna, NTS scholars again rely on views of selected authorities from the past such as Ahmed Ibn Hanbal (d. 241 A.H.) who is considered to be a major proponent of *ahl-hadith manhaj*.[60] Hanbal's approach to the nature and the scope of the concept of Sunna is clearly demonstrated in his treatise *Tabagatul-Hanabilah* in which he states: "And the Sunna with us are the athar (narrations) of the Prophet" (*wa-s-Sunnatu 'indana atharu resulillah)*"; there is no analogical reasoning in the Sunna and examples or likenesses are not to be made for it (*wa laysa fi sunneti qiyas, wa la tudrebu laha al-amthal*) and "nor is it [Sunna] grasped and comprehended by the intellects or the desires (*wa la tudrebe bi 'uqaw'li wa la 'l ahwa'*)."[61] Elsewhere he has reportedly said that an unreliable hadith was dearer to him than the use of reason.[62]

As part of their overall claim to be the sole custodians of the *salaf-ul-salih's* understanding of the scope and the nature of the concept of Sunna, NTS also maintain that the way in which the nature and the scope of the Qur'an and Sunna indicants (*'adilla/dalil*) were understood and interpreted from the time of the Prophet until now remained the same and is adhered to in its original form by the ahl-hadith. This is the view of Al-Madkhalee, for example, who in the chapter of his book on *Who is the Ahl-Hadeeth?*, writes: "They[Ahl-Hadith] after all of the Companions—and the head of them the rightly guided Caliphs—are the leaders of the taabi'een and at the head of them [sic]."[63] We are then told that the following authorities amongst the second generation of Muslims belonged to the ahl-hadith movement:[64] Al-Musayyib (d. 90 A.H.), M. ibn Hanafiyah (d. 80 A.H.), Ibn Mas'ood (d. 94 A.H.), Al-Basri (d. 110 A.H.), Umar ibn Abdul Aziz (d. 101 A.H.) and Al-Zuhri (d. 125 A.H.). Finally, among the followers of tabi'in (*atbaa'at-tabi'in*), or the third generation of Muslims faithful to the *ahl-hadith* methodology of interpretation of Qur'an and Sunna, the following people are included: Imam Malik (d. 179 A.H.), Awza'i (d. 157 A.H.), and Abu Hanifah (d. 150 A.H.). Al-Madhkhalee also mentions people belonging to subsequent generations who, according to him, follow in the footsteps of previously stated authorities, including scholars such as Shafi'i (d. 204 A.H.), Ibn Hanbal (d. 241 A.H.), Bukhari (d. 256 A.H.), Muslim (d. 261 A.H.), Ibn Salah (d. 643 A.H.), and Ibn Taymiyyah (d. 728 A.H.).[65]

Furthermore, NTS scholars also identify themselves with the efforts of the modern *ihya as-Sunna* movements. For example, Zaynoo clearly states this by asserting that it is the task of his and those who belong to the Saved Sect identified as the *ahl-hadith* to "revive the Sunna of the Messenger (saw) in their worship, their dealings and their lives..."[66]

Another closely related concept in the discussion of the concept of Sunna in NTS literature is that of *bid'ah*. According to the NTS thought *bida'ah* is the antonym of Sunna, thus it is defined as heretical innovation in religion without any precedent found in the "authentic" hadith literature. The *madhhab* approach to the concept of *bid'ah* is more nuanced and conceptualizes it in terms of both good and bad *bid'ah*,[67] as based upon a report on the actions of the Caliph 'Umar[68] and the opinion of *madhhab* scholars such as Shafi'i who is said to have divided *bid'ah* into an approved (*mahmuda*) or blameworthy (*madhmûma*) *bid'ah*. The former is said to be in conformity with the Sunna and the latter is not.[69] The madhhab-based definition also takes recourse to a major madhhab-based authority on hadith in Sunni Islam that of Ibn Hajar Asqalani whose five-fold classification of *bid'ah* is defined as follows:

> The root meaning of innovation is what is produced without precedent. It is applied in the law in opposition to the Sunna and is therefore blameworthy. Strictly speaking, if it is part of what is classified as commendable by the law then it is a good innovation (*h.asana*), while if it is part of what is classified as blameworthy by the law then it is blameworthy (*mustaqbaha*), otherwise it falls in the category of what is permitted indifferently (*mubâh*). It can be divided into the known five categories.[70]

NTS scholars interpret away the report on the actions of the Caliph 'Umar as being "relative and subjective not original or absolute." I might add that this is the only insistence in the NTS literature that I have consulted in which such a methodological/hermeneutical distinction between that specific and general or absolute and contingent was made in relation to any issue. Instead, they advocate for a comprehensive definition of *bid'ah,* which by definition can only be blameworthy. This they do on the basis of another hadith according to which the Prophet of Islam reportedly warned Muslims to be aware of the newly invented matters because every such matter is a *bid'ah* and that every *bid'ah* leads astray to Hellfire.[71] Furthermore, Al-Madkhalee and Al-Atharee describe the methodologies of those Muslims from the past and the present, including the followers of the *madhahib,* who do not follow or oppose the *ahl-hadith manhaj* as guilty of *bid'ah.* For example, Al-Atharee states that "whoever hates Ahlul-Hadith, ancient and new, old and young, then he is upon innovation." Elsewhere he quotes Shah Walli Allah(d. 1762 A.D.), a noted hadith scholar from India, who in his book on the history of the ahl-hadith accuses the *madhahib* of being innovators.[72] Similarly, Al-Madkhalee includes a number of other Muslim groups such as the Khawarij, the Rawafid (i.e., the Shi'a), the Sufis, and the *ahl-kalam* as those who belong to the innovators based on their *manhaj.*[73] In the same vein, Ibn Amir Ar Ruhaylee, Professor at the Islamic University of Madinah and teacher in the Prophet's mosque in Medinah, in his short treatise titled "Advice to the Muslim Youth" considers all other Muslims who do not belong to the Ahl Sunna *'ulama,* which he does not define in any specific manner, but given his elsewhere stated definition of Sunna, it can be concluded that he conflates the Ahl Sunna *'ulama* with that of the Ahl-Hadith,[74] as people of *bid'ah* and people who have deviated from Sunna.[75]

Therefore we can conclude that the nature and the scope of the concept of Sunna according to the NTS school of thought are such that it considers *sahih* hadith its only vehicle of transmission and embodiment. Thus, on this they are again in agreement with the premodern *ahl-hadith*. Furthermore, NTS scholars claim that by adhering to the *ahl-hadith manhaj* of Sunna they automatically hold on to the *salafi manhaj* of the same. Finally, the NTS scholars have a unique concept of *bid'ah* that is conceptualized as an antonym of Sunna and is very comprehensive in covering all issues that fall outside of their definition of *'ilm*.

Another important aspect of the debates that have unfolded in history in relation to the relative status of the various sources of legal authority and their authenticity is the legitimacy and the scope of nontextual sources in conceptualizing and interpreting the Islamic tradition that affected the definition of what constitutes valid or legitimate religious knowledge and its sources (*'ilm*). On this issue, the NTS school of thought is again in accordance with the premodern *ahl-hadith* in their claim of the sole legitimacy of the Qur'an and hadith texts as sources of *'ilm*. In particular, they oppose the doctrines of *taqlid, ijtihad* in presence of text (i.e., the Qur'an and hadith), *istihsan, qasd, maslaha mursala, ra'y,* and *qiyas*.[76] Instead, they advocate for and promote the institution of *ittiba'*, defined as unflinching adherence to "authentic" hadith. According to the NTS community of interpretation, nontextual sources of knowledge can be used only if "there is no clear and explicit text which would allow the verification of the correctness of various opinions."[77] Furthermore, according to the NTS *manhaj*, reason and reason-based sources of knowledge, which are relied on to some extent in the broader *madhhab*-based traditional Islamic scholarship,[78] are considered to function outside the scope of the "valid" religious knowledge contained in the Qur'an and the hadith-based Sunna. In this context an NTS scholar Al-Madanee asserts:

> One who puts forward his ijtihad in a matter of fiqh, or analogy (qiyas) from the intellect, or an opinion derived from philosophy, or ta'weel, or tahreef, or a belief of shirk, or an innovated desire in the belief, statement or action—over even the smallest of clearly established Prophetic Sunna found in the authorised reliable books of ahaadeeth, after coming across it in them—then he is not from the Saved Sect which the truthful Messenger specified.[79]

As such,

> There is no need to go to what has been collected by the people of opinions and people of ijtihad, from their many judgments and their papers on

subsidiary issues. Most of them have no supporting proof for the declaration in them of what is lawful and what is unlawful, the permissible and the impermissible...[80]

Legal sources of knowledge based on reason or reason-based opinion such as *istihsan, qiyas,* and "the methods of the *ahl-kalam*" are not recognized as valid.[81] Al-Madanee quotes the opinion of a classical scholar Al-Maliki (d. 390 A.H.) to support the view that *taqlid* is forbidden and that *ittiba'* is considered one of the foundations of the Islamic religion.

> Ibn Kuwaizmin said al-Maalikee said, "Taqleed in the legislation is going back to a statement which has no proof from its sayer and ittibaa' is what is established to contain proof. Ittibaa' in the religion is a foundation and taqleed is forbidden."[82]

and,

> The da'wah of the Ahlul-Hadith to take from the Book and the Sunna alone, without performing blind following (taqleed) of anyone in particular...[83]

Bin Baz echoes this view by listing narrations of the Imams of the four Sunni *madhahib* that imply that the "blind following" of their opinions is not warranted by the Imams themselves and that they prefer hadith over their own opinions.[84] Arguing against the need for *taqlid* in the field of theology and law, Al-Madanee similarly maintains that the textual indicants (*'adillah*) present in the Qur'an and the Sunna can be determined on the basis of hadith compilations of the "pure Sunna like al-Bukharee, Muslim and others from authentic books," which are "sufficient and satisfactory for all events and judgments up to the Day of Judgment."[85] This view is echoed by Al-Atharee.[86]

Elsewhere strong criticism of the institution of the *taqlid* present in the *madhahib* is evident in the NTS literature.

For example, Al-Albanee writes:

> This is the taqleed which rejects hadith in giving victory to the madhhab. The likes of this is prohibited by the caller of the Sunna.[87]

On the other hand, NTS school of thought endorses the concept of *ittiba'*. For example, Al-Albanee, basing himself on a report from Ibn Hanbal considers that the institution of *ittiba'* is to be equated with that of *ahadith/athar*.[88] Indeed, the entire religion is said to be restricted to *ittiba'*.[89]

The arguments over *taqlid* and *ittiba'* have lead to numerous debates between the proponents of the *madhahib* and that *ahl-hadith/*NTS scholars, which are still ongoing.[90]

2.4 NTS Manhaj as Described by NTS Scholars

At the beginning of this chapter using several examples from the book by Al-Hadadee on what he terms the Salaf *manhaj*, I made some preliminary remarks regarding the main features of the NTS *manhaj* and characterized it as a collection of (segments of) Qur'anic verses and "authentic" hadith, at times buttressed with short commentary from *ahl-hadith*-minded scholars without or with little analysis or attempts at contextualization. Moreover, as a rule, NTS scholars do not discuss their *manhaj* in any great detail nor do they base it on any theory of interpretation. Furthermore, NTS scholars often employ very vague and general language not only when attempting to explain their methodology but also when discrediting the methodology of others using terminology such as "people of desires," "the strayed," "the innovators," etc., as will be noted below. How do NTS scholars themselves characterize their *manhaj*?

Zaynoo, for example, portrays the NTS *manhaj* as supposedly clinging to the methodology adopted by the Messenger during his lifetime and the methodology of his Companions after his death and equates this methodology with the "authentic" hadith. In his own words, the correct *manhaj* to which NTS adhere is as follows:

> This methodology is the Qur'an which Allah revealed to His Noble Messenger (saw) who then explained it to his Companions in the authentic narrations from him.[91]

Furthermore, more specifically, Zaynoo considers that the correct methodology when disputes and differences arise is to "return to the Speech of Allah (i.e. the Qur'aan) and the speech of His Messenger (i.e. the authentic narrations)." Zaynoo then immediately quotes two Qu'ranic verses, giving no contextual background behind them, one of which enjoys the Muslims to obey Allah, His messenger and those who are in authority (4:59), and the other verse according to which Muslims are said to not have faith unless they are willing to have their disputes between them settled by the Messenger (4:65) to evidently substantiate his above made claim of what the correct methodology entails.[92] This approach is very representative of other NTS literature I consulted. For example, Al-Albanee in the context of discussing a hadith according to which the Prophet Muhammad reportedly said that Christians and Jews were split into seventy-two and seventy-one sects, respectively, and that his Muslim community (*umma*) would split into seventy-three, all of which would go to Hellfire expect the one that follows the *jama'a* (i.e., the early community of Companions) and considers this hadith to be clear and true on the basis of immediately quoting verses 3–4 from Sura *An-Najm*, which states that the Prophet does not speak out of desire and that he is indeed receiving revelation from God. Therefore his method solely consists of linking the hadith with the Qur'anic verse, which presumably supports his explanation of the hadith.[93] Similarly, in the context of arguing the importance of not "innovating into religion that which has not been permitted by Allah nor prescribed by His Messenger even if people see it as something good because the religion has been perfected,"[94] Al-Atharee, to seemingly support this assertion, quotes verse 32 from Sura *Yunus,* which he translates, "And what is there after the truth, expect misguidance." Again, as in the case with the previous two examples, the NTS scholars' *manhaj* consists solely of quotation of hadith or isolated Qur'anic verses without any attempts at developing a systematic theory of interpretation or any systematic attempt at contextualization.

Al-Hadadee gives us one important insight into the NTS *manhaj* by quoting a prominent NTS scholar Al-Fawzan who asserted that he would never dare to place an introduction[95], to the Prophetic hadith. Al Hadadee continues to write that these words of Al-Fawzaan "are a great lesson in veneration of the prophetic Sunna."[96]

The methodology of Sunna in particular, as mentioned above, consists entirely in ascertaining and following authentic hadith as defined by early Muslim hadith scholars. Any new or modern methodologies are considered illegitimate. This is evident in the following statements found in the postscript of Al-Madanee's book:

> The prophetic manhaj [is that] which is found in the Qur'an, the Saheeh of Muslim and Bukhari and the remaining books of Sunna[97] and the sayings and actions of Salafus-Saalih, not the various new and pretentious methodologies.[98]

A comparable statement is found in Al-Atharee's book where the NTS methodology is defined against other groups including "intellectuals" and "modernists" who are accused of "softening" or "watering down" (*mumayyi'un*) the religion. Al-Madkhalee makes a comparable assertion by stating that the correct methodology entails following the *manhaj* of authorities such as Abd ul Wahhab, Ibn Taymiyya, and Ibn Al-Qayyim in contrast to those who "oppose the truth and tawheed from among the secularists, Jews, Christians, communists, and deviant innovators such as those who form into sects, parties and movements."[99]

Al-Albanee characterizes the NTS methodology as consisting of *tazki-yah wa tarbiyah* (purification and education) and restricts it to primarily the understanding of science of hadith, which entails "distinguishing the saheeh from the da'eef, so that we do not base our worship upon faulty ahkaam which many Muslims have fallen into because they relied upon weak ahaadeeth."[100]

The NTS methodology not only considers new or modern methodologies espoused by "intellectuals" and "modernists" as illegitimate but also defines its own *manhaj* largely by opposing those *manahij* adopted by other Muslim or non-Muslim groups. For example, in his ringing endorsement of Abd ul Wahhab's *manhaj*, which he considers to be based upon the true Qur'an and Sunna[101] teachings that are in and of themselves sufficient on the essential of *'aqidah*, Zarabozo states the following:

> However, over the years, many are the Muslims who have sought to ignore this pristine methodology [of Abd ul Wahhab] and follow instead the ways of the philosophers, mystics, Jews, Christians and so forth. [102]

Elsewhere in the book he characterizes the true salafi *manhaj* as based on the avoidance of the discussions of the "philosophers" and "dialecticians" in matters of faith (*'aqidah*). The correct *manhaj* is linked, instead, to the "clear teachings of the Qur'an and Sunna." What that actually meant was left unexplained.

In another statement in the same book, Zarabozo is more specific and describes the *manhaj* using again what we could call a form of oppositional dialectics by asserting:

> In the arena of aqeedah (creed) the Salaf us-Saalih follow a particular methodology, which is opposed to that of other than them, such as the Ash'arees, the Mu'tazilah and their likes whose hallmark is to raise the intellect and kalaam (theological rhetoric) over the texts of the Book and the Sunna and the well-known sayings of the Imaams of this ummah.[103]

Similarly, in the arena of *'ibadah* (worship), the NTS are said to follow the *salaf-us-salih* by adhering " to a methodology opposed to that of the intoxicated Soofees and grave worshippers, who invent and innovate into the religion that for which Allaah sent down no authority."[104] In the realm of *da'wah* (calling to Allah) and current affairs, the NTS *manhaj* is described as being opposed to and is "distinguished from the innovated and pretentious methodologies of the political activists'.[105] Elsewhere the opponents of the NTS *manhaj* are characterized as being "rationalists."[106]

In one of the most specific references as to what the NTS methodology entails Al-Madkhalee lists a number of books and authors who in his view call to the manner and methodology of the *Ahl-Sunna Wa'l Jamaa'ah*.

Because of its specificity and the insight it offers into the NTS *manhaj,* the comment warrants a complete quotation:

> O people! Read what the imams of hadeeth from Ahl-Sunna wal-Jamaa'ah wrote. Read what Imaam Al-Bukharee wrote in "Khalq Af'aal-il-'Ibadd" and what imam Ahmad and his son, 'Abdullah wrote. Read what Al-Khallaal and Ibn Khuzaimah wrote in their respective book "As-Sunna" and 'At-Tawhhed". Read "Al-Ibaanah" and "'Ash-Sharsh wal-Ibaanah" of Ibn Battah, "Sharh 'Itiqaad Ahlis-Sunna wal-Jama'ah of Al-Laalikaa'ee, the introduction of "Sharh-us-Sunna of Al-Baghawee," the introduction of Ibn Majah (to his "Sunnan"), the chapter on the "Sunna" by Abu Dawood in his book "As Sunan" and "Al-Hujjah fee Bayaan-il-Mahajjah" of Abul Qasim At-Taymee Al-As-Bahaanee. Read the books of Ibn Taymiyyah and Ibn Al-Qayyim, such as "As-Sawwa'iq-ul-Muesalah" and 'An-Nooniyyah". Read the library of books from Muhammad bin 'Abdil-Wahhaab.[107]

From this statement it is evident that the boundaries of *'ilm* and its *manhaj* according to NTSm is restricted to the books of 'aqidah and hadith/ sunan written by primarily early classical Hanbali *muhaddithun* or and those who largely followed their *manhaj* later on such as Ibn Taymiyyah and Abd ul Wahhab.

Another important aspect of the NTS *manhaj/aqidah* identified in the writings of NTS scholars is the concept of *al wala' wal bara'.* This concept, it is important to note, has no explicit mention as developed and employed by NTS scholars either in the Qur'an or in the hadith body of texts. *Al-wala'* lexically means alliance with, friendship, showing preference for, and associating with one of the parties engaged in a conflict. *Al-bara'* on the other hand is its antonym, meaning severance, to walk away, or distance oneself from or to be free of obligation from something or someone. According to al-Qahtani, a contemporary NTS writer, the concept of *al-wala' wal bara'* is part of *'aqidah* constituting a fundamental principle of Salafi belief, "one that is firmly founded in both the Book of Allah [i.e. the Qur'an] and the Sunna of His Prophet."[108] Similarly, for Al-Madhkhalee this principle of Salafi doctrine is the firmest handhold of belief "for the sake of Allaah and to the methodology of Allaah and those who adhere to it."[109] Elsewhere Al-Madkhalee writes that this *al wala' wa l bara'* doctrine is under great threat and has been weakened by the new methodologies of innovators.[110] Because the interpretational implications of this concept are primarily in relation to the concept of *'iman,* I shall discuss it in more detail in publication three in the context of NTS understanding of the concept of a "Believer" in Chapter 4. For the purposes of this section of the chapter, it is sufficient for us to mention the fact that *al wala' wal bara'* is one component of the NTS *manhaj* as identified by them.

To summarize this section it is evident that the NTS scholars, when describing their own *manhaj* use very vague and unspecific language. More often then not they resort to a form of oppositional dialectics when doing so. They view new methodologies of "intellectuals" and "modernists" to be illegitimate as well as those of the philosophers and Sufis. Instead they believe that they follow the true Qur'an-Sunna *manhaj* by adhering to the authentic narrations in form of *sahih* hadith as defined by classical *ulum-ul hadith*.

2.5 Conclusion

From our preceding discussion, a number of conclusions can be drawn. First, NTS scholars can be considered as the contemporary incarnation of the premodern *ahl-hadith* school of thought in relation to how they conceptualize *'ilm*, Salafism, Sunna, and its relative status in relation to the Qur'an and hadith bodies of knowledge, as well as in relation to non-textual sources of knowledge such as *'aql, ra'y, istihsan, taqlid,* etc. Second, NTS school of thought was found to advocate a completely textual legal hermeneutic expressed best in their definition of *ittiba'* as an unflinching adherence to *sahih* hadith, which, in turn, is conflated with following the true salafi Qur'an-Sunna *manhaj*. Third, the NTS *manhaj*, as identified and described by themselves, is often nonspecific and vague, consisting of amalgamations of Qur'anic verse and *sahih* hadith and at times with a commentary of classical scholars who themselves espouse the *ahl-hadith manhaj*. It shows no evidence of being consciously grounded in, or even aware of, any modern theory of interpretation. Fourth, the NTS *manhaj* is often disclosed by means of oppositional dialectics where it is contrasted in general terms with "new methodologies of modernist and intellectuals" or that of the *madhahib* or Sufis. Finally, one important part of the NTS *manhaj* is its subscription to the concept of *al wala' wal bara'*, which is considered part of the *'aqidah*.

Chapter 3

The Delineating Features of Premodern Embedded *Manahij* and Their Interpretational Implications

This chapter is divided into two sections. The first part identifies the assumptions informing the premodern embedded *manahij* with respect to the Qur'an and presents a critical analysis of the interpretational implications of these assumptions. The second section examines the interpretational assumptions behind the NTS Sunna *manhaj* and their interpretational implications. As far as the assumptions of premodern Qur'an *manhaj* are concerned, I rely upon the scholarship that primarily was addressing the *madhhab*-based scholarship.

To understand the suitability of this methodology, we need to recall our discussion in the first two chapters on the difference between the NTS and *madhhab*-based *manahij*. First, despite the fact that the majority of premodern *madhhab* approach to *usul-ul-fiqh* had "a distinctly egalitarian, open-ended, non-deterministic, and cumulative evolutionary character," while its NTS version, "has become deterministic, closed, resolute, and authoritarian,"[1] both of them operate, as far as their respective *usul-ul fiqh* theories are concerned, within an entirely premodern episteme. Second, NTS thought and its *manhaj* is an epistemologically narrower subset of the premodern *madhhab*-based approach to conceptualizing and interpreting the Islamic tradition. Therefore because of the above two points, the Qur'an assumptions present in the *madhhab*-based approach would apply to the NTS *manhaj* too. This is even more so the case for the NTS thought given the NTS self-confessed view[2], of the illegitimacy of employing new methodologies for the purposes of interpreting the Islamic tradition and their very restrictive view of the role of reason in the same.

As stated in the introduction, the criteria this study employs in identifying, comparing, and contrasting the assumptions governing NTS and progressive Muslim *manahij* and their interpretational implications relate to the following issues:

- the function and nature of language in the Qur'anic text and the nature of Revelation;
- the process of derivation of meaning of the Qur'anic text
- the extent of the recognition (or otherwise) of the role of context in the shaping of the Qur'anic content;
- the role, legitimacy, and scope of reason in Qur'anic interpretation and the nature of ethical value in the Qur'an;
- the extent of the employment of a thematic or holistic approach to the Qur'an's interpretation or lack thereof of (i.e., prevalence of what here is termed textual segmentalism);
- the scope of an objective, aim-based approach (*qasd*) to Qur'anic interpretation; and
- The interpretational implications of the NTS *manhaj* of Sunna.

3.1   NTS Qur'an Manhaj—Conceptual Assumptions, Presuppositions, and Their Interpretational Implications

3.1.1   The Premodern Embedded View of the Function and the Nature of Language in Qur'anic Text and the Nature of Revelation

During the most of the preclassical period of Islamic thought extending to the first two and a half centuries of the Islamic calendar, a conceptual differentiation between the Qur'an as oral discourse and the Qur'an as text (*mushaf*) was made.[3] This resulted in important differences in interpretative strategies employed by preclassical and classical Islamic scholars.[4] The Qur'an's textualization and its subsequent standardization[5] and proliferation of hadith compendia brought into the foreground a philologically centered approach to Qur'anic interpretation.[6] By philologically centred approach to Qur'anic interpretation I mean that various philological sciences and their role in the process of derivation of (Qur'anic) meaning came to be considered as the Qur'an's most decisive and hermeneutically powerful interpretational tools.[7] This aspect of the premodern-embedded approaches to the legal theory methodology originating in the writings of Shafi'i (d. 204 A.H.)[8] was based on a type of reasoning that assumes that:

> The language is a series of exterior signs representing a pre-existing string of internal thoughts…It is the absolute signifier, 'clear text' (*nass*), and signified, elucidation (*bayan*), that coalesces and transparently constitutes the articulated truth of God as embodied in the eternal language of the Qur'an…where all arguments are indeterminately shaped by a logic that is derived from the grammar of the Arabic language with its implicit logical premises.[9]

This approach to the nature of the function and nature of language is described by Jackson as *formalism*, that is,

> the tendency to stress the essential relationship between the observable features of language(e.g. morphological patterns) and specification of meaning, to strive to preserve a systematic relationship between meaning, textual items and the syntactical structure of sentences.[10]

Furthermore, argues Jackson, this *manhaj* is predicated on the assumption that there is an objectively identifiable relationship between morphology, syntax, and meaning that permits us to have access not simply to the meanings of words and sentences but to the actual thoughts in the minds of speakers.[11] In other words, interpretation is largely restricted to observable features of language. In the opinion of Auda, "[T]his added to the general literal character of linguistic evidences, which were also given priority over all other rational evidence."[12]

This premodern embedded interpretational method, therefore, had a strong positivistic foundation and orientation according to which "the understanding of the Qur'anic text derived from the Companions from the Prophet is regarded as univocal and objective…[t]he meaning disclosed is for all times and cultures…" and as a corollary, "the proper task of the exegete is to engage in exegesis not eisegesis—a reading and interpretation *of* the Qur'anic text, not a reading *into* the text."[13] In the context of examining the legal epistemology and methodology of Saudi Arabian scholars, Bramsen refers to this aspect of *manhaj* as "literalism," which assumes fixity of meaning and adherence to the canonical text's wording alone.[14]

Another characteristic of the premodern approaches to *usul-ul-fiqh*, its view of the nature of language, and thus the nature of the Qur'anic text, is the belief in the "uncreatedness" of the Qur'an and its metaphysical existence prior to the actual event of Revelation. The standpoint is closely linked to the concept of the Qur'anic language and text being operational outside, originating prior to reality and history, and thus not being subject to interpretation against this background. According to this "revelationist" theory, the origin of language is a result of Divine designation (*tawfiq*) rendering its formation outside the space-time dimension.[15] This belief is based upon an assumption that Divine Speech (*goettlische Rede*) is not subject to rational, human methods of analysis.[16]

An additional characteristic of the premodern *manahij* concerns the nature of Revelation or *wahy*. The premodern embedded concept of *wahy* and the role of the Prophet in it is based on a mechanical, nonsymbiotic, independent dynamic between the two, a relationship that posits God as a Speaker (in an anthropomorphic sense) and the Prophet as the God's loudspeaker whose persona, psychological makeup, mind, and "situatedness" in history do not affect the nature and the content of Revelation whatsoever.[17]

There are several interpretational consequences of the formalistic approach to the nature and the function of language in interpretation of the Qur'anic text combined with the ahistorical view of the concept of revelation. First, they lead to the adoption of the view of the Qur'anic text as being largely and in essence *fixed in meaning* (not just in text) and the imposition of Qur'anic interpretational reductionism and uniformity considered to be the norm. Second, the dominant premodern notion of the "uncreatedness" of the Qur'anic text further reinforces this interpretational method as it places Revelation outside the domain of linguistic/literary criticism and reason and considers the Scripture to be on a higher epistemological plane than that of the reality and human beings as Scripture's interpreters.[18] This leads us to the issues pertaining to the assumptions present in the premodern approaches to the discipline of reading hermeneutics.

3.1.2   Premodern Embedded *Manahij* and the Closed Derivation/Determinacy of Qur'anic Meaning

Hermeneutics is a study of interpretation theory. In the context of religion it refers to the study of the interpretation of sacred texts, especially texts in the areas of theology and law.[19] Although difficult to define hermeneutics is a process comprising of "both the understanding of the rules of exegesis and the epistemology of understanding—the study of the construction of meaning in the past and their relationship to the construction of meanings in the present."[20] According to the leading Western theoretician of hermeneutics of the twentieth century, Hans-Georg Gadamer (1900–2002), hermeneutics is "the classical discipline concerned with the art of understanding texts."[21] Reading, as part of the hermeneutical process, put simply, is a process whereby a reader derives meaning from a piece of text. The outcome of this process, termed *determinacy of meaning*, is governed by the following factors:

- The nature of the reader (previous bodies of knowledge—termed *schemata*—gender, experience, and personality/character/moral sense/development of the reader, sociocultural norms governing the society in which s/he lives);
- The (intent of) the author; and
- The nature of the text (i.e., context and mechanics of language).

Every time a reader is engaged in the process of reading, these factors contribute to its determinacy. So, put briefly, reading Qur'anic hermeneutics relates to the study of theories of interpretation and understanding of the Qur'an, especially in relation to how meaning is derived and the role of the reader, author (or the author's intent to be more specific), and the text in this dynamic.

Due to the premodern *manhaj*, embedded scholars' reluctance to tap into the knowledge fountains of the modern episteme as they apply to the textuality of the Qur'an and hadith-based Sunna, those approaches, are oblivious to issues of the "ontology, character and identity of text and textuality, literary theory and deconstructionism."[22] This particularly applies to the NTS school of thought, which, as demonstrated in previous chapters, is based upon its broader aversion to epistemologies and methodological constructs that originate in Western modern traditions.

The premodern embedded Qur'anic interpretation was shrouded in broader interpretational inclination that Weiss terms textual "intentionalism." *Intentionalism* is a widespread hermeneutical tendency of the scholars operating within the premodern embedded *usul-ul-fiqh* to focus on authorial intent as the object of *all* interpretation and its *principal* potential discoverability.[23] The premise that the derivation of meaning rests heavily on the side of the author and the belief in the *principal* discoverability and accessibility of the author's intent meant that the role of the nature of the text itself or that of the reader/interpreter in the overall process of meaning derivation is considerably marginalized.[24] This is how Bremsen characterizes the methodology of interpretation of Saudi religious scholars.[25]

Formalism, an ahistorical view of the nature of Qur'anic language and a hermeneutical tendency of intentionalism, contributed to the development of a *manhaj* that was premised upon the assumption of a fixed, stable nature of the meaning of the Qur'anic text residing in totality in the mind of its Originator. This propensity was further reinforced and extended to that of the Prophet by the proliferation and subsequent canonization of the vast Hadith-based Sunna literature which acted as the ultimate reference point in the determinacy and derivation of the meaning of the Qur'anic text. Consequently, premodern-based *manahij* did not fully recognize the inherently subjective nature of the reader in the process of determining meaning as well as the essentially subjective nature of the entire reading hermeneutics process. [26]

This in turn resulted in the view of the essential semiotic monovalency of the nature of the Qur'anic text and a failure to recognize the interpretational importance of the epistemic communities in the process of interpretation and derivation of Qur'anic meaning. Sharify-Funk describes this approach as "minimalist hermeneutics" in which the interpreter "suppresses textual ambiguities while claiming that the text speaks for itself."[27] This approach also contributed to the phenomenon of "interpretational authoritarianism" and monopolization of God's words.[28]

In summary the majority of the premodern-embedded *manahij*, in essence assume that it is possible to interpret Qur'anic text with complete objectivity without presuppositions or preconceived ideas.[29] As such the quintessential characteristic of these approaches to derivation of meaning can be characterized by their tendency to "restrict the loci of meaning to the observable features of language, such that the perspective or presuppositions of any would-be interpreter are neutralized or at least limited."[30] It is this approach to the derivation of meaning of the Qur'anic text that we refer to as *closed*.

3.1.3   The Context-Content Qur'anic Dynamic in Premodern-Embedded *Manahij* and Its Interpretational Implications

All of the aforementioned aspects of the premodern *manahij* to *usul-ul fiqh* largely resulted in the decontextualization and marginalization of Qur'anic revelatory background and the importance this context played in the very shaping of the Qur'anic content, thus in discerning of its actual nature and aims. The historical embeddedness of the Qur'anic content[31] was de-emphasized, and the interpretational approaches based on a historical approach to the Qur'an were not fully developed.[32]

In other words, the interpretational consequences of this methodological approach governing the premodern *manahij* of the Qur'anic revelation vis-à-vis its revelatory context, resulted in an inadequate appreciation of the importance of the sociocultural milieu and the prevailing norms, customs, beliefs, and traditions of pre-Qur'anic Arabia (i.e., the entire pre-Qur'anic worldview) in the understanding of the actual intent, nature, and character of Qur'anic revelation and its interpretation.[33] Some of the most pertinent aspects of this pre-Qur'anic *Weltanschauung* in which the Qur'an was revealed would include an andocentric, patriarchal society based on certain cultural understandings of gender/sex, the prevalence of slavery, the wide availability of female concubines and prostitutes,[34] social-class distinctions, culturally based notions of proper and improper human conduct, virtues and vices, religious beliefs and customs, tribal economics, and rules governing tribal armed conflict.[35] In this context the words of Younis are very instructive:

> Most lacking in classical legal hermeneutics was the articlation of context based theory or legal hermeneutics that genuinely read the text both in letter and spirit.[36]

An inadequate understanding and appreciation of these sociocultural, political, and economic forces within which the Qur'an operated yield an approach that fails to understand the actual nature of Qur'anic revelation and the intent behind the newly developing Qur'anic worldview[37]. On the other hand by adhering to a largely decontextual and ahistorical meaning of the sociohistorically contingent verses in the language of much of the Qur'anic texts did not only result in the distortion of the actual reality itself but also in the misrepresentation or lack of recognition of the underlying objectives of the Revelation.[38]

The interpretational implications of interpretational aspect of the premodern embedded *manahij* are two-fold. First, it is not capable of hermeneutically distinguishing, in a systematic manner, between the universalist and sociohistorically contingent elements of the sacred scripture. Second, it considers the historically contingent as part of the universal, metahistorical dimension of Revelation.[39]

The premodern approaches to Qur'anic interpretation *did* recognize the need for contextualization of (certain) Qur'anic verses as evident in the Qur'anic science of *asbab al-nuzul* (occasions of revelation) and *naskh wa mansukh* (abrogation and abrogated).However there are two problems that are associated with these premodern Islamic sciences. First, in essence they to a large extent depend upon the hadith bodies of knowledge that themselves, as discussed in the first chapter, are based upon certain methodological and epistemological assumptions.[40]

Secondly, the way the content of these Revelation contextualizing reports and the purposes of abrogation were employed, however, was such that their full *interpretational leverage* was not fully realized.[41]

This fundamental and principal lack of recognition of the historical dimension of Revelation in premodern-embedded *manahij* for the

purposes of its actual interpretation is unable to break the shackles of the
Qur'an's revelatory historicity in order to free it from the spatiotemporal
constrains within which it initially operated. This led to the development
of premodern *usul-ul-fiqh* theory, which "fell short of integrating the time
space factor into the fabric of its methodology."[42]

3.1.4   The Premodern-Embedded *Manahij* and Their Views of the Nature of Ethical Value, the Role of Reason in Qur'an and Its Interpretational Implications[43]

Does the Qur'an advocate ethical subjectivism,[44] ethical objectivism,[45] or
ethical voluntarism[46]? In other words does the Qur'an assume that what
is right can *always* be known by revelation-independent reason[47] alone[48];
what is right can be known in *some cases* by revelation-independent reason
alone and in others by revelation and revelation-derived sources whereby
both of these sources are complementary and in agreement,[49] or in order
to know what is right, humans must always rely only on revelation and
revelation-derived sources and can *never* know what is right by independent reason.[50]

This leads us into the widely discussed theme in Islamic tradition of
the nature of the relationship between reason and revelation (whose exact
relationship is yet to be systematically arrived at).[51]

In the first chapter, I demonstrated that the legitimacy and the place
of reason in conceptualizing the nature and the interpretation of Qur'an
and Sunna during the first three to four generations of Muslims was much
broader and reason inclusive than in postformative Islamic thought. I
argued that it was only in the middle of the second century of the Islamic
calendar that the epistemological-methodological framework behind the
concept of the nature of the relationship between reason and revelation
and revelation derived-sources started to initiate the mechanisms that ultimately resulted in introducing a qualitative change to the reason-revelation
dynamic. This change completely subordinated ontologically, epistemologically, and methodologically the scope and the legitimacy of reason and
reason-derived opinion (*ra'y*) to that of the textually based sources of revelation, i.e., Qur'an and Hadith. With this process in completion by the
middle of the third century of the Islamic calendar, reason was primarily
used in a derivative sense to assist in arriving at the consensus of opinions
(*ijma'*) of the Muslim Community or in its analogical (*qiyas*) function.

The above described tendency toward ahistorical, decontextualized,
and philologically oriented *manahij* to Qur'anic interpretation was based
upon a particular concept of the nature of the primary sources of Islamic

Weltanschauung. Once Sunna was conceptually equated with Hadith and made epistemologically and methodologically *dependent* upon canonical hadith compendia and the hadith-based hermeneutic of the Qur'an was elevated to the highest ranks of the interpretational endeavor, the role of reason in the overall Qur'anic hermeneutic was relegated to the background. The reason-based interpretation had now to function within the boundaries of the entirely *textually* based interpretational framework. This narrowing of the interpretational scope of reason was hermeneutically incapable of going beyond the text and searching for the possible moral trajectories, rationale, and objectives (*maqasid*) of the Qur'anic revelation.[52]

Furthermore this *manhaj* permitted only a derivative use of reason in the form of an analogy (*qiyas*), which was epistemologically and methodologically embedded firmly in the normative textual indicants. The role of reason, thus, was seen as strictly instrumental. The Divine Will, as embodied in the normative texts, was considered by the majority of legal philosophers as the sole determinant in the realm of law and "no concept of human reason as [being] author of ultimate source of law" was developed.[53] Indeed, in the context of characterizing classical Islamic law, argues Weiss, that "between human reason and the law of God there stretched an essentially unbridgeable gap."[54] Weiss terms this hermeneutical tendency in premodern *manahij* as *voluntarism*. It permeated the way in which nature of law, ethics, morality, and ontology was conceptualized.[55] A subscription to voluntarism has important interpretational implications. Firstly, it affects the way in which the nature and the character of Qur'anic revelation is perceived and interpreted. Voluntarism was responsible for infusing the Revelation with a comprehensive legalistic *ethos* and subsequent marginalization of some of its other dimensions such as those that could be broadly termed ethicoreligious in nature. This distorted the way in which the overall nature, character, and "purpose" of the Qur'anic Revelation and its message were perceived and subsequently conceptualized. Voluntarism also implies a *legalistic* expression of the Will of God that can only be known from commands and prohibitions. This approach renders the law entirely dependent upon a sovereign and unbound divine will that denies any rational element in it as well as views humanity as not being capable of comprehending independently of the help of revelation.[56] An interpretational model premised on voluntarism also assumes that the text includes the complete knowledge and that the role of reason in interpretation of the text is minimal. All four Sunni premodern major schools of jurisprudence and theology adopted in various degrees a "voluntarist" view of the relationship between reason and revelation. As argued in the second chapter NTS school of thought went further by even disputing the legitimacy of *analogical* reason in any branches pertaining to 'ilm may that be in *usul-ul-fiqh* or theology. Therefore NTSm has a more pronounced voluntarist approach to Qur'an-Sunna interpretation. This voluntaristic hermeneutic, as espoused by the most widespread theology of Sunni *Asha'rism,* is ultimately responsible for the subversion of rational ethics and authority in Islamic law and ethics according to which "an act can be gauged as good from a certain perspective and detestable from another,"[57] and "both analysis would be in accordance with the sovereign will of God."[58] Al-Attar describes this view of ethics and morality as being based on a "Divine Command Theory," which presupposes that "divine commands and rules have to be obeyed regardless of the social or moral implications, as there is no rationale beyond their being divine commands."[59]

3.1.5   The Premodern *Manahij* and Qur'anic Textual Segmentalism

As it is commonly known, the gradual, piecemeal process of Qur'anic revelation lasted over a period of more than 20 years. The subsequent act of canonization of the Scripture in form of a *mushaf* and an attempt to give structure and form to the Qur'anic contents not only altered the nature of the Qur'anic revelation itself from being largely perceived as an oral discourse[60] to that of a pure text but also imposed a particular method and technique when reading and interpreting the Qur'anic *text*. The traditional "authentic" division of the Qur'an into a particular sequence of *surahs* (Qur'anic chapters) was neither chronologically nor thematically ordered. The *nature* of the Qur'anic discourse, however, was such that the concepts, ideas, and the moral and ethical lessons internal to the Qur'an were dispersed throughout the Scripture and are often repeated. This nature of the Qur'anic discourse has been traced to the specific linguistic-cultural characteristics/requirements of its first recipients to ensure Qur'an's comprehensibility and optimize what in essence was/is the ethicoreligious and didactic nature of its message.[61]

The premodern *manahij* to the interpretation of the Qur'an mainly adopted a *lemma plus comment* exegesis, that is, a word for word, verse-by-verse, *surah* by *surah*, linear, segmental analysis of the Qur'anic text.[62] This is known as a *tajzi'i* or *tariqa tahliliyya* method that involves a chronological analysis of the *mushaf uthmani* Qur'anic codex.[63] This interpretational technique has certain interpretational implications. Several scholars argue that it largely ignored the Qur'an's thematic coherence and underlying unity of the revelatory message and thereby "prevent[ed] the generation of a Qur'anic *Weltanschauung* on its own terms.[64] Echoing this view is Mir who argues that the premodern Muslim exegetes' predominant methodology was such that it studied verses in isolation from the preceding and the following [verses] that resulted in the neglecting of the Qur'anic "thematic and structural *nazm* [coherence]."[65] Abdul-Raof concurs with this by saying that the classical Islamic scholarship on *al-munasaba*, i.e., conceptual and textual chaining in the Qur'an necessary for appreciating its overall consonance, themes, and gist, was very limited and superficial.[66] I refer to this aspect of premodern *manahij* as textual segmentalism. Auda terms this feature of premodern *usul-ul fiqh* theory as "decompositional" characterized by their partial orientation, traditional logic, and a static perspective.[67]

Thus, this, in the words of F. Rahman, "atomistic" approach to Qur'anic interpretation not only overlooked underlying Qur'anic themes and its gist/ spirit but was also not conducive to the development of a (more) holistic approach to Qur'anic hermeneutics.

A corollary to this feature of premodern-embedded *manahij* is the interpretational tendency to form opinions on the basis of particularistic, isolated Qur'anic injunctions, which are then applied generally by being considered universal in nature regardless of either the contextual factors, which might have "occasioned" it, or without due consideration of other relevant Qur'anic evidence.[68] I call this aspect of premodern *manahij* the "universalization of the contingent."

3.1.6   The Premodern *Manahij* and the Legitimacy and Scope of an Objective, Aim-Based Approach (Qasd) to Qur'anic Interpretation and the Concept of Maslaha

The focus on textual segmentalism, formalism, and the marginalization of revelationary context combined with ethical voluntarism and a purely derivative function of reason vis-à-vis Revelation and revelation-derived sources as the delineating features of a premodern-based *manahij* inevitably result in a Qur'anic interpretational model and an *usul-ul-fiqh* theory that is incapable of conceptualizing (or recognizing)—or even distorting[69]— the underlying purposeful, objective-based approach to the nature and the character of the Qur'anic purposive and its interpretation. Kamali notices this dimension of the premodern *usul-ul-fiqh* by stating:

> Another aspect of the conventional methodology of *usul*, which merits attention, is its emphasis on literalism and certain neglect, in some instances at least, of the basic objective and the rationale of the law. The early formulations of *usul* have not significantly addressed this issue and it was not until al-Shatibi (d.790 A.H.) who developed his major theme on the objectives

and the philosophy of Shari'ah (*maqasid al-shari'ah*). Al-Shatibi's contribution came, however, too late to make a visible impact on the basic scheme
and methodology of *usul*.[70]

Echoing this sentiment is Muhammad Fathi al-Darimi, a contemporary
Syrian legal scholar, who maintains that there has been no inductive or
logical study of the *philosophy* and the *purposes* of the premodern Sunni
Muslim jurisprudence in the discourse of law and legal theory.[71]

Analogous to what was discussed in relation to the reason-revelation
dynamic, the concept of a *maqasid*-based approach to understanding the
nature of Qur'an-Sunna teachings and their interpretation embodied
in the concept of *maslaha mursala*—a legal mechanism that considers
that a rationally suitable benefit that in the interest of public welfare is
operational even in the absence of any *nass/dalil*—although not systematically developed as a principle in Islamic jurisprudence, featured much
more dominantly in the thinking of the first three to four generations of
Muslims.[72]

As *usul-ul-fiqh* became more systematized in the course of the second,
third, and fourth centuries, the concept of *maqasid* and *maslaha* were
marginalized and were given largely a subsidiary function in the hierarchy
of sources in *usul-ul-fiqh*.[73] Thus, they were considered hermeneutically
inferior to textually based tools as well as to the principals of *ijma'* and
qiyas.

Therefore, according to this approach the nature of Qur'an-Sunna
teachings was neither seen as *essentially* and *principally* aiming to promote
public interest and welfare based on giving hermeneutical primacy to these
considerations over that of *nass* nor to have underlying objectives in form of
certain ethicomoral values or norms. Instead, like any other atextual source,
their hermeneutical force was heavily limited in these approaches.[74]

Indeed, as argued in the second chapter the NTS *manhaj* is entirely
textually based, thus it subscribes to the view of a complete illegitimacy,[75]
, of the concept of *maqasid/maslaha mursala* to conceptualizing the nature
of Qur'anic discourse/text or subsequently its interpretation.

3.2   NTS Sunna *Manhaj*—Conceptual Assumptions, Presuppositions, and Their Interpretational Implications

This section of the chapter investigates the interpretational implications
of epistemological and methodological coalescing of the concept of the

nature, the scope, and the definition of Sunna with that of hadith, a feature of the NTS *manhaj* on their Qur'anic interpretation.

It is important to recall that, as we saw in the first chapter, the NTS's methodology for ascertaining the validity and authenticity of *ahadith* functions completely within the traditional *'ulum-ul-hadith* sciences as developed by the *early* masters of hadith sciences, which are largely based upon the analysis of their *isnad* authenticity in isolation from assessments pertaining to their epistemological value or issues pertaining to the broader *usul-ul-fiqh* questions.[76] I argued that the NTS, unlike the broader *madhhab*-based *manhaj*, considers *ahad hadith* as having a priori normative value in all aspects of Islamic thought, including that of theology and law.

The canonical collections of hadith literature, the so-called *al-kutub al-sitta* present a picture of the Prophet as having a say on a vast number of issues concerning dogma, law, theology, ethics, and morality, even to the extent of laying down rules concerning the most private spheres of an individual's life. Those who uphold the a priori Sunna *value* of these narrations, such as the NTS proponents, consider nearly all aspects of Prophet's behavior found in the authentic hadith as having a normative Sunna precedent,thus to be binding on all Muslims.

Therefore, the *mutawatir 'amal*, ethicoreligious and values-based concept of the nature and the scope of Sunna that was organically linked to that of the Qur'an during the first three to four generations of Muslims, prior to what I described in the first chapter as the process of traditionalization of Islamic thought, was substituted by a voluminous, largely non-mutawatir, written-based, hadith-dependent Sunna imbibed with a legal ethos.[77] This process, in turn, distorted and changed the original nature and scope of the concept of Sunna and is based upon a number of assumptions.

First, it assumes that the scope of Sunna is epistemologically dependent upon and constrained by hadith, i.e., that its epistemological value is the same as that of each "authentic" hadith and that the existent "authentic" hadith body of literature is the sole depository and the sole vehicle of Sunna's perpetuation. Second, it assumes that Sunna is methodologically dependent on hadith. By *methodologically dependent on hadith*, it is meant that the Sunna compliance (or otherwise) of certain (legal, ethical, or theological) practices or principles is and can only be determined by sifting through numerous narratives reportedly going back to Prophet Muhammad via an authentic chain of narrators (*isnad*). Third, as a corollary to the second premise, coalescing and substituting the nature and the scope of the concept of Sunna with that of hadith breaks the symbiotic and organic relationship between the concept of the Qur'an and Sunna as it existed during the first four generations of Muslim making the Qur'an increasingly more hermeneutically dependent upon the hadith compendia.

A new hadith-based Sunna was seen as something additional to, a necessary exegetical supplement to and explicator of the Qur'an rather than the other side of the same coin.[78] The traditional post-Shafi'i function of Sunna was based on this reasoning and was expressed in the well-known maxim in Islamic jurisprudence affirming that the Qur'an's interpretational need of Sunna (in form of its sole vehicle, the hadith) is greater than the Sunna's interpretational need of the Qur'an.[79]

Sunna's function and purpose became increasingly positively legalistic rather than ethicoreligious or principle-based in nature.

Since, as argued in the second chapter, a qualitative distinction between the nature, scope, and character of pre- and postclassical concepts of Sunna existed, this affected the epistemologico-methodological parameters within which Qur'anic interpretation could develop. Moreover, because the preclassical concept of Sunna, apart from its 'amall'ibadiyyah component, was primarily conceived in abstract ethicoreligious and principle-based terms and was reason constitutive and conceptualized in terms of the broader objectives and purposes (maqasid) of the Qur'an, it permitted a wider Qur'anic interpretational framework than that based on the hadith-dependent Sunna championed by NTS.

We'll discuss the interpretational implications of this conceptual coalescing of Sunna and hadith bodies of knowledge on the construction of normative "Believer" and "Muslim Woman" concepts in the next chapter where we present a number of ahad hadith NTS scholars employ to construct their version of the same.

3.3 Conclusion

This chapter discussed the assumptions governing the premodern manahij in relation to conceptualization and interpretation of Qur'an and Sunna and their interpretational implications. These were found to include: a philologically centered, interpretational orientation; textual "intentionalism," i.e., the subscription to a voluntaristic view of law, ethics, morality, and ontology; the belief in the fixed, stable nature of the meaning of the Qur'anic text residing in totality in the mind of its Originator; decontextualization and the marginalization of Qur'anic revelationary background for the purposes of its interpretation; the "voluntarist–traditionalist" view of the relationship between reason and revelation; textual segmentalism; and the lack of a thematic, principle- and aim-centered (maqāṣid) approach to

Qur'anic hermeneutics. It also discussed the interpretational implications of the NTS *manhaj* of Sunna.

The interpretational implications of these assumptions were found to lead to the Qur'an's interpretational reductionism and uniformity; a deemphasis of the historical dimension of the Qur'anic revelation; a development of a hermeneutic premised on a view of a fixed, stable nature of the meaning of the Qur'anic text residing in totality in the mind of its Originator leading to the development of minimalist hermeneutics; an interpretational theory that assumes that it is possible to interpret Qur'anic text with complete objectivity; a *manhaj* that is not capable of hermeneutically distinguishing, in a systematic manner, between the universalist and sociohistorically contingent elements of the sacred scripture; a *manhaj* that considers the historically contingent as part of the universal, metahistorical dimension of Revelation; a voluntaristic approach to the nature of ethical value in the Qur'an that was responsible for infusing the Revelation with a comprehensive legalistic *ethos,* resulting in a subsequent marginalization of its ethicoreligious elements; and a *manhaj* in which the role of reason in interpretation of the text is minimal and that ignored the Qur'an's thematic coherence and underlying unity of the revelatory message. All of these, in turn, resulted in interpretational tendencies that are incapable of conceptualizing (or recognizing), or even undermining, the underlying purposive, objective-based approach to the nature and the character of the Qur'anic discourse and its interpretation. Finally, NTS Sunna *manhaj* lead to the development of a Qur'anic hermeneutic that combined with the above premodern approaches to the Qur'anic interpretation and was increasingly hermeneutically dependent on the hadith, thus severing the symbiotic, hermeneutical relationship between the Qur'an and Sunna that existed prior to the process of traditionalization of Islamic thought and conflation of Sunna and hadith bodies of knowledge epistemologically and methodologically so that the latter was considered the former's sole method of perpetuation and embodiment.

Chapter 4

NTS Religiously Ideal "Believer" and "Muslim Woman" Concepts

In this chapter, I explain how the NTS *manhaj* provides the interpretational foundation for the views of NTS scholars pertaining to the issue of what constitutes a religiously ideal "Believer" (Part One) and "Muslim Woman" (Part Two) concepts. In order to do so, I will present relevant Qur'an-hadith textual indicants employed by NTS scholars and analyze which aspects of their NTS *manhaj* inform their opinions on these two normative concepts.

PART ONE: NTS Concept of a Religiously Ideal "Believer"

As outlined in the introduction, by the term *a normative concept of a "Believer,"* I mean what the Qur'an and Sunna teach about the religious status of the religious Other, especially the Christians and the Jews. By *religious status* I mean the boundaries of the concept of belief (*'iman*) in Islamic theology and, in particular, whether or not the adherents of the Christian and the Jewish religious traditions can be considered as either Muslims (*muslimun*) or Believers (*mu'minun*) in the Qur'an-Sunna sense and thus attain salvation.

4.1 The Religious Self and the Other in the Qur'an and Sunna: The Importance of Context

Before I turn my attention to the issue of a normative "Believer" concept, according to the NTS school of thought, more needs to be said about the revelatory environment in which the revelation (and the Prophet's embodiment of it in reference to the question of the identity of the Self and of the Other) occurred, especially in the Medinan period. This is because it was primarily in Medinah that Prophet Muhammad's message—and, therefore, the Muslim identity—became more Self-conscious. But, also, it is the Medinan model of the Prophet and early Muslim community that many Muslims consider worthy of emulation in many respects, including that of the relationship with the (religious) Other. Furthermore, even a cursory examination of the Qur'anic content (and, therefore, of the Prophet's legacy) was organically linked to this context, especially the dimension of the Qur'anic content bearing on the relationship between Muslims and the religious "Other."

Several general points need to be considered in attempting to understand from a religious perspective the concept of the identity of Self and Other as understood during the Prophet's time in light of the Qur'an and the Prophet's embodiment of it. First, the Prophet Muhammad's message arose within the context of well-established religious communities, most important of them being—apart from the pre-Qur'anic paganism—Judaism, Christianity, and Hanifiyyah.[1] The Qur'an itself describes several instances of the Muslim community's attitude toward the non-Muslim Other[2] and vice-versa.[3]

Second, the Qur'anic attitude (and Muhammad's conduct) toward the non-Muslim Other is highly contextual in nature and, therefore, possibly ambivalent.[4] Namely, as noted by Weldman there seems to be a process of development of what she refers to as accumulated meanings[5] of certain important concepts in the Quran (such as that of the kufr) that are highly contextually contingent. In the context of systematically examining these accumulative meanings Weldman argues that the development of the meanings of kufr "Perhaps more than any is tied to the history of Muhammad's preaching appeal."[6]

Also, during much of the Muslim community's formative period, in terms of formation of their religious/confessional identity in Medina, a climate of political and theological/religious friction and hostility between the Muslims on the one hand and the mushrikun, large Jewish tribes, Christians,[7] and hypocrites (munafiqun)[8] on the other prevailed. Under these circumstances, Muslims were constantly concerned about the survival of their newly founded religious community. These factors converged and can be said to be responsible for Muslims (as well as various non-Muslim groups) of that time occasionally adopting reactionary attitudes as well as antagonistic stances vis-à-vis the religious Other. For example, Watt describes the circumstances and motives behind the relationship between Muslims and non-Muslims, especially between the Prophet of Islam and the Medinan Jews:

> In Muhammad's first two years at Medina the Jews were the most danger-ous critics of his claim to be a prophet, and the religious fervour of his fol-lowers, on which so much depended, was liable to be greatly reduced unless Jewish criticisms could be silenced or rendered impotent .... In so far as the Jews changed their attitude and ceased to be actively hostile, they were unmolested.... [9]

This is well attested to by the Qur'an itself.[10] This context-dependency of the scriptures toward the view of the (religious) Other lead Waardenburg to assert that "looking back at the interaction of the new Islamic religious movement with the existing religious communities, we are struck by the importance of socio-political factors."[11] Similarly, Friedmann asserts that the attitudes Muslims formulated toward other communities they encountered was shaped by the historical context in which that encounter occurred as well as, to a certain extent, the nature of the respective non-Muslim religious tradition.[12]

Besides the sociopolitical factors, religious ideas were also signifi-cant, since the Qur'anic progressive consolidation of Islamic religious identity is inextricably linked with the religious identity of the Other, notably of Jews and Christians.[13] The aspects of religious identity's continuity and commonality with other faiths[14] in the Qur'an are intertwined with those of the emergence of, and the emphasis on, the Muslim identity's originality and distinctiveness.[15] Thus, the religious aspects of, and interactions between, various religious communities in the Qur'anic milieu led to the genesis of the construction of the reli-gious/confessional identity of Muslims and played a very important role in its construction.[16]

In his study of the extent of the Prophet Muhammad's and the Qur'an's emphasis on confessional distinctiveness, Donner has demonstrated that, in the Islamic scripture and in early Islam, "the community of Believers was originally conceptualized independently of confessional identities," and that

> it was only late—apparently during the third quarter of the first century A.H., a full generation of or more after the founding of Muhammad's community—that membership in the community of Believers came to be seen as confessional identity in itself when, to use a somewhat later formula-tion of religious terminology, being a Believer and Muslim meant that one could not also be a Christian, say, or a Jew.[17]

Elsewhere he writes:

> As used in the Qur'an, then, islam and muslim do not yet have the sense of confessional distinctiveness we now associate with "Islam" and "Muslim"; they meant something broader and more inclusive and were sometimes even applied to some Christians and Jews.... [18]

Donner adduces a substantial amount of evidence to support the argument that Qur'anically (some) Jews and Christians would qualify as *mu'minun* (believers) besides the *muslimun* (those who submit to God).[19] Friedmann confirms this by averting that some evidence in the Islamic legal tradition exists suggesting that early on when the boundaries of the Muslim community were not precisely demarcated, Jews and Christians were considered to be part of the Muslim community.[20]

Another significant trend in the "historicity" of the development of the Muslim religious Self was the gradual but ever-growing religious self-consciousness of the Prophet of Islam and his early community. While attempts to find common ground and a syncretic base featured more frequently during the earlier periods of Muhammad's life,[21] later periods stressed "features constituting specific identity and what distinguished one [i.e. Muslims] fundamentally from others."[22] Miraly asserts that "whereas pluralism was an essential foundation of Islam, exclusivism was a later addition. In the centuries following the Revelation, the original pluralist impulse that prompted the Constitution of Medina was usurped by politically motivated factions who propounded exclusivist interpretations of the Qur'an in order to justify warfare and territorial expansion."[23] Echoing this observation while discussing the context of the early Muslim view of the Byzantines in the days of the Prophet Muhammad, Shboul says that the attitudes of the Muslims developed from sympathy and affinity, reflected in the early Qur'anic verses, to awe and apprehension of Byzantium's military power, scorn of Byzantine wealth and luxury, and, finally, anticipation of open antagonism and prolonged warfare.[24] Jews and Christians were eventually recognized by Islam as recipients of previous revelations (*Ahl-Kitab*) and were awarded by it the status of protected/secured minorities (*dhimmis*).

An additional point to be considered in relation to the question under examination is the Qur'anic concept of a *hanif/millat* Ibrahim.[25] Qur'anically, this notion may be called the primordial, monotheistic Urreligion based on the belief in the One, True God as embodied in Abraham's message (Arabic millat Ibrahim), considered as the universal belief system and as potentially Muhammad's final attitude toward the religious Self and the Other.[26] It is, however, unclear whether the Prophet of Islam himself identified "historical Islam" "as the only or merely one possible realisation of the primordial religion, the Hanifiyyah, on earth."[27]

An "Islamocentric view" of Muslim perceptions of the religious Other stems from a certain interpretation of the Qur'an-Sunna teachings. This view is based on the premise that the Qur'an is a source of empirical knowledge of the religious Other that is to be applied universally, ahistorically, and without regard to context.[28]

Having outlined the general trends and circumstances that shaped the Qur'an-Sunna view of the religious Other, we will now examine statements from the Qur'an and hadith pertaining to the religious Other and analyze them in relation to the NTS *manhaj* in order to gain an insight into how they construct the concept of a "Believer."

4.2   NTS *Manhaj* in relation to the Concept of a Religiously Ideal "Believer": Relevant Qur'ano-Hadithic Texts

Here we investigate how several Qur'anic verses,[29] when interpreted on the basis of the NTS *manhaj*, give rise to a particular view of the religious Other. Along with the quotation of the verses, a brief description of the historical period in which they were revealed will be given in order to contextualize them.

I. Qur'anic Verses[30]

Never will the Jews or the Christians be satisfied with thee unless thou follow their form of religion. Say: 'The guidance of Allah that is the (only) guidance.' Wert thou to follow their desires after the knowledge which hath reached thee then wouldst thou find neither protector nor helper against Allah. (Q 2:120)

O ye who believe! Take not into your intimacy those outside your ranks; they will not fail to corrupt you. They only desire your ruin: rank hatred has already appeared from their mouths; what their hearts conceal is far worse. We have made plain to you the Signs if ye have wisdom. (Q 3:118)

O ye who believe! Take not the Jews and the Christians for your friends and protectors (*awliya*): they are but friends and protectors to each other. And he amongst you that turns to them (for friendship) is of them. Verily Allah guideth not a people unjust. (Q 5:51)

> But when the forbidden months are past, then fight and slay the Pagans wherever ye find them, and seize them, beleaguer them, and lie in wait for them in every stratagem (of war); but if they repent, and establish regular prayers and practice regular charity, then open the way for them: for Allah is Oft-forgiving, Most Merciful. (Q 9:5)

> If anyone desires a religion other than Islam (submission to Allah, never will it be accepted of him; and in the Hereafter He will be in the ranks of those who have lost (All spiritual good). (Q 3:85)

Traditional Qur'anic exegesis has documented the context behind these verses and *sūras* (chapters).[31] Broadly speaking, at the time of the revelation of these verses —and the larger chapters in which they are embedded—the sheer survival of the small Muslim population residing in Medina was under constant threat, from both within and without. The internal threat came from those that the Qur'an on numerous occasions calls as *munafiqūn* (religious hypocrites), who cooperated with the external sources of threat and attempted to sabotage the Muslim community from within. The external threat, apart from the Meccan tribe of Quraysh, was increasingly felt, particularly from the Jewish tribes living on the outskirts of Medina. These tribes at first signed a joint peace treaty known as the Constitution of Medina[32] and swore allegiance to Muhammad. According to this document, all of the inhabitants of the city where considered as one community (*umma*) whose religious difference was respected as attested and endorsed by the Qur'an.[33] Furthermore, the Constitution stipulated that there was to be "sincere friendship, and honorable dealing, not treachery" between Muslims and Jews. All the signatories of the document were also to "help against whoever suddenly attacks[ed] Yathrib [Medina]."[34] However, as the Muslim community grew in numbers and strength and became more self-reliant and self-aware, these Jewish tribes withdrew their support and started to openly cooperate and conspire with the Meccans against the Muslim community.[35] Thus, they broke the constitutional agreement by committing treason. This inevitably prompted responses both in the Qur'an and by the Prophet as to how Muslims should deal with these tribes and individuals. In this context, the execution of (some of) the men of a Jewish tribe[36] and the expulsion of another are often used as examples of an exclusivist orientation in Muhammad's policies and the Qur'an.[37] That the above quoted verses are, indeed, contextually embedded and are not universal in nature is borne out not only by the fact that the Qur'anic discourse pertaining to Jews and Christians contains a large number of conciliatory verses that will be discussed below but also, as Miraly argues, by the fact that Muhammad's actions against the Jewish tribes from Medina "[were] not motivated by any sense of religious exclusivism" but "were the result of irresolvable civic tensions that had no bearing on the

Qur'an's position on religious pluralism."[38] Furthermore, Armstrong, a distinguished non-Muslim scholar of the Abrahamic faiths, asserts in this context that, after the expulsion and execution of the two Jewish tribes in question, "the Qur'an continued to revere Jewish prophets and to urge Muslims to respect the People of the Book. Smaller Jewish groups continued to live in Medina, and later Jews, like Christians, enjoyed full religious liberty in Islamic empires."[39]

In relation to Q 3:85, Esack argues that, while the verse in the pre-classical or early stages of Islamic was considered to afford salvation to groups outside the Muslim community, much later, the exegetes used more sophisticated exegetical devices, such as the theory of abrogation (*naskh*), to "secure exclusion from salvation for the Other."[40]

Furthermore, the specific rather then general nature of Q 9:5 is based not only upon contextual considerations but also upon grammatical ones. Namely the use of the definite article (*al-mushrikina*) in *flight* and *slay the pagans* (*faqtulu al-mushriqina*) limits the application of the verse to specific tribes and is not to be understood as universally prescriptive and normative.[41]

II. Hadith

A reflection of the context described above is also found in many hadiths reportedly going back to the Prophet, in which the emphasis is on the difference between Muslims on the one side and Jews and Christians on the other, with the noticeable engendering of a reactionary, clearly delineated and antagonistic identity is noticeable. Here are several examples:

Narrated Abu Hurayra: "'The Prophet said, 'Jews and Christians do not dye their hair so you should do the opposite of what they do.'" (Bukhari, Ṣaḥīḥ, 7.786)

Narrated 'Abd Allah ibn 'Amr ibn al-'As: "Allah's Messenger (peace be upon him) said, 'He does not belong to us who imitates other people. Do not imitate the Jews or the Christians, for the Jews' salutation is to make a gesture with the fingers and the Christians' salutation is to make a gesture with the palms of the hands'" (Tirmidhi, 4648, classified as weak).

Narrated Abu Hurayra: "Suhayl ibn Abu Salih said: 'I went out with my father to Syria. The people passed by the cloisters in which there were Christians and began to salute them. My father said: 'Do not give them salutation first, for Abu Hurayrah reported the Apostle of Allah (peace be upon him) as saying: Do not salute them (Jews and Christians) first, and when you meet them on the road, force them to go to the narrowest part of it'" (Abu Dawud, 5186).[42]

> Narrated Abu Hurayra: "The Prophet (peace be upon him) said:
> 'Religion will continue to prevail as long as people hasten to break the fast,
> because the Jews and the Christians delay doing so'" (Abu Dawud, 2346).

It is not difficult to understand how these Qur'anic verses and hadiths, reportedly going back to the Prophet, if taken at face value without taking into account the historical circumstances and the background to the revelation outlined above, would result in construction of a very negative view of the religious Other, which could then come to be considered as normative. This is exactly what has happened with those who adhere to the NTS interpretational model of Qur'an Sunna teachings, which, as described in the previous chapter, is characterized by the marginalization of contextual background regarding the nature, content, understanding, interpretation, and objective of these Qur'anic injunctions and hadith texts. Furthermore, the interpretational proclivity to generalize and universalize these contextually based injunctions, which is another feature of the NTS approach to the interpretation of Qur'an-Sunna teachings, would result in the application of these verses to all Muslim, Christian, and Jewish communities both during the Prophet's lifetime and after his death. Furthermore, the NTS atomistic or segmentalist approach to textual evidence, which does not systematically consider all the textual evidence on a particular theme in order to develop a coherent and holistic view, combined with the use of the principle of abrogation (*naskh*) as espoused by classical Islamic legal theory, is also responsible for the development of this view. In addition, the NTS hadith-dependent Sunna hermeneutic and their *ahl al-ḥadīth manhaj* in relation to hadith criticism construe these hadith as normative and thus religiously binding.

So, for example, in the context of discussing the concept of *al wala' wa l bara'* examined in the third chapter, Qahtani,[43] a contemporary NTS scholar, writes that *al wala' wa l bara'* concept is a theological rather than just a political one having "primary importance in matters of faith." A "matter of belief and disbelief," he adds, furthermore, that "tawhid will never be achieved without it." Then he goes on to quote the Qur'anic verse 5:51 mentioned above to suggest that all Jews and Christians, those of the past and those of the present, fall outside the boundaries of "Belief."[44]

Moreover, on discussing the verse in the Qur'anic chapter titled Al Mutmahinah verse 1, "O you who believe do not take my enemies and your enemies as allies showing them affection," without any due regard for contextualization, again a hallmark of the NTS *manhaj* as argued in the previous chapter, Qahtani comments the following:

> When Allah granted love and brotherhood, alliance and solidarity to the
> believers He also forbade them totally from to allying themselves with

disbelievers of whatever hue, be they Jews or Christians, atheists or polytheists (emphasis mine).[45]

Here Qahtani, by using the words *believers* and *disbelievers* clearly forms
the view that "belief" only resides within reified socioreligious and historical community of the followers of Prophet Muhammad.

Similarly, in the context of commenting on the Qur'anic verse (109:6)
in which Prophet Muhammad is instructed to say to the Arab "pagans,"
"You have your own religion and I have mine" (*lakum dinukum wa li-a
dini*), quoting Ibn Taymmiyya (d. 728)[46] who, as we discussed in the third
chapter, is considered by the NTS scholars as remaining faithful to the
true belief and understanding of Islamic creed thus espousing the NTS
manhaj,[47] Qahtani states:

> There is no basis here for the assumption that the Prophet was somehow
> approving of the religion of these pagans; neither with that of the Jews and
> the Christians nor other People of the Book, as some secular minded people
> have suggested (emphasis mine).[48]

Here Qahtani, again on the basis of a lack of historical context informing
the NTS *manhaj* and on the basis of its *manhaj* mechanisms, such as textual segmentalism and generalization of the contextual/specific, the belief
of pagans are linked with that of all the Jews and Christians, past and present, to argue that the religion of Jews and Christian is not valid, therefore
denying them the religious status of "Believers."

Another instance that gives us an insight into the NTS concept of a
"Believer" discussed by Qahtani is in relation to a number of verses found
in the second and the third chapters of the Qur'an that mention people of
the book and Jews and Christians,[49] and on the basis of "generalizing the
particular" aspect of the NTS *manhaj*, Qahtani states the following:

> These verses and others like them make clear that scheming and ill will
> they [people of the book, Jews and Christians,] hold towards Islam and
> its followers. For this reason too, many verses were revealed which warned
> the believers, indeed forbade them, from associating with the disbelievers
> generally, and the people of the Book, especially.[50]

Here Qahtani not only considers People of the Book as disbelievers but
throughout the book he partially equates them with all Jews and Christians,
past and present, and views them to be especially strong in their disbelief.

Other examples include the quoting of medieval scholars such as Ibn
Hazm (d. 456),[51] Ibn Qayyim (d. 751),[52] and At-Tabari[53] (d. 310), who
in the context of the Qur'anic verse 5:51 given above consider that those

believers who make alliances with Jews and Christians, understood again in the universalist sense, have lost their faith.[54]

Similarly, Al-Madkhalee, another NTS scholar, views Jews and Christians as "disbelievers" and considers that Allah has described them "using the vilest of attributes," and He threatened them with the severest of threats without mentioning any of their good qualities because of their "disbelief and rejection of Muhammad and what they committed of disbelief and distortion of their revealed books."[55] In the context of discussing the ruling on one who befriends innovators and supports them against the adherents of the Sunna, the same scholar after quoting *sura* Ali 'Imran, verse 118 refers to the following commentary of the verse by Al-Qurtubi[56] (d. 671):

> Allah prohibits the believers, with this ayah, from taking the disbelievers, Jews and followers of vain desires, as trusted companions and confidants whom they could turn to for their opinions and entrust their affairs to.[57]

On a well-known NTS Web site, www.calgaryislam.com, one finds a short treatise titled "Are Christians and Jews Believers? The Islamic Position Concerning the People of the Book" written by Rashad Abdul Muhaimin, who frequently quotes prominent NTS scholars such as 'Abdur-Rahman ibn Hasan Aal-Ash-Shaykh, Saalih ibn al-'Uthaymeen, and in accordance with the broader NTS *manhaj* quotes, the Qur'anic verses, such as 9:31[58] and 5:17, 72,[59] and concludes that :

> Judaism, Christianity, and indeed all other ways of life have been excluded from what is accepted by Allah because in reality, they are rooted in disbelief and shirk.[60]

Ar Ruhalyee[61] in his book that advises the youth of Ahl-Sunna endorses this view by writing that Muslim minorities "live in the lands of the Kufaar," by which he means the West.

In a similar vein Al-Uthaymeen in his collection of fatawa on living in the land of disbelievers, which is targeting Muslim living in the West, clearly considers non-Muslim Westerns to be disbelievers.[62] A fatwa issued by the Saudi Arabian Standing Committee on Academic Research and Issuing Fatwas (al-Lajnah al-Daa'imah li'l-Buhooth al-'Ilmiyyah wa'l-Iftaa') is very clear and reads as follows:

> one of the basic principles of belief in Islam is that we must believe that every Jew, Christian or other person who does not enter Islam is a kaafir,

and that those against whom proof is established must be named as kaafirs and regarded as enemies of Allaah, His Messenger and the believers, and that they are the people of Hell....[63]

Based on this, we can conclude that the NTS concept of a "Believer" excludes all those who as known today or have been known as Muslims in a reified sense of the word.

In addition to the above, there are several Qur'anic verses and a number of hadiths that, when taken out of their original context described above and applied decontextually, impact upon the view of the religious Other, as they emphasize the tension and enmity that existed between Muslims and Jews and Christians during the time of the Prophet's early Medinan community expressed, for example, by invoking God's curses on them. Here we consider several of these.

III. Qur'anic Verses[64]

Strongest among men in enmity to the believers wilt thou fined the Jews and Pagans... (Q 5:82).

Fight those who believe not in Allah nor the Last Day nor hold that forbidden which hath been forbidden by Allah and His apostle nor acknowledge the religion of truth (even if they are) of the People of the Book until they pay the Jizya with willing submission and feel themselves subdued (Q 9:29).

IV. Hadith

Narrated 'Abd Allah ibn 'Umar: "Allah's Apostle said, 'You [i.e. Muslims] will fight with the Jews till some of them will hide behind stones. The stones will (betray them) saying, 'O 'Abd Allah [i.e. slave of Allah]! There is a Jew hiding behind me; so kill him'" (Bukhari, 4.176).

Narrated by 'Abd Allah ibn Mulayka: "Aisha said that the Jews came to the Prophet and said, 'As-Samu 'Alaikum [death be on you].' 'Aisha said (to them), '(Death) be on you, and may Allah curse you and shower His wrath upon you!' The Prophet said, 'Be calm, O 'Aisha! You should be kind and lenient, and beware of harshness and fuhsh [i.e. bad words].' She said (to the Prophet), 'Haven't you heard what they [the Jews] have said?' He said, 'Haven't you heard what I have said (to them)? I said the same to them, and my invocation against them will be accepted while theirs against me will be rejected [by Allah].'" (Bukhari, 8:57)

The conflictive and reactionary nature of these Qur'anic verses and hadith texts, again if considered from the NTS interpretational perspective, can have very grim implications and provide a religious foundation for a purely oppositional, discordant Muslim Self vis-à-vis the religious Other.

One example of this type of mentality and approach to Jews and Christians is promoted by the NTS scholar al-Albani, who considers that the Prophet forbade the initiation of greetings with Jews and Christians and said that Muslims should not develop genuine, human-based relationships with non-Muslims.[65] He bases his decisions upon a completely decontextualist and ahistorical approach to a couple of isolated (*ahad*) hadiths, including the one cited above on the authority of 'Aisha and disregarding other hadith that report prophet Muhammad's greeting of non-Muslims.[66] Noting the two different approaches and the disagreement among the traditional Muslim scholars on this issue of greeting, Qahtani nevertheless quotes At-Tabari who was of the view that the hadith prohibiting the greeting of non-Muslims was general in nature, thus is to be upheld, and the other specific, thus to be abandoned.[67]

Similarly, Al-Fawzan in his treatise Al Wala' wal Bara' cites, among others, verses 5:51 and 60: 1[68] to argue that Muslims ought not to be friends or seek support from non-Muslims.[69]

Thus, based on the above discussion, the NTS school of thought, based upon their *manhaj*, engenders a reified concept of a "Believer" that only encompasses the socioreligious and historical community of Prophet Muhammad and emphasizes an oppositional, discordant relationship between Muslims and the religious Other.

4.3   Qur'an-hadith Texts on the Boundaries of Faith according to the NTS *Manhaj*

In this section, we shall investigate how the NTS approach to the interpretation of the Qur'an and Sunna draws and demarcates the boundaries of belief and unbelief and applies them to non-Muslims, especially Christians and Jews. As in the previous section, before we begin with the textual analysis, the historical development of the concept of faith/belief (*īmān*) and unbelief (*kufr*)[70] requires some explanation in order for the NTS understanding of these concepts to be appreciated and situated in the broader Islamic tradition.

4.3.1   The Qur'anic Concepts of Kufr and Īmān

Izutsu, drawing upon his theory/methodology of Qur'anic historical semantics, gives several components of the implied/related meanings of the root k-f-r, based upon its Qur'anic usage, namely:

1. To cover, ignore knowingly, or be unthankful for received benefits—philological meaning;
2. Attitude of ingratitude toward and acts of rebellion against the Benefactor;
3. Giving lie (*takdhīb*) to God and God's Apostle and the divine message;
4. *Disbelief* if used as an antonym of *īmān*;
5. Man's denial of the Creator manifesting itself in acts of insolence, haughtiness, contentiousness, and presumptuousness (Izutsu 2002, 119–155),
6. Kufr associated with shirk or the practice of associating other gods with the One true God—the practice of the Arab polytheists termed *mushrikūn*,
7. Kufr in the sense of going astray (*ḍalāla*).

Building on the work of Izutsu but on the basis of a more chronologically fine-tunned approach to the development of meanings of kufr Waldman traces the accumulative development of the meanings of the root of KFR from that of being very 'adaptive, and undergoing an interesting development connected with Muhlammad's own changing views of his opponents' to its semantic field being primarily determined as the opposite of the root AMN (from which the word iman is derived of course) to it being increasingly linked with the concept of shirk and finally it being referred to in the context of 'the class of people to be fought by the mu'minin'.[71]

For the purposes of our study, three important points need to be highlighted at this stage. First, the concept of kufr presupposes the belief in God. Second, it can be applied to those who give the lie to God (i.e., meaning number 2 above), God's Apostle, and his Message and thus have gone astray. Third, as is commonly known, Jews and Christians in the Qur'an are primarily referred to as belonging to the *ahl al-kitāb* (People of the Book), but in several instances (Q 5:17, 98:1, 5:57), the root k-f-r is also used, as shown below. It is important to note in this context that given the above various meanings of kufr, it does not necessarily imply lack of faith but could be some form of incorrect thinking/action even on behalf of Muslims as in Q: 9:49 ("Among them is (many) a man who says: 'Grant me exemption and draw me not into trial.' Have they not fallen into trial already? and indeed Hell surrounds the Unbelievers (kafirin)"), which according to traditional Muslim exegesis applied to those Muslims who refused to take part in the expedition of Tabuk. However, unless one adopts a holistic and thematic approach to Qur'anic interpretation, there is a degree of "ambivalence" when it comes to the Qur'anic attitude toward Jews and Christians in relation to the "salvific status" of their faith.

As Izutsu has pointed out, the Qur'anic concept of the muslim/kāfir[72] relationship is based on a rather clear semantic dichotomy. However, subsequent Muslims changed the nature of the muslim/kāfir dialectic and introduced an additional element, namely the concept of the grave sinner (murtakib kabīra) or fāsiq. For example, the Khawarij, the first Muslim sect and first Muslim puritans, considered all those Muslims who did not subscribe to their view of Islam to be fāsiq and unbelievers, that is as kāfirūn. Murji'ites, the "pacifists" considered fāsiqūn to be Muslims, while the Mu'tazilites regarded them as an independent category.[73] Fisq, kufr and nifāq (religious hypocrisy) are Qur'anically closely related concepts. Indeed, fisq and nifāq are regarded as types of kufr.[74] Keeping the above distinctions in mind, we are in a position to analyze several Qur'anic verses that deal with the issue of faith boundaries and how to behave toward the religious Other.

I. Qur'anic Verses

> Let not the believers take for friends or helpers unbelievers rather than believers; if any do that in nothing will there be help from Allah; except by way of precaution that ye may guard yourselves from them. But Allah cautions you (to remember) Himself for the final goal is to Allah. (Q 3:28)

> Those who reject (Truth) among the People of the Book and among the Polytheists will be in hell-fire to dwell therein (for aye). They are the worst of creatures. (Q 98:6)

> O ye who believe! Take not for friends and protectors those who take your religion for a mockery or sport whether among those who received the Scripture before you or among those who reject faith; but fear ye Allah if ye have Faith (indeed). (Q 5:57)

> In blasphemy [kafara] indeed are those that say that Allah is Christ the son of Mary... (Q 5:17)

> Those who reject [kafara] (the truth) among the People of the Book and among the Polytheists were not going to depart (from their ways) until there should come to them Clear Evidence. (Q 98:1)

II. Hadith

> Narrated Abu Hurayra: "The Messenger of Allah (peace be upon him) observed: 'By Him in Whose hand is the life of Muhammad, he who amongst the community of Jews or Christians hears about me, but does not affirm his belief in that with which I have been sent and dies in this state (of disbelief), he shall be but one of the denizens of Hell-Fire.'" (Muslim, 284)

Due to the enmity and tension that existed between Muslims and some of the *ahl al-kitāb* described above, the application to *ahl al-kitāb* of verses that referred to the *fāsiqūn* and *munāfiqūn* (especially in the light of Q 5:57, 5:17and 98:1 and the above hadith) could easily result from using the NTS interpretational model. More will be said about this after we analyze the concept of *īmān* (faith).

Much like the concept of *kufr*, the concept of *īmān*, from the Qur'anic perspective, is closely related to the context of the unfolding of the Qur'anic revelation. It has undergone a transformation of meanings in the Qur'an itself and various Qur'anic commentaries.[75] Similarly, the subsequent understandings of *īmān* on the part of various Muslim factions were triggered by the turbulent sociopolitical and theological schisms that featured prominently and significantly shaped the formative period of Islamic thought.[76]

Izutsu maintains that the semantic field of *īmān* revolves around the concept of *kufr* occupying the negative side of the semantic field and the concepts of muslim (one who has willingly surrendered/submitted to God), *ihtidā'* (right guidance), *taqwā* (God consciousness/"fear" of God), and *shukr* (thankfulness [to God]) being positively related to it.[77]

Izutsu refers to the "essential structure of the concept of *'iman*"[78] and its essential components as a theological concept that is concerned with answering the following three questions:

- Subject of belief (i.e., who is the believer?)
- Essential means of expressing belief (i.e., how is to be believed?)
- Object of belief (i.e., what is to be believed in?)

According to Izutsu, Muslim theologians, as representatives of past communities of interpretation, considered *īmān* to be a byproduct of the following elements:

- Knowledge (*ma'rifa*) of God
- Assent by heart (*taṣdīq bi-al-qalb*)
- Verbal acknowledgment or confession in words (*iqrār bi-al-lisān*)
- *'Amāl* or acts of obedience or good works.[79]

Muslim interpretative communities have differed significantly as to what constitute the essential elements of belief[80] and what is the hierarchy of these constituents of *īmān*. For example, as we have already noted, the *fāsiqūn* were considered by some sections of the Muslim community to be Muslims and by others not to be.

As we demonstrated in the previous section, the NTS interpretation of the above Qur'an-hadith textual indicants in relation to the concepts of *īmān* and *kufr*, following the NTS *manhaj*, is that both the *ahl al-kitāb* referred to in the Qur'an and the contemporary adherents of the Christian and Jewish faith as unbelievers. Furthermore, NTS conceptual coalescing of the concepts of Sunna and "authentic" hadith, and in particular its view on the epistemological and hermeneutical value of *ahad hadith*, renders the above hadith narrated on the authority of Abu Hurayra as "authentic," thus having a normative bearing upon how the concept of the "Believer" is formulated in NTS thought. According to this view, the religious/confessional identity of non-historical Muslims, such as the Jews and Christians, would not come under the purview of what it means to be a "Believer" in a Qur'an-Sunna sense.

PART TWO: NTS Concept of a Religiously Ideal "Muslim Woman" Concept

How do NTS construct their concept of a religiously ideal "Muslim Woman" concept? Which elements of their *manhaj* may be seen as responsible for such a concept? Before I attempt to answer these questions, I need to elaborate on the criteria I employ in the construction of such a concept. The justification of the criteria was explained in the introduction part of the study.

4.4   The Criteria Used for the Construction of a Religiously Ideal "Muslim Woman" Concept

The interpretational implications as they pertain to the construction of a religiously ideal "Muslim Woman" concept that will help us in answering these questions, are structured around the NTS and progressive Muslim view of: the nature of the female (and by implication male) gender, especially female sexuality; Muslim woman's position in broader society/public sphere, in particular the purpose and function of segregation of sexes and covering (hijab/niqab) for women; and spousal rights and obligations and the purpose of marriage. Several assumptions underpin the NTS and progressive Muslim construction of a religiously ideal "Muslim Woman" concept at these three levels. It is in relation to these questions, as we argued in the introduction, that competing and divergent religiously ideal "Muslim Woman" concepts are particularly evident. As in the previous chapter, the assumptions regarding the premodern understanding of a religiously ideal "Muslim Woman" in relation to the three criteria apply to both *madhhab* and NTS *manahij*.

4.4.1   The Nature of Female (and Male) Sexuality according to *Madhhab* and NTS Thought

In order to understand the NTS and progressive Muslim construction of a religiously ideal "Muslim Woman" concept, it is important to first discuss the classical/traditional meaning, within which NTS school of thought operates, of the concept of female, and by implication male, sexuality. The first assumption that governs NTS and classical view of the female and the male sexuality is their essential difference.[81] According to this view, sexuality is a crucial locus of construction of masculinity and femininity.[82] These sexual differences are said to be based on biological and mental functions and capacities that differentiate the sexes. This gender dualism considers the female nature to be derivative vis-à-vis the male whose superiority is both ontological and sociomoral.[83] The female body is, furthermore, considered as sexually corrupting. As a corollary, the male sexual nature is seen as "polymorphously pervasive and aberrant."[84] As such, men are considered "as having an insatiable sexual desire aroused by sight, smell or voice of a woman, thereby distracting and diverting their energy from productive endeavours to wasteful sexual activity."[85] Furthermore, the premodern views of women are posited on (an artificial) slip between body and mind, sexuality, and spirituality. The category of the female gender is constructed primarily in sexual terms. Women are identified with the "irreligious" realm of sexual passion, as repositories of all "lower" aspects of human nature, the very anti-study of "illuminated" sphere of male (religious) knowledge, which is the sole sources of religious authority.[86]

Mernissi, among others, has lucidly discussed this understanding of the female (and male) sexual nature in many of her works. On the basis of classical Muslim literature she argues that Muslim civilization, unlike the modern Western one, developed an active concept of female sexuality regulating female sexual instinct by "external precautionary safeguards" such as veiling, seclusion, gender segregation, and constant surveillance. What underpins this view is the "implicit theory" based on the notion of the woman's *kayd* power, that is, the power to deceive and defeat men, not by force but by cunning and intrigue.[87] This theory considers the nature of woman's aggression to be sexual, "endowing [the Muslim woman] with a fatal attraction which erodes the male's will to resist her and reduces him to a passive acquiescent role."[88] As such women are a threat to a healthy social order (or *ummah*), which, as we shall subsequently see, is conceptualized as being entirely male.

4.4.2   Muslim Woman's Position in the Broader Society/Public Sphere and the Purpose of Veiling and Gender Segregation according to *Madhhab* and NTS Thought

The above briefly sketched gender dualism based on the essential difference in sexual natures between the two genders and the aggressive, morally corrupting (that is, for men) nature of female sexuality are employed to impose a number of restrictions upon the female both in the public and private spheres. According to the view of an active, morally harming (again for men) female sexuality, women are considered sources and causes of *fitna* or social and/or moral chaos.[89] In the words of El-Fadl, "women are seen as walking, breathing bundles of fitna" and womanhood is artificially constructed into the embodiment of seduction.[90] Thus, as a result of this view of female sexuality, women become symbolic of *fitna* and are considered antidivine and antisocial forces. The requirement for adopting the practice of *hijab/niqab* is seen as a proof a dangerous (i.e., for men's chastity) female sexuality, her immorality, and inferiority vis-à-vis the male, as well as an attestation to an aberrant male sexuality that is irresistibly and helplessly drawn to it. Basing her assertion on the work of the classical Muslim scholar Abu Hamid Al-Ghazali (1058–1111 CE), who, on this issue, embodies both the classical *madhhab and* NTS view, Mernissi asserts that the entire Muslim view of civilization revolves around "the struggle to contain the woman's destructive, all absorbing forces." As such women are to be "controlled to prevent men from being distracted from their social and religious duties" by "creating institutions which foster male dominance through sexual segregation." The purpose and the function of the head and/or face covering (*hijab/niqab*) serves a similar function to that of gender segregation and is based upon the same understanding of female and male sexualities. Veiling, according to Mernissi, is in actual fact "a symbol of sexual segregation." This is so because the classical understanding of Muslim sexuality is also "territorial" in a sense that "its regulatory mechanisms consist primarily in a strict allocation of space to each sex." The public sphere belongs solely to the males while the domestic sphere, the sphere of sexuality, to the female.[91]

4.4.3   Spousal Rights and Obligations and Purpose of Marriage according to *Madhhab* And NTS Thought

Linked to the first two points discussed above, the premodern Islamic jurisprudence developed a system of sharply differentiated, interdependent, gender-based spousal rights and obligations.[92] According to Ahmed, the historical context in which this system evolved played a major role in which spousal relations were determined by classical Muslim jurisprudence and inherited by NTS.[93] The institutions of patriarchy, social stratification, and slavery in particular had a major impact on the role and the status of the wife and the husband in marriage.[94] Ali, for example, argues that according to classical Islamic jurisprudence, marriage, in essence, was seen as a type of ownership (*milk*) based upon a contract between the parties giving rise to mutually dependent gender-based rights and obligations. At the core of this contract was a transaction whereby a wife's sexual availability was exchanged for her right to be financially supported and maintained by her husband.[95] Furthermore she states that "at its most basic, the[classical] jurists shared a view of marriage that considered it to transfer to the husband, in exchange for the payment of dower, a type of ownership(milk) over his wife, and more particularly over her sexual organ (*farj, bud'*)."[96] Based on this concept of marriage, women's constant obligation to be sexually available to her husband resulted in granting to the husband a total control over his wife's mobility so much so that he could prevent her from going to the mosque, visiting her parents, or even from attending the funeral of her immediate family, including her parents and children.[97] This view of marriage, in addition to other laws pertaining to divorce and child custody, and the strictly associated gender differentiated marital rights and obligations, resulted in the creation of a hierarchical, authoritarian marital relationship and a creation of a classical Islamic tradition based on male epistemic privilege.

4.5   The Interpretational Implications of the NTS Qur'an-Sunna *Manhaj* on the Construction of a Religiously Ideal "Muslim Woman" Concept

How are the above outlined interpretational assumptions governing the NTS Qur'an-Sunna *manhaj* employed by NTS in the construction of their version of a religiously ideal "Muslim Woman" concept?

4.5.1   NTS View of the Nature of Female (and Male) Sexuality

There are no Qur'anic verses that would support the classical view of female sexuality described above. NTS scholars do employ several Qur'anic verses in order to construct such a view. For example, in his book *The Veil:Evidence of Niqab*, Ibn Ismail uses verse 14 in *Sura Al-'Imran*; [98] An-Nur, verse 2; [99] At-Taghabun, verse 14; [100] and Yousuf, verse 28 in order to prove that "the Qur'an has pointed to the danger of the temptations of women."[101] There are a number of hadith that directly link women to the concept of *fitna*, some of which will be quoted below. Although they are not of the highest authenticity even by the classical hadith criticism standards,

> these traditions lay the foundation for most of the determinations regulating a woman's appearance and conduct...becom[ing] the vehicle for symbolisms placing women in the role of the distrusted or treacherous, and for associating them with the construct of a menace that must be restrained.[102]

This is primarily so because of the NTS (and classical) hadith and hadith-based Sunna *usul-ul-fiqh* which, as we saw in the third chapter, conceptually conflates the two regarding Sunna as epistemologically and methodologically hadith dependent. In addition to this, even if these *ahad hadith* are not considered as *"sahih"*[103] for legal purposes, both are deemed by the premodern *manahij* as probative on issues of morality, ethics, and theology.[104] Here are several:

> Abu Sa'id al-Khudri narrated that the Prophet said:...When it comes to [the temptations of] this world be cautious, and as to women be cautious [as well] for the first fitna that befell the Israelites was [the fitna of] women.
>
> Abd Allah b. Masood narrated that the Prophet said, [The whole of] the women are 'awra and so if she goes out, the devil makes her the source of seduction.
>
> Abd Allah b. Umar narrated that the Prophet said, I have not left in my people a fitnah more harmful to men than women.

Ibn Baz cites Al-Khudri's and Abd Allah bin Umar's second hadith to warn men not to sit in privacy with women, to not visit them privately, and to not travel with them without having any male-guardian present.[105] He adds that all of this leads to immorality and temptation.[106] Al-Madkhalee cites the first hadith on the authority of Abd Allah b.

Masood and concurs with this opinion.[107] Ibn Ismail quotes all three
hadith to argue the same point.[108] So does Mahmood.[109] Based upon
the above, argues El-Fadl, it is not surprising to come across classical
commentaries on these and similar traditions, which use the following
language:

> Since God has made men desire women, and desire looking at them, and
> enjoy them, women are like the devil in that they seclude men towards the
> commission of evil, while making evil look attractive [to men].We deduct
> from this that women should not go out in the midst of men except for a
> necessity, and that men should not look at their cloth and should stay away
> from women altogether.[110]

Thus, religiously ideal female Muslim identity, as we shall argue
subsequently, would be constructed along the lines of their complete
"invisibility" in the public domain of males. For example, based on the
women as sources of *fitnah* argument, a NTS scholar Maymani considers it unlawful for women to drive cars, walk in the middle of the
road, travel alone, or work in radio or television stations.[111] In the same
vein, Shaikh Ibn Jibreen, a prominent NTS scholar, forbids, on the
basis of the temptation argument, any kind of correspondence between
men and women, including exchange of letters, looking at non-*mahram*
men/women (even on television), and speaking over the phone because
"correspondence between men and women is a great temptation and
something very much to be avoided."[112] Sheikh Ibn Baz uses the same
reasoning to argue that women are not allowed to drive cars or work
alongside men.[113]

4.5.2   NTS's View on the Female Identity Vis-À-Vis Broader Society/Public Sphere, Especially the Purpose And Function of Hijab

The last sentence of the above quotation leads us to the issue of the religiously ideal "Muslim Woman" concept in relation to their function in
the broader society. By subscribing to the theory of active female sexuality
described above and considering the female body as inherently morally
and socially corrupting, the classical and NTS schools of thought impose a
number of sociospatial regulatory rules and regulations on women including the religious obligation of hijab[114] or niqab,[115] seclusion of women and
segregation of sexes, which are premised upon following Qur'an-hadith
evidence.

I. Veiling/'Awra

i.Qur'an:
33:59–60
O prophet! Tell thy wives and daughters and the believing women that they should cast their outer garments over their persons (when abroad): that is most convenient that they should be known (as such) and not molested: and Allah is Oft-Forgiving Most Merciful.

24:30–31
Say to the believing men that they should lower their gaze and guard their modesty: that will make for greater purity for them: and Allah is well acquainted with all that they do. (30) And say to the believing women that they should lower their gaze and guard their modesty; that they should not display their beauty and ornaments except what (must ordinarily) appear thereof; that they should draw their veils over their bosoms and not display their beauty except to.... (31).

24:60
Such elderly women as are past the prospect of marriage, there is no blame on them if they lay aside their (outer) garments, provided they make not a wanton display of their beauty: but it is best for them to be modest: and God is One Who sees and knows all things.

33:32–33
O Consorts of the Prophet! Ye are not like any of the (other) women: if ye do fear (God), be not too complacent of speech, lest one in whose heart is a disease should be moved with desire: but speak ye a speech (that is) just. And stay quietly in your houses, and make not a dazzling display, like that of the former Times of Ignorance; and establish regular Prayer, and give regular Charity; and obey God and His Messenger. And God only wishes to remove all abomination from you, ye Members of the Family, and to make you pure and spotless.

33: 53
And when ye ask (his ladies) for anything ye want ask them from before a screen: that makes for greater purity for your hearts and for theirs. Nor is it right for you that ye should annoy Allah's Apostle or that ye should marry his widows after him at any time. Truly such a thing is in Allah's sight an enormity.

For example, Shikh Ibn Jibreen quotes 24:30–31 to argue that women must cover their faces and makes a following observation:

Allah has ordered them [in the verse above] to lower their head-covering from their heads over the opening in front of their chest. It comes down from the head, it covers both the face and the neck and front chest area.[116]

Ibn Baz in turn cites verses 33:59–60, 33:32–33 and 33:53 to argue that the Qur'an commands all believing women and not just prophet's wives to stay in their homes and forbids them from indecently exposing themselves as the women would do in the Days of Ignorance (*Jahiliyyah*). He defines indecent exposure of believing women to include the bodily features such as "the head, the face, the neck, the chest, the forearm, the shin and so on." As a reason for this Ibn Baz considers that exposing these part s of the body by women leads to "great mischief, overwhelming temptation and an incitement of male hearts towards embarking on the means of fornication."[117] In relation to 24:30–31 Ibn Baz defines the operative word *jilbab* to include all of the women's body including the hair and the face "so that they may be known for their chastity."

In a similar vein Al-Uthaymeen and Al-Madkhalee cite 24:30–31, 24:60, 33:55–60 in support of the veiling of women including the face by stating that wearing of *khimaar* over the *juyub* entails covering of the face because wearing of "khimaar necessitates that or because it is understood from general reasoning."[118]

ii. Hadith

In the booklet on the obligation of veiling authored by leading NTS scholars Ibn Baz, Al-Uthanymeen, and Al-Madkhalee, a number of hadith are cited to argue in favor of obligation of veiling for women including the covering of their face.

i.   Ali bin Abee Talhah reported from Ibn Abbas that he said: Allah has commanded the believing women, when they come out of their homes due to a necessity, to cover their faces by placing their jalaabeeb over their heads, and only exposing one eye.[119]

ii. 'Aisha in the story of the great Slander against her, veiled her face (with her khimaar) when she heard the voice of Safwaan bin al-Mu'attal As-Sulamee'.[120]

iii. Prophet said: There are two types of people from the dwellers of the Fire that I have never seen before. [The first is] women who will be clothed yet naked... [121]

iv. Prophet said: The eyes commit *zinaa* (fornication) and their *zinaa* is looking... The heart ardently desires and waits, and private parts either confirm it or deny it.[122]

v.   Abu Hameed reported that the Prophet said: When one of you (believers) intends to marry a woman, there is no sin on him if he looks at her, so long his looking at her is only for the purpose of the intention of marriage. And this is even if she is unaware of it.[123]

vi. After commanding the women to come out of the *musalla* (place of prayer) for 'Eid, the prophet was asked by one of the women (Umm 'Aatiyah): o Messenger of Allah! If a woman has no veil, is there any sin if she does not come out (on 'Eid day)? The Prophet said: Let her sister (in islam) cover her with her *jilbaab* (veil), and the women should participate in the good deeds and in the religious gatherings of the believers.[124]

vii. 'Aa'ishah reported what has been confirmed in the two saheeh collections that the Prophet would offer the *fajr* prayer (in congregation) and then witness that the believing women, wrapped up with their shawls, has prayed with him. They would return to their homes, and no one would recognize them due to the darkness (of dawn). Then 'Aa'ishah said: If the Prophet would see the women that I see (in my time), he would have surely restricted them from going to the masjid, just as women of the tribe of Israa'eel were restricted.

xiii. Ibn 'Umar reported that the prophet said: Whoever trails his garment out of pride, Allah will not look at him on the Day of Judgment. So Umm Salamah asked, Then what should the women do with hems of their dresses? The Prophet said: Let them extend their hems the length of a hand span. She said: But their feet would still be exposed. So he replied: Then let them extend it a forearm's length and no more.[125]

ix. 'Aa'ishah said: Male raiders would pass by us while we (wives of the prophet) were in the state of *ihram* with the messenger of Allaah. When they would approach us, (each) one of us would let her jilbaab fall down from (the top of) her head over her face. And when they had passed on, we would uncover our faces.[126]

x. Prophet said: Muhrimah shouldn't wear the face veil or gloves.[127]

xi. Abd Allah b. Masood narrated that the Prophet said, "[The whole of] the women are 'awra and so if she goes out, the devil makes her the source of seduction."[128]

Al-Hashimi, cites additional *ahadith* to argue for obligatory nature of veiling for women, including the covering of faces by citing 24:30–31 and 'Aa'ishah commentary of it as follows:

> May Allah have mercy on the muhaajir women. When Allah revealed that they should draw their veils over their bosoms—they tore their wrappers and covered their heads and faces with them.[129]

Ibn Baz cites hadith i to argue for the obligatory nature of veiling that includes that of the face by asserting, on the authority of M. Ibn Sireen and 'Ubaydah as-Salmani, that the words "to cast their jalaabeeb upon themselves" (*judnina 'alayhinna min jalabibihinna*) in 33:59 means veiling the face and head and exposing only one eye; Ibn Baz cites hadith ii to argue that after the *ayah of hijab* was revealed (referring to 33:59), the women were not able to be recognized because of the veiling of their faces. Finally Ibn Baz cites hadith iii in conjunction with hadith given in previous section dealing with the nature of female sexuality to chastise Muslim women who "imitate disbelieving women, such as Christians by wearing short garments, exposing hair and other body parts, getting hairstyles according to the fashion of the people of disbelief and wickedness, adding hair extensions and wearing manufactured hairpieces, known as wigs."[130]

Al-Uthaymeen, on the other hand, uses the hadith iv as a commentary and explanation/clarification of 24:30 to argue that "the means that lead to guarding the private parts is the veiling of the face" as this can lead to finding pleasure in looking at the attractive features of the face and possible communication and intercourse between men and women.[131] Al-Uthaymeen cites the hadith v to assert that beauty is the suitor's objective when wishing to marry and that face is the main aspect of beauty. To support this claim he cites another hadith on the authority of bin Shu'aba in which the Prophet suggested to bin Shu'aba to look at his future wife prior to proposing to marry her.[132] Basing himself on hadith vi and vii, Al-Uthaymeen forms the view that *hijab* and covering of the face was the customary practice of the female companions of the prophet who are the role models of all Muslims so it is also incumbent on Muslim women to follow this example.[133] Al-Uthaymeen considers that hadith viii mandates the obligatory covering of the feet for women. Al-Uthaymeen cites hadith ix and x and defers to the opinion of ibn Taymiyyah to argue for the obligatory nature of covering the face and wearing of gloves for women when not on pilgrimage.[134] Al-Madkhalee cites hadith xi to support his view that women ought to cover all parts of their body, including the face and the gloves "as they are sought after by men and the areas of encitement from women."[135] Al-Uthaymeen also uses what he calls evidence from general analogy, mainly based on the *fitnah* argument described above and supported by hadith evidence.[136] In addition, he further supports his view of the obligatory nature of veiling including that of the face by referring to opinions of Ibn Taymiyyah, later Hanbali scholars such as Ibn al-Najjar al-Futuhi (d. 980 A.H.), Al-Bahuti al-Hanbali (d.1051 A.H.) and Shafi'i scholar M. Ash-Shawkani (1834 CE).[137] Al-Uthaymeen also refutes the evidence employed by other madhahib, mainly in form of hadith, used for nonobligatory nature of covering of the face, hands, and feet as in the *hanafi madhhab*.[138]

II. Public space and gender segregation:
i. Qur'an
33:32–33
O Consorts of the Prophet! Ye are not like any of the (other) women: if ye do fear (God), be not too complacent of speech, lest one in whose heart is a disease should be moved with desire: but speak ye a speech (that is) just. And stay quietly in your houses, and make not a dazzling display, like that of the former Times of Ignorance; and establish regular Prayer, and give regular Charity; and obey God and His Messenger. And God only wishes to remove all abomination from you, ye Members of the Family, and to make you pure and spotless.

33: 53
And when ye ask (his ladies) for anything ye want ask them from before a screen: that makes for greater purity for your hearts and for theirs. Nor is it right for you that ye should annoy Allah's Apostle or that ye should marry his widows after him at any time. Truly such a thing is in Allah's sight an enormity.

b. Hadith:
Narrated by Abd Allah b. Umar that the prophet said: "The prayer of a woman in her room is better than her prayer in her house and her prayer in a dark closet is better than her prayer in her room."

   Narrated by Abu Bakrah, the Prophet is reported to have said: "Those who entrust their [sociopolitical] affairs to a woman will never know prosperity."

   Narrated Abu Hurraira that the Messenger of Allah, may Allah bless him and grant him peace, said, "It is not halal for a woman who believes in Allah and the Last Day to travel the distance of a day and night without a man who is her mahram.

Based on this and similar Qur'an-hadith texts, public participation of women, even for the purposes of attending the mosque, are considered resentful, provocative, and offensive to the public domain that belongs solely to males.

   Emplying the above and similar other Qur'an-hadith evidence the above graduate thesis on *fiqh* presented to Imam Saud Islamic University in Riyadh entitled *Wilayah al-mar'ah fi al-Fiqh al-Islami* (*Leadership of Women in the Islamic Law*) written by H. Anwar, based on NTS *manhaj*, considers that *wilayat* of women is to be restricted only to women's responsibility over their own money, women working in specific gender segregated educational or medical jobs, and women leading other women in prayer. Leadership roles in areas of social, political, economic, legal, judicial, educational, and media are rendered unlawful.[139] He does so on the basis of, among others, the hadith of Abu Bakra cited above. Al-Hashimi[140] and Ibn Baz[141] cite the haidth of Abu Hurraira as support to prevent free mixing of men and women, which can lead to spread of immorality. Similarly, Al-Uthaymeen prohibits women from assuming political roles on the basis of the hadith according to which the Prophet had reportedly stated that women were inferior in intellect and religion and the historical evidence that women did not participate in the election of any of the caliphs.[142]

Which NTS *manhaj* principals are responsible for this interpretation of the above quoted Qur'anic and hadith-based material?

One of these principals is the concept of voluntarism, discussed in the third chapter, that implies a legalistic expression of the Will of God. It has important implications on how the above quoted Qur'anic textual indicants are interpreted. For instance, the Qur'anic injunction in 24:30–31 given above pertaining to women's (and men's) dress has been read/interpreted largely as a legal injunction—rather than an ethicomoral exhortation—to be enforced by the "Islamic state," giving women no choice in the matter. Therefore the normative construct of a woman image—whose *'awrah*[143] has been interpreted to be different to that of men and according to the majority view of classical jurisprudence[144]—within which NTS *usul-ul fiqh* operates, included the covering of an entire body except for face and hands (*hijab/khimar/jilbab*) or in some cases including that of the face (*abaya* and *niqab*), is constructed in relation to that of a veiled woman.

Another feature of the NTS *manhaj* was its decontextualist or (at best) superficially contextualist approach to interpretation and conceptualization of the nature of the Qur'ano-Sunnaic indicants. Concerning the construction of a normative "Muslim Woman" concept, this is particularly evident in relation to the issue of the NTS view of the *jilbab/hijab* and the practice of segregation. These Qur'anic injunctions seem to be highly contextually based.[145] Thus, the NTS is informed by a decontextualist, textual segmentalist *manhaj* that does not seek to make a distinction between a possibly specific nature of 33:59–60 and the more general nature of 24:30–31. The NTS interpretations in this context are therefore based upon what I called in the previous chapter "the universalisation of the particular" aspect of their *manhaj* and the dehistorization of the 33:59–60. A lack of *maqasid* approach is also another *manhaj* element of NTS that leads to this type of reasoning. Namely, the Qur'anic verses pertaining to veiling could be understood to promote certain underlying principles such as modesty and decency and that veiling was a culturally sensitive means toward achieving these moral principles and not an end in itself. Furthermore, NTS conceptual coalescing of the concepts of Sunna and hadith, and in particular its view on the hermeneutical value of *ahad hadith* renders the above hadith as "prescriptive" in relation to the religiously ideal "Muslim Woman" construct. Based on these features of the NTS approach to interpretation of Qur'an-Sunna teachings, the religiously ideal "Muslim Woman" concept is constructed in reference to that of a veiled, secluded woman who remains within the privacy space of her home and rarely ventures into the public space of the male ummah.[146]

4.5.3   View of Spousal Rights and Obligations in Marriage

In order to construct this dimension of a religiously ideal "Muslim Woman" concept, the NTS proponents use several Qur'anic verses and numerous *ahadith*.[147]

I. Qur'an

4:34

Men are the protectors and maintainers of women because Allah has given the one more (strength) than the other and because they support them from their means. Therefore the righteous women are devoutly obedient and guard in (the husband's) absence what Allah would have them guard. As to those women on whose part ye fear disloyalty and ill conduct admonish them (first) (next) refuse to share their beds (and last) beat them (lightly); but if they return to obedience seek not against them means (of annoyance): for Allah is Most High Great (above you all).

2:228

Divorced women shall not wait concerning themselves for three monthly periods nor is it lawful for them to hide what Allah hath created in their wombs if they have faith in Allah and the Last Day. And their husbands have the better right to take them back in that period if they wish for reconciliation. And women shall have rights similar to the rights against them according to what is equitable; but men have a degree (of advantage) over them and Allah is Exalted in Power Wise.

II. Ahadith:

There are many other *ahadith* of this genre that highlight the importance of blind obedience of wives to their husband/s as their religious duty and a precondition to their religious salvation, including the inability to refuse sexual intercourse initiated by the husband or do voluntary[148] fasts or the view that women lack in intelligence or are not as who primarily provides sexual pleasure for the husband, which also forms the rationale behind the *nikah,* or the marriage contract.[149] A collection of these misogynist *ahadith* is found for example in above quoted work *The*

Righteous Wife by an NTS scholar M. Shooman, Ash-Shahawi's *Marital Discord: Causes and Cures*, as well as the book titled *The Choice of Every Woman* by another NTS scholar named Abu Saif, in which these ideas are based upon by "authentic hadith." We quote here only several representative examples.

Abu Hurrayra reports that Allah's Messenger said:

> "The rights of the husband over the wife is such that if he had a wound, or his nostrils were pouring forth pus or blood, then she were to swallow that down—then she would (still) not have fulfilled his right."[150]

Abu Sa'id al-Khudri said:

> "The Messenger of Allah went out to the prayer ground for the prayer of Adha or Fitr, and he passed by the women and said :"O Women! Give in charity, for I have been shown that you shall be the majority of the People of the Fire. So they asked," Why is that, O Messenger of Allah? He replied," You curse frequently and are ungrateful to your husbands."[151]

The Messenger of Allah said, "Allah will not look at a woman who does not give thanks to her husband and she cannot do without him."[152]

In Abu Saif'ss book we find the following *ahadith* with the similar theme.

The Prophet said :

> If a woman knew what right her husband has (over her) she would not sit down while his lunch and dinner are served to him until he finishes (his meal).
>
> Were I to order anyone to perform prostration (out of respect and honour and not as an act of worship) to another person, I would have ordered a woman to perform prostration to her husband, because of the great right he has upon her.
>
> As for two (people) ,their prayers do not go beyond their heads : a slave who runs away from his owners, until he returns to them, and a woman who disobeys her husband, until she returns.[153]

Ash-Shahawi cites the following hadith from *sahih hadith* collections and remarks that "a man has the right to derive physical pleasure from his wife at all times."

> When a man invites his wife to his bed and she then refuses to come, the angels curse her until the morning.

> If a man invites his wife (to have sexual relations with him), then let her come to him, even if she is (watching) over the oven.[154]

M. Shooman in his *The Righteous Wife* quotes Dhahabi[155] who in his Al-Kabaair is quoted as having said the following (d. 748) in relation to the concept of a "righteous woman":

> What is obligatory upon the woman is that she seeks the pleasure of her husband, and avoids angering him, and does not refuse him whenever he wants her. The woman must also know that she is like a slave to her husband, so she should not do anything affecting herself or her husband's wealth except with his permission. She should give precedence to his rights over her rights, and the rights of his relatives over the rights over relatives, and she should keep herself clean and be ready for him to enjoy her. She should not boast at his expense of her beauty, nor rebuke him for any ugliness found in him. The woman must also be always modest and reserved in the presence of her husband, lower her eyes in front of him, obey his commands, remain silent when he speaks, keep far away from everything which angers him, avoid treachery in his absence, with regard to his bed, his wealth and his house.[156]

Which interpretational assumptions governing the NTS *manhaj* are responsible for the adoption of this view as being based on normative Qur'an-Sunna teachings?

Apart from the already discussed hadith-dependent Sunna *manhaj*, a number of Qur'anic interpretational assumptions engender this aspect of the NTS version of a normative "Muslim Woman" concept. For example, the interpretational tendency of "intentionalism" that was discussed and defined in the previous chapter as a focus on authorial intent as the object of all interpretation and its principal status discoverability in essence assumes that it is possible to interpret Qur'anic text with complete objectivity without presuppositions or preconceived ideas. Alongside the entirely premodern episteme of NTS *manhaj*, intentionalism results in an approach that considers that premodern communities of interpretation understanding/s of a normative Muslim image as either not interpretation/s at all but the actual unmediated commandments of God's Will, or considers these interpretations as the only legitimate interpretational possibilities the relevant Qur'an (and hadith) evidence can yield. For example, the above Qur'anic verses (3:34; 2:228) that deal with the issue of the relationship between husbands and wives are understood/interpreted as conferring onto men inherent God-given superiority over women whose only duty is to obey her husband because that is the manner in which the classical body of exegesis and jurisprudence interpreted them. They are viewed as having eternal applicability regardless of changing social, cultural, legal, or political contexts.

As such, Shooman, a contemporary proponent of NTS thought quotes the interpretation of a prominent Saudi Arabian *fiqh* scholar As-Sa'di (d. 1307) who with regards to 4:34/2:228 maintains the following:

> That is due to the excellence of man over women, and the eminence which they have been given over them. So the pre-eminence of the men over the women is from many aspects: holding positions of leadership and authority is particular to men, likewise to Prophethood and Messengership. . . . Also due to the characteristics given to them by Allah, the like of which are not possessed by women such as sound intellect, composure, patience and endurance. . . . So from all this it is known that the man is like a governor and master for his wife, and she is with him like a captive. So his [husband's] role is to take care of that which Allah has placed him in charge of, and her role is to be obedient to her Lord and to obey her husband.[157]

Another feature of the NTS *manhaj* discussed in the previous chapter was that of textual segmentalism referring to verse-by-verse, surah by surah, linear, segmental analysis and commentary of the Qur'anic text and the relative neglect of the Qur'anic thematic and structural *nazm*. The implications of this textual segmentalist approach for the construction of a religiously ideal "Muslim Woman" construct can, for example, be seen in relation to NTS *manhaj* that hermeneutically disregards/downplays the significance of gender egalitarian verses present in the Qur'an[158] and focusing on few verses such as 4:34 and 2:228 quoted above to foreground male dominancy over that of gender egalitarianism. In this context Shehadeh, when delineating what she describes as fundamentalist Islam, argues that its proponents exhibit a "willful prejudiced interpretation of Qur'an and hadith, emphasizing a handful of verses and hadiths that could be interpreted pejoratively while ignoring numerous other verses and hadiths that stress clearly and unambiguously gender equality."[159]

Furthermore, the literal and philologically oriented NTS *manhaj*, based on a blend between ethical voluntarism and the strictly instrumental role of reason, results in a hermeneutic that considers any textual indicant found in "authentic" hadith bodies of knowledge such as those quoted above pertaining to women as being equated with the concept of Sunna, even if they run counter to reason or are ethicomorally (as values based on objective reality), repugnant. Therefore another aspect of a religiously ideal "Muslim Woman" concept, according to the NTS view, is that of an obedient, immobile, and silent wife whose religious duty is to please and satisfy the (sexual) needs of her husband.

Chapter 5

Progressive Muslims—Conceptualizing and Engaging the Islamic Tradition

This chapter consists of four sections. In the first part, the aim is to present a discussion on some defining themes underpinning progressive Muslim worldview. The second and the third section historically contextualize and place progressive Muslim thought in relation to their intellectual predecessors coming from both the non-Muslim majority and Muslim majority worlds. The last part outlines progressive Muslim approach to conceptualizing and engaging with the Islamic tradition and the concept of modernity/modern episteme.

5.1   Progressive Muslims: General Themes Characterizing Progressive Muslims' Worldview and Its Proponents

In this section, I will present some general themes that characterize and underpin progressive[1] Muslims' overall worldview. It is important to state at the very outset that the concept of "progress" in progressive Muslim thought is not conceptualized in its Hegelian-Fukoyamian teleological view of history/time in a sense of inevitability of change. "Progress" is rather framed in the realm of the "possibility" of change.[2] Moosa, one of the most prominent intellectual theoreticians behind progressive Muslim thought, employs the concept of "progress" in a sense of something that is "fortuitous, rather then inevitable, hold[ing] the promise that change might occur in diverse and multiple forms." Thus, according to this under-standing of the concept of "progress" is not premised on the "totalitarian narrative of progress driven by scientism [and] liberal capitalism" or that of the notion of "deterministic or apocalyptic theory of progress" embed-ded in the larger framework of singular modernity.[3] Instead, history and historical inquiry is approached from a Foucaultian genealogical perspec-tive according to which "ideas, institutions and practices are regarded as unique products of specific historical confluences, perfect in and of them-selves, without reference to extra-historical values or ideals in relation to which they either succeed or fail to conform."[4] Importantly, progressive "Islam" is not, as Moosa warns, "a ready-made ideology or an off-the shelf creed, movement or pack of doctrines." It is not a school of thought as it is more than a systematic theory of interpretation of the entire Muslim law, theology, ethics, and politics. Progressive Muslims' worldview is founded on more than "identity, texts, practices and history"[5]. As much as those elements are important to being a progressive Muslim, it also includes an additional, undefined element that "involves all those things that make one feel that you belong."[6] Being and feeling to be a progressive Muslim is, argues Moosa further, at best a practice, a package of loyalties and commit-ments, a work in progress.[7]

Furthermore the progressive Muslims' "cosmovision,"[8] to use the words of F. Esack, one of its leading intellectual designers and proponents, is best characterized by its commitments and fidelity to certain ideals, values, practices, and objectives that are expressed and take form in a number of different themes. These themes primarily concern issues pertaining to the progressive Muslims positioning in relation to: i. the dominant or hege-monic economic, political, social, and cultural forces often termed "The Empire"; ii. their own inherited Islamic tradition; and iii. its conceptual-ization of the notion of modernity.

One of the most prominent of these ideals and practices is the com-mitment to what Esack terms "principled or prophetic solidarity," i.e., the engagement with the marginalized and the oppressed communities of the world that are confronted with the actual context of injustice. This prin-cipled solidarity ought not be confused with and must be distinguished from what Esack labels the "expedient or situational ethics" that, in his view, dominate current Muslim public discourses, which are strategic, utilitarian, and accommodationist in character.[9] In the words of Esack, the primary concerns of Progressive Muslims

> [r]elate [far more directly] to global structures of oppression whether eco-nomic, gender, sexual etc., and ensuring that the oppressed are once again active agents of history. This fight for us [Progressive Muslims] involves the

centrality of God, the imagining of mankind as *al-nas-* *a* carrier of the spirit of God and an appreciation of Islam as a liberatory discourse.[10]

In this context, the hegemony of the modern free-market–based economics and political and social structures, institutions, and powers ("The Empire") that support, maintain, or are not critical of the (unjust) status quo are strongly resisted and are seen by progressive Muslims as antithetical to their overall Weltanschauung including their understanding of Islam. This is so because "The Empire" is considered to have brought about the transformation and the reduction of a human (*al-insan*), a carrier of God's spirit, into a primarily economic consumer (*homo aeconomicus*) producing great economic disparities between the majority world of the poor South and the minority world of the rich North. According to Safi, this "Empire" consists of a multitude of forces, "among them the oppressive and environmentally destructive forces of multi-national corporations whose interests are now linked to those of neo-imperial, unilateral governments...that put profit before human rights and 'strategic interest' before the dignity of every human being."[11]

Another central theme that permeates progressive Muslim thought is its wish to bring about the centrality, the uniqueness, and inherent worthiness of each and every human being as the recipient and carrier of God's spirit. This view is perhaps best illustrated with the following statements of Safi:

> [A]t the heart of a progressive Muslim interpretation is a simple yet radical idea: every human life, female or male, Muslim and non-Muslim, rich or poor, "Northern" or "Southern" has exactly the same intrinsic worth.[12]

and

> A progressive Muslim agenda is concerned with the ramifications of the premise that all members of humanity have this same intrinsic worth because, as the Qur'an reminds us, each of us has the breath of God breathed into our being.[13]

Thus, progressive Muslims emphasize God's universal nature and the universality of the faith itself through demonstrating God's concern for humanity in general over that of the petty minutiae of earthly squabbles.

Another prominent theme that is present in progressive Muslim thought concerns the issues of democracy and human rights. The discourse on democracy and human rights stemming from the geographical regions of the Empire's center is viewed by progressive Muslims with a great deal of suspicion as it is seen as often functioning as a "Trojan Horse of Recolonisation."[14] It is viewed with suspicion also because it is considered not to be living up to its own ethicomoral standards, especially (but not only) in relation to issues directly affecting Muslims.[15]

In this connection, one important aspect and objective of being a progressive Muslim, argues Esack, is the "speaking truth to power" by engaging: i. "in relentless self-critique that enables the adherent of progressive Muslim thought to be true to the ideals of a just society in a way that also prevents his or her cooptation by those who have their own agendas or the expansion of the Empires as their primary reason for wanting to engage Islam"; ii. engaging the Empire in the light of i. without jeopardizing the inherent humanity of those comprising it; and iii. engaging the *ummah* by confronting those within it who in the guise of protecting Muslim societies from the Empire violate Muslims' basic human rights.[16]

This means that progressive Muslims are engaged in a "multiple critique" that "entails a multi-headed approach based on a simultaneous critique of the many communities and discourses we [Progressive Muslims] are positioned in."[17] To be a progressive Muslim, thus, means to challenge, resist, and seek to overthrow the structures of injustice regardless of the ideational origins and phylogeny.

In conjunction with the emphasis on the inherent dignity of every human being, the values of social and gender justice and religious pluralism are the main driving forces behind the progressive Muslim ethicoreligious outlook. As such progressive Muslims are characterized by their

> striv[ing] to realize a just and pluralistic society through critically engaging Islam, a relentless pursuit of social justice, an emphasis on gender equality as a foundation of human rights, a vision of religious and ethnic pluralism, and a methodology of nonviolent resistance.[18]

Gender justice and equality in particular, play a very important part in the overall progressive Muslim thought because they are seen as "a measuring stick for the broader concerns of social justice and pluralism."[19] Gender justice and equality are, therefore, regarded as sine qua non of progressive Muslim thought. In the words of Safi

> ...the Muslim community as a whole cannot achieve justice unless justice is guaranteed for Muslim women. In short there can be no progressive interpretation of Islam without gender justice. Gender justice is crucial, indispensable and essential. In the long run any progressive Muslim interpretation will be judged based on the amount of change in gender justice it is able to produce in small and large communities.[20]

As such progressive Muslims strive for a legitimately recognized Islamic feminism.

The much debated and frequently misunderstood concept of *jihad* in progressive Muslim thought is closely linked to that of its etymologically related concept of *ijtihad*. Indeed, an essential component of progressive Muslim thought according to Safi is their struggle (*jihad*) "to exorcise [our] inner demons and bring justice in the world at large by engaging in a progressive and critical interpretation of Islam (*ijtihad*)".[21] By subscribing to this view, progressive Muslims wish to shift the current discourses on *jihad* from being primarily embedded in overly geopolitical and security-terrorist analytical and conceptual matrixes to that of inner intellectual and ethical and primarily nonviolent struggle and resistance to forces that conflict with their overall Weltanschauung.[22]

At the core of this progressive Muslims "cosmovision" is also a very strong emphasis on spirituality and interpersonal relationships based on the teachings of some of the "romantic or idealistic" Sufi ethics of dealing with fellow human beings in a way that "always recall[s] and remember[s] the reflection of Divine Presence and qualities in one another.[23]

As Bamyeh argues, this aspect of the progressive Muslims' worldview[24] in many ways represents a modern intellectualization of Sufism.[25]

Another important facet of progressive Muslim thought is its emphasis on grassroots activism that reflects its ideals and values. In the words of Safi,

> A progressive commitment implies by necessity the willingness to remain engaged with the issues of social justice as they unfold at the ground level in the realities of Muslim and non-Muslim communities. Vision and activism are both necessary. Action without vision is doomed from the start/vision without activism quickly becomes irrelevant.[26]

In other words, progressive Muslims consider that there is a very strong link between orthopraxis and orthodoxy in which the former leads to the latter.[27] Therefore, progressive Muslim thought can be seen as a persuasive public philosophy of modernizing religious life based on activism, spelling out what a spiritual (not secular) life ought to look like in modern society.[28]

The proponents of progressive Muslim thought are to be found spread throughout the Muslim and non-Muslim world. In this context, Safi in his article "What is Progressive Islam"[29] writes the following:

> It would be a clear mistake to somehow reduce the emergence of progressive Islam to being a new "American Islam." Progressive Muslims are found everywhere in the global umma. When it comes to actually implementing a progressive understanding of Islam in Muslim countries, particular

communities in Iran, Malaysia, and S. Africa are leading, not following, the United States.

Apart from those scholars whose work has been cited in this chapter so far, they include Hasan Hanafi, professor of philosophy at Cairo University in Egypt; Nasr Hamid Abu Zayd, a professor of "Islam and Humanism" in the University of Humanistics in Utrecht, in Netherlands; A. K. Soroush, a prominent Iranian scholar and intellectual based in Washington;[30] F. A. Noor, political scientist and human rights activist in Malaysia;[31] the late Nurckolish Majid (d. 2005), a prominent Islamic thinker and intellectual in Indonesia; Ali Ashgar, engineer, rights activist, and Muslim scholar in India;[32] Enes Karic and Mustafa Ceric, Professors of Islamic Studies at the Faculty of Islamic Sciences in Sarajevo in Bosnia;[33] Abdul Qadir Tayoub and Sa'diyya Shaikh, lecturers of Islamic Studies at the University of Cape Town in S. Africa;[34] Kacia Ali, an Assistant Professor of Religion at Boston University;[35] Asma Barlas, Professor of Politics and Director of the Center for the Study of Culture, Race, and Ethnicity Ithaca; Amina Wadud, Associate Professor of Islamic Studies at the Virginia Commonwealth University[36] in the United States; and many others. Many of the leading progressive Muslim intellectuals live in the West and teach at Western universities. Some of them obtained their graduate and postgraduate qualifications from these institutions and, in some cases, have also received traditional training in the Islamic sciences.[37] Importantly, progressive Muslim intellectuals and activists include a significant number of those of the female gender and their thoughts are considerably informed by the discourses surrounding contemporary critical feminist studies and gender justice. In the words of Safi:

> Unlike their liberal Muslim forefathers, progressive Muslims represent a broad coalition of female and male Muslim activists and intellectuals. One of the distinguishing features of the progressive Muslim movement as the vanguard of Islamic (post)modernism has been the high level of female participation as well as the move to highlight women's rights as part of a broader engagement with human rights.[38]

Another delineating attribute of the progressive Muslims worldview is their understanding of the concept of Islam. In general, Islam is not viewed within a framework of a reified religion or culture but as, to borrow Karamustafa's phrase, a civilizational project in progress, that is,

> dynamic and beyond reification; a truly global phenomenon adoptable across cultural, national and ethnic divides; both a supracultural construct

that is inclusive of and interactive with culture (i.e. inclusively interactive); a treasure trove of civilisational riches serving all humanity; and constantly in progress but having a core set of beliefs and practices that are ultimately linked to the historical legacy of Prophet Muhammad.[39]

The historical reified Islam or what Arkoun terms "The Islamic Fact" as embodied in the historical Islamic tradition, in turn, is considered " a result of a continuous historical and social construction of human actors;...a series of political, intellectual, cultural, economic, and juridicial *faits accomplis*...[40]
Another prominent aspect of progressive Muslim thought is that besides awarding a vital role to the concept of the sociocultural embeddedness of certain aspects of the Islamic tradition and its primary sources, ethicoreligious and moral considerations are the highest hermeneutical tool in the progressive Muslim approach to interpretation of Qur'an-Sunna indicants.[41] As such progressive Muslim thought is characterized by a "search for moral and humane aspects of Islamic intellectual heritage and [a force] against moral lethargy."[42] Indeed one of its central guiding principles is "to reclaim beautiful in the vast and rich moral tradition of Islam and to discover its moral imperatives."[43] As part of this approach, progressive Muslim thought calls for a "careful analysis of some of the more complex and foundational presumptions in Muslim legal and ethical philosophy" and the necessary epistemological and paradigm shift in, what Moosa terms, the post-Empire Islam climate.[44] In this respect progressive Muslim thought strongly opposes, accounts for, and challenges the "great impoverishment of thought and spirit brought forward by all Muslim literalist-exclusivist groups such as (but not only) Wahhabism."[45] Being a progressive Muslim, argues Safi further, means "to issue an active and dynamic challenge to those who hold exclusivist, violent and misogynist interpretations [of the Islamic tradition].[46] Progressive Muslims, in this context, see it as their task to revive the tradition's "vibrancy, intelligibility and diversity."[47]
As shall be discussed in more detail in the next chapter, the progressive Muslim *manhaj*, unlike what we described in the previous chapter as minimal hermeneutics employed by NTS and NTS-like communities of interpretation, is comprehensively contextualist or historical in nature.
Another important trait of progressive Muslim thought is that it purports to move beyond the apologetic discourses indulged in by not only modernists but other traditionalist and revivalist groups that have emerged over the last two-three decades.[48] An apologetic approach is based on a process that "reduces complex problems and practices to their bare essentials in order to score an ideological point."[49] This methodology is,

furthermore, ahistorical and in actual fact, distorts history by attempting to apply today's standards onto the past. Instead, progressive Muslim thought aims to be ever conscious of history.

Progressive Muslim worldview is also based upon certain view of ethics and religion. As shall be argued in more detail in the next chapter, progressive Muslims are advocates of ethical objectivism whose starting point is a philosophical reflection on the actual experience of social existence, rather than merely on the holy text. Concepts such as truth, justice, or morality are seen as intuitively embodying self-evident virtue and do not necessarily emerge from any transcendental realm. According to this view, religion does not teach "justice" or morality but is accepted because it is just and moral.[50]

The above outlined characteristics are a crosssection of the major themes, ideas, and values underpinning progressive Muslim worldview, which serve as a heuristic device to delineate and describe a particular way of "being and feeling a Muslim," a progressive Muslim way at that.

5.2   Western Intellectual Predecessors of Progressive Muslims' Conceptualization and Engagement with the Islamic Tradition[51]

From what was asserted above, it is clear that progressive Muslims do not subscribe to commonly employed dichotomies such as, tradition vs. modernity, secularism vs. religion, or simplistic generalization such as modernity =Western or Judeo-Christian intellectual /civilizational tradition. In order to better understand the way progressive Muslims engage and conceptualize the Islamic tradition and the manner in which they approach modernity and its epistemology (which is the task of the subsequent two sections of the chapter), progressive Muslim thought needs to be placed in the broader context of not only the past intellectual movements based on the indigenous Islamic tradition stemming from the Muslim majority world but also those intellectual streams originating from the non-Muslim majority realm that can be considered as its predecessors in relation to how they deals with the questions pertaining to interpretation of religion and sacred texts and as a corollary interpretation of history and time. This is so because progressive Muslim thought, as shall be argued below, is marked by epistemological pluralism and methodological fluidity and self-consciously incorporates modern episteme when self-defining itself.

Wright in his PhD thesis "Modern Qur'anic Hermeneutics" makes a compelling case for the hermeneutical and intellectual linking of what he refers to as European Romantic Criticism and Philosophy with some contemporary Muslim intellectual streams, especially in the case of the 'Egyptian Literary Renaissance' embodied by the works of Egyptian scholars such Amin Al-Khuli (1895–1966) and Nasr Hamid Abu Zayd (1943–2010). It is my contention that this also applies to progressive Muslim thought as defined in this study.

Wright argues that in the wake of the what M. G. S. Hodgson terms the "Technicalist Revolution"[52] of the sixteenth century Europe, Romantic intellectuals, and thinkers such as G. B. Vico (1688–1744), R. Lowth (1710–1787), J. C. Eichhorn (1752–1827), J. G. von Herder (1744–1803), and Victor-Marrie Hugo (1802–1885) developed "reading strategies designated to account for a new modern or contrapuntal sense of time" that for the first time in history consciously become aware of and "feel the distinction between natural and historical or cultural temporality" or change.[53] This new conceptualization of time ushered in novel intellectual patterns and ways of thinking about themes such as the nature and study of history/ the past, human agency, religion, and the interpretation of sacred texts.[54]

This modern sense of time, not evident in the thinking and the writings of the pretechnicalist revolution writers/thinkers, had very important implications in which human beings conceive of and talk about the past and history. For example, the premodern sense of time was thought to be world over uniform and monolith. Those actors living during the medieval epoch were not aware of and thus did not make a distinction between natural and cultural or historical time.[55] As such they had not experienced the "contrapuntal rhythms of technicalist age." They considered the past to be finalized, fixed, and "eternally present" in the present. The past's presence in and, as we argued in the third chapter in the context of NTS worldview, imposition upon and the privileging over the present had an important function of vouchsafing the "cultural memory as a potent source of present authority."[56] History and engaging in historical writing was seen as a simple act of retrieval.

Equipped, aware of and in tune with the modern, contrapuntal sense of time the Romantic thinkers "psychologically underwrote the historicist conclusion [of the Romantic thinkers] that history has a history—or as we would say today—that cultural memory is as much constructed as it is found."[57] Wright argues that according to Koselleck, two crucial historicist conclusions were derived from this modern sense of time, namely that: "history is an open-ended process rather than a closed science and a fatality"; and "that there exists a gap between the historical events and the language used to represent them—both by the agents involved in these events and by historians retrospectively trying to reconstruct them."[58] This new way of thinking casts a critical eye on the past treatments of the past and considers that "no past treatment of the past ought to be accorded continuing authority in the present without careful scrutiny."[59] This approach thus emphasizes the importance of human agency in ways in which past and history have been treated.

Romantic philosophy, embedded in this contrapuntal conceptualization of time and revisionary history, is founded on what Wright terms the practice of "re-description" (term borrowed from Rorty[60]) that engenders "new vocabularies" and "makes possible the consideration of things not previously considered—it makes possible the saying of things of previously left unsaid, or previously said, but now forgotten or ignored."[61] Moreover, the task of re-description, importantly, is to offer alternatives to hegemonic traditions and to "construct (hopefully) compelling counternarratives to the selective cultural memory that characterizes hegemonic tradition."[62]

Romantic philosophy has also developed a unique approach to interpretation of religion and sacred texts. Unlike the tradition of the European Enlightenment and its "higher criticism," Romantic thought/philosophy does not consider religion as a useless, wrong-headed, or dangerous remnant of premodern times, but its relationship to it, according to Wright, is best described in the words of C. West's notion "of critical alignment with an enabling tradition."[63] Wright sees this relationship as a "project of reconciliation with temporality" that he terms *secularization*.[64]

Another important feature of Romantic thought, thus, is that of "secularization" of inherited theological ways of thinking and the putting into operation of secular historical scholarship to sacred books. The term *secularization* here is not linked to its contemporary overly political meaning of separating religion from societal institutions but is defined by Wright as referring to "an acute sensitivity to historical context" brought about by the rise of technicalism in Europe in the sixteenth century.[65] In other words, "secularism" here refers to a type of comprehensive contextualization and humanization of sacred and religious books and writings.

This Romanticism's approach to religion and sacred texts, thus, signifies a "move from theology to cultural and anthropological hermeneutics" and a discursive shift from "the timelessness of theological truths to historicism."[66] The words of Herder in the context of biblical scholarship are instructive of the Romantic philosophical approach to religion and sacred writings:

> Read the bible in the human [*menschlich*] way: For it is a book written through human agency for human beings; human is the language; human were the external means whereby it was written and preserved; human, finally, is the sense with which it must be grasped and every aid that elucidates it; as well as the entire purpose and use to which it should be applied.[67]

The Romantic thinkers, argues Wright, were the precursors of modern literary historians. Modern literary historians regard any text, including sacred texts, as a historical artifact that linguistically 'encodes' aspects of extratextual environment in which it is produced and as such becomes a form of a "palimpsest" to be carefully scrutinized so as to reveal data of interest.[68] That is to say that any text, including sacred scriptures, has to operate within a spatiotemporal dimension. The premodern approach to history, on the other hand, argues Wright "did not seek to disembed the sacred text from theological presumptions designated to insulate it from its historical context" considering that there exists an intimate and immediate link between the history-bound reader and the ahistorical text.[69]

The belief in the secular history of sacred scripture, i.e., the belief in the embedding of a sacred text in a specific sociocultural reality embodied in a specific linguistic system, however, does not necessarily deny its Divine provenance. The Romantic thinkers, argues Wright, furthermore, subscribe to the view of "literariness" of Scripture that, however, does not undermine the validity of the text's connection to something that stands outside history.[70] According to this view, the sacred text, operates at an intersection between the ahistorical, premodern theological vertical "axes" and that of the time-bound, contextual horizontal axes, which are as conceived as being able to coexist.

The processes and ideas propelling European technicalism were not constrained to Europe and the West but also profoundly influenced the Muslim majority world. The sixteeth and the seventeenth centuries in particular witnessed an era of the export and the establishment of European technicalism and its technicalist revolution by means of European military and economic dominance and the colonization of much of the Muslim majority world. Dubbed "The Great Western Transmutation" by Hodgson, this "modernization" impetus was, argues Wright, to have an enormous effect on how some Muslim intellectual and scholars were to view and deal with their culture-religious Islamic heritage (Islamic tradition). Although the response to this "intrusion," as mentioned in the third chapter, varied from an enthusiastic embrace to pessimism and sustained disdain, the intangible dimension of the technicalist revolution and its the contrapuntal flow of time, in what Wright creatively describes as a "Trojan Horse fashion," affected the Muslim thinkers' perception of time, which started to reflect itself in the manner in which they channeled their mental and cognitive energies to the study of the Islamic past. The adoption and the adaptation of European Romantic thinking among some twentieth century Muslim thinkers in the Muslim world such as T. Husayn (1889–1973), A. Al-Khuli(1895–1966), and, most recently, N. H. Abu Zayd (1943–2010) and A. K. Soroush (1945–) manifested itself in the increasing employment of sophisticated and nuanced literary-historical tools developed by literary historians based on the recognition of the need for comprehensive contextualization and historically embed the traditional Islamic sciences beyond those developed by the classical Muslim scholarship. Progressive Muslim scholarship and thought is in great affinity with the views and the intellectual fruits of European Romantic Criticism as they relate to the study of the past, religion, and sacred texts. This will become more evident in the next chapter where I discuss progressive Muslim interpretational assumptions of the primary sources of the Islamic tradition, the Qur'an and the Sunna.

5.3   Situating Progressive Muslims in the Historical Context of Islamic Thought since the Era of Classical Modernism

The previous section briefly outlined the modern roots and antecedents of progressive Muslim thought stemming from the non-Muslim intellectual tradition of European Romanticism.This section of the chapter historically contextualizes progressive Muslim thought especially in relation to what in the third chapter we described as the classical modernist thought, its closest predecessor in terms of its approach to conceptualizing and interpreting the Islamic tradition.

Progressive Muslims are, as we discussed in the third chapter, not the first generation of Muslims who have grappled with the issues of Islamic tradition and modernity. Safi in this context argues that progressive Muslim thought can be seen as both a continuation as well as a radical departure from the 150-year-old tradition of "liberal Islam," the Islam of the major nineteenth and twentieth century reformers such as M. Abduh (d. 1905), Jamal Al-Afghani (d. 1897), Sir Sayyid Ahmed Khan (d. 1898), R. Rida (d. 1935), A. Shari'ati (d. 1977), and others.

When talking about the phenomenon of classical modernism, we have referred to the attempts of the above named classical modernist reformers to come to terms with the advent of modernity and the modern episteme. In many ways, classical modernists are the most historically recent forerunners of progressive Muslims.[71] Progressive Muslims consider that these reformers made the first steps in "advancing a synthesis between Islamic and modern Western values with the impulse stemming from within the Islamic tradition and culture itself as the integrating framework for modernity,"[72] a feature that progressive Muslim thought aims to uphold and build on. Modernity's most precious gift of rationality to the classical modernists of the nineteenth and twentieth century, however, argues Moosa,[73] did not, result in their embrace of the modern episteme in the realms of the humanities and social sciences as employed by the above described modern literary historicism. Progressive Muslim thinkers form the view that classical modernism was not an organized intellectual movement that developed a systematic methodology of interpretation of the Islamic tradition that could dislodge the firmly entrenched premodern ontology of traditional Islam. As such progressive Muslim thinkers regard that the classical modernists engaged in reform only in a segmented and diffused manner and consider that the many problems the challenge of modernity brought to its shores were not addressed by classical modernists at the root level but only symptomatically.[74] The method of knowledge employed by the classical modernists, furthermore, is regarded by progressive Muslims as being largely ad hoc, reactive, and partial.Thus, progressive Muslim thinkers regard that the solutions that classical modernist thought proffered, if any, were often very general, if any, and were incompatible with the tradition itself.

In the words of Bamyeh classical modernists "assumed that the meaning of Islam was self-evident (or at least should be), and all one needed to do was simply learn the early traditions of the faith."[75] However, progressive Muslims believe that the challenges that modernity presented to classical modernist thinkers often required significant rethinking of the premodern bodies of knowledge on which the edifice of traditional Islam stood.

Furthermore, the theoreticians behind progressive Muslim thought maintain that classical modernists did not only fail to employ the tools of modern literary historicism (outlined in the previous section) in relation to the Islamic tradition but that the entire movement and its intellectual aspect was in essence a diffuse phenomenon of cultural revival brought to life by the painful experience of colonialism and its sociopolitical, economic, and cultural aftershocks and not a methodical and systematic attempt, in a critical light, to reexamine and where deemed necessary significantly reform the Islamic tradition from within.

In this context Moosa remarks

> With some exceptions, the critical light of modern knowledge developed in the humanities did not illuminate the Muslim modernists' theories, as applied to the interpretation of the scriptures, history and society, the understanding of law, and theology. What they [Muslim modernists] did not undertake or in some instances refused to undertake was to subject the entire corpus of historical Islamic learning to the critical gaze of the knowledge-making process (episteme) of modernity...They still felt that

the premodern Muslim epistemology as rooted in dialectical theology (*'ilm al-kalaam*) and legal theory (*usul al-fiqh*) was sufficiently tenacious, if not compatible with the best in modern epistemology.[76]

Such an approach, argues Al-Azmeh, did not seek to radically question ancient interpretations. The fact that it did not seek to historicize the canonical texts themselves made this approach in his view "furtive, hesitant, self-contradictory, and in many ways vulnerable to the fundamentalist attacks that have gathered force in the past two decades."[77]

Therefore the Islamic intellectual legacy in the hands of these classical modernist scholars was not subject to the critical insight of the (post) modern episteme something that progressive Muslim thought purports to subject itself to.[78] The epistemological boundaries and contours of progressive Muslim thought, as I shall argue in the next section are inclusive of both the premodern traditional Islamic as well as the modern literary historicism whose phylogeny was briefly described above in the context of European Romantic thinkers.

On the other hand, progressive Muslims assert to be aware and believe that they can overcome the shortcomings of classical modernist thought by engaging in a holistic and systematic reform of the inherited premodern Islamic tradition addressing its root causes through "examining the interaction of theoretical underpinnings of ethical, theological, legal, social and political problems" with the objective to provide a cohesive framework which would enable "methodical, logically harmonious and rationally defendable solutions."[79]

This brings us to the question of how exactly progressive Muslim thought considers to achieve this aim and, more specifically, on basis of which approach to conceptualizing the Islamic tradition and the concept of modernity.

5.4   Progressive Muslims Approach to the Islamic Tradition (Islamic tradition) and the Notion of the Late Modern Episteme

In this section progressive Muslim thought is defined in relation to what Moosa terms the "innovation, discontinuity and continuity"[80] of the accumulated Muslim tradition (Islamic tradition) and its approach to and the understanding of the notion of late[81] modernity and its underlying worldview. In this context I am not interested in discussing the concept of late modernity and its episteme[82] from a philosophical vantage point but define it by some of its most important defining characteristics in relation to its social, cultural, political, and religious elements including the emphasis on critical thought, dynamism,[83] rationality, and epistemological/methodological pluralism.

The first point that needs to be made is that progressive Muslims' concept and engagement with the Islamic tradition rejects the NTS assumption of the regressive character of history/time and the static nature of the Islamic tradition described in the second chapter. Apart from subscribing to the view of history and time as advocated by European Romantic thinkers discussed above,[84] Progressive Muslims' understanding of tradition is based on its dynamism and "constructed-ness." One of its fundamental premises is that the concept of tradition, including its primary normative textual sources, are subject to humanly constructed interpretational processes and that a distinction between "religion and religious knowledge,"[85] "normative and historical Islam" (to use Rahman's terminology[86]), or, in the parlance of Islamic jurisprudence, between shari'ah (divine worldview) and *fiqh* (human understanding of it) ought to be made. Progressive Muslims approach makes a claim to recognize that "[b]etween scripture and the pronouncement of a legal ruling lies a complex interpretive and constructive process administered by the human agent."[87] Thus, the knowledge of the tradition is not confused with the tradition itself.[88] Moreover, tradition and the knowledge of it are considered to be subject to "expansion and contraction" to use Soroush's terminology.[89] Religion is seen as evolving alongside humanity's reason, as such it cannot be frozen according to a single, authoritative, and immutable understanding.[90] In other words, progressive Muslim thought emphasizes the role of human agency in the essentially humanly constructed and mediated processes of reading/understanding history and sacred texts. This is the reason why progressive Muslim thinkers primarily employ the phrase, Progressive Muslim and not Progressive Islamic thought. This interpretational awareness of progressive Muslim thought translates itself in the importance and emphasis given by it to examining the epistemological and methodological dimensions underlying and determining the validity and soundness of various inherited interpretational models of the overall Qur'an-Sunna teachings. This will form the subject matter of the next chapter.

The concept of tradition is apart from being conceptualized as operating on a human epistemological plane, also viewed as very complex and multi-faceted. Tradition is considered as consisting of a number of competing interpretations which, at times, can be mutually exclusive all of which, nonetheless, are regarded as being constitutive of it.[91] Tradition, according to this view, is like a rich dense tapestry consisting of many interlacing or at times parallel running threads all of which put together give the tapestry its unique design. The progressive Muslim thought, therefore, considers the concept of the Islamic tradition as a result of a fluid exchange of ideas and acknowledges a wide spectrum of interpretations that are inherent to it.[92] Thus, the nature of the concept of tradition is not seen as being static but something that is subject to vicissitudes of human history, something that is subject to interrogation, correction, and advancement.[93] Moosa uses an apt analogy from the science of biology to describe this nature of the concept of tradition in a following manner:

> Tradition is unlike palingenesis where certain organisms only reproduce their ancestral characters without modification. Rather tradition works more like kenogenesis: it describes how in biology an organism derives features from the immediate environment in order to modify the hereditary development of a germ or organism.

According to this view, every tradition, Islam included, is viewed as a tradition-in-becoming.[94] In other words Muslim thought is not conceptualized as a "pre-fabricated design of being"[95] but as a dynamic construct, "manifesting itself in the relationship between the past, which produced the Islamic tradition, and the present in which the Islamic tradition still lives.[96] The question of authenticity (*asala*) of the Islamic tradition in progressive Muslim thought is constructed along the lines outlined in the Fourth Statement of the Final Declaration on the question of heritage and authenticity by the Arab Muslim intellectuals who convened in Kuwait in 1974. With its emphasis on values and the importance of creativity and criticality of the human spirit, the statement asserts:

> Authenticity does not consist in literal clinging to the heritage but rather in setting out from it to what follows and from its values to a new phase in which there is enrichment for it and development of its values. Real revivification of the heritage is possible only through a creative, historical ,critical comprehension of it; through transcending it in a new process of creation; through letting the past remain past so that it may not compete with the present and the future; and through a new assimilation of it from the perspectives of the present and the future.[97]

Based upon this dialectical relationship between the past and the present, progressive Muslim thought "studies Islamic tradition in the light of the present, its problems, its questions and its needs."[98] Bamiyeh, who uses the term *hermeneutic Islam* as the equivalent to progressive Muslims term employed in this study, argues that this approach to the Islamic tradition and its primary texts acknowledges that they could not be approached "selectively and defensively."[99] As shall be argued in more detail in the next chapter, the proponents of the progressive Muslim *manhaj* consider that the Qur'an does not stand above the modern reader who would simply digest it passively. The process of understanding is considered, instead, to begin with the believer himself. The relationship between the believer and the tradition is conceived as a dialogue. This is so because progressive Muslim thought asserts that only in that sense could the Islamic tradition and its primary sources live on across vastly different epochs and speak to exceedingly diverse minds.[100]

In line with the genealogical approach to history described in the first section of this chapter, the Islamic tradition is conceived as consisting of contending forces and ideas, not as a picture perfect and flawless entity. In particular, the ideologically vulnerable legal discourses embedded in the larger framework of culture, are seen as ideologically laden and are-nas where power relations are constantly (re)negotiated.[101] Thus, in accordance with Asad, progressive Muslims consider tradition to be discursive in nature embedded in the broader framework of power relations, conflict and contestation of competing interpretations or subtraditions each based on shared set of assumptions linking the Islamic past and the future to particular Islamic practice in the present.[102]

Criticality is another delineating feature of how progressive Muslim thought approaches the concept of tradition.[103] Unlike some tradition eschewing approaches[104] to the Islam, the progressive Muslim approach to tradition is that of serious engagement with the full spectrum of Islamic thought and practices.[105] In the words of Safi

> There can be no progressive Muslim movement that does not engage the very 'stuff' (textual and material sources) of the Islamic tradition…we [PM] believe that it is imperative to work through inherited traditions of thought and practice. In particular cases, we might conclude that certain pre-existing interpretations fail to offer us sufficient guidance today. However, we can fruitfully claim that position after-and not before-a serious engagement with tradition. To move beyond certain past interpretations of Islam, we have to go critically through them.[106]

Serious engagement with the inherited Islamic tradition with a willingness to cast it in critical light is one important feature of how progressive Muslim thought situates itself in the dynamic between tradition and modernity. Progressive Muslims, therefore, consider themselves to be "critical traditionalists." That is to mean that they "constantly interrogate tradition and strive to ask productive questions."[107]

Importantly, premised on the above described concepts of "progress" and "tradition," progressive Muslims, unlike some nontraditional approaches to Islam, do not claim an epistemological rupture and a clean break from the Islamic tradition.[108] Progressive Muslim approach, argues Safi, is based on a critique that derives its inspiration from within the heart of Islamic tradition. According to this view progressive Muslim thought is a graft that must ultimately grow in the soil of Islam and nowhere else.[109] Indeed, for progressive Muslims, the Qur'an continues to assume a central position to the contemporary Muslim debates and is considered the ultimate legitimizing text of the Islamic tradition.[110] In the words of Jahanbakhsh who employs the term *Neo-rationalists*, being the equivalent term for what here are termed *progressive Muslims*, advocates an Islam that draws upon "the rich religious, ethical and intellectual heritage but is responsive in appositive and serious sense to the imperatives of modern human values." It is a project characterized by a critical adoption of selected elements of the inherited tradition whose foundation is an epistemological principle of historicity of religion and the dynamic nature of religious knowledge.[111]

Apart from embracing modernity's emphasis on criticality and dynamism, rationality also features prominently in progressive Muslims approach to the conceptualization and interpretation of the Islamic tradition. In this context progressive Muslims call for a "rational authentication of Islamic tradition [as] a methodological tool for making Islamic tradition the product of a dynamic fertilization of textual assets by means of innovative hermeneutic activity..."[112] Progressive Muslims advocate a new rationalist theology especially in the realm of ethical theory and theology. This is so because rationalist theology can serve as a basis for legal and jurisprudentic reform and as a hermeneutical springboard for employing modern methods on interpretation that are inclusive of rational and historical assumptions favoring a critical analysis of the inherited tradition including its sacred texts.[113]Progressive Muslim thought, therefore, welcomes critical rationalism as a way of empowering one's faith and making it relevant to present and ever changing contexts.[114]

Progressive Muslims' view of the tradition-modernity dynamic is also based upon epistemological or methodological pluralism by subscribing to the view that different epistemological methodologies are necessary if one is to better approximate truth.[115] This is characterized by progressive Muslims' willingness to adopt and incorporate sources of knowledge and methods outside of the traditional Islamic sciences and affirm their potentially normative status. As such progressive Muslims' cosmovision is inspired and in varying extents shared by other spiritual and political movements,[116] including those associated with liberation theology, secular humanism, and social and gender–justice based movements in Latin America, the United States and Europe and embodied in the works and philosophy of thinkers such as Gustavo Gutierrez, Leonardo Boff,

M. L. King (Jr.), Rebecca Chopp, Edward Said, and Noam Chomsky to name but a few.

Progressive Muslims' also have developed a particular understanding of and attitude toward the concept of (late) modernity. Moosa, for example, asserts that progressive Muslims' approach and attitude toward modernity is characterized by an acute, contrapuntal awareness that the modernity they are facing now is radically different to what their Muslim forerunners experienced.[117] Progressive Muslims are fully cognizant of the epistemological ruptures modernity brought about. They are attentive to the philosophical and conceptual foundations of modernity and its profound affects on disrupting and challenging the premodern theological and ethical systems of thought.[118] However, they do not wish to conflate these modern systems of thinking and being with their actual outward manifestations in the Western societies known as modernization.[119] Additionally, progressive Muslims do not consider "culturo-intellectual assimilation of western modernity as the basis for [Islamic] reform."[120] As such unlike many of the classical modernist Muslim thinkers progressive Muslims no longer "look to the prevalent notion of Western modernity as something to be imitated and duplicated in toto."[121] Progressive Muslims' approach to an engagement with modernity is rather characterized by an attempt to problematize the history of debate between Islam and modernity or Islam and the West by critical and selective adoption and adaption of modern ideas and concepts in contemporary Muslim discourses.

As such it is important to note that progressive Muslims are critical of the metanarratives underpinning classical modernity and the Age of Enlightenment characterized by the notions of a universal legislative, secular, and objective reason and objective truth.[122] Instead, they advocate what Benhabib would describe as a form of moderate postmodernism[123] where truth is sought in a dialectical relationship between revelation, reason, and the sociohistorical context in which both are embedded. According to this view,

> [r]ationality and belief, human rights and divine obligation, individual and social justice, collective reason and religious morality, human mind and divine revelation are living peacefully together.[124]

Furthermore, progressive Muslims' understanding of the historical processes leading to modernity considers them a result of transcultural and transpolitical intercivilizational processes thereby demonopolizing the often made claim that modernity is a pure, universal, and monopolar Western civilizational product.

In this context the words of Esack are instructive:

> Here we [progressive Muslims] are not merely attempting to break the monopoly of the west in the production of the discourses of modernity. We also attempt to reclaim modernist discourses of feminism, socio-economic justice and restating them in Islamic terms. We are simultaneously engaged in the task of articulating interpretative traditions within Islam that embody these values thus challenging the notion that modernity is distinctly a Western project.[125]

Progressive Muslims' understanding of modernity is therefore based upon a cultural theory of modernity according to which modernity unfolds within a specific cultural (or civilizational) context having different starting points and leading to potentially different, multiple alternative "modernities."[126] Progressive Muslims, thus, subscribe to the view that the sociopolitical and cultural processes that have brought about epistemological and ontological changes in the Western worldview and resulted in the advent of modernity as we know it today are considered a result of a dynamic process of civilizational interaction and mutual construction through transcultural, transpolitical, and transsocial spaces. Additionally, progressive Muslims believe that this late modern episteme could be also applied within the framework of the sociocultural context of the Muslim majority societies resulting in the genesis of another distinct type of modernity.

5.5   Conclusion

This chapter attempted to: i. paint a picture of important themes underpinning progressive Muslim worldview; ii. historically contextualize and place progressive Muslims thought in relation to their Western intellectual predecessors coming from both the non-Muslim majority and Muslim majority worlds; iii. outline progressive Muslim approach to conceptualizing and engaging with the Islamic tradition and the concept of modernity.

In the first section it was claimed that progressive Muslim thought and "cosmovision," as developed by the contributors to the book "Progressive Muslims," is best characterized by a number of commitments, ideals, and practices that the adherents of progressive Muslim thought subscribe to. These include a strong commitment to social and gender justice and a belief in the inherent dignity of every human being as a carrier of God's spirit. It was argued that one pertinent and important feature of progressive Muslim worldview is their critique of the dominant political, economic, and cultural forces that are responsible for perpetuation of a contemporary politico-economically unjust status quo of the poor South and the rich North. Another prominent feature of progressive Muslims though is that of the centrality of spirituality and the nurturing of interpersonal relationships based on Sufi ethicomoral philosophy, termed *Islamic humanism*.[127] Bringing about the multifaceted and dynamic aspects of the classical Islamic scholarship and resisting its reductionism and exclusivist interpretation founded on patriarchy and misogyny was seen as an additional trait of progressive Muslim thought. Moreover, it was asserted another important attribute of the progressive Muslim thought is that it is syncretically arranged and engaged in permanent dialogue with the progressive agendas of other cultures drawing inspiration from liberatory movements such as liberation theology and secular humanism.

Based on the progressive Muslim employment of modern literary historicism whose intellectual predecessors were the European Romanticist thinkers, in the second section, progressive Muslim thought was historically contextualized in relation to western intellectual and philosophical thinking of the seventeenth and the eighteenth centuries, especially in relation to how the way they conceptualize and interpret history, historical inquiry, and sacred literature. It was contended that many ideas to which progressive Muslims subscribe especially in relation to historical inquiry and the study of sacred literature are in affinity with those developed and espoused by the European Romanticist thinkers and can be seen broadly as an intellectual continuation of their ideas the different time periods and contexts notwithstanding.

In the third part of the chapter the intellectual phylogeny of progressive Muslims in relation to Muslim intellectual movements indigenous to the Muslim majority was presented. Here it was argued that the ideas and values of classical modernists of the early twentieth century were most closely related to the objectives of progressive Muslim thought. However, also a number of important differences between the two were noted.

In the final fourth section progressive Muslim conceptualization and engagement with the Islamic tradition and the concept of late modernity and its episteme was the subject of discussion. Herein, it was argued that progressive Muslims consider the nature of the concept of tradition to be a dynamic, humanly constructed product of many past and present communities of interpretation. Furthermore, it was asserted that the concept of culture-religious authenticity (*asala*) in progressive Muslims thought is not based upon a literal clinging to the Islamic tradition but on a creative, historical, critical engagement with it. As such serious, critical engagement with the Islamic tradition was considered to be another distinguishing attribute of progressive Muslim thought.

As far as epistemological and methodological boundaries and contours of progressive Muslim thought are concerned, it was demonstrated that they are inclusive of both the premodern traditional Islamic episteme as well as the modern episteme. I also contended that progressive Muslims consider modernity a result of transcultural and transpolitical intercivilizational processes. As such we maintained that progressive Muslims do not subscribe to the view that modernity is a pure, universal, and monopolar Western civilizational product but conceive of it multiple, civilizationally distinct types of modernity. It was argued that this progressive Islamic consciousness is firmly rooted in usable traditions but is uncompromisingly universal in its outlook with the ability to redefine the very meaning of Islam in light of modernity without abandoning the parameters of faith. As such the often employed tradition-modernity dichotomy in the context of discourses pertaining to Islam and Muslims is considered as artificial and false by the proponents of progressive Muslim thought. Lastly, I argued that progressive Muslims distance themselves from the metanarratives and universalistic claims of the Age of Enlightenment and classical modernity and that they can be considered as adherents of Benhabib's moderate form of postmodernism according to which the truth resides in a dialectical relationship between revelation, reason, and context. Moreover, it was maintained that progressive Muslims strive for a synthesis between late modernity and the inherited Islamic tradition and a crosscultural dialogue based on equal partnership with the ultimate goal of a culturally polycentric world founded on economic socialism and gender equality.

The next chapter will discuss the delineating features of the progressive Muslims' Qur'an and Sunna hermeneutic and its interpretational implications.

Chapter 6

Progressive Muslims' Model of Interpretation (*Manhaj*) and Their Interpretational Implications

Analogous to what was outlined in the fourth chapter about the NTS *manhaj*, the aim of this chapter is to discuss the delineating features of progressive Muslims' Qur'an and Sunna *manhaj* and its interpretational implications.

6.1   Progressive Muslims' Qur'an *Manhaj* and Its Interpretational Implications

As outlined in the previous chapter, progressive Muslims conceptualization and engagement with the *turath* is not based on an epistemological break with the classical Islamic scholarship and its episteme. Most, if not all, of the "higher textual criticism" interpretational mechanisms on the nature of sacred texts and history discussed in the previous chapter have real precedents in classical scholarship.[1] Progressive Muslims *manhaj* builds upon the pre-modern classical *usul-ul-fiqh* sciences but importantly it also incorporates this "higher textual criticism." As outlined in the fourth chapter, the below mentioned criteria are used in juxtaposing, contrasting, and explaining the differences between the PM and NTS *manahij* and their respective assumptions:

- the function and nature of language in the Qur'anic text and the nature of Revelation;

- the process of derivation of meaning of the Qur'anic text;
- the extent of the recognition (or otherwise) of the role of context in the shaping of the Qur'anic content;
- the role, legitimacy, and scope of reason in Qur'anic interpretation and the nature of ethical value in the Qur'an;
- the extent of the employment of a thematic, corroborative-inductive (or systematic) approach to Qur'an's interpretation or lack thereof of (i.e., prevalence of what here is termed *textual segmentalism*);
- the scope of a purposeful, aim-based approach (*qasd*) to Qur'anic interpretation; and
- the nature and the scope of the concept of Sunna and its interpretational implications

6.1.1   Progressive Muslims View of the Function and Nature of Language in Qur'anic Text and the Nature of Revelation

While the NTS's view of the nature and the function of language in the Qur'anic text is based upon the notion of a metahistorical view of language as a code whose meaning is largely to be deciphered according to rules of Arabic grammar, the progressive Muslim concept of the nature and function of language in the Qur'anic text and its interpretation is founded upon its essential literariness in accordance with a "conventionalist" theory of the origins of language. According to this theory the Qur'an is, despite being a Divine text to Muslim faithfuls, a linguistic, literary text[2] whose language in essence is socioculturally produced, i.e., is an outcome of human convention and not of Divine designation.[3] Consequently, following in the footsteps of the Mu'tazilites, the meaning of God's speech is considered *by necessity* bound to the accepted standards of linguistic semantics.[4] This is in contrast to the premodern mainstream Sunni tradition (inherited by NTS), which maintains that God can constrain the addressee of His speech to know its meaning (*yadtarruhu ila- mura-dihi bi-l-khita-b*).[5]

According to this view the nature and the function of language is such that it considers texts, including the "Divine text" as integral to the reality and the culture that moulded the process of its very formation.[6] In the words of Hanafi, "Language without reality is void, the reality without language is blind."[7]

Furthermore progressive Muslim thought subscribes to the view that the religious texts are in the final analysis just like any other literary texts in the sense that they belong to a particular cultural structure. They are the result of that cultural system whose central system of meaning is the language (author's translation).[8]

As such progressive Muslim thought considers that there is an organic link between language, meaning, culture, and history. Additionally, as based upon the analysis of Qur'anic composition, form, and stylistic character inherent in its text, the progressive Muslim *manhaj* highlights the essential oral nature of the (precanonical) Qur'an, which is considered as emerging out of a virtually communicative process underlying its discursive aspect whose essential function is "the explicit moral or theological edification of the community... of how the true Believer acts in certain situations."[9] Moreover, in doing so, it aims to preserve/recover the "tensions" that have shaped its very content and takes their full interpretational leverage into account.[10]

Furthermore progressive Muslims do not subscribe to the notion of a legalistic Divine Will in which human beings are trapped within the dualistic framework of being either "predetermined to do one thing by command [or] desist from another by prohibition."[11] In addition, progressive Muslims, following in the footsteps of the Mu'tazilah, do not subscribe to the notion of "uncreatedness of the Qur'an," as elaborated upon in the fourth chapter, but maintain that the "createdness of the Qur'an" "defreezes," to use Abu Zayd's term, its meaning through the processes of *Verstehen* (understanding) and Interpretation.[12] In the words of Abu Zayd:

> If the insistence on the view of the uncreatedness of the Qur'an and the eternal character of the revelation freezes the religious content then the conception of the Qur'an's createdness at a particular point in time and that of the historicity of revelation revives the texts and, through the process of understanding and interpretation, liberates the religious content from the state of suspension in a particular historical period making it relevant to the needs of, throughout history, the dynamic nature of human society (author's translation).[13]

As such progressive Muslim thought considers that the Qur'an stands in a dialectical relationship with the pre-Islamic norms, practices, and culture that had their own previous assessment, presuppositions, and assertions and that this aspect of the nature of the Qur'an is of critical importance when developing a Qur'anic hermeneutic and Islamic legal theory.[14]

Furthermore, progressive Muslim concept of Revelation (*wahy*) and the Prophet's role in it is more in tune with that of the view of the classical Islamic philosophers (*falsafa*) and/or mystics such as Ibn Sina (d. 1037),

Ibn Rushd (d. 1198), and J. Al-Rumi (d. 1273) who saw the two are intimately linked, existing in a symbiotic, interdependent, and dialogical relationship. This view is in contrast with that of what became to be known as the mainstream view that insists on the clear mechanical separation between the recipient of Revelation (the Prophet) and its Originator (God) where Prophet's agency, mind, and psychological makeup in shaping the content and the nature of Revelation is marginalized and reduced to that of a "parrot," to use Soroush's expression.[15]

This understanding of the nature of the Revelation permits an epistemologically and methodologically more flexible and fluid interpretive framework that can engender authorized and authenticated interpretations of the Qur'anic enunciations, which although at times contradictory to their literal meaning are justified with reference to the Qur'an's (and Sunna's) overall ethos and objective (*qasd*).[16]

6.1.2 Progressive Muslims' Approach to the Process of Derivation of Meaning in the Qur'anic Text and Its Interpretational Implications

By considering Qur'an, for interpretational/hermeneutical purposes, as a piece of literature, the progressive Muslim *manhaj* renders it subject to modern literary criticism like any other culture specific text. Qur'an is still albeit considered to be of Divine origin yet not requiring any special methods when attempting to understand and interpret it.[17]

The Qur'an is also considered to be capable of sustaining various interpretations. The human understanding of its text is considered to be dependent upon human knowledge of human sciences, which itself is sociotemporarily contingent.[18]

By being largely oblivious to the discourses of modern literary theory, premodern-NTS approach to derivation and determining of Qur'anic meanings has largely focused on the role of authorial intent[19] and its principal discoverability when engaging in this process. Progressive Muslims do not share this presupposition. They argue that the task of hermeneutics is not the recovery of elusive authorial intention but a study of and a contribution to the ongoing and ever varying approximations of it.[20]

Furthermore, there has been a shift of focus on the history of literary criticism from being author centric to that of reader centered with its attendant implication that the role of the reader of a text is not so much understood as a process of reproduction of meaning but that of its production.[21] In this context a young Indonesian scholar and proponent of progressive

Muslim *manhaj* Y.Rahman notes:

> It is considered that meaning of the text may lie in the author, the text, the context, or the reader, that the task of hermeneutics is not only to discover but also to create the meaning of the text. Given the many possibilities of locating the meaning of the text, the methods and approaches used to ascertain the analysis are consequently diverse.[22]

As such the progressive Muslim view of the nature of language and its function in *usul-ul-fiqh* is more akin to the theory of New Legal Formalism whose underlying premise is that "meaning is not discovered but rather fashioned or created by the interpreter."[23] Consequently, the meaning of a word is not just given "by the one who posits the word [God] but rather by a human being [reader] who is a subject of his own visions, presuppositions and experiences."[24] In other words, as Abu Zayd argues, the receiver of the text, the human being conditioned by her sociohistorical reality, is the starting and the end point of this process.[25] As Ashraf notes any Holy Text, including the Qur'an, ultimately speaks through its reader since religious texts do not interpret themselves but people do and they do so not in an epistemological or methodological vacuum but always bring their own insights, biases and knowledge into the interpretational process. As a result the meaning of a religious text is more often than not only as moral as the reader/interpreter.[26]

Wahyudi, in his study of the thought of three contemporary Muslims scholars, namely, Al-Jabiri, Hanafi, and Majid, remarks that all three authorities subscribe to the view that a text withstands or accommodates a pluralistic interpretation "in more or less direct proportion to the sociopolitical and cultural backgrounds of the interpreter."[27] Furthermore, Abu Zayd argues that the spiritual and cultural horizon of the reader plays an important role in her/his understanding the language of the text and in the extraction of its meaning (author's translation).[28] That the understanding of the text is dependent upon the reader is also implied by an Iranian progressive Muslim scholar Soroush who argues that the understanding of the Qur'an and Sunna is dynamic and changes along with the knowledge of its interpreter because "every understanding of religion is founded upon knowledge that is outside the scope of religion itself" (author's translation).[29]

The implications of this aspect of literary theory with regards to the process of meaning derivation is that the full meaning of any text is in essence partially indeterminate or relative to that of the interpreter. In this context, Mabrook makes an important observation by considering a reader to be "in history, of history and for history"; a reader who is limited by his or her own history and epistemology is affected in his or her role in understanding, assimilating, and reshaping the reading matter. Therefore, the progressive Muslims *manhaj* takes into consideration that the consciousness of the context of that which is being read as well as the consciousness of the reader engaged in the process of interpretation will determine its outcome.[30]

Consequently, due to the dynamic nature of the readers it is to be expected that a text, such as the Qur'an, exhibits semiotic polyvalence, that is, it can withstand various interpretative strategies eliciting different readings of the same (piece of) text all of which can be seen as contextually legitimate.

This is not to say that the proponents of progressive Muslim *manhaj* consider that any and every reading of the text can be justified but it does provide an insight into why and how various readings of the same text developed, thus allowing for its subsequent criticism and revision. It should also be noted that when readers share many of the factors governing the "nature of a reader" (e.g., same sociocultural norms), a notion of "interpretive communities,"[31] that is, a group of individuals who share similar interpretive strategies in reading, arises. These communities of interpretation impose some reading uniformity in an inherently divergent process of meaning derivation, thus curbing and narrowing down alternative readings. They in the words of El-Fadl "objectify the subjective" and marginalize "unreasonable interpretations."[32] Hence, commitment to textual polysemy does not mean having to embrace unrestricted interpretational relativism, because texts can withstand only "a limited field of possible constructions." Furthermore, El-Fadl, drawing upon Ricour,[33]Echo,[34] and Wolterstoff,[35] argues that communities of interpretation can "resist imposed interpretations in details" and only certain interpretations of texts can be considered as " contextually legitimated."[36]While this understanding of how interpretative communities function has validity, it must be kept in mind that when societies and cultures undergo [radical] changes, they also have an impact on how contemporary communities of interpretation deal with the efforts of the past interpretative communities. These would require close scrutiny as every new community of interpretation might not share the same sociocultural assumptions, norms, and values as previous ones. Thus, in the words of Barlas, "the interpretive process is [always] both imprecise and incomplete…and open to critique and historicization."[37] Therefore, meanings, according to progressive Muslim *manhaj* are only fixable in the context of a given historical period characterized by a particular hermeneutical method.

As a corollary to the above it follows that the reader is never in the position to completely identify her [his] opinion with that of the author.

Amirpour, who describes the nature of Soroush's Qur'anic hermeneutic, asserts this by saying, "That which humans consider being the meaning/intent of the Qur'anic text and its actual meaning/intent can never be considered to be the same."[38] In other words one can never afford to monopolize the interpretation of God's Word/s. Rahman asserts that this concept of derivation of meaning "challenges, for instance, the absolutists who claim to know the true meaning and the true interpretation of the text."[39] According to progressive Muslim *manhaj*, therefore, interpretation is never fully divine "but a kind of divinely inspired human value."[40] Progressive Muslim thought, thus, in words of Saeed, "recognises the complexity of meaning" in its approach to Qur'anic interpretation.[41]

The implications of the progressive Muslim approach to derivation of meaning and interpretation is based upon a polysemic nature of the Qur'anic text that not only leaves scope for and accommodates multiple interpretational strategies of the Qur'an but it renders it applicable for future communities of interpretation as the act of interpretation of a text (i.e., its meaning) is essentially pluralistic and significantly determined by the reader. Thus, it reaffirms the widely held Muslim belief, conceptualized, albeit very differently, but shared by both NTS and progressive Muslim proponents, of the Qur'an's timeless and perpetual quality/relevance to human concerns.

6.1.3 The Context-Content Qur'anic Dynamic in Progressive Muslim Thought and Its Interpretational Implications

While the NTS approach to the interpretation and conceptualization of the nature of the Qur'anic revelation leads to marginalization of the role of the context in the shaping of its content and its interpretation, a foundational premise of progressive Muslim *manhaj* is that "at a closer scrutiny [of canonical texts] would show that history, embodiment, linguistics, time, and space are all alluded to in the sources of Islamic Law and ethics."[42] Progressive Muslim *manhaj* is also based upon the idea that historical process according to human experience is the medium through which God chose to convey his message with full interpretational implications for the "historicality" of the Qur'anic text. In this context Esack argues:

> Sociohistorical and linguistic milieu of the Qur'anic revelation is reflected in the contents, style, objectives and the language of the Qur'an. Revelation is always a commentary on a particular society.[43]

This essential sociohistorical embeddedness of much of the Qur'anic content and its interpretive importance as a feature of the progressive Muslims' *manhaj* is also argued by Saeed who asserts that the sociohistorical context of the Qur'an in the pre-Islamic and early Islamic periods, including the "spiritual, social, economic, political and legal climate and the associated norms, laws, customs, manners, institutions and values [in addition to] housing, clothing, food, social relations, such as family structure, social hierarchy, taboos and rites of passage" of the region at that time is not to be "ignored" for the purposes of a better understanding of the nature of the Qur'anic message.[44] This view is echoed by Abu Zayd who maintains that the interpretation of the sociohistorical elements of the canonical texts is a precondition for the "defreezing" of the meaning of the texts themselves. This entails reaffirming of what he terms the fundamental, the essential, core elements of the scripture and the leaving out of those elements deemed to be embedded in a particular time and place.[45] Similarly, in this context Soroush makes a distinction between the "accidentals" and the "essentials" of religion incorporating into the former aspects of the Scripture such as Arabic language and culture and the concepts stemming from them employed in it including those pertaining to natural as well as legal sciences and into the latter what he terms the Prophet's goals, which are restricted to purely religious matters in a narrow sense of the word such as religious salvation and minimalist guidance.[46]

The progressive Muslim approach also stresses the radical changes in the context between the communities of interpretation at the time when the Qur'an was revealed and that in which contemporary interpretative communities operate in.[47] The progressive Muslim interpretational methods, therefore, place strong emphasis on the role and the importance of context in the process of formation of Revelation as its essential inherent methodological characteristic.[48] This approach to the underlying nature of the Qur'anic content and its interpretation could be termed as "comprehensively contextualist" or historical.[49] A comprehensively contextualist heuristic consists of two elements, as identified by Barlas: reading behind the text, that is, reconstructing the historical context from which the text emerged, and reading in front of the text, that is, recontextualizing the text in light of present needs.[50]

The intrinsic contextuality of the Qur'anic Revelation, according to progressive Muslim *manhaj*, stems from the very process of its formation and its actual content.[51] Namely, as Wadud argues, the Qur'an's revelationary period spanned over more than two decades and the process of its gradual, progressive revelation as evident in the content of the scripture itself, point to its contextuality and due regard for the prevalent worldview of its immediate audience when attempting to bring about change. Furthermore, this type of Qur'anic hermeneutic is considered to force its readers/interpreters to adopt a teleological reading and the purpose of the text. This delineating element of progressive Muslim interpretational model will be discussed subsequently.[52]

A number of progressive Muslim scholars have noted the importance of recognizing this aspect of the nature of the Qur'anic discourse/text when developing their models of Qur'anic interpretation and/or Islamic legal theory. For example, Moosa maintains that the Qur'an without its' direct recipient audience would cease to be the Qur'an.[53] Achrati elsewhere argues that the oral-based culture of the Arab Bedouins strongly influenced the character and the nature of the Qur'anic discourse.[54] Similarly Abu Zayd considers that the Qur'anic discourse reflects the dialectical relationship between the Qur'an and the reality of the early Muslim community.[55] Soroush goes even further by asserting that the experiential, evolutionary, and dialogical nature of the prophetic experience had a very significant impact on the nature and the content of the revelation itself.[56]

According to the progressive Muslim *manhaj*, analyzing the overall context in which the Qur'anic content was revealed and taking into account the importance it had on the shaping of the Qur'anic content itself would provide an indispensable insight into character and the aims of the emerging Qur'anic Message as a whole. Such a heuristic, would be able to deduce the élan and the foundational principles of the Qur'anic Weltanschauung with the aim of the breaking of the shackles of the Qur'an's revelatory historicity and freeing it from the spatiotemporal constrains within which it initially operated.

Furthermore, in the traditional *asbab-ul-nuzul* and *naskh wa mansukh* sciences progressive Muslim interpretational methodology sees further evidence for a strong contingent relationship between the Qur'anic text and context in which the text was revealed.[57] The comprehensive contextualization of Qur'anic verses, however, is not the end of the interpretational process itself. Based on the information provided by the above two classical Qur'anic sciences with the use of reason and a values-based approach to Qur'anic interpretation[58], general principles, which transcend contexts, could be deduced. However, this did not eventuate in the premodern *usul-ul-fiqh*. Kamali, in the context of the role and nature of *naskh* in classical *usul ul-fiqh*, adopts the following view:

> [A] brogation which was originally meant to maintain harmony between the law and social reality began to be used contrary to its original purpose. The classical jurists advocated abrogation as a juridical doctrine in its own right rather than seeking it as an aid to the role of the time-space factor in the development of law.[59]

The ultimate aim of this comprehensively contextualist or historical approach to Qur'anic interpretation is, according to progressive Muslim theoreticians, to be able to interpretationally/hermeneutically distinguish between universal ethicoreligious and socioculturally contingent elements of Qur'anic revelation allowing for a development of a systematic, coherent, and hierarchical model of general and universal Qur'anic values that, hermeneutically, would be its most powerful interpretational tools.[60]

6.1.4   Progressive Muslims and the Systematic, Thematicoholistic, Corroborative, Inductive Approach to the Qur'anic Interpretation

In the third chapter, I described the NTS's segmentalist, atomistic, verse-by-verse approach to Qur'anic text and its interpretation. I also referred to the lack of internal connectivity of concepts and themes in the Qur'anic text due to the nature of its formation, subsequent textualization, and canonization as well as the didactic nature of its message. Progressive Muslims believe that this exegetical method of both classical and NTS approaches to Qur'anic interpretation "by the very nature of their procedure cannot yield insights into the cohesive outlook on the universe and the life which the Qur'an undoubtedly possesses."[61]

Progressive Muslims instead argue for a systematic, thematicoholistic and corroborative, inductive approach to interpretation of Qur'anic content based on not only the insights stemming from the traditional Islamic scholarship[62] referred to as *al-munasaba* (i.e., conceptual and textual chaining in the Qur'an)[63] and *istiqra'* (corroborative induction) but also on that of modern textual linguistics that enable the reader to discover Qur'an's textual coherence, sequentiality, and progression.[64] This is known as a *maudhu'i* method of interpretation, which collects all of the related verses from all of the Qur'anic *suras* and analyzes their interconnectivity before reaching a conclusion.[65] This approach to understanding the Qur'anic worldview is based on neither the fact that at the time of the Qur'an's collection its content was organized neither chronologically nor content-wise. Concepts, ideas, and the moral and ethical lessons derived from it are dispersed throughout the Qur'an. This absence of internal connectedness evident in the canonized Qur'anic text is made more intelligible, argue progressive Muslim theoreticians, if we keep in mind the didactic nature of its message and timeframe in which the Qur'an was revealed and, as mentioned above, the assertion that the Scripture was originally thought of as being suited to the oral-based culture of the Arab Bedouins. These factors, in turn, are thought to have strongly influenced the character, the content, and the nature of the Qur'anic discourse as being essentially oral, disjointed, and narratively parsimonious in nature, which "spurns linear thinking."[66] It is due to this apparent lack of correlation between different

Qur'anic parts that a thematicoholistic, corroborative, inductive approach to it is necessary.[67]

Furthermore, this approach is based on the premise that a proper understanding of a Qur'anic concept is gained only if all [68]the relevant verses dealing with that concept are analyzed and subsequently synthesized into a larger framework of its interpretation by means of a corroborative induction. This is referred to as thematic or systematic method of interpretation.[69] According to this view, the text is conceived as being web-like within which ideas are interwoven and the task of reading is to uncover what Mabrook terms "the comprehensive constant" (*thabitan kulliyan*) through thematic and corroborative inductive approaches. The eventual uncovering of the *thabitan kulliyan* would, in turn, be the aim or the objective of the reading/interpreting process.[70] In the words of Esack, progressive Muslims recognize

> a need for a hermeneutical theory which enables us to go beyond examining the "occasions" of isolated texts into one which examines the Sitz im Leben of the Qur'an as an entirety.[71]

In other words, according to this approach, the Qur'anic textual indicants (*dalil*) do not function as a self-contained entity to make a particular provision of the law manifest but are to be understood within their contexts, which must always be placed within the setting of the whole.[72] Derivation of meaning and explication of laws is therefore a result of a "relationship to a universe of meanings and values that were [are] inductively extrapolated from an aggregate of texts. On this understanding, legal matters were to be resolved by reference to inductively-established values and principles, even in the absence of explicit texts."[73] As such the Qur'anic text is to be studied in its textual unity and this unity can only be arrived at through a thematic approach to the Qur'an. Barlas asserts in this regard the following:

> The principles found within the Qur'an reveal a preference for reading the text as a cumulative, holistic process, that is, as a whole, a totality. Traditional Muslim views that the Qur'an is its best interpreter and that we need to interpret the Qur'an by the Qur'an are hermeneutical principles implicit in the Qur'an itself, which suggests textual holism as the basis of intra-scriptural investigation.[74]

Hasan Turabi's *Al-Tawsir al-Tawhidi* (The Unifying Exegesis) is another contemporary example in which a thematic approach to Qur'an is applied. Turabi does so at a level of unifying Qur'anic language that is considered as an integral whole, unifying the language of the Qur'an with that of the language of it direct recipients; on the level of Qur'anic structure unifying of topical content regardless of order of verses and unifying law with morality and spirituality.[75]

Indeed, progressive Muslims point to the fact that in the Qur'an itself one can deduce the principle of textual unity as a methodological tool to be applied to its reading .For example, Barlas makes reference to Qur'an 15: 91–93, "Those who break the Qur'an into parts. Them, by thy Lord, We shall question, everyone, of what they used to do."[76] Furthermore, Barlas argues that according to the Qur'an itself (39:23), revelation is characterized by continuity, self-consistency, and internal clarity.[77] This intra-textual, thematic approach to Qur'anic hermeneutics is, according to the progressive Muslim *manhaj*, also rooted in the Prophet's own method of interpretation of the Qur'an.[78]

Auda, in the context of developing a philosophy of Islamic Law, refers to this *manhaj* as a "systems approach," which is characterized by cognition, holism, openness, interrelatedness, hierarchy, multidimensionality, and purposefulness.[79]

As in the case of the comprehensively contextualist dimension of the Qur'anic interpretation its underlying aim is to develop a purely Qur'an-centered ethics. This, in turn, is necessary since proponents of progressive Muslim thought point to the fact that

> One cannot point to a single work of ethics squarely based upon the Qur'an. [But also] for without an explicitly formulated ethical system [based solely upon the Qur'an], one can never do justice to Islamic Law... [as Islamic] Law has to be worked out from the ethical systematisation of the teaching of the Qur'an and the uswa (sunna) of the Prophet, with regard to the situation currently obtaining.[80]

Thematicoholistic, corroborative-inductive, and comprehensively contextualist approaches to understanding the nature and the interpretation of Qur'an are also linked to another characteristic or element in the progressive Muslim *manhaj* to understanding the nature and the interpretation of Qur'anic text, namely, its underlying purposes and objectives.

6.1.5   Progressive Muslims' *Manhaj* and an Ethicoreligious Values and Aim-Based Approach (*Qasd*) to Qur'anic Interpretation

While all the elements of the NTS interpretive model discussed in the fourth chapter obstruct an aims and ethicoreligious values-based approach to Qur'anic interpretation, all of the principles of the progressive Muslims *manhaj* elaborated on above are based upon a broader hermeneutical assumption that the actual nature and character of the Qur'anic discourse seeks to realize and reach an underlying objective (*qasd*) in the form of certain ethicoreligious values considered as fundamental principles of the Qur'anic worldview. Progressive Muslims believe that this exegetical method of both classical and NTS approaches to Qur'anic interpretation did not seriously incorporate the notion of purposefulness of Islamic law in *usul-ul-fiqh* theory based on principles justice, equality, and righteousness understood in ethically objectivist terms.[81] For example, Ibn Ashur, a contemporary proponent of such an approach argues that premodern *usul* legal theories:

> disregard[ed] the purposes of the law, not including them in the fundamentals [of Islamic legal methodology], and merely studying them in a partial way within sections of analogical reasoning, under appropriateness and unrestricted interests, even thought they were supposed to be the fundamental of the fundamentals.[82]

Purposive nature of Islamic law is considered to be the definitive task of the interpretational process. [83] According to this view:

> The human is the aim and the purpose of all duties, laws [and legislation] which were introduced by different religions for the purpose of establishing harmonious social life between various peoples (author's translation).[84]

This aims-based, purposive nature of Qur'anic discourse is believed by progressive Muslim thought to be embedded in its actual content, especially its historical narratives, which form the bulk of the revelationary content.[85] As such the task of the contemporary reader opines avers Mumisa is to "search and recover the original audience of the Qur'anic text, along with its original message and intent."[86]

Thus *maqasid*-(aims/purpose) based approaches to the Qur'an by progressive Muslims are embedded in the broader interpretational framework that considers the ultimate objective of canonical texts to be facilitation of general welfare (*maslaha*). Therefore, according to this approach, *maslaha*, unlike the way it was understood and applied in Islamic legal theory in premodern times, becomes the highest governing hermeneutical principle.[87] In this context, El-Fadl argues that the general purpose of the Islamic Law is to serve the general welfare (*al-maslaha*) of the people, which, in turn, is to be conceptualized in terms of certain moral objectives such as justice and goodness.[88] Furthermore, according to this view, the ethical or moral values themselves will become contingent on their ability to serve the general welfare/wellbeing of people or be deemed invalid.[89] Similarly, Esack argues that the purpose of the Islamic law is to facilitate actualization of dignity and justice and considers that

> when the law fails to do this then it must be reinterpreted, amended or abandoned, in order to fulfil this objective. People as repositories of God's spirit, precede law.[90]

In this context the words of Ashrof are also representative of this approach:

Every expression of law must be subject to the requirements of justice and compassion. Because the law, wherever it originated from, is always approached and interpreted by human beings, it must be interpreted in terms of ever approximating and evolving notions of justice and compassion, the pivotal values that make them truly Islamic (Quran 5:8, 4:135).[91]

These views adopted by progressive Muslim scholars are also based upon careful analysis of the early Muslim community's attitude to legal innovation. Souaiaia has demonstrated this in reference to legal rulings of the first four caliphs in which *maslaha* in many instances overruled clear Qur'anic injunctions or precedents left by the Prophet.[92] Souaiaia has also adduced sufficient evidence that early Muslim scholars attempted to, for example, determine inheritance rights on principles of justice and fairness by adjusting the letter of the Qur'anic law.[93] There are a number of other examples, which I shall provide below. In other words, progressive Muslim *manhaj* is informed by the premise that the first generations of Muslims were characterized by flexible interpretational approaches to the Qur'an and Sunna that ably set the model of comprehensively contextual interpretation of sacred texts.[94]

Auda in his comprehensive treatment of the concept of *al-maqasid al-shari'ah* has compiled an extensive amount of evidence of *maqasid*-based *ijtihad* from the time of the Prophet and the Companions to that of the more systematically developed *maqasid* theories from the fifth to the eight century hijri and to the present.[95] Auda's examples include, for instance, the fact that although the Qur'an (59:7) clearly stipulates distribution of part of the booty to those who participated in wars ensuing from the early Arab conquests and this was a practice endorsed by the Prophet himself, 'Umar, the second caliph, however, decided not to distribute immovable property as in the case of lands of Iraq, in accordance with the verse because this was in the interests of the greater good and benefit (*maslaha*) of society in general. Similar decisions based on the principal of *maslaha* and *maqasid* were taken in the cases of impermissibility of enslavement of the original inhabitants of conquered lands; suspension/ abrogation of spending of the portion of zakat, the obligatory tax on non-Muslims (as a Qur'anic incentive for conversion, 9:60); and the outlawing of the practice of selling of female slaves who bore the children of their masters although these practices occurred during both the time of the Prophet and that of the first caliph.[96] Similarly, Islamic law pertaining to inheritance often diverges from explicit Qur'anic enunciations.[97] Similarly, some of the early jurists continued with this trend. Examining the works of Ibrāhīm al-Nakha'ī, al-Ḥijwī argues that although the rulings of the law were based on firm grounds and rationales (*qawā'id wa-'ilal thābita*) that were in fact meant to serve the interests (*maṣāliḥ*) of the people. Furthermore, he considered that these rationales were discernible from the Qur'ān and the Sunna, in addition to reason, which can distinguish between good and evil.[98]

Progressive Muslim theoreticians justify the validity of this approach also on the basis the example of a number of premodern legal theorists who developed legal theories whose aim was to be freed from the entirely textually based Qur'an-Sunna hermeneutic that was applied since the triumph of the forces of traditionalization and the development of the classical hermeneutic as explained in the second chapter.

They cite works which had more rudimentary conceptions of *maqasid* such as Al Tirmidhi Al-Hakim's (d. 296/908) *Al-Salah wa Maqasiduha*,[99] Abu Zayd Al-Balkhi's (d. 322/930), *al-Ibanah 'an 'ilal al-Diyanah /Masalih al-Abdan wa al-Anfus*,[100] Ibn Babawayh al-Qummi's (d. 381/991) *'Ilal al-Shara'i*,[101] Al-'Amiri al-Faylasuf' *al-I'lam bi-Manaqib al-Islam*[102] to those classical works that deal with the concept of *maqasid* more systematically such as Abu Al-Ma'ali Al-Juwayni's (d. 478/1085) *Al-Burhan fi usul al-Fiqh*,[103] Abu Hamid Al-Ghazali's (d. 505/1111) *Al-Mustasfa*[104], Al-'Izz Ibn Abd AL Salam's (d. 660/1209) *Qawa'id al-Ahkam fi masalih al-Anam*,[105] Shihab al-Din Al-Qarafi's (684/1258) *al-Furuq*,[106] Ibn Al-Qayyim's(d. 748/1347) *I'lam al-Muwaqqi'in*,[107] and Al-Shatibi's (d.790/1388) *Al-Muwafaqat fi usul al-Shari'ah*,[108] and those *maqasid*-oriented works among modern Muslim scholar's such as R. Rida's (d. 1354/1935) *Al-Wahi al_Mohammadi; Thubut al-Nubuwwah bi al-Qur'an*,[109] Ibn Ashur's *Maqasid al-Shari'ah al-Islamiyyah*,[110] Y. Al-Qaradi's *Kayf Nata'aamal Ma'a al-Qur'an al-'Azim*,[111] and T. Al-Alwani's *Maqasid al-Shari'ah*.[112]

Auda, for example, avers that in Al-Juwayni's *Al-Burhan* the notion of the protection (al-'ismah) of people's faith, souls, minds, private parts, and money as the purpose of Islamic law was developed.[113]

According to Moosa, Abu Hamid al-Ghazali, although at first not taking the principle of *maslaha* as one of the sources of *usul-ul fiqh*, considered that in several instances the *maslaha* doctrine "secures the purpose of revelation (*mahafaza 'ala maqsud al-shar*).[114] Moosa summarizes Ghazali's approach to the question of *maslaha* by stating:

> If one examines the primary sources—The Qur'an and Sunna—carefully, he [Ghazali] said, one will find that maslaha is indeed implicitly and explicitly evident as the purpose of the law. Ghazali thus endorsed maslaha stealthily, progressing from disparaging it as 'fanciful' at first, to viewing it later as the grounds of all legal pronouncements to be found in the canonical sources.[115]

Abd Al-Salam's Qawa'id, according to Auda, linked the validity of rulings to their purposes and considered that purposes of law can exist independently of any specific evidence from the scriptures, consensus, or analogy.[116]

In addition , Auda forms the view that Al-Qarafi also developed a theory according to which the concept of *al-maqasid* was linked to the purposes/intents of Prophet's actions.[117]

One of the first classical Muslim scholar who fully endorsed the concept of *maslaha* as the essence of and the ultimate purpose in interpretation and objective of the Qur'an and Sunna was by the name of Najmal-Din Al-Tufi (d. 716 A.H.). In Moosa's examination of Al-Tufi's work, Moosa comes to the conclusion that Tufi considered *maslaha* as having a regulatory function over all other established sources[118] and gave it "a universal and humanist status in the [Islamic] law" by giving preference to public interest (*maslaha*) over clear meaning of the text thereby "subordinating the text to the divination of the universal intentions and purposes of the Shari'ah." [119]

Furthermore, Moosa maintains that in Tufi's thought

> In terms of function and philosophy, the sources of law were actually representations of public interest...and stressed that ethical values and the priority of the sociological purposes of law over epistemology, in line with the meta-purpose of law.[120]

Ibn Al-Qayyim's emphasis on Shari'ah being based on wisdom, justice, mercy, good, and the achievement of people's welfare in this and the afterlife is considered by Auda as another important example of *maqasid*-oriented juridicial methodology espoused by premodern Muslim thinkers.[121]

Abu-Ishaq al-Shatibi (d. 790), whose Islamic legal theories, according to Hallaq, represent the culmination of the intellectual development starting in the fourth century A.H., is another important classical Muslim scholar whose thought and approach to Qur'ano-Sunnaic teachings and their interpretation were strongly influenced by the concept of *maqasid* and whose work is often referred to by progressive Muslim scholars when championing the importance of *maqasid* in their overall hermeneutical theory.[122]

Shatibi, Auda maintains, considered *al-maqasid* to be "the fundamentals of religion, basic rules of the law, and the universals of belief" (*usul al-din wa qawa'id al-shari'ah wa kulliyah al-millah*).[123]

Progressive Muslim thought considers itself to be building upon the maqasid oriented *usul-ul-fiqh manahij* approaches but with important differences. Namely, the premodern maslaha-based approaches were still restricted and operated within the broader juristic empiricism, to use prof. Jackson's terminology that is legal epistemology based on objectivism. Progressive Muslim approach goes beyond the premodern maqasid al-shari'ah and maslaha interpretational theories. In this context Auda asserts that the premodern theories of maqasid were studied as a secondary topic within *usul-ul fiqh* under the category of unrestricted interests (*al-masalih al-mursalah*) or the appropriate attribute for analogy (*munasabah al-qiyas*) and not as a independent discipline or as premised on the basis of forming "fundamental methodology."[124]

Wahyudi forms the view that for contemporary Muslim thinkers such as H. Hanafi, Al-Jabiri, and Madjid the concept of *maqasid-maslaha* is seen as the essence of the Qur'an and that it can take precedence over the clear Qur'anic text.[125] Same holds true for Ibn Ashur, perhaps a leading proponent of *maqasid*-based approach to Islamic law[126].

Auda himself has developed a universalist *maqasid*-based philosophy of Islamic law according to which:

> The validity of any method of ijtihad is determined based on its degree of realization of maqasid al-shari'ah. The practical outcome is Islamic rulings which are contusive to the values of justice, moral behaviour, magnanimity, co-existence and human development, which are 'maqasid' in their own right.[127]

Progressive Muslims' departure from this premodern scholarship on *maqasid* is also based on certain assumptions pertaining to ontology and epistemology. In the words of Johnstone

> It implies a primary ontological and epistemological shift—a step away from the classical Sunni-Ash'ari tendency toward ethical voluntarism, and a step toward granting human reason more latitude in interpreting and applying the 'general edicts' of the texts (*al-ahkam al-'amma or al-usul al kulliyya*).[128]

These interpretational strategies are discussed in the following section.

6.1.6   Progressive Muslims' View of the Nature of Ethical Value and the Role of Reason in the Qur'an and its Interpretational Implications

In the fourth chapter, I briefly described the triumph of traditionalization forces that have resulted in a particular *usul-ul-fiqh* methodology in the third century A. H. As a result of these forces of traditionalization, Hourani maintains that the inherently Qur'anic principles of ethical objectivism and partial rationalism were transformed into ethical voluntarism (ethical concepts understood only in terms of God's will[129]) and traditionalism (humans can never know what is morally right by independent reason, but only by revelation and revelation-derived sources),[130] thereby changing the epistemologico-methodological character of both Qur'an and Sunna [131]. In this context Reinhart asserts that "[at] this point in time [after the victory of the forces of traditionalization,] Islam itself became the standard and the congruence of reason and religion, which once served to justify religion, now, at best, justified reason."[132] Furthermore, the overriding principles of the premodern textual hermeneutics also meant that "Revelation must categorically alter morality and epistemology..." and by inference "[b]efore or without Revelation there can be no moral knowledge."[133]

Hourani's finding also implies that this was not the case during the formative period of Islamic thought. What concerns us here is to describe this change in the way the nature of ethical value in the Qur'an was understood as well as the scope of reason used in its interpretation during the first half of the formative period of Islamic thought. The reason being that the progressive Muslim *manhaj* considers itself to be a continuation and extension or a progression of this reason-inclusive approach to interpretation based on ethical objectivism.[134]

In terms of epistemologico-methodological boundaries of Sunna at the time of the Prophet, Hourani states that in terms of ethical knowledge, the Qur'an "considers" revelation its major source but that "it is probable, but unproved, that natural reason is also capable of forming ethical judgments [independent of revelation]."[135] Furthermore, argues Hourani that in terms of the boundaries of ethical epistemology the Qur'anic nature of ethical value is generally objective, "the use of independent reason in ethical judgments is never ruled out explicitly in the Qur'an, and there are some considerations that favour implicit assumptions of its use." It is further maintained that:

> Qur'an and Muhammad both display a common sense attitude and that we
> should not expect either of them to claim that for every ethical judgment

he makes, a man must consult a book or a scholar, or work out an analogy when the book or scholar gives no direct answer to the problem.[136]

Furthermore, he asserts that the Qur'anic and Prophetic attitude of ethical objectivism discussed above were taken up and embodied by the generation of his Companions.[137]

According to Reinhart the essential common-sense "attitude" of the Qur'an and its message are evident in its discourse of "nature, 'aql, the cosmos, and their patterns— all [are] appealed to say that the message of the Qur'an is reasonable."[138] Draz in his exhaustive investigation of the moral world of the Qur'an echoes this view by concluding that, according to the Qur'anic moral world, the human consciousness is prior to Revelation and is capable of divorcing right from wrong without it.[139] The same applies to the concept of Sunna. Guraya in his close analysis of the concept of Sunna in early Islam maintains that speculative, free thought was considered as genuine, valid, and authoritative constituent of Sunna.[140] Thus, rationality and ethical objectivity certainly cannot be considered as alien to the overall spirit of Qur'an-Sunna teachings.

Reason, reason-based opinion (ra'y), as well as qiyas (analogical reason) were essentially seen as legitimate, pragmatic tools for extrapolating law and had a positive connotation to them throughout the first century A. H.[141] Ansari considers that the personal judgments of the earliest Muslim jurists were considerably influenced by subjective considerations and were accompanied by a broad understanding of the spirit and goals of Islam playing a fairly important part in the early Islamic legal thinking.[142] Moreover, Schacht maintains that ra'y had been an integral part of regional Sunna and an essential element of Islamic thought from its very inception.[143] Hallaq, furthermore, asserts that meaning of ra'y during the entire first century of Hijrah and a portion of the next "was a major source of legal reasoning and judicial rulings"[144] and furthermore was "very close to and, in fact, couldn't be separated from Sunna."[145]

During the second century A. H., a similar narrowing down of the legitimacy and scope of the use of ra'y based on 'aql was starting to take place, but this process, just like in the case of Sunna, was incomplete. [146]Reinhart, for example, argues that, throughout the Abbasid era, the Islamic worldview existed in a symbiotic relationship with the religious ideology characterized by the belief that all human beings shared moral common sense and that the Revelation supplemented and confirmed 'aql.[147] Additionally, the numerous fuqaha, who died during the second and the third decade of the second century relied heavily on exercising personal opinions based on reason/'aql rather than being involved in hadith transmission.[148]

The positive connotations of *ra'y* were still in operation in the middle of the second century Hijri although they had started to develop negative ones too.[149] As the hadith body of literature was gradually expanding, views not based on these, now entirely textual sources of Sunna, increasingly started to denote "arbitrary opinion" in the minds of those engaged in the process of the written documentation of the Sunna.[150]This mixed trend of good and bad ra'y, for example, was still evident at the time of two prominent Muslim jurists, Abu Yusuf (d. 182) and Shaibani (d.189). Emon has also shown that several authorities in the post-formative period of Islamic thought also considered reason to be source of moral obligation in addition to revelation.[151]

Progressive Muslim thought considers these prevalent views on the scope and the use of reason and the nature of ethical value in the Qur'an (and by implication Sunna) prior to the triumph of the classical Muslim view to be the normative and distances itself from the classical. For example, Sachedina avers similarly that "the purpose of the divine message, according to the Qur'an, is none other than to complement the innate reason in human beings, in order to seek the right guidance for establishing an ideal society on earth that would reflect God's Will for humanity."[152]

Another argument that gives credence to the objective nature of ethical values in the Qur'an refers to its assumption regarding the meaning and the usage of moral principals. In the famous Qur'anic maxim of enjoying the good (*ma'ruf*) and forbidding the evil (*munkar*), which forms the basis for political governance of a Muslim state, El-Fadl argues that the word *ma'ruf* means that which is commonly known to be good. "Goodness, in the Qur'anic discourse, is part of what one may call a lived reality—it is a product of human experience, and constructed normative understandings." The same applies to the word *munkar* or the word *ihsan* (kindness). Furthermore, El Fadl maintains, that the "Divine is the very embodiment of all that is moral, ethical , good, and right and therefore, the presence of the Divine as an objective reality necessarily means the existence of ethical values such as justice and goodness as an objective reality."[153] Therefore, maintains El-Fadl, in regards to every ethical obligation, "the Qur'anic text assumes that readers will bring pre-existing, innate moral sense to the text." [154]

To Gabiri rationality, furthermore, is seen as the aim/objective/purpose of Revelation ("*Zweck der Offenbarung*").[155]

Al-Attar provides a number of arguments in the support of ontologically objective status of ethical values in Islamic thought, especially the Qur'an. Her first argument is based upon her analysis of the Qur'an's usage of ethical terms in a manner that its audience could understand, which presupposes, in her view, their objective nature. The fact that ethical attributes in the Qur'an are predicated of God leads Al-Attar to assert that they are as such "impossible to interpret in terms of obedience to His [i.e., God's] own commands." She corroborates her view further by maintaining that if God was not just and good in a human sense then the divine attributes would be "meaningless and unappealing to human moral feeling and religious devotion." Al-Attar, among others, finds further evidence for objective nature of ethical values in the Qur'an in the nature of the God's covenant with humans as described in the Qur'an and the fact that God has instilled Divine breath in human beings all of which are indicative of human beings possessing "a consciousness that distinguishes good from evil."[156]

Furthermore, progressive Muslims are of the view that both "reason and history play roles in determining values, those revealed as well as those that were non-revealed."[157] As such progressive Muslims' position is more aligned and can be considered a continuation and logical elaboration of the views espoused by Mu'tazilah, Muslim speculative rationalists.[158]

6.1.7 Progressive Muslims Ethicoreligious Values-based Approach to Interpretation of Qur'an

Hudan li-l-nas, guidance for the human kind, is a Qur'anic self-description of its essential function and nature of revelation according to progressive Muslim thought. As described in the fourth chapter, in its function as a "guide," Qur'anic content can be said to deal with issues that pertain to theology/faith and worship (*aqidah* and *'ibadah*), those related to ethico-moral realm (*akhlaq/adab*), social relations/transactions (*mu'amalat*), and law/jurisprudence (*fiqh*).

As argued above the progressive Muslims comprehensively contextualist, thematic-holistic, and *maqasid-maslaha* approach to its interpretation was based upon a view that in the very nature and permeating through substantial portions of the Qur'anic content are non-*aqidah/'ibadah* elements that mirrored and presupposed/assumed the continuation of certain sociocultural, political, legal, and economic norms of the region at that time. Although Qur'an attempted to mitigate and attenuate the effects of some of these prevalent norms, it did not eradicate them completely. This is because of its evolutionary rather than revolutionary and mitigatory rather than abolitionist character.[159] Progressive Muslim thought considers that based upon this mitigating effect and the Qur'an's overwhelming, what Saeed terms, "ethico-theological" nature of Qur'anic language,[160] the primary function and the rationale behind all non-*aqidah/'ibadah* elements of the Qur'an (and Sunna) can be reduced to the deduction or derivation of certain normative ethicoreligious values or general principals arrived at by using above stipulated methodological/hermeneutical tools. Thus, the core of the non-*aqidah/'ibadah* Qur'an (and Sunna message) can be reduced to a set of hierarchical values that would in the overall hermeneutical model, occupy the highest position and govern all other interpretational tools.[161]

In such an approach, the upper levels of a hierarchical model are based on the fundamental Qur'anic ethicomoral concepts such as Justice (*al-adl*), freedom of belief, equity (*al-qist*), and mercy (*rahmah*) just to name a few, which themselves, in turn, are based on, what Barlas refers to as the principle of God's "Self-Disclosure" as a concrete manifestation of "Divine Ontology" whose anchor is the Qur'anic concept of *Tawhid*.[162] These principles then act as guides in the interpretation (higher order principles of interpretation) of Qur'anic injunctions to which all other norms/values/injunction, especially those which are socioculturally relative (lower-order principles), including those in the Qur'an, are subservient. Thus, if there is an apparent Qur'anic (or Hadithic) textual conflict between the higher- and lower-order principles, the higher order principle must prevail.[163]

In summary, progressive Muslims approach to understanding the nature and interpretation of Qur'an is based upon a number of epistemological and methodological assumptions, which, in many cases, are diametrically opposed to that of the NTS's model and are outside the "thinkable" realm of both the classical Muslim and NTS thought.

What is the progressive Muslims *manhaj* regarding the nature and scope of the concept of Sunna? I turn my attention to this question next.

6.2   The Nature and Scope of the Concept of Sunna in Progressive Muslim Thought—Conceptual Assumptions and Their Interpretational Implications

The concerns of this part of the chapter are two-fold. First, I will refer to the scholarship of Muslims scholars who have distinguished the concepts of Sunna and hadith. The reason behind this is that progressive Muslims are revisiting the historical debates behind the tensions that exists between the *ahl-hadith manhaj* of Sunna (to which NTS subscribes) and that of other Muslim groups such as the various *madhahib* and the Islamic legal theorists aiming to problematize and question the *ahl-hadith manhaj* of Sunna, which, as we demonstrated in the fourth chapter, operates entirely within the premodern *ulum-ul hadith* sciences and conceptually, methodologically, and epistemologically conflates the two. Second, I discuss the methodological mechanisms of contemporary Muslim scholars who go beyond traditional *ulum-ul hadith* sciences in order to evaluate the validity and the authenticity of hadith in order to determine what is Sunna. As such the methodologies employed by these scholars would come under the umbrella of progressive Muslim thought as defined in this study.

During the formative period of Islamic thought an ontological, epistemological, and methodological differentiation between the concepts of Sunna and Hadith was made. This was, for example, evident in the concepts of regional or *'amal-* (practice) based Sunna in the Maliki school of thought or that of Sunna *al-ma'rufa al-mahfuza* in Hanafism.[164]

Ahmed Hasan in his "The Early Development in Islamic Jurisprudence" points to this difference when he says:

> It is not necessary that Sunna be always deduced and known from a Hadith. Early texts on law show that the term Sunna was used in a sense of the established practice of the Muslims claiming to have come down from the time of the Prophet. That is why Sunna sometimes contradicts Hadith and sometimes Hadith documents it.[165]

Numerous modern Muslim scholars [166] have alluded to the semantical and conceptual differences between the Hadith and Sunna, during the first two centuries of Islamic calendar. For example, Dutton's study of Malik's Muwatta led him to conclude that according to Malik Sunna was seen as:

> a normative practice established by the Prophet, put into practice by Companions and inherited from them as 'amal (in this sense the practice of Companions in Medina) by the Successors and their Successors up to the time of Malik.[167]

A unique definition of Sunna that does not depend upon its written-based documentation (i.e., hadith) is argued by contemporary Pakistani scholar Moiz Amjad. He defines Sunna as:

> a set of actions or practical rules (excluding beliefs) which Prophet initiated, promoted and performed among all of his followers as a part of God's religion (din) and that have been perpetuated from one generation to another practically.[168]

Having examined the use of Hadith in Malik's Muwatta, and writings of Awza'i Rahman makes an important conclusion in saying that:

> Awza'i regards the Hadith of the Prophet as being endowed with funda-mental obligatoriness but the Sunna or the living practice[169] is of same importance to him. His appeals to the practice of the Community or its leaders are to judge from the extinct materials, the most regular feature of his legal argumentation. Malik adduces Hadith (not necessarily Prophetic Hadith) to vindicate the Medanise Sunna but regards Sunna in terms of actual importance, as being superior to the Hadith.[170]

Rahman goes on to develop his own hadith-independent definition of Sunna describing it as a general umbrella concept, a dynamic action-behavioural system that permitted interpretation that included non-pro-phetic ijtihad in it.[171]

Similarly, the notion of practice as indicator of Sunnah is also evident in Abu Yusuf's writings who lived in Kufa. The practice- based Sunnah derives, in his view, from "those norms which were recognised as such by the Muslims in general, were accepted by the fuqaha and which had come down through reliable and learned people (al-sunnah 'an rasul Allah 'an al-salaf min ashabih wa min qawm fuqaha). The same can be said about early Ibadi authorities methodology of filtering hadith on the basis of al-haqq al-ma'ruf fi kitab Allah wa sunnat nabiyhi wa athar al-salihin i.e. al-a'imma wa'l-ulama.[172] What is of importance to this thesis is that progressive Muslim thought approach to the nature and scope of Sunna revisits these early discussions on Sunna and hadith in order to develop a new Sunna hermeneutic that does not epistemologically, methodologically, or ontologically depend upon hadith.

Additionally, traditional sciences of hadith criticism (*ulum-ul-hadith*) within which *madhhab*- and NTS-*manahij* are conceptually framed have primarily focused on *isnad* analysis when attempting to determine the authenticity of hadith.[173] Progressive Muslim approach to hadith criticism goes beyond these sciences and includes for example analy-sis of hadith according to methods found in the works of Muslim[174] and non-Muslim scholars such as G. H. A. Juynboll, H. Motzki, and G. Schoeler. [175]

As such they do not restrict themselves primarily to *isnad* criticism, but they award more scope to the role of reason and ethicomoral consid-erations[176] and a more stringent *matn* criticism in the overall sciences per-taining to hadith criticism. Additionally, *ahad hadith* are not considered as binding in any of the Islamic sciences including that of theology and law as in the case of NTS (but not the broader *madhhab*-based tradition).[177]

In addition to revisiting the debates on the conceptual difference between the concepts of Sunna and hadith, progressive Muslim scholars are employing a number of the same methodological tools when interpreting the Qur'an to that of Hadith as mentioned above. In particular they use: a. comprehensive contextulisaton, b. thematicoholistic approach, c. ethicoreligious values -based approach, and d. objective- or purpose-based approach to interpretation of hadith. What follows is a discussion of these in some of the progressive Muslim works, especially as they relate to the issue of gender.[178]

In his controversial book *Tahrir Al Mara'a fi al Asr al-Risala*, Abu Shuqqa's *manhaj* combines comprehensive contextualization with a thematicoholistic approach alongside specification of what classical Muslim thought considered to be general and vice-versa, and a quasi-physiological hermeneutic that aims to recover the real intents behind the words of the Prophet found in some of the hadith pertaining to women—such as those pertaining to women's deficiency in religion and intellect or women forming a majority in Hell discussed in Chapter 5—in order to invalidate the traditionally patriarchal and misogynistic interpretations of the same. For example, after thematically analyzing the full context behind the historical events pertaining to the hadith in describing women as lacking in intellect, religion, and forming the majority of people in Hell, he asserts the following:

> As for the [Prophet's] text formulation, it is not such that implies a general ruling stipulation nor it is general in nature.[179]

Himself being committed to the direct Qur'an and Sunna (hadith) *manhaj*, he also cites some women-friendly hadith such as "Women are men's twins"[180] in order to strengthen his argument for gender equality.

In her article titled "Knowledge, Women, and Gender in the hadith: a Feminist Interpretation," S. Shaikh argues that hadith literature can serve as a mirror of the formative civilization reality of the first three centuries of Islam. She also avers that hadith literature is a window into the dominant conceptions of sociopolitical, religious, and cultural norms and values of the Islamic community, especially in relation to gender and the category of a woman. She is also interested in exploring the manner in which hadith body of knowledge in time became ideologically functional in defining ideals of gender. By contextualizing the hadith body of knowledge and by being sensitive to the gender ideology embedded in it, she explores how hadith can be used to offer alternative (to traditional approaches) possibilities of interpretation providing counter leverage to the dominant discourses.[181] Faqihudin Abdul Qadir in his "Hadith and Gender

Justice—Understanding the Prophetic Traditions" adopts a similar contextualist approach by considering that a proper understanding of hadith, especially in relation to the role and the status of women, is obtained only in terms of their original sociopolitical contexts requiring comprehensive contextulization and the inquiry into the circumstance behind the emergence of hadith *('ilm asbab l-wurud)*.[182]

The principle of corroborative induction examined above in the context of Qur'anic interpretation is also applied to hadith interpretation. Qadir for example laments the selectivity of employment of hadith by traditional scholarship by stating that "in essence, certain hadith and indeed, specific decisions by the Prophet have been typically selectively invoked as authoritative references instead of being examined comprehensively and in totality."[183]He is of the opinion that Qur'ano-hadith texts are to be "interpreted and applied according to the broader transformative spirit that characterizes the Qur'an and the hadith as a whole" by taking resort to what we term a thematicoholistic or corroborative inductive approach to interpretation of hadith.

Again as in the case of the Qur'anic interpretation hadith are to be interpreted in a way to facilitate certain ethicoreligious values. In this context Qadir asserts that "regarding women issues references to the hadith must be based on an awareness of the crucial values he [Prophet Muhammad] brought: the oneness of Allah, the equality of all human beings (rich or poor, men or women), justice and mercy."[184] The principle of justice and equality in particular play a prominent role in this type of reasoning and interpreting of hadith. A values-based approach to interpretation of hadith is best exemplified by the following statement of a contemporary progressive Muslim scholar Qadir:

> Contemporary interpretations of many [of these] hadith continue to engender inequality and unfairness in the relationship between men and women. This inequality, moreover, violates the most fundamental principles of the Qur'an and the hadith.[185]

El-Fadl has also introduced two novel methodological principals with the view of conceptually, methodologically, and epistemologically divorcing Sunna and hadith termed "authorial enterprise" and "a conscientious pause" when dealing with hadith interpretation. According to El-Fadl, the term *authorial enterprise* refers to the process of determining to what extent the Prophet's role in the historical transmission of the report can safely be established. This is based upon the fact that, as per the classical Islamic scholarship's view of hadith as not being the actual words of the Prophet but recollections and interpretation of Prophet's words that retained the core meaning by individuals reporting them, hadith can be a result of several authors and various collateral influences each impacting upon both the structure and the meaning of the report. When interpreting the report, argues El-Fadl further, a principle of proportionality of correlation between the role of the Prophet and the normativeness of the report is to be put in place. The higher the Prophet's authorial enterprise in the report the higher its normative effect and vice-versa. Additionally, he applies another regulatory mechanism relating to the normative effect of the report. According to this rule, reports having "widespread moral, legal, or social implications must be of the highest rank of authority…and requiring heaviest burden of proof."[186] Lastly, as the very last methodological resort, he introduces three concept of a "conscientious pause," a faith-based objection to textual evidence[187] based upon the overall understanding of the Qur'an-Sunna Weltanschauung and its élan/ethos.

Hadith texts, instead, are seen in their function of furthering justice and the general welfare understood as the foundational principles of Islam and as the ultimate interpretational ends of the interpretational process.[188]

Auda's *maqasid* approach to philosophy of Islamic law introduces new epistemological principles to the issue of resolving opposition of juridical evidences (known as *ta'arud/ikhtilaf*), which often are based on opposing hadith evidence. He takes recourse to the idea of multidimensionality, as one component of his *maqasid* approach, to ground his methodology beyond the premodern binary approaches to legal theory based on the dichotomy of certain (*al-qat*) vs. uncertain (*al-zann*) categories in juridicial evidences, which, in his view, were responsible for "a narrow ,out of context and partial view of many fiqhi rulings." In this context, he asserts the following:

> … [t]he quest for "absolute certainty" [yaqin] in juridical thinking, whether it takes the form of linguistic implication, historical authenticity, or logical implication, is unsubstantiated, and should be dealt with ,theoretically speaking, according to a continuous (probability) spectrum, rather than the binary certain/uncertain classification.

Multidimensionality, on the other hand, entails "a spectrum of levels between binary opposites" in which the probability increases in a non-linear mode with the number of available evidences. Auda argues for a continuous approach to certainty, which when forming a part of a *maqasid* approach to Islamic law can offer a better methodology in resolving issues pertaining to *ta'arud*. For instance, Auda gives an example of opposing hadith with respect to the rights of custody of children to mother divorcees who remarry. According to some, a hadith woman loses her custody while others suggest that they could keep the children even after they get married. Auda goes on to say that the vast majority of premodern schools of thought, relying on the first group of narrations, which they considered as being more authentic/certain due to the fact that they are found in Bukhari's and Ibn Hanbal's hadith collections, simply eliminated others and concluded that custody of children is automatically transferred to the father if the mother gets married.

Auda, arguing against the binary certainty/uncertainty dichotomy as a methodological principle in the area of *ta'arud* proposes a methodology that gives due regard to the context and the juridical *maqsid* of "fulfilling the best interest of people" as "the key to interpreting these narrations." With respect to this he asserts that "a maqasid approach could fill the gap of missing contexts in the narration of hadith" and "moreover, al-maqasid, in the sense of the intents of the prophet, could also be utilized in contextualizing narrations."[189]

He states further that in case of multiplicity of *maqasid* arising when dealing with *ta'arud* evidences a kind of hierarchy of *maqasid* needs to be developed with those of highest order being given priority.[190]

Fadel's article "Is Historicism a Viable Strategy for Legal Reform: The Case of 'Never Shall the Folk Who Have Appointed a Woman to Rule Them'"[191] employs what he terms *hermeneutical historicism* to analyze the hadith found in most major hadith Sunni collections narrated on the authority of Abu Bakra that the Prophet had stated, "Never shall a folk prosper who delegate their affairs to a woman." Fadel's "hermeneutical historicism" is premised on the concept of history as a source for textual interpretation and consists of a number of sub-methodologies applied to the treatment of hadith by examining the assumptions governing classical Islamic legal hermeneutics and its assumptions regarding the nature of language, especially the principle that general terms must not be applied generally until care has been taken to exclude the possibility that circumstantial evidence indicates a more specific intent (*takhsis al-'amm*); contextualization of hadith genres, their narrative frames, and its interpretational implications; and by examining how this hadith was used in substantive law. Here he argues that it is possible, in the case of the hadith under analysis by exploring literary history, Islamic legal hermeneutics, and substantive Islamic law, to create a more gender-egalitarian version of Islamic law by remaining within the classical/traditional, epistemological, and methodological frameworks and without relying on arguments outside of it and without raising more controversial theological questions that would be less likely acceptable to traditional Muslim minds.[192]

In summary progressive Muslims form the view that, as in the case of the Qur'an, the above principles when applied to hadith are assumed to promote the broader interpretational principles of an aims-based function of the nature of the hadith. In the words of Qadir,

> ...in the light of the fundamentally contextual character of the hadith, a number of scholars have adopted an understanding of the hadith which is informed by the essential purpose of the text and the root problem it addresses. The meaning inscribed in the literal language of the text is not regarded as definitive and need not be applied in an unconditional manner.[193]

Chapter 7

Progressive Muslims' Religiously Ideal "Believer" and "Muslim Woman" Concepts

This chapter aims to explain how progressive Muslims' *manhaj* is employed to engender the progressive Muslims' understating of religiously ideal "Believer" and "Muslim Woman" concepts. It uses the same methodology as the one adopted in the fifth chapter.

PART ONE: Progressive Muslims Concept of a Religiously Ideal "Believer"

In the first part of this section, I identify the relevant Qur'an and hadith texts employed and the most commonly applied hermeneutical tools and methods by progressive Muslims with regards to their view on the normative principals and the decorum adopted when dealing with the religious Other.

Here and in the next section, I primarily discuss the work of Esack and Shahrur, which, as discussed in the first chapter of this study, are the only extant works that directly link the issue of Qur'anic hermeneutics with that of the religious status of the religious Other.

Esack based on his "contextual hermeneutic of religious diversity for libration" outlines a number of "general attitudes" evident in the Qur'an that are to be considered when attempting to understand the Qur'an's relationship with the religious Other. First, by taking recourse to the importance of "overall historical context," Esack considers that the Qur'an embraces religious inclusivism by "present[ing] a universal, inclusivist perspective of a divine being who responds to the sincerity and commitment of all of His servants."[1] In this context, he develops a hermeneutically important idea of a gradual and contextual development of the Qur'anic position toward the religious Other to argue that there is no final or universal Qur'anic position on the issue. Second, Esack emphasizes the importance of the Qur'anic constant wedding of issues of dogma with that of social justice to argue that the Qur'an develops a very intimate and strong connection between orthodoxy and orthopraxis. Third, he considers that the Qur'an only denounces the religious exclusivism characterized by the Jewish and Christian communities encountered by Prophet Muhammad in Hijaz. Fourth, basing himself on a thematic approach to the Qur'an quoting a large number of relevant verses that shall be presented in the next section of this chapter below, Esack asserts that the Qur'an is explicit in its acceptance of religious pluralism and the *de jure* legitimacy of all revealed religion by "taking into account the religious life of separate communities coexisting with Muslims, respecting their laws, social norms, and religious practices and it accepts that the faithful adherents of these religions will also attain salvation."[2] Fifth, Esack forms the view that the Qur'anic portrayal of the relationship between Muslims and the religious Other is based on "the socio-religious requirements" of the Muslim community such as security and community building and not on faith convictions or lack thereof. Sixth, quoting Qur'an 22:40,[3] he asserts that, on the basis of this verse alone, the Qur'an's acceptance of Other's spirituality and salvation through Otherness is revealed.

Furthermore, Esack's view of what he terms *prophetic responsibility* to the religious Other stemming from the religiously inclusionary stance of the Qur'an is postulated on two levels:

i. as a challenge to existing communities with scriptures about their commitment and faithful adherence to their own tradition, and
ii. more generally to humanity, to present the Qur'an's own guidance for consideration and acceptance.[4]

In this context he asserts:

> Muhammad's basic responsibility in inviting was to call to God. For some components of the other, the response to this call was best fulfilled by a commitment to [reified] Islam. Thus they were also invited to become Muslims. For others, the call was limited to [non-reified] *islam*.[5]

In line with its method of understanding the nature, objectives, and the context-content dynamic behind the unfolding of Qur'an-Sunna teachings, progressive Muslims consider Qur'anic verses and hadith discussed in the context of NTS interpretation of the concept of a "Believer" in the fifth chapter (and similar others) as being contextually contingent—and, hence, specific to the time of the Revelation and to the communities at the time of the Revelation encountered by the prophet Muhammad. In other words, by making a hermeneutical distinction between universalist and historically contingent aspects of the scripture, the Qur'an and hadith texts are not considered as being universal in their scope. [6] Progressive Muslims rely not only on the comprehensively contexualist approach to their interpretation to them but maintain that, with respect to the religiously hostile hadith vis-à-vis the religious Other presented in the fifth chapter, they contradict the concept of *Sunna* as based on the *overall* Qur'anic attitude (thematic and corroborative/holistic approach) toward the *religious Other* as well as on the Prophet's praxis, which is an embodiment of that attitude. These religiously antagonistic *ahadith*, in turn, are considered to be reflective of the community attitudes among some of the members of (the early) Muslim community.[7] Furthermore, progressive Muslim's conceptual, methodological, and epistemological divorcing of the Sunna from the hadith body of knowledge is also used as a hermeneutical tool to argue against the normative character of the reactionary *ahadith* presented in the fifth chapter. Moreover the hermeneutical recourse to "authorial enterprise," "proportionality of correlation" and "conscientious pause," (all discussed in the previous chapter), to argue against the normative nature of these *ahadith* can also be taken.

In addition to the above, by adopting a thematic/holistic approach to the Qur'anic verses cited below, progressive Muslims develop an inclusionary concept of a "Believer" that legitimizes the religious claims of the religious Other.[8] As such, progressive Muslims consider "the ethic of pluralism," including the religious, to be intrinsic to the Qur'an and its worldview.[9]

In reference to what the normative Muslim attitude toward the religious Other should be, progressive Muslims consider a number of verses to be more reflective of the spirit and ethos of the overall Qur'an–Sunna teachings such as the following:

> Invite (all) to the way of thy Lord with wisdom and beautiful preaching; and argue with them in ways that are best and most gracious: for thy Lord knoweth best who have strayed from His Path and who receive guidance. (16:125)
>
> And dispute ye not with the People of the Book except with means better (than mere disputation) unless it be with those of them who inflict wrong

> (and injury): but say "We believe in the Revelation which has come down to us and in that which came down to you; Our Allah and your Allah is one; and it is to Him we bow (in Islam). (29:46)

> Allah forbids you not with regard to those who fight you not for (your) Faith nor drive you out of your homes from dealing kindly and justly with them: for Allah loveth those who are just. (60:8)

According to the progressive Muslim thought these verses lay down the general and universal principles underlying the decorum to be observed in dealing with, and the attitude to be taken toward, the religious Other whether in conditions of peace or in a situation of conflict.[10] As such, these verses are considered by the theoreticians of progressive Muslim *manhaj* as higher-order hermeneutical principles superseding the exclusionary and antagonistic Qur'an-hadith body of texts presented in the fifth chapter.[11]

I will now consider how the progressive Muslim approach to interpretation of the Qur'an and Sunna demarcates the boundaries of belief in order to construct their understanding of the concept of a religiously ideal "Believer."

Based on a comprehensively contextualist and thematico-holistic aspects of the progressive Muslim *manhaj*, Esack considers that there exists an urgent need to reexamine and rethink the Qur'anic terms *islam,'iman, kufr, din, ahl-kitab ,mushrik* and *wilayah,* which are crucial in understanding the Qur'anic position on the religious Other in the light of the broader principles and objectives underlying his "hermeneutic of religious pluralism for liberation." One of these principals, Esack asserts, is that these terms are "dynamic," meaning that they ought to be considered as being "embodied in certain qualities of individuals in different stages of their lives,"[12] multi-dimensional, i.e., having a number of meanings and connotations ranging from an intensely personal/spiritual to doctrinal, ideological, and sociopolitical, but all of which are *inextricably intertwined*; that they have a number of meanings that have changed over a period of time; that they are inherently linked to issues of righteous deeds and conduct, i.e., to orthopraxis; and that they can exist at abstract and reified levels. [13]

In arguing this, Esack wishes to "redefine, rediscover and re-appropriate the subsumed meanings of these terms including those which appear to encourage religious exclusivism." He considers that there exists "a frayed relationship" between majority premodern and contemporary understandings of the relationship between the Qur'an and the religious Others and how they are employed in the Qur'an.[14]

Taking recourse to a thematic and comprehensively contextualist interpretive method in relation to the dynamic between *islam-iman-kurf,* Esack notes that one important aspect of the "process of rigidification of Islamic theology" occurred by the means of reification of these concepts and their association with a particular socioreligious and historical community. Additionally, Esack forms the view that this narrowing of the boundaries of belief in Islamic theology emerged as a later developed theological trend of substituting, *in their reified forms,* the particularly metaconfessional concept of *iman/mu'min* with that of islam/muslim as a key term for self-identification. In this context, by basing himself on a thematic approach to the Qur'anic text analysis, Esack asserts that this process took hold despite the fact that the term *iman* is much more central to Qur'an and its worldview than is *islam,* which is quite marginal. These occurrences, as noted above in the context of work by Donner in Chapter 5, resulted in a narrowing of confessional identity denied a status of a "Believer" to those outside the prophet Muhammad's socioreligious and historic community. Furthermore, by adopting a thematic and comprehensively con-textualist approach to the Qur'an, Esack considers concepts of iman, din and islam in their nonreified form as metahistorical universalist concepts to be primarily understood within the framework of a "deep inner and personal conviction" that cannot be linked to institutionalized religion.[15] For example, in relation to the concept of islam,[16] he offers three nuanced meanings, two of which are nonreified, namely the Qur'anic *islam* of pre-Muhammadan prophets, *islam* as personal submission to the Will of God and a reified *Islam* in individuals and communities who share common space, geography, or time with the adherents of reified Islam[17] (i.e., those known today as Muslims). Iman is also seen as essentially a nonreified concept. In the words of Esack as "a personal recognition of, and an active response to, the presence of God in the universe and in history," character-ized by dynamism and fluctuation and existing at various levels (such as "perfect" and "diluted" iman). Esack also conceives of the concept of iman as multidimensional in nature incorporating the spiritual, the religious, and socieconomic dimensions, all of which form a symbiotic whole. [18]

Consistent with his analysis of other Qur'anic terms already discussed above, the Qur'anic concepts of *kufr/shirk* are rethought by Esack in a simi-lar manner and are linked to issues of the Qur'anically intimate relation-ship between doctrine and ideology, i.e., orthodoxy and orthopraxy;[19] its sociohistorical boundedness and a prior recognition of yet willful rejection of the acknowledgment of God's unity and Muhammad's prophethood. He considers that the premodern Muslim exegetes have failed in making a dis-tinction between *kufr* "as an active attitude of individuals (or a collection of individuals) and the socio-religious (and often) ethnic identity of a group." Esack does not deny its doctrinal dimension but calls for a "contemporary application of the term *kufr* and not the mere transference of labels."[20]

Another hermeneutical tool Esack uses to (re)define the Qur'anic view of the religious Other and construct it in an inclusionary manner is to bring to the fore the Qur'nic concept of the symbiotic relationship between orthodoxy and orthopraxy. Forming the view that the Qur'an's primary concern is for the latter and not the former, Esack considers that the basis of Qur'anic pluralism is in what he terms "liberative praxis." Based upon a comprehensively contextualist and holistic *manhaj* in this context he interprets the Qur'anic texts dealing with the concept of *'wilayah*[21] (e.g., 5:51) not as a doctrinal issue but an ideological-political one and argues that "when understood in their historical contexts, [they] offer a radically different perspective to that which a casual and decontextualized reading render" adding that "far from preventing Muslims from entering into relationship of solidarity with the religious Other, they actually facilitate and inspire the progressive Islamists' pursuit of a hermeneutic that accommodates the religious Other and liberative praxis."[22]

Esack also questions the contemporary definitions and understandings of the Qur'anic term *ahl-kitab* as referring to distinct contemporary religious groups. Contextualizing comprehensively, he first notes the situation boundedness of all of the Qur'anic categories in relation to the terms dealing with the religious Other, the gradual shift in understanding in it as to who constitutes such a group and the importance of the ideological dimension in it. Second, he discusses the lack of consensus among classical exegetes in relation to the definition of *ahl-kitab*. In the context of saying the former, he asserts the following:

> The Qur'an naturally dealt only with the behaviour and the beliefs of those of the people of the Book with whom the early Muslim community were in actual social contact. To employ the Qur'anic category of the people of the Book in a generalized manner of simplistic identification of all Jews and Christians in contemporary society is to avoid the historical realities of Medinian society, as well as the theological diversity among both the earlier and contemporary Christian and Jews. To avoid such an unjust generalization, therefore, requires a clear idea from their sources of their beliefs, as well as many nuances, that characterized the various communities encountered by the early Muslims.[23]

In this regard, we may also note the view of Abu Zayd, who maintains that one major characteristic of Qur'anic discourse that of negotiation, an inclusionary mode of discourse, applies to the *ahl al-kitab*. In fact, he argues that Qur'anic discourse does not repudiate the scriptures of Jews and Christians, only the Jews' and Christians' understanding and explanation of them. The exclusivist mode of Qur'anic discourse, Abu Zayd maintains further, only applies to the *mushrikun, i.e.* the Arab polytheists.[24]

Shahrur's distinction between al-islam and al-iman follows closely to that of the work of Esack. However it has a number of novel aspects on which I will focus here. Shahrur, based on his linguistic principle of nonsynonymy of words in the Al-Kitab, which itself is derived though a thematico-holistic approach it, and the philosophical principle of evolution of religious thought considers that the only two prerequisites of belonging to a group of people the Al-Kitab refers to as "muslims," (i.e., those who possess the quality of al-islam) and thus attain religious salvation, are the belief in God and the Last Day and doing what is righteous (al 'amal al-salih). However, "mu'mins" or those who have al-iman, are those who have a specific religious belief as well as particularistic ethics based on this belief, which is traced back to Prophet Muhammad. He terms the former Muslim-Assenters and the former Muslim Believers. Furthermore, Shahrur, on the basis of a thematico-holistic approach to Revelation, considers al-islam to be a manifestation of the universalist urreligion of din al-hanif, or the universalist religion and ethics that coincides with the natural predisposition of not only the humanity but the entire universe. The relationship between al-islam and al-iman is summarized by Shahrur as having the following characteristics: al-islam always takes precedents over al-iman; they mean two different types of faith; divine reward is given to both types of believers, i.e., muslims as well as mu'mins; the term al-iman is always linked to a relationship with a specific messenger; and al-iman is a specific type of piety. He goes on to assert that what traditionally have been understood to be the pillars of al-islam such as the testimony of faith, paying of zakat, performance of hajj, and daily prayers, in addition to the Qur'anic principles of consultation and fighting in the way of God, are in actual fact the pillars of al-iman.

Importantly, Shahrur also makes a distinction between two types of kufr. One type of kufr exists in the sphere of al-iman and the other in the realm of al-islam. Whereas the latter negates the minimal prerequisites of al-islam, the former rejects the belief in the Prophethood of Muhammad and in Al-Kitab being of Divine origin. He then goes on to state that for someone to be branded a kafir his/her disbelief must be expressed:

> in deliberate, fully articulate and publicly stated views by which disbelievers antipathetically oppose either kind of faith.

Based on the above Shahrur concludes that some but no all muslims can indeed be mu'mins and importantly that religious salvation is not restricted to the sociohistorical community of Prophet Muhammad.[25]

We will now consider some examples that the progressive Muslim employ, based upon its interpretational model, to regard religious pluralism as the normative paradigm of the Qur'an-Sunna teachings:[26]

> Let there be no compulsion in religion. Truth stands out clear from error; whoever rejects evil and believes in Allah hath grasped the trust worthiest handhold that never breaks. And Allah heareth and knoweth all things. (2:256)
>
> If their spurning is hard on thy mind yet if thou wert able to seek a tunnel in the ground or a ladder to the skies and bring them a Sign (what good?). If it were Allah's will He could gather them together unto true guidance: so be not thou amongst those who are swayed by ignorance (and impatience)! (6:35)
>
> To thee We sent the Scripture in truth confirming the scripture that came before it and guarding it in safety; so judge between them by what Allah hath revealed and follow not their vain desires diverging from the truth that hath come to thee. To each among you have We prescribed a Law and an Open Way. If Allah had so willed He would have made you a single people but (His plan is) to test you in what He hath given you: so strive as in a race in all virtues. The goal of you all is to Allah; it is He that will show you the truth of the matters in which ye dispute. (5:48)
>
> If it had been the Lord's Will they would all have believed all who are on earth! Wilt thou then compel mankind against their will to believe! (10:99)
>
> (They are) those who have been expelled from their homes in defiance have right (for no cause) except that they say "Our Lord is Allah." Did not Allah check one set of people by means of another there would surely have been pulled down monasteries churches synagogues and mosques in which the name of Allah is commemorated in abundant measure? Allah will certainly aid those who aid His (cause); for verily Allah is Full of Strength Exalted in Might (Able to enforce His Will). (49:13)
>
> Those who believe (in the Qur'an) and those who follow the Jewish (Scriptures) and the Christians and the Sabians and who believe in Allah and the last day and work righteousness shall have their reward with their Lord; on them shall be no fear nor shall they grieve. (2:62)
>
> Those who believe (in the Qur'an) those who follow the Jewish (Scriptures) and the Sabians and the Christians any who believe in Allah and the Last Day and work righteousness on them shall be no fear nor shall they grieve. (5:69)
>
> Those who believe (in the Qur'an) those who follow the Jewish (scriptures) and the Sabians Christians Magians and Polytheists Allah will judge between them on the Day of Judgment: for Allah is witness of all things. (22:17)

hadith:

> By God, I am the messenger of God and I do not know what God will do with me.

> Previous prophets and I are like a man who built a house, set it right and made it comely except for one brick, so that people said when passing by the house, "How lovely this house would be if it were not for that brick." I [i.e., Muhammad] am that brick and the seal of the prophets.

For example, a contemporary Syrian scholar Al-Habash, basing himself on a thematic-holistic approach to the above given Qur'anic and hadith evidence[27] argues that the Islamic revelation came to confirm and not abrogate previous prophecy and that non-Muslims can attain salvation though their own religions.[28]

Based on the hermeneutical principles outlined in the previous chapter, the above given Qur'anic verses are viewed as being hermeneutically superior to any other Qur'an-Sunna/hadith evidence, and as forming the foundation of the Islamic perspective on the issue of faith. They are also invoked to argue that the "necessity of diversity" is intended by God and is a sign of His wisdom and will. Furthermore, progressive Muslims subscribe to the view that, as Qur'an 22:17 suggests, the ultimate arbiter in matters of belief/unbelief is God, not human beings. In this context, El-Fadl writes:

> Moderates[29] argue that not only does the Qur'an endorse principle of diversity, but it also presents human beings with a formidable challenge, and that is to know each-other [Qur'an, 49:13]. In the Qur'anic framework, diversity is not an ailment or evil. Diversity is part of the purpose of creation, and it reaffirms the richness of divine. The stated Divine goal of getting to know one another places an obligation upon Muslims to cooperate and work towards specified goals with Muslims and non Muslims alike...In addition to the obligation of tolerance, the Qur'an obliges people to work together in pursuit of goodness.[30]

Concluding his discussion on the Qur'an's approach to the religious Other, Esack similarly asserts that the Qur'an, proceeding from the premise that the notion of inclusiveness is superior to that of exclusiveness, the religious Other is recognized on the basis of certain principals such as struggle for justice, righteous conduct and competing in goodness and not their acceptance of a reified Islam and Muhammad's prophethood.[31]

As such, Progressive Muslims are of the view that religious pluralism is divinely willed and is central to the Qur'an's vision of society giving salvational significance to all human communities.[32] Thus, unlike the NTS, progressive Muslims construct a concept of a "Believer," which encompasses the belief of those who are not part of the socioreligious and historic community of the followers of Prophet Muhammad.

How are the features of the progressive Muslim *manhaj* employed in order to develop a progressive Muslim version of a religiously ideal "Muslim Woman" concept?

PART TWO: A Progressive Muslims' Religiously Ideal "Muslim Woman" Concept

Progressive Muslims' View of the Nature of the Female Sexuality

Progressive Muslims' view maintains that the question of the NTS concept of female gender status and role in society, including that of female sexuality is socioculturally contingent and tainted.[33] Thus, they reject the classical view of the inherently active female sexuality and the concept of the female body being innately morally corrupting as discussed in the fourth chapter. They also consider the NTS conceptual linking of women to the notion of causing social chaos (*fitna*) is based on flawed assumptions concerning the nature of female (and by implication male) sexuality. The misogynistic hadith evidence outlined in the fourth chapter on which this view of female gender and sexuality is based is considered essentially as remnants of the patriarchal nature of the interpretative communities in the past echoing the view of Bellamy that the "sexual ethics in Islam" were worked out by men."[34] Ashraf in this context notes the following:

> Progressive Muslims have long argued that it is not religion but the patriarchal interpretation and implementation of the Quran that have kept women oppressed.[35]

A detailed and systematic discussion on the issue of the nature of female sexuality and gender from the progressive Muslims *manhaj* is that of Barlas. Employing the full array of the progressive Muslims methodological tools outlined above, especially the contextualist and thematico-holistic approach to the interpretation of the Qur'an and Sunna and the notion of an ethicoreligious values-based approach to Qur'anic interpretation as its most hermeneutically powerful tool, Barlas argues that the Qur'an does not only endow humans with a fixed nature but that is also considers males and females to have essentially the same sexual natures (30:21; 24:26). She highlights the Qur'an's emphasis on the ethicomoral equality before God (such as 33:35) to argue that Qur'an:

> Does not distinguish between the moral and social praxis of men and women, hold[ing] them to the same standards, and judges them on the basis of the same criteria...does not ascribe a particular type of sexual identity, drive or proclivity for certain types of behaviours to

either sex... or does not advocate either the idea of a sexually corrupt or passive female nature or a polymorphously perverse or aberrant male sexuality.[36]

She further maintains that the Qur'anic concern with bodily modesty is based on the view of the body, male or female, as being erotic or sexed not with the purely pudendal female body per se as conceptualized by the mainstream premodern and modern classical Islamic scholarship.[37] Using the same *manhaj* outlined in this section, Barlas argues further that the Qur'an does not define men or women in certain absolute, unique terms apart from recognizing sexual specificity of female and male bodies. She concludes by asserting that "whatever ideas Muslims may have of women and their bodies and of sex and sexual differentiation, the Qur'an itself does not suggest that sex or sexual differences are a determinant of moral personality, gender roles or inequality."[38]

Progressive Muslims' View of the "Muslim Woman's" Position in Broader Society/Public Sphere, Especially the Purpose and Function of The Veiling, Women's Seclusion and Gender Segregation

The Qur'an-hadith evidence used by classical and NTS approaches to interpretation of Qur'ano-Sunnaic indicants to justify the practices of veiling, seclusion, and segregation of sexes outlined above is interpreted significantly differently by progressive Muslims. They do so by taking recourse to methodological tools such as the comprehensive contextualization of the normative sources' legislative dimension; a hermeneutical privileging of ethical objectivism over legalistic expression of the Will of God; the thematico-corroborative approach to textual evidence and the purpose- (*maqasid*) and ethicoreligious values-based approach to interpretation of Qur'ano-Sunnaic teachings as outlined in the previous parts of the chapter.

I. 'Awra and Veiling

A very good example of the utilization of several of these interpretational tools in reference to the issue of veiling that characterizing progressive Muslims' *manhaj* is found in Barlas with regards to the Qur'anic verse pertaining to the dress code for women (33:59–60).

Taking into account the "occasion of this particular revelation" (one facet of the principle of contextualization mentioned above) and apart from arguing that these verses are specific rather than general in nature (employing the above mentioned principal of distinguishing between universal and contingent Qur'anic elements), thus are to be seen in the context of another Qur'anic verse (24:30–31).[39] Moreover, she opines that forcing "moral praxis upon a person " is contrary to the larger Qur'anic attitude (thereby employing the principles of thematico-holistic as well as ethico-objective *manhaj*); she goes on to contextualize this verse by saying that a *jilbab* served the purpose of recognition/protection ("be known and not molested"—in the words of the Qur'an) of women from the still evident *jahili* mental attitude prevalent among the "hypocrites in whose hearts is disease" as the Qur'an puts it. Barlas extends this line of thought by saying that:

> [In] mandating the jilbab, then, the Qur'an explicitly connects it to a slave-owning society in which sexual abuse by non-Muslim men was normative, and its purpose was to distinguish free, believing women from slaves, who were presumed by jahili men to be non-believers and thus fair game. Only in a slave -owning jahili society, then, does the jilbab signify sexual non-availability, and only then if Jahili men were willing to invest in such a meaning (emphasis hers).[40]

Barlas further argues that "conservative" interpretations not only fail to distinguish between the specific nature of 33:59–60 and the general nature of 24:30–31 but also that their interpretations based upon unwarranted generalization and dehistorization of the 33:59–60 in addition to "subverting their [verses'] openly stated intent and purpose."[41]

Similarly, El-Fadl, in his analysis of the verse 33:59–60 after scanning the views of the early Muslim jurists on the interpretations of these verses, echoes the sentiments of Barlas, and points to the essential function of the *jilbab* as a marker of distinction between free and slave women. Additionally, taking recourse to what I termed above comprehensive contextualization of the Qur'anic revelatory milieu and the socially and culturally acceptable norms prevalent in the contemporary society, El-Fadl argues that slave women according to these early jurists, for example, were not required to cover their hair, neck, arms, and even, according to some, chest and had different *'awra* requirements applying to them to that of the free women whose *'awra* according to majority of jurists included the whole body except, generally speaking, the hands, face, and feet. He, therefore, concludes that the *jilbab* constitutes a call for modesty and mandates the covering of legs or the bosom (but not hair). El-Fadl further argues that based upon this distinction, it was the social norms that dictated the *'awra* norms.

In this context he maintains,

> What is the basis for this distinction? Is the hair, arms, or chest of a slave girl less capable of inciting seduction than that of a free woman? The response cannot be in the affirmative: the body parts of a slave girl are no less enticing than their counterparts in a free woman. The response largely depends on social norms. The social norms of the time did not consider it immodest for slave-girls to leave their hair uncovered, while it was considered shameful for a free woman not to have jilbab that would cover her body and perhaps a part of their hair.[42]

As a result of his comprehensive contextualization, El-Fadl and Barlas deduce, from 33:59–60, a general principle of call for modesty and a principle of safe conduct. Hence their scholarship epitomizes an objective and ethicoreligious-based *manhaj*.

El-Fadl's and Shahrur's analysis of 24:30–31 is another example of a multifaceted approach to interpretation anchored in comprehensive contextualization and an aims or values-based *manhaj*. Starting with an etymological and philological analyses of the phrase *wal yadribina bi khumurihinna 'ala juyubihinna*, El Fadl argues that this verse calls for women to cover their bosom area (*juyub*) with their head cloths (*khumur,sg. khimar*). He avers further that a likely reason for this is the fact that in pre-Islamic times, the *khimar* worn by women on the neck was thrown backward leaving the head and chest exposed and that this verse instructs "that the piece of cloth normally worn on the head or neck to be made to cover the bosom or to descend down to the point of touching the cloth." He also points out that Qur'anic commentators had often mentioned that women in Mecca and Medina were in habit of exposing all or most of their chests, even if their hair was covered and that this revelation quit possibly calls upon women to cover their chests. El-Fadl also argues that although the verse under consideration does not explicitly require the covering of hair, it is possible that it assumes so. Moreover, he also includes into his analyses other parts of the verse such as the phrase *illa ma dhahara minha* (that which normally appears) and argues that the purpose of this Qur'anic phrase allows for accommodation of various customs and social standards that may have different notions of propriety and modesty as acknowledged in the principles of Islamic jurisprudence under the name of *'urf/ada* (customary practice). His examination of this verse includes the aims-based interpretational orientation according to which the juristic principal of the removal of hardship needs to be balanced against the requirements for modesty and that what constitutes hardship is to be decided by women and not men.[43] Shahrur employs his novel linguistic methodology (to keywords such as *hijab, juyub* and *zina, zawj,ba'l, ar-rijal, an-nisa*), the theory of limits with comprehensive contextualization, a thematico-holistic and a values-based *manhaj* to argue that women's (and men's) dress is primarily culturally conditioned and not a question of haram and halal, and that women need not cover their heads in front of non-mahram men.[44]

With reference to the hadith employed to justify the normative nature of veiling for women El-Fadl, upon analyses all of the version of the hadith (thematico-holistic approach) points to not only the questionable authenticity of the hadith even by the criteria of classical *ahadith* criticism but also to the existence of other hadith evidence that narrates that women of Medina responded to the Qur'anic verses regarding veiling by covering of their bosoms and not their hair or face.[45] Of course, progressive Muslims hadith *independent* concept of Sunna and the employment of postclassical *ulum-ul-hadith* methods discussed in the previous chapter can also be applied in this case to establish that veiling does not constitute a part of normative Qur'an-Sunna teachings.

Gender Segregation and Seclusion of Women:

A similar array of hermeneutical tools to that of veiling is used by progressive Muslim theoreticians to question the embedded view of the necessity and legitimacy of the practice of gender segregation and the seclusion of women in the public sphere. These include comprehensive contextualization, the differentiation between Hadith and Sunna and the hermeneutically privileging of the ethicoreligious values-based Qur'an-Sunna hermeneutic.

For example, comprehensive contextualization and making of the distinction between universal and contingent/specific Qur'anic injunctions is evident in the progressive Muslims' analysis of the Qur'anic verse (33:53) that is utilized by NTS scholars to advocate for the normative nature of gender segregation. According to progressive Muslim thought this verse is not only specific to the Prophet's wives but was a result of a particular incident as evident by its occasion of revelation and is not to be applied universally.[46] Furthermore, again relying on the methodological principals of comprehensive contextualization and a thematio-holistic approach to interpretation, as far as gender segregation and attitude to women in public spaces is concerned, progressive Muslims point to the historical fact that during the early Muslim community in Medina while the Prophet was alive, as testified by a large number of traditions and on the basis of historical evidence of the Prophet's *sira* (i.e., life), women lead a very active social life. Progressive Muslims point to a number of widespread social practices that were women inclusive. For example, this includes the prevalent practice of women attending the mosque; the idea that men who came late to the congregational prayer would pray behind women and their prayers would be considered valid; the nonexistence of a physical barrier in the Prophet's mosque that would separate woman and men and, importantly, the evidence that some early Muslim jurists maintained that a physical barrier between men and women during the prayer would invalidate women's prayers.[47]

The in the fourth chapter given *ahad hadith* evidence used by the NTS scholarship to argue for the normative character of gender segregation is interpreted away by progressive Muslim in the context of the more systematic and corroborative historical evidence (thematico-holistic approach) and by rendering the practice contrary to the established practice at the time of the Prophet (distinction between Sunna and hadith)[48]. As such these hadith are considered not to be in accordance with Sunnaic teachings but reflecting the patriarchal sociocultural context within which Islamic legal thought developed and subsequently became canonized. Additionally, based progressive Muslims consider the institution of gender segregation to be a later introduced practice essentially entrenching itself only at the time of the Abbasid caliphate.[49]

Based on the above features of the Progressive Muslim *manhaj* practices of seclusion of women, segregation, and that of veiling are not considered normative parts of a religiously ideal "Muslim Woman" concept.

Progressive Muslims' View of Spousal Rights and Obligations and the Purpose of Marriage

Progressive Muslims reject a number of assumptions that inform the NTS view concerning the nature of gender equality, especially in the context of marriage and its purpose. As discussed in the fourth chapter, by developing a theory of aggressive and sociomorally corrupting nature of female sexuality, the classical Islamic scholarship depicted women as essentially *sexual* rather then *social* beings. Progressive Muslims consider that this view was formulated based on the fact that socially and culturally gender inequality was taken as, a priori, matter of principle, and as a natural order of things.[50] Progressive Muslims also argue that these views were based upon a presupposition that woman's biology determined her destiny as well as on a downright completely distinct theory of gender roles.[51] Progressive Muslim theoreticians aver that women's rights were only discussed in the context of a marriage contract, which was likened to that of slave contract or an exchange (*bay'*) according to which, in essence, a woman's sexual and reproductive rights are exchanged for her maintenance. Similarly, women's sexuality was considered a commodity.[52] As such progressive Muslims believe that this state of affairs fundamentally shaped questions pertaining to wife's rights to her body/reproductive organs/sex (and by extension mobility) rendering it under the complete authority (*'isma*) of her husband and determining the spousal rights and obligations. As we demonstrated in the fourth chapter, these views can also be linked to NTS interpretational model (*manhaj*) of the Qur'an and Sunna.

Based on their *manhaj* progressive Muslims argue that the presupposition of the patriarchal nature of one *dimension* of the Qur'anic content reflecting its revelatory context in relation to issues concerning society and culture was embedded in a broader process of attenuation and mitigation of the entrenched androcentric nature of the society at the time of revelation and that on this basis a moral trajectory toward a completely gender egalitarian Qur'anic concept in the sociocultural and political realm is possible to be deduced.[53] In this context El-Fadl asserts:

> The thorough and fair-minded researcher would observe that behind every single Qur'anic revelation regarding women was an effort to protect the women from exploitative situations and from situations in which they are treated inequitably. In studying the Qur'an it becomes clear that the Qur'an is educating Muslims how to make incremental but lasting improvements in the condition of women that can only be described as progressive for their time and place.[54]

The in the fifth chapter quoted verses 4:34 and 2:228 that seem to sanction a Qur'anic, androcentric worldview are interpreted by the progressive Muslims based upon this concept of Qur'anic mitigation and evolutionary moral reform. Progressive Muslims' consider the "superiority" and the "protectorship"[55] mentioned in these verses to be functional, socially contingent not inherent in nature as understood by the classical scholarship approaches. To argue for this point progressive Muslim also insist on a complete reading of the verse 4:34[56], which links this protectorship to males' economic role of breadwinners and the overall male-female dynamics of the seventh century Medina.[57] Moreover, in relation to discussing the same Qur'anic verses progressive Muslims that recourse to ethicoreligious oriented Qur'an-Sunah *manhaj* to argue that the genuinely Qur'anic value[58] of "justice" embedded in the overall Qur'anic worldview ought, to be considered as its most hermeneutically privileged tool and that these verses, like any other that pertain to Qur'anic legislative dimension, are to be interpreted in this light. In other words this is another example of the employment of what I term *ethicoreligious values* and *maqasid cum maslaha*–based approach to interpretation of these verses in order to argue against the normative value as advocated by NTS thought.

As far as the misogynist hadith evidence presented in the fourth chapter in relation to the issue of purpose of marriage and the marital rights and responsibilities is concerned, one of the hermeneutical tools taken recourse to by progressive Muslims scholars such as El-Fadl is that of the "authorial enterprise" and "a conscientious pause" to argue that these reports cannot be considered as emanating from the Prophet and do not come under the purview of the teachings of Sunna. Again, this is another instance where a hermeneutical recourse to refer to ethicoreligious and values-oriented *manhaj* is utilized by progressive Muslim scholars to question the normative status of the hadith evidence in question.

Based upon these principles El-Fadl rejects all of the hadith quoted above,[59] advocating segregation, seclusion of women, their linking to the concept of *fitna* and their "removal" from the public spaces and prohibition of gender mixing.[60]

In this context he asserts:

> Quite aside from the issues of technical, chain of transmission-focused authenticity of these traditions, they are indicative of a dynamic and highly negotiative process. In fact I believe that as to the overwhelming majority of traditions dealing with the role of women in society, the role of the Prophet in the authorial enterprise is minimal... [And] that there were too many patriarchal vested interests circulating, advocating and embellishing these types of reports.[61]

An additional methodological tool that is used to dismiss the Sunna compliance of the above misogynist hadith is the fact that progressive Muslims consider Sunna and hadith not to be semantically, etymologically, conceptually and epistemologically identical bodies of knowledge. They argue that the *'ibadah/'amal* elements of Sunna have, in the early period of Islamic thought, been ultimately derived from a particular Qur'an-Sunna hermeneutic rather then later developed *ulum-ul hadith* sciences. According to this view the Sunna compliance or otherwise of a particular hadith is not merely established on the basis of epistemological and methodological constraints and weaknesses inherent in the classical *ulum-ul hadith isnad-* and *rijal*-based sciences but on overall considerations stemming primarily from the *usul-ul-fiqh* sciences. In other words the questions regarding the authenticity/reliability of the transmission are no longer critical in establishing the "value" of the hadith as it its ultimate "applicability" rests on the broader considerations relating to Qur'ano-Sunnaic hermeneutics.[62]

In addition progressive Muslims bring additional Qur'an and hadith evidence to advocate for an alternative understanding of husband-wife dynamic to be more indicative of the Qur'an-Sunna spirit. The representative examples include:

I. Qur'anic verses:
30:21
And among His Signs is this that He created for you mates from among yourselves that ye may dwell in tranquility with them and He has put love and mercy between your (hearts); verily in that are Signs for those who reflect.

7:189
It is He who created you from a single person and made his mate of like nature in order that he might dwell with her (in love).

49:13
O mankind! We created you from a single (pair) of a male and a female and made you into nations and tribes that ye may know each other (not that ye may despise each other). Verily the most honored of you in the sight of Allah is (he who is) the most righteous of you. And Allah has full knowledge and is well acquainted (with all things).

16:97
Whoever works righteousness, man or woman, and has Faith, verily, to him will We give a new Life, a life that is good and pure and We will bestow on such their reward according to the best of their actions.[63]

II. Hadith:
"Women are but sisters (or twin halves) of Men,"
"The best of you are those who behave best to their wives."
and
"The more civil and kind a Muslim is to his wife, the more perfect in faith he is."[64]

On the basis of the above verses, which they consider universal and in accordance with the overall objectives of the Qur'an-Sunna worldview, progressive Muslims argue that the principle of sameness and similarity are the defining characteristics of the spousal relationship that wives and husbands are equal in.[65] For example, Kodir, cites 30:21 and 2:187 to argue that

The Qur'an has outlined several principles that guarantee the achievement of successful marriage. One of these requires that a husband-wife relationship ought to be a joint or two-way relationship in which one side is equal to the other. In such as even and equal relationship, one side acts as a companion who completes the other, with no superiority or inferiority issues involved. The picture of such a harmonious and parallel relationship of husband and wife is portrayed in an extremely beautiful poetic language by the Qur'an as in "your wives are a garment for you and you are a garment for them (Al-Bakarah, 187).[66]

Moreover, the purpose and the goal of marriage, largely conceptualized in classical jurisprudence as a transaction as I argued in the fifth chapter, apart from copulation, is the achievement of the Qur'anic concept of *sakina*, (i.e., serenity and tranquility).[67] Furthermore, progressive Muslims maintain that the only criteria for distinction between *all* people are that of God consciousness and righteousness (*taqwa*). In words of Al-Hibri, "there is no metaphysical, ontological, religious, or ethical primacy for the male over the female."[68] Also for Ashraf Quran (30:33) is the basis for full equality of genders confirmed by the prophets attitude who 'treated women as equals and was very responsive to their thoughts and needs.'[69] As such according to progressive Muslim thought the normative "Muslim Woman" concept is based on a premise that women are fully autonomous, human beings inherently equal to men and that women's religious identity is based upon their level of *taqwa* without it hinging upon their blind obedience or satisfaction of their husband's demands.

In relation to hadith Kodir cites the above given hadith to form the view that a just and good treatment of women was fundamental to the Prophet's mission based on justice and equality.[70]

In summary, progressive Muslims reject the premodern, and in their view, socioculturally tainted view of female sexuality as conceptualized in classical Islamic works. They also dismiss the patriarchally embedded practices of veiling, seclusion, and gender segregation as being normative parts of a religiously ideal "Muslim Woman" construct. Instead progressive Muslims subscribe to the concept of a religiously ideal "Muslim Woman" concept, which is metaphysically, ontologically, religiously, and ethically equal to that of male Muslims by basing themselves on a comprehensively contextualist, thematico-holistic, ethico-religious values, and objectives-based approach to interpretation of Qur'an and Sunna.

Conclusion

The concern of this study has been to explore how on the basis of different *manahij*, and the assumptions that inform them, the two contemporary Islamic schools of thought, NTS and progressive Muslims, conceptualize their respective versions of a religiously ideal "Believer" and "Muslim Woman" concepts. A particular focus of the study was to highlight the crucial importance of the act of interpretation and its underlying methodological, epistemological, and hermeneutical assumptions in the formulation of the NTS and progressive Muslims representation of these concepts. The broader context of the thesis was informed by the contemporary intra-Muslim debates on the issues of religious authenticity, legitimacy, and the authority to speak for, and thus, define the very nature and future of Islam. In this context, I pointed out that the existing scholarship suggested that, due to the forces of globalization and modernization, which favor democratization of religious knowledge and facilitate the fragmentation of religious authority, these debates have intensified with a number of actors who have emerged asserting their right to authoritatively speak on behalf of Muslims and Islam. I also argued that this state of affairs left us with a perplexing phenomenon of "normative Islams," which at times can be mutually exclusive on certain issues. The concepts of a "Believer" and "Muslim Woman," the focus of this study, are two such issues.

In order to situate the intense and highly contested contemporary debates and discourses on the issue of the nature of the Islamic tradition and to show their essential continuity/discontinuity with the experiences of the previous communities of interpretation, the first chapter outlined the broad contours of the historical background behind the debates surrounding the status and the authenticity of the various sources of its legal authority with a particular emphasis on the *madhhab* and *ahl-hadith*-based *manahij*. In particular, I examined the various approaches to the question of the nature and the authenticity of Prophetic authority (Sunna) and its relationship with the hadith and Qur'an bodies of knowledge.

In the second chapter, I situated the NTS community of interpretation in relation to this historical context and argued that the NTS scholars can be considered as the contemporary incarnation of the premodern *ahl-hadith* school of thought in relation to how they conceptualize the concepts of *'ilm*, Salafism, Sunna, and its relative status in relation to the Qur'an and hadith bodies of knowledge, as well as in relation to nontextual sources of knowledge such as *ra'y* and *taqlid*. Furthermore, the NTS school of thought was found to advocate a completely textual legal hermeneutic expressed best in their definition of *ittibaa'* as an unflinching adherence to *sahih* hadith, which in turn is conflated with following the true salafi Qur'an-Sunna *manhaj*. I tried to show that the NTS *manhaj* as identified and characterized by themselves is often unspecific and vague, consisting of amalgamations of Qur'anic verse and *sahih* hadith and at times buttressed with a commentary of classical scholars who themselves espouse the *ahl-hadith manhaj*. Moreover, I attempted to show that the NTS *manhaj* shows no evidence of being consciously grounded in any theory of interpretation. I maintained that the NTS *manhaj* is often disclosed by means of oppositional dialectics where it is contrasted in general terms with "new methodologies of modernist and intellectuals" or that of the *madhahib* or Sufis. Lastly, I noted that one important part of the NTS *manhaj* is their subscription to the concept of *al wala' wa l bara'*, which they consider as is part of the *'aqidah*.

Based on the delineating features of the NTS *manhaj*, a subject matter of the third chapter, the NTS was found to subscribe to very specific concepts of a "Believer" and "Muslim Woman." Based upon their *ahl-hadith salafi* revivalist *manhaj*, I demonstrated in the fifth chapter that, according to the NTS thought, the concept of a Believer was restricted only to the historical Muslim community who recognized the claim of Prophethood of Muhammad, thus forming the view that religious salvation was permanently not to be extended to any other non-Muslim community such as the Jews and the Christians. In the same chapter with respect to the NTS concept of a religiously ideal "Muslim Woman," the study found that such a concept was constructed in relation to that of a secluded and completely veiled Muslim woman whose primary, if not exclusive, functions are considered to be that of a wife and a mother and whose religious duty is to obey her husband at the cost of her religious salvation.

Another community of interpretation within the Islamic tradition that this thesis focused on is that of progressive Muslims. In the fifth chapter, I described important themes underpinning progressive Muslim worldview. In this context, I maintained that progressive Muslim thought and "cosmovision," is best characterized by a number of commitments, ideals, and practices that the adherents of progressive Muslim thought advocate and adhere to. These included a strong commitment to social and gender justice, religious pluralism, and a belief in the inherent dignity of every human being as a carrier of God's spirit. I also historically contextualized and placed progressive Muslim thought in relation to their Western predecessors of the eighteenth and nineteenth century such as the European Romantic intellectuals and, in particular, with respect to the ideas and values of *classical modernists* of the early twentieth century Muslim reformers whose worldview and *manhaj* was most closely related to that of progressive Muslim thought. However, also a number of important differences between the latter and progressive Muslims were noted such as the classical modernists inability to go beyond what was termed "the theological verticalism" of the premodern embedded religious worldview. I also maintained that progressive Muslims consider the nature of the concept of tradition to be dynamic, humanly constructed, a product of many past and present communities of interpretation. Furthermore, I found that the concept of culture-religious authenticity (*asala*) in progressive Muslims thought is not based upon a literal clinging to the *turath*, as in the case of NTS, but on a complex, creative, historical, critical, and serious engagement with it. I argued that this progressive Muslims' consciousness purports to be firmly rooted in usable traditions but is uncompromisingly universal in outlook with the ability to redefine the very meaning of Islam in light of modernity without abandoning the parameters of faith. As such the often employed tradition-modernity dichotomy in the context of discourses pertaining to Islam and Muslims, to which NTS thought was found to subscribe to, is considered as artificial and false by the proponents of progressive Muslim thought. As far as epistemological boundaries and contours of progressive Muslim thought are concerned, it was asserted that they are inclusive of both the premodern traditional Islamic as well as the modern episteme. It was also contended that progressive Muslims consider modernity a result of transcultural and transpolitical intercivilizational processes. As such I maintained that progressive Muslims, subscribe to the view of civilizationally distinct types of modernity. Lastly, I argued that progressive Muslims distance themselves from the metanarratives and universalistic claims of the Enlightenment and that they can be considered as adherents of moderate form of postmodernism. Moreover, it was maintained that progressive Muslims strive for a synthesis between modernity and the inherited Islamic tradition and a cross-cultural dialogue based on equal partnership with the ultimate goal of a culturally polycentric world founded on economic socialism and gender equality.

The delineating features of the progressive Muslim *manhaj*, which constituted the subject matter of the sixth chapter, were found to be characterized as being comprehensively contextualist/historical and holistic in nature, hermeneutically privileging ethicoreligious values of the tradition such as justice and equality over the literalist (or at best semi-contextualist) hermeneutic embodied by the NTS *manhaj* and endorsing the view present in the formative period of Muslim thought of not conceptually conflating Sunna and hadith bodies of knowledge. Based upon this *manhaj,* I attempted to show, in the seventh chapter, that the progressive Muslims do not restrict the concept of a "Believer" to the historical, reified community of Muslims and extend and recognize salvific plurality as part of the Qur'an's and Prophet's normative teachings and with respect to their normative religiously ideal "Muslim Woman" concept I asserted that progressive Muslims do not consider the practices of veiling, seclusion of women, gender segregation, and husband's religiously sanctioned dominion over his wife to be the part of the religiously normative "Muslim Woman" concept. Instead, I contended that they promote and advocate an alternative concept that highlights women's complete autonomy and their full metaphysical, ontological, ethical, religious, moral, and sociopolitical agency vis-à-vis the men.

I would like to conclude my study with one last idea regarding the importance of the study.

In the second chapter, I briefly pointed to the fact that the forces of modernization and globalization have ushered a new era in which fragmentation of religious authority and democratization of religious knowledge have resulted in a proliferation of the debates on the very nature of Islam. Furthermore, I alluded to the literature that has detected the increased importance the competing versions of "normative Islams" based on variant conceptualizations and interpretations of the primary sources of the Islamic worldviews are playing in the battlefield for the heart and the minds of Muslims as espoused by a number of different Muslim groups and schools of thought. Although occurring at a much larger scale this contemporary situation in terms of its interpretational fluidity and vibrancy as well as its highly contested nature is somewhat reminiscent, of that of the time of the Prophet himself.[1] The continuing importance of studies examining this contested nature of the Islamic tradition dynamic and rather than historical roots is aptly summarized with the following words of Afsaruddin.

> For the believing Muslim, this historical-hermeneutic project remains a worthwhile and even urgent today. Given the fact that Islam's formative period remains contested among many, reclamation of this past in a responsible and historically defensible way must remain part and parcel of every contemporary reformist project that wishes to gain broad legitimacy and acceptance...this project of reclamation is being done more credibly today by those we have termed "modernist" and/or "reformist" Muslims (called "liberal" or "moderate" by others) than by the hard-line Islamists. These modernists have imbibed more than a drop of their illustrious forbearers'

penchant for robust faith, creative thinking, and fidelity to core principles
of their religion. In contrast, the illiberal and radical Islamists, for all their
protestations to the contrary, have to a large degree undermined these core
principles and betrayed the legacy of the earliest Muslims in their nihilistic
quest for political power.[2]

Similarly, El-Fadl argues that the future of Islam as far as Muslims go, for
the next few generations will be defined by two broadly defined approaches
or schools of thought he refers to as modernists and puritans. He goes on to
say that question of interpretation will play an increasingly important part
in terms of which one of these will set root among the contemporary and
future generations of Muslims.[3] It is hoped that this study has shed some
light on this problem and has contributed to these debates in a constructive manner.

Notes

INTRODUCTION

1. Throughout the study the word manhaj/manahij will be used in the sense of interpretational assumptions governing certain methodologies of interpretation of the Qur'an and Sunna, especially in the field of Islamic legal theory (*usul-ul-fiqh*) and Qur'anic hermeneutics.
2. See among many J. Esposito and D. Mogahed, *Who Speaks for Islam? What a Billion Muslims Really Think* (Gallup Press, 2008).
3. S. Allievi and J. Nielsen, ed., *Muslim Networks and Transnational Communities in and across Europe* (Leiden: Brill, 2003); Also the special issue in *The Muslim World* 96, no. 4, Frank Peter and Elena Arigita, ed., "Authorizing Islam in Europe" (2006).
4. A. Duderija, Literature Review on religious identity construction in the context of being a new immigrant minority religion: "The Case of Western Muslims," *Journal of Immigrants and Minorities* 25, no. 2, (2007):141–162.
5. D. F. Eickelman and J. Piscatory, *Muslim Politics* (Princeton, NJ: Princeton University Press, 1996).
6. M. Mamdani, *Good* Muslim, Bad Muslim: *America, the Cold War, and the Roots of Terror* (New York: Pantheon Book, 2004).
7. What I mean by the term *communities of interpretation* will be explained in the main text below.
8. A. Saeed, "Trends in Contemporary Islam: A Preliminary Attempt at a Classification," *The Muslim World* 97, no. 3 (2007): 395–404.
9. M. Sharify-Funk, *Encountering the Transnational: Women, Islam, and the Politics of Interpretation* (Aldershot: Ashgate, 2008), 23, 38.
10. Sharify-Funk, *Encountering the Transnational.*
11. Ibid., 21.
12. The spelling of the names and the books of NTS scholars consulted in this study will be kept as they appear in the NTS literature and on their web sites.
13. Based on my review of NTS literature, I noticed that there is a certain reluctance on behalf of Western-based NTS scholars to write books on *manhaj*.
14. On the link between theology and legal theory, see A. Emon, *Islamic Natural Law Theories* (New York: Oxford University Press, 2010).

15. F. Hussein, "The Ideal and Contextual Realities of Muslim Women," in F.Hussein, ed., *Muslim Women* (London: Croom Helm, 1984), 3–6.

16. M. Cooke, "Deploying the 'Muslimwoman,'" *Journal of Feminist Studies in Religion* 24, no. 1 (2008): 91–119. Also see the responses to this article by leading contemporary Muslim "feminists" in the same issue.

17. Ibid., 91–92.

18. A. Barlas, *Believing Women in Islam: Unreading Patriarchal Interpretations of the Qur'an* (Austin: University of Texas Press, 2002); A. Wadud, *Qur'an and Woman: Rereading the Sacred Text from a Woman's Perspective*, 2nd ed., (Oxford: Oxford University Press, 1999).

19. B. Stowasser, "The Status of Women in Early Islam," in F. Hussein, ed., *Muslim Women*, 11–43.

20. L. Al-Faruqi, *Women, Muslim Society and Islam* (Indianapolis, IN: American Trust Publications, 1991), 1–17; Stowasser, "The Status of Women in Early Islam," 11–43;

21. See A. Duderija, "Identifying Factors Determining Religious Identity Constructions among Western born Muslims," 371–400.

22. Hussein, *Muslim Women*, 1.

23. C. Kurzman (ed.), *Liberal Islam: A Sourcebook* (Oxford: Oxford University Press, 1998), 5.

24. K. El Fadl, *Speaking in God's Name: Islamic Law, Authority and Women* (Oxford: Oneworld, 2001), 122–125.

25. For example, I will argue that Shaikh Nasir Al-Albani belongs to the NTS community of interpretation based on his overall Qur'an and Sunna *manhaj* described in detail in Chapter four of this study, and can, thus, be considered as a representative of it, although, unlike the vast majority of NTS scholars, he does not consider the face-veil to be a normative requirement for Muslim women mandated by the Qur'an and the Sunna.

26. Wadud, *The Qur'an and Woman*.

27. F. Rahman, *Islam and Modernity: Transformation of an Intellectual Tradition* (Chicago: University of Chicago Press, 1982).

28. In this context, she again acknowledges her intellectual debt to F. Rahman's double movement theory developed in his "Islam and Modernity," which consists of two steps. The first movement consists of moving from the present situation to the Qur'an to elicit and to arrive systematically at its "general principles, values and long-range objectives'; the second movements entails moving from this derived general principle and apply it to the specific that is to be formulated and realized in the present. Ibid., 5–7.

29. F. Rahman, *Islam*, 2nd ed., Chicago University Press, 1979.

30. Wadud, *Qur'an and Woman*, 1.

31. Ibid, ix–7.

32. Barlas, Believing Women in Islam.

33. Ibid., 203.

34. Ibid., 87.

35. Ibid., 204.

36. Ibid., 205.

37. See notes 20–22

38. Barlas, *Believing Women*, 22–23.

39. A. Saeed's Interpreting the Qur'an: A Contemporary Approach (New York: Routledge, 2006).

40. Barlas, *Believing Women*, 204.

41. M. Arkoun, The Unthought in Contemporary Islamic Thought (London: Saqi Boks, 2002).

42. Fadl, *Speaking in God's Name*, 170–177.

43. U. Eco, *The Role of the Reader: Explorations in the Semiotics of Texts* (Bloomington: University of Indiana Press, 1979), 47–65.

44. El Fadl, *Speaking in God's Name*, 88.

45. F. Esack, *Qur'an, Liberation and Pluralism: An Islamic Perspective of Interreligious Solidarity against Oppression* (Oxford: Oneworld, 1997), 14.

46. These terms will be left deliberately undefined here. A discussion of their meaning will be presented in the seventh chapter.

47. Ibid., 13.

48. Ibid., 15.

49. Here it is noteworthy to point out that Esack has spent several years studying Biblical hermeneutics in Germany in the 1990s.

50. Esack, *Qur'an, Liberation and Pluralism*, 90.

51. Ibid., 97.

52. M. Shahrur, *The Qur'an, Morality and Critical Reason: The Essential Muhammad Shahrur,* trans. Andreas Christman (Leiden: Brill, 2009).

53. Shahrur, as part of his broader linguistic methodology, does not consider the words al-Kitab to mean the same as al-Qur'an. By al-Kitab he actually means the fixed text of the mushaf. To reflect this I will also use the word Al-Kitab instead of the al-Qur'an in this review section of Shahrur's work.

54. M. Iqbal, The Reconstruction of Religious Thought in Islam, Oxford University Press, Humphrey Milford, 1934.

55. Shahrur, *The Qur'an, Morality and Critical Reason.*

56. See his *Mafhūm al-Nass: Dirāsah fī 'Ulūm al-Qur'ān*, Beirut and Cairo 1991, 5th edition 1998.

57. More on this in Chapter Two.

58. Shahrur, *The Qur'an, Morality and Critical Reason*, 16.

59. Shahrur, The Quran,Morality and Critical Reason, 17.

60. Ibid., 72

61. What we precisely mean by this phrase will be extensively dealt with in the second and fourth chapters.

62. Ibid.,pp.101-102.

63. Ibid., 108.

64. E. Fadl, *The Great Theft: Wrestling Islam from the Extremists* (New York: Harper Collins, 2005), 203.

65. On this see Chapter Four.

1   Genealogy of Debates on the Relative Status and the Authenticity of the Various Sources of Legal Authority in the Sunni Islamic Tradition

1. C. Abrahamov, *Islamic Theology: Traditionalism and Rationalism* (Edinburgh: Edinburgh University Press, 1998), vii.
2. I. Abu Rabi'i, *Intellectual Origins of Islamic Resurgence in the Arab World*, (New York: SUNY Press, 1996), 42.
3. M. H. Kamali, "Methodological Issues in Islamic Jurisprudence," *Arab Law Quarterly* 11, no. 1 (1996): 3–33.
4. A. Ahmad, "The Structural Interrelations of Theory and Practice in Islamic Law : A Study of Takhrij al-Furu ala al-Usul Literature" (PhD. Study, Harvard University, 2005), 31.
5. W. Hallaq, *A History of Islamic Legal Theories* (Cambridge, Cambridge University Press, 1997), 82–206.
6. Few Muslim groups, such as the nineteenth and twentieth century *Ahl-i-Qur'an* groups in the subcontinent or proponents of the contemporary Qur'an alone, have rejected the concept of Sunna as being normative because of their rejection of hadith. In their minds these two concepts, as according to the classical Islamic scholarship, were conceptually the same, hence, the rejection of the concept of Sunna as a source of Islamic Law. See D. Brown, *Rethinking Tradition in Modern Islamic Thought* (Cambridge: Cambridge University Press, 1996), 38–39. More on these movements in the main text below.
7. Y. Wahyudi, "The Slogan "Back to the Qur'an and Sunna"—A Comparative Study of the Responses of Hasan Hanafi, Muhammad Abid Al-Jabiri and Nurcholish Madjid" (Ph.D. Study, McGill University, Canada, 2002).
8. A. Al-Azmeh, "The Muslim Canon from Late Antiquity to the Era of Modernism," in A.van der Kooijand, *Canonization and Decanonization,* ed. K.van der Toorn (Leiden: Leiden University Press, 1998), 191–228, 199.
9. F. Rahman, *Revival and Reform in Islam: A Study of Islamic Fundamentalism*, (edited and with an introduction by E.Moosa), Oneworld, Oxford, 2000, 30.
10. W. Madelung, *The Succession to Muhammad* (Cambridge: Cambridge University Press, 1997).
11. Hallaq, *History of Islamic Legal Theories*, 3–7.
12. Rahman, *Revival and Reform*, 30–69.
13. M. Hodgson, *The* Venture of Islam, *Volume 1: The Classical Age of* Islam (Chicago: University of Chicago Press, 1958).
14. E. Dickinson, *The Development of Early Sunnite Hadith Criticism: The Taqdima of Ibn Abi Hatim Al-Razi* (E. J. Brill: Leiden, 2001).
15. A. Duderija, "The Evolution in the Concept of Sunna during the First Four Generations of Muslims in Relation to the Development of the Concept of an Authentic Hadith as Based on Recent Western Scholarship" (peer-reviewed conference paper, unpublished).

16. M. Y. Guraya, "The Concept of Sunna in the Muwatta of Malik B. Anas," (unpublished PhD. study McGill University, 1969), Introduction; cf.U. F. Abd-Allah, Malik's Concept of "Amal in the Light of Maliki Legal Theory" (unpublished Ph.D. Study, University of Chicago, 1978).

17. Journeys undertaken by pious Muslims who wanted to preserve Prophet's words and put them in writing. Also referred to as *rihlah*, the journeys.

18. N. Abbott, "Studies in Arabic Literary Papyri," *Qur'anic commentary and tradition*, Vol. 2, no. 56.

19. W. Hallaq, *The Origins and Evolution of Islamic Law* (Cambridge, Cambridge University Press, 2005), 53. Cf.Ali S.Ali, Tafsir al Ma'thur: The Qur'anic Exegesis of Prophet Muhammad, His Companions and Successors ,Ph.D.Thesis, University of Michigan,1996, 96–97

20. Rahman, *Revival and Reform*, 102–103. Even the recognition of *istihsan* or considering something to be good in and of itself, i.e., based on reason, was either a type of *qiyas* and necessity- *(darura)* based (Hanafism), ijma-based (Hanbalism), or maslaha-based (Malikism). Shafi'is completely reject it because of its reason-based nature. M. H. Kamali, "Istihsan and the Renewal of Islamic Law," http://www.google.com.au/search?hl=en&rlz=1T4IRFA_en AU319AU321&q=madhahib+istihsan&aq=f&aqi=&aql=&oq=.accessed May 24, 2011.

21. Ch. Melchert, "Ibn Mujahid and the Establishment of Seven Qur'anic Readings," *Studia Islamica* 91 (2000): 5–22; For a more complex picture of the *ahl-hadth-ahl-ra'y* divide, see A. Osman, "The History and the Doctrine of the Zahiri Madhhab," (PhD thesis, Princeton, 2010), 106–161.

22. I. Goldziher, *Muslim Studies*, vol.II, trans. C. R. Barber and S. M. Stern (London: George Allen & Unwin Ltd: 1971), 81; J. Schacht, "Ahl-Hadith," in *The Encyclopaedia of Islam*, Volume one (Leiden: E. J. Brill, 1960), 258.

23. Such as in the case of Zahirites or the Hashwiyya, which were often given the epithet Ahl-Hadith.

24. Sh. Jackson, "Literalism, Empiricism, and Induction: Apprehending and Concretizing Islamic Law's Maqâsid al-Sharî," *2006 Mitch. St .L. Rev.*, 1469–1486.

25. M. Abu Zahra, *Tarikh al-Mathahib al-Islamiyyah* (Cairo: Dar al Fikr al-'Arabi, n.d.), 458.

26. Melchert, "Ibn Mujahid," 6.

27. I. Goldziher, *The Zahiris—Their Doctrine and Their History* (Leiden: E. J. Brill, 1971), 3.

28. Ch.Melchert, *The Formation of the Sunni Schools of Law in the Ninth–Tenth Centuries* (Leiden: E. J. Brill, 1997).

29. Goldziher, *The Zahiris*, 3; Hallaq, *The Origins,* 122–28. Hallaq refers to this as the "Great Synthesis".

30. Goldziher, *The Zahiris,* 4–5.

31. Duderija, "The evolution in the canonical Sunni Hadith."

32. Daniel Brown, *Rethinking Tradition in Modern Islamic Thought* (Cambridge: Cambridge University Press, 1996), 20.

33. Brown, *Rethinking Tradition,* 20.

34. A. Zysow, *The Economy of Certainty: An Introduction to the Typology of Islamic Legal Theory* (PhD Dissertation, Harvard University, 1984), Introduction.

35. Souaiaia defines *accretive* in a sense that Islamic law expanded through time through the interaction between the oral discourse with the static Qur'anic enunciations to adapt to changing times and circumstances. A. Souaiaia, *The Function of Orality in Islamic Law and Practices:* Verbalizing Meaning (New York: Edwin Meller Press, 2006), 163.

36. Ibid. Meaning that Islamic Law is neither entirely founded on what Muslims consider as divine scripture nor on the letter of the written documents.

37. Ibid., 164. Meaning that Islamic law was significantly shaped by social, economic, and political forces present during its formative period.

38. Ahmed Souaiaia, *The Function of Orality in Islamic Law and Practices: Verbalizing Meaning* (Lewiston, New York: Edwin Meller Press, 2006).

39. Ibid.

40. W. Hallaq, *Authority, Continuity, and Change in Islamic Law* (Cambridge: Cambridge University Press, 2001), 257.

41. Ibid., 239.

42. Ibid., x–xi.

43. This consensus should not be confused with the later definition of it in form of *ijma'* but should be understood in terms of the agreed living practice constituting Sunna. Cf. W. Hallaq, *The Origins,* 110–112.

44. Brown, *Rethinking Tradition,* 20.

45. One of the reasons for this is the fact that the schools of law gained high prestige in society and awarded a great deal of authority and reverence to their founding fathers. On this see W. Hallaq, *Authority, Continuity, and Change.*

46. Ibid.

47. Brown, *Rethinking Tradition,* 28–29. More on this in the second chapter.

48. J. Robson, "Tradition: Investigation and Classification," *Muslim World* 41 (1951): 98–112, 101

49. A. A. Islahi, *Juristic Differences and How to Resolve Them in an Islamic State,* trans. S.A.Rauf (Lahore: Islamic Publications, 1986), 69–71; Khalīfa Bābakr al-Ḥasan, *al-Ijtihād bi-l-Ra'y fī Madrasat al-Ḥijāz al-Fiqhiyya* (Cairo: Maktabat al-Zahrā', 1997), 266–267.

50. Remaining Qur'anic sciences, such as rhetoric and style or syntax, deal with aspects that are internal to Qur'an itself and largely do not rely on transmitted body of knowledge in form of hadith.

51. I. Goldziher, *Die Richtungen der islamischen Koranauslegung* (Leiden: Brill Press, 1952).

52. See R. Ahmed, "Qur'anic Exegesis and the Classical Tafsir" in E. Karic, *Kur'an u Savremenon Dobu,* (*Qur'an in the Contemporary Context*) (El-Kalem: Bosanski Kulturni Centar, 1997),113–179.

53. Ibid.

54. H. Berg, ed., *Method and Theory in the Study of Islamic Origins* (Leiden: E. J. Brill, 2003).

55. E.g., evaluating the nature of the character of a person or his memory differed from one scholar to another, affecting the level of authenticity of the hadith in question.

56. See S. Guenther, "Assessing the Sources of Classical Arabic Compilations: The Issues of Categories and Methodologies," *Br. J. Middle Eastern Studies* 32, no. 1 (2005): 75–98. This also holds true for the epistemological evaluation of hadith discussed next in the main text.

57. Wheeler Brennon, *Applying the Canon in Islam—The Authorization and Maintenance of Interpretive Reasoning in Hanafi Scholarship* (Albany, NY: SUNY Press, 1996).

58. Zysow, *The Economy of Certainty.*

59. As in the case of divergences inherent in the *muḥaddith*-based methodology there is a range of differences between various schools of thought pertaining to their epistemological value that are in turn based on differences stemming from the very criteria that these methodologies are based on. See Guenther, "Assessing the Sources."

60. Ibn Habban, *al-Ihsan fi taqrib sahih Ibn Habban* vol.1, ed. Sh. Arna'ut (Beirut: Mu'assaset al-Risalah, 1998), 156; M. b. Ja'far al-Kattani, *Nazm al-mutanathir min al-hadith al-mutawatir,* (Beirut: Dar ul-kutub al-'ilmiyya ,1987), 15. W. Hallaq, "The Authenticity of Prophetic Ḥadith-A Pseudo-problem," *Studia Islamica* 99 (1999), 75–90.

61. Guenther, "Assessing the Sources." Here again problems with the standardization of terminology resurface as the definition of a *mutawatir* hadith reached a consensus some time in the ninth century Hijri. Ibid.

62. Zysow, *The Economy of Certainty,* 32–49.

63. This hadith has been related in many hadith collections such as Ibn Hanbal, Bukhari, and Tirmidhi. See N. Al-Abanee, *The Principals of Salafi Methodology,* (Toronto: T.R. O.I.D., 2003), 21n1.

64. See J. A. Haywood, "Al-Suyuti," in *Encyclopedia of Islam,* 12th edition (Leiden: E. J. Brill, 1954–2003), 900–901, 913–916.

65. G. F. Haddad, *Albani and His Friends—A Concise Guide to the Salafi Movement* (Birmingham: Aqsa Publications, 2004), xiii–xiv. Other dates such as 132 AH (until the end of the Umayyad caliphate) are also given.

66. For as more detailed study of the conceptual ambiguity of *as-salafiyya,* see H. Lauziere, "The Construction of Salafiyya: Considering Salafism from the Perspective of Conceptual History," *Int. J. Middle East Stud.* 42 (2010): 369–389.

67. S. A. Mourad, *Early Islam between Myth and History* (Leiden: E. J. Brill, 2006), 9–15 and 199–200. Mourad asserts that an additional reason, which is not of a direct concern to this chapter, behind the recourse to past for purposes of (self) legitimization is that of the sudden spread of Islam resulting in "Muslims' awareness of their distinct identity,along with their exposure to hostile polemics by religious groups in the Near East and Persia, that forced them[Muslims living in that age] to shape Islam's external parameters." Ibid., 9–10.

68. Whether these words can indeed be attributed to Al-Basri is not of crucial importance to our argument since they can be seen as providing an insight

into how the early Muslim community interpreted the events of the first century of the Islamic calendar. Ibid.

69. Cf. Lauziere, "The Construction of Salafiyya."
70. *Sunnism* is defined as any believing adult Muslim who, even for a moment, saw the Prophet. M. Al-Bukhari, *Sahih al-Bukhari, Kitab fada'il al-sahaba,* bab 1.
71. M.S. Mathnee, Critical Reading of Fazrul Rahman's Islamic Methodology in History, M.A. Study, University of Cape Town, 2005.
72. E.Chaumont, "al-Salaf wa'l-Khalaf" 901; cf. Mourad, *Early Islam,* 199.
73. Goldziher, *Muslim Studies,* 31.
74. Chaumont, "al-Salaf wa'l-Khalaf," 901.
75. In this study termed the *madhhab*-based approach.
76. In this study referred to as *ahl hadith manhaj.*
77. Chaumont, "al-Salaf wa'l-Khalaf," 901.
78. More on this in the next chapter.
79. The first hadith is found in Al-Bukhari and Muslim hadith collections and the second one in Al-Tirmidhi collection.
80. Chaumont, "al-Salaf wa'l-Khalaf," 900.
81. Al-Azmeh, "The Muslim Canon," 215–216.
82. A. Al-Azmeh, *Islams and Modernities,* (London:Verso, 1993), 48.
83. Brown, *Rethinking Tradition* , 60–108.
84. M. Arkoun, The Unthought in Contemporary Islamic Thought (London: Saqi Books, 2002).
85. Sh. Jackson, "Taqlid, Legal Scaffolding and the Scope of Legal Injunctions in the Post-Formative Theory: Mutlaq and 'Amm in the Jurisprudence of Shihab al-Din al-Qarafi,'" *Islamic Law and Society* 3, no. 2 (1996): 165–192, 168.
86. Hallaq, *Authority, Continuity, and Change.*
87. Jackson, "Taqlid," 168. Jackson defines "juristic empiricism" as a legal methodology of interpretation which rejects all a priori claims to knowledge of the Islamic law that go beyond and cannot be explicitly documented in the textual sources of the Qur'an and hadith. As a corollary, "juristic empiricism" desires to establish the primacy of texts and to eliminate all extratextual biases, speculations, and presuppositions. Zahiris or the Hashwiyya developed this *manhaj* to their logical extremes. See Sh. Jackson, "Literalism, Empiricism."
88. P. Rudolphs, "Idjtihad and Taqlid in 18th and 19th Century Islam," *Die Welt des Islams* 20 (1980): 131–145, 136.
89. Brown, *Rethinking Tradition,* 21–22.
90. F. Rahman, "Islam: Challenges and Opportunities," in A. T. Welch and P. Cachia, eds., *Islam: Past Influence and Present Challenge,* (Edinbrugh: Edinburgh University Press, 1979), 315–330, 317.
91. Brown, *Rethinking Tradition,* 27–32.
92. Rahman, "Islam: Challenges and Opportunities," 319.
93. B. Haykel, "On the Nature of Salafi Thought and Action," in R. Meijer, ed., *Global Salafism: Islam's New Religious Movement* (New York: Columbia University Press, 2009), 33–51.
94. Rahman, "Islam: Challenges and Opportunities," 317.
95. Brown, *Rethinking Tradition,* 29.

96. Ch. Kurzman, ed., *Modernist Islam, 1840–1940*, (Oxford: Oxford University Press, 2002).

97. M. Kh. Masud, "Islamic Modernism," in M. Kh. Masud, A. Salvatore, and M. Bruinessen, eds. *Islam and Modernity—Key Issues and Debates* (Edinburgh: Edinburgh University Press), 237–261, 257.

98. I. Abu Rabi'i, ed., *The Blackwell Companion to Contemporary Islamic Thought* (Oxford: Blackwell, 2006), 8.

99. Kurzman, *Modernist Islam*, 3–27.

100. M. Bamyeh, "Hermeneutics against Instrumental Reason: National and Post-National Islam in the 20th century," *Third World Quarterly* 29, no. 3 (2008): 555–574, 563.

101. Brown, *Rethinking Tradition*, 32–37.

102. Rudolphs, "Idjtihad," 131.

103. Kurzman, *Modernist Islam*, 4.

104. El-Fadl, *Speaking in God's Name—Islamic Law, Authority and Women* (Oxford: Oneworld, 2003), 174–175.

105. Kh. Abou El-Fadl, "The Ugly Modern and the Modern Ugly: Reclaiming the Beautiful in Islam," in O. Safi, ed., *Progressive Muslims* (Oxford: Oneworld, 2003), 33–78, 55.

106. Rahman, "Islam: Challenges and Opportunities," 320.

107. Kurzman, *Modernist Islam*, 9–14.

108. Brown, *Rethinking Tradition*, 41.

109. Rahman, "Islam: Challenges and Opportunities," 321.

110. Brown, *ReThinkingTradition*, 31.

111. J. Al-Qasimi, *Qawa'id al-tahdith min funun mustalah al-hadith* (Bayrut: Dar Ihya' al-Sunnah al-Nabawiyah, 1979).

112. T. Al-Jaza'iri', *Tawjih al-nazar ila usul al-athar*, ed. 'Abd al-fattah Abu Ghudda, Aleppo, Maktabat al-matbu'at al-Islamiyya, 1995.

113. See, for example, 'Abdallah Al-Ghumari, *Tawjih al-'inaya li-ta'rif 'ilm al-hadith riwaya wa diraya*, ed. Safwat Jawdah Ahmad (Cairo: Maktabat al-Qahira, 2002); Ahmad Al-Ghumari, *Dar 'al –da'f 'an hadith man 'ashiqa fa-'aff*, ed. 'Iyad al-Ghawj, (Cairo: dar al-Imam al-Tirmidhi,1996).

114. Kurzman, *Liberal Islam*, 5–26.

115. Rahman, "Islam: Challenges and Opportunities," 320.

116. Ibid.

117. B. Tibbi, *The Challenge of Fundamentalism—Political Islam and the New World Disorder* (Berkeley: University of California Press, 2002), 30.

118. A. Dahlen, *Islamic Law, Epistemology and Modernity—Legal Philosophy in Contemporary Iran*, (New York: Routledge, 2003),106.

119. M.Gaebel, *Von der Kritik des arabischen Denkens zum panarabischen Aufbruch: Das philosophische und politische Denken Muhammad Abid Gabiris* (New York: Klaus Schwarz Verlag, 1995), 18.

120. Rahman, "Islam: Challenges and Opportunities," 320–322.

121. A similar approach to hadith can be found in the writings of a Israr Ahmad Khan and Amin Ahsan Islahi, contemporary South Asian hadith scholars. In his book *Authentication of Hadith: Redefining the Criteria* (London: IIT,

2010), Dr. Khan considers that a more *matn*-focused criticism of hadith is necessary in the light of the following three principles: a) examining certain hadith in light of Quranic principles and instructions; b) *matn* criticism of hadith in the light of some "highly authentic prophetic hadith" (which he elsewhere describes as sunnah mutawatirah); and c.) reason, p.i–xxiii.

Islahi in his *Mabadi Tadabbur-e- Hadith* (Fundamentals of Hadith Interpretation, trans. T. M.Hashmi (Al-Mawrid: Lahore, 2009) has developed a more elaborate and sophisticated methodology of fundamentals of Hadith interpretation, which consists of the following five fundamental principles of understanding hadith (35–43):

a.)　Five fundamental principles in understanding the hadith:

　　1. all ahadith are to be interpreted in the light of the Quran (citing 42:17,57:25,5:48). Hadith are a branch and Quran is the root
　　　　– Hadith can only explicate the themes of the Quran and therefore must be in accordance with it because whatever the Prophet did or said was always in perfect accordance with the Quran.
　　　　– we should look into the basis of hadith in the Quran and understand it in the light of it.
　　2. hadith are not to be interpreted individually but in the light of the entire corpus of hadith and thematically i.e., part is interpreted in the light of the whole not other way around.
　　3. a mastery of hadith language and terminology is required for their proper understanding.
　　　　– in syntactic and morphological analysis of hadith we need to rely on the judgement of expert grammaticians and lexicographers.
　　4. understanding hadith always requires proper understanding of the instances of specifications and generalizations, situation and context, and the nature of address
　　　　– student of hadith needs to fully appreciate the implications of both the textual and situational context of the hadith
　　5. hadith must be in accordance with (collective) reason and human nature (*fitrah*).

b.)　six additonal principles employed in sifting sound from unsound hadith (44–56):

　　1. a hadith abhorrent to understanding and religious taste of the believers and pious scholars is to be rejected.
　　2. a rare practice which is not in accordance with the customary practice of Muslims will not be accepted
　　3. hadith which contradict the Quran in any manner cannot be acccepted as genuine
　　4. hadith which contradict the well known sunnah (*sunna ma'luma or sunna ma'rufa*) will also be rejected.
　　5. any hadith which is not in accord with reason will be rejected
　　6. any hadith running counter to 'conclusive and definite evidence' is not to be acccepted.

122. M. Al-Ghazalli, *Al-Sunna al-nabawiyya bayna ahl al-fiqh wa ahl-hadith,* 13th edition (Cairo: Dar al-Shuruq, 2005).
123. Ibid., Introduction.
124. Ibid., 14–15.
125. Y. Qaradawi, *Approaching the Sunnah: Comprehension & Controversy* (International Institute of Islamic Thought, 2007).
126. Ibid., 12.
127. Ibid., 91–182.
128. Brown, *Rethinking Tradition,* 42.
129. http://www.ahl-alquran.com/English/main.php, accessed October 15, 2009.
130. Abu Rabi'i, *Intellectual Origins,* 1–62.
131. Ibid., 44.
132. Ibid., 40–62.
133. Ibid.
134. El-Fadl, "The Ugly," 49–55, 50.
135. El-Fadl, "The Ugly," 52.
136. Abd AL Wahhab, *Kitab Al-Tawhid.* An electronic copy of the book in English can be found http://islamicweb.com/beliefs/creed/abdulwahab/, accessed October 16, 2009.
137. On the influence of Ahl-i-Hadith on Wahhabism, see A. Al-Bassam, *'Ulama Najd khilal themaniyat qurun,* vol. 2 (Riyadh: Dar al-Asima), 223.
138. El-Fadl, "The Ugly," 52–62.
139. O. Roy, *Globalized Islam-The Search for the New Ummah* (New York: Columbia University Press, 2004), 233–243.
140. Here defined in the sense of attempts to remould the Islamic tradition with an epistemological break that is without taking recourse to a systematic rethinking of its premodern dimension.

2 NEOTRADITIONAL SALAFISM: ITS MAIN PROPONENTS AND ITS MANHAJ

1. Its synonym would, thus, be Neo-Ahl-hadith Salafism. I decided against the usage of this term since it is very long to use as a descriptor.
2. Taught hadith among others at University of Medina. For more I. M. Al-'Ali, *Muhammad Nasir Al-Din al-Albani: muhaddith al'asr wa nasir al-sunna* (Damascus: dar al Qal'a, 2001).
3. Former Grand Mufti of S. Arabia. For more, see http://www.fatwa-online.com/scholarsbiographies/15thcentury/ibnbaaz.htm, accessed May 25, 2011.
4. Ibid. Taught Religious Fundamentals at the Shar'ah Faculty of Ibn Sa'ud Islamic University, Riyadh. Also a member of the PCIRF.
5. Student of Bin Baz and Al-Albani.
6. Currently he is based in the Bay Area California and teaches Islamic and Arabic Language classes, translated books on fiqh by Middle Eastern NTS

scholars such as Dr. Salih Sadlan's, Professor of Shari'ah at the Islamic University in Riyadh, book titled *Taysir Fiqah.*

7. Obtained postgraduate qualifications from King Saud University in Riyadh in Islamic Theology. Has authored a number of books on *fiqh,* hadith, and *'aqidah,* as well as translated books by salafi *ahl-hadith*-minded scholars such as Ibn Taymiyya and Ibn Jawziya. http://www.bilalphilips.com.

8. Their followers are many and include a number of influential NTS scholars of the present day such as: Ali Abdul Hamid Al-Halabi (Palestinian), Shaykh Ash-Shaqanti (Mauritarinan), Marzuq al-Banna (Egyptian), Abu Bakr Al-Jaziri (Algerian), Fawzee Al-Altharee (Saudi/Kuwait), 'Abdul Qadir al-Arna'oot(Syrian). See O. Roy, *Globalized Islam—The Search for the New Ummah,* New York: Columbia University Press, 2004), 241.

9. See Roy, *Globalized Islam,* 234–243.

10. For a full list of NTS Web sites and their scholars' Web sites visit, http://www.salaf.com/.

11. http://www.usc.edu/dept/MSA/introduction/understandingislam.html.

12. http://www.uh.edu/campus/msa/home.php

13. http://www.qss.org/. Formerly known as *The Salafi Society of North America.*

14. http://qssc.org/

15. http://www.jimas.org/. Also see Roy, *Globalized Islam,* 241–242.

16. For the list, see F. Al-Atharee, *Clarification that the Ahlul-Hadeeth Are the Saved Sect and Victorious Group.* (Toronto: T.R.O.I.D., 2003), 178–182. It ought to be emphasized that the list given includes scholars that do not necessarily fall into the category of *ahl-hadith* scholars as identified by the proponents of NTSm. On this see, G. F. Haddad, *Albani and his Friends—A Concise Guide to the Salafi Movement* (Birmingham: Aqsa Publications, 2004). Additionally, it seems as if Al-Atharee has fallen out of favour with other NTS scholars recently, however, his *manhaj* is identical to the rest of the NTS scholars and his books are available for purchase on their Web sites. For the reason behind this split from the other NTS scholars' point of view, see http://www.siratemustaqeem.com/phpBB/viewtopic.php?f=28&t=4704, accessed January 26, 2011.

17. Teacher in Riyadh and Imam and Khateeb at Masjid 'Aisha bint Abi Bakr in the Urajah area of Riyadh, accessed October 28, http://www.salafitalk.net/st/viewmessages.cfm?Forum=28&Topic=9693, 2009.

18. Abu Khadeejah Abdul-Waahid, trans., *The Book of Forty Hadeeth Regarding the Madhhab of the Salaf* (Birmingham: Minhaaj As-Sunna Publications, 2005).

19. Ibid., 1.

20. Ibid., 24.

21. Ibid.

22. Ibid., 27.

23. M. Zaynoo, *The Methodology of the Saved Sect,* trans. Aboo Nasir 'Abid bin Basheer (London: Invitation to Islam, 1999), 18.

24. Al-Atharee, *Clarification,* 44.

25. Usually considered to be the first three generations of Muslims.

26. B. Baz, *A Statement and Clarification of Al-Salafiyyah: Concepts and Principals,* trans. M. Mohar Ali (Ipswich: Jam'iat Ihyaa Minhaaj Al-Sunna, 2000), 11.

27. Albanee, *The Principals of the Salafee Methodology: An Islamic Manual for Reform* (Toronto: T.R.O.I.D. Publications, 2003), 21–22.

28. M. bin Al-Uthaimeen, A Reply to the Doubts of the Qutubiyah concerning Ascription to Sunna and Salafiyyah, 47, accessed June 30, 2006, www.salafi-publications.com.

29. Ibid, 5.

30. Athar is usually a synonym for hadith; that is, it is a narrative going back to the Prophet but also at times to that of the Companion. *Ahl-hadith* and *ahl-athar* are often used interchangeably.

31. Al-Atharee, *Clarification,* 29.

32. Al-Madkhalle, *The Methodology of Ahlus-Sunna Wal Jamaa'ah: On Criticizing Individuals, Books and Groups,* 44.

33. Ibid.

34. Al-Uthaiymeen, A Reply to the Doubts of the Qutubiyyah *Concerning Ascription to Sunna and Salafiyyah,* www.salafibuplications.com. accessed on of June 30, 2006, 88.

35. M. Al-Majdub, *'Ulama' wa mufakkirun 'araftuhum: al-juz al-awwal* (Cairo: dar al I'tisam, 1980), 290.

36. See A. Ibn Muhammad al-Shamrani, Thabatu mu'allafat al-muhaddith al-kabir al-imam Muhammad Nasir al-Din al-Albani, accessed last January 15, 2011, www.dorar.net,p.17.

37. Sufyan al-Thawri ibn Said (d. 161 A.H.) was a tabi'i Islamic scholar, hafiz, and jurist, founder of the now extinct Thawri madhhab. He was also a hadith compiler.

38. I. Baz, *The Obligation of Acting upon the Sunnah of the Messenger and the Unbelief of Those Who Reject It,* trans. Abu Talhah Dawood (Birmingham: Minhaj As-Sunnah Publications, 2004), 22.

39. Al-Atharee, *Clarification,* 108–111.

40. Al-Albanee, *The Principles,* 81

41. Mainly hadith experts such as Abu Zur'ah ar-Razi (d. 264 A.H.) and As-Asbahani (d. 430 A.H.).

42. This is a standard formula used in front of the actual content of the hadith implying usually oral transmission of knowledge via a chain of narrators reportedly going back to the Prophet or in some cases the Companions only.

43. Al-Madkhalee, *The Methodology,* 193–194.

44. Here he makes a distinction between Ahlul-hadith and Zahiris who differ form the former in their acceptance of only the basic or literal meaning and not what is implied by it.

45. Al-Madkhalee, *The Methodology,* 156–157.

46. Al-Albanee, *The Principles,* 34, 36, 41.

47. Al-Albanee, *The Hadith is Proof Itself in Belief and Laws* (The Daar of Islamic Heritage Publication, 1996).

48. Al-Albanee, *The Principles,* 35–36.

49. M. Zaynoo, *The Methodology of the Saved Sect* (London: Invitation to Islam, 1999), 82.

50. Al-Albanee, *The Principles*, 33–34.

51. Abu Talib al-Makki, Muhammad ibn 'Ali (d. 386/996 in Baghdad). A hadith scholar, Maliki jurist and a Sufi Mystic, set down the foundation of Sufi practices.

52. Al-Madkhalee, *The Methodology*, 182.

53. Al-Albanee, *The Principles*, 26.

54. Bin Baz, *The Obligation*, 6.

55. M. M. Al-A'zami, *Studies in Ḥadīth Methodology and Literature* (Kuala Lumpur: Islamic Book Trust, 2002), 6. Professor Emeritus at King Sa'ud University where he also chaired the department of Islamic Studies. He holds Saudi citizenship.

56. Al-Atharee, *Clarification*, 98–99.

57. R. Al-Madkhalee, *The Status of the People of Hadeeth (the Ahlul-Hadeeth): Their Feats and Praiseworthy Effects in the Religion*, trans. Abu Hakeem Bilal Davis (UK: Salafi Publications, 2001), 7; Al-Atharee, *Clarification*, 29; Zaynoo, *The Methodology of the Saved Sect*, 15.

58. Al-Atharee, *Clarification*, 65; Al-Madkhalle, *The Status* of the People, 37; Zaynoo, *The Methodology of the Saved Sect*, 13.

59. Al-Atharee, *Clarification*, 13.

60. Al-Madkhalee, *The Status* of the People; Al-Atharee, *Clarification*.

61. Abu Zahra, *Ibn Hanbal,* 232.

62. Abu Zahra, *Ibn Hanbal,* 239.

63. Al-Madkhalee, *The Status* of the People, 10.

64. For the full list, see Ibid., 11–12.

65. Al-Atharee, *Clarification*, 178–182.

66. Zaynoo, *The Methodology of the Saved Sect*, 17; Al-Madkhalee, *The Methodology*, 112.

67. For a *madhhab*-based definition of *bid'ah*, see cf. Nuh Ha Mim Keller http://www.masud.co.uk/ISLAM/nuh/bida.htm, accessed November 24, 2010.

68. Report is found in Al-Bukhari's sahih according to which 'Umar approved of an action (uniting people in prayer during the fasting month under one prayer leader), describing it as a good (*bid'ah hasana*) with which he was pleased.

69. G. H. Haddad, http://www.abc.se/~m9783/n/sdb_e.html, accessed May 25. 2010.

70. Ibn Hajar, *Fath al-Bârî* (Beirut: Dar al-Ma'rifa, 1989), 4, 318; cf. Ibn 'Abd al-Salâm, *al-Qawâ'id al-Kubrâ* (Beirut: Dar al-Ma'rifa), 2, 337–339.

71. Al-Uthaymin, *Bid'ah And Their Evil Effects—The Unique Nature of the Perfection Found in the Sharee'ah and the Danger of Innovating into It*, trans. Aboo 'Abd-illaah as-Sayalaanee (Salafi Publications, 1999), 11–16.

72. Al-Atheree, *Clarification*, 32, 71–2.

73. Al-Madkhalee, *The Methodology*, 46.

74. Ar Ruhaylee, quotes Al-Halaby Al- Altharee, a student of Al-Albanee, who endorses the same definition of Sunna as Al-Albanee. See http://www.indonesiaindonesia.com/en/f/6872-liabilities-hold-true-by-sunna-and-prohibition-doing-bid-ah-in-religion/, accessed January 14, 2011.

75. Ibraheem Ibn Am'ir Ar Ruhaylee, Advice to the Youth of Ahlus Sunah, http://abdurrahman.org/family/Advice_to_the_Youth_of_Ahlus_Sunna. pdf, accessed January 14, 2011.
76. N. Al-Albanee, *The Hadith*; A. Al-Dawish, ed., Fatawa al-lajna al-da'ima lil-buhuth al 'ilmiyya wal ifta' (Riyadh: Maktabat al-Ma'arif, 1412), 20, 176.
77. That is either a Qur'anic verse or an "authentic" hadith. See Uthaimeen, *A Reply*, 88.
78. See, for example, Hallaq, *The Origins*.
79. Al-Madanee, *The History of Ahl-Hadith—A Study of the Saved Sect and that It Is The People of Hadeeth*, trans. Aboo 'Ubaidah ibn Basheer (Birmingham: Salafi Publications, 2005), 136.
80. Ibid., 128.
81. Al-Atheree, *Clarification*, 25, 100.
82. Al-Madanee, *The History*, 133.
83. Al-Madanee, *The History*, 28.
84. Bin Baz, *The Obligation*, 23; cf.Albani, *The Hadith*, 88–89
85. AL-Madanee, *The History*, 125.
86. Al-Atharee, *Clarification*, 61, 81, 91.
87. Al-Albanee, *The Principles*, 91. cf. Albani, *The Hadith*, 83–109.
88. Al_Albanee, *The Principles*, 29n1.
89. Al-Atharee, *Clarification*; Al Madkhalee, *The Methodology*.
90. Al-Abanee, *The Principles,* has a section on the exchange between Tantawi the Head of Al-Azhar University and Al-Albanee (78–101). Also these debates can be found on the Internet. One example is http://www.themodernreligion. com/basic/madhab/madhab-debate.htm, accessed October 29, 2009.
91. Zaynoo, *The Methodology*, 15.
92. Ibid., 15–16.
93. Al-Albanee, *The Principles*, 19.
94. Al Atharee, *Clarification*, 45.
95. Therefore not any commentary or analysis.
96. Al-Hadadee, *The Book of Forthy Hadeeth*, 3.
97. i.e., Hadith compilations primarily those compiled in the third, fourth, and fifth century of the Islamic calendar. For some examples of these books, see Al-Atharee, *Clarification*, 184–192.
98. Al-Madanee, *A History*,170; Al-Uthaymeen, *Bida'ah*, 26.
99. Al-Madkhalee, *The Methodology*, 24.
100. Al-Albanee, *The Principles,* 9–10.
101. Zarabozo conflates the concept of Sunna and hadith and follows the *ahl-ha-dith manahj* in relation to the nature and the scope of the concept of Sunna. See his J. Zarabozo, Life, Teaching, *and Influence of Muhammad Ibn Abdul Wahhab* (Riyadh: Ministry of Islamic Affairs, Endowments, Dawah, and Guidance, Kingdom of Saudi Arabia, 2005), 81–82.
102. Zarabozo, *Life,* Teaching, *and Influence,* 106.cf.; I. Baz, *Statement and Clarification of Al-Salafiyyah: Concept and Principles.* trans. M. M. Ali, Jam'iat Ihyaa 'Minhaj Al-Sunnah, (Riyadh:1996),14; Al-Suhaymee, *The Methodology of the Salaf in Aqidah and Its Influence on Muslim Unity,* trans. Aboo Aaliyah Dwight, (New York: Tarbiyyah Publishing, 2002), 73.

103. Zarabozo, *Life, Teaching, and Influence*, 85.
104. Ibid.
105. Ibid.
106. Madkhalee, *The Methodology*, 155.
107. Ibid., 112.
108. M. Qahhani, *Al-Wala' wa'l -Bara' according to the 'aqeedah of the Salaf*, London: Al-Firdous, 1999, 12–19.
109. Madkhalee, *The Methodology*, 155.
110. Al-Madkhalee, *The Methodology*, 112, 26.

3   THE DELINEATING FEATURES OF PREMODERN EMBEDDED MANAHIJ AND THEIR INTERPRETATIONAL IMPLICATIONS

1. K. El-Fadl, "The Place of Ethical Obligations in Islamic Law," 4 *UCLA, J. Islamic and Near E. L.*1 (2005): 23 [1–40].
2. See previous chapter.
3. H. N. Abu Zayd, *Re-thinking the Qur'an—Towards a Humanistic Hermeneutic* (Utrecht: Humanities University Press, 2004), 11; M. Arkoun, "Rethinking Islam Today," in ed. Ch. Kurzman, *Liberal Islam, A Sourcebook* (Oxford: Oxford University Press, 1998), 205–222. A. Souaiaia, "On the Sources of Islamic Law and Practices," *Journal of Law and Religion*. 20, 1 (2004–5): 125–149.
4. Souaiaia, "On the Sources."
5. In the case of the Qur'an, the last official decision closing any discussion on the various versions of the "orthodox" Uthmani codex was made by qadi Ibn Mujahid in the fourth century Hijrah/tenth century A.C.; Arkoun, "Rethinking Islam Today," 214.
6. As based on Arkoun's survey of some 80 categories (*naw'*) pertaining to *ulum-ul*, Qur'an as found in Suyuti's *Itqan*. See M. Arkoun, "Introduction: An Assessment of and Perspectives on the Study of the Qur'an." in *Formation of the Classical Islamic World*, V. 24, ed. I. Conrad (London: Ashgate, 2004), 297–332.
7. B. G. Weiss, *The Spirit of Islamic Law* (Athens: University of Georgia Press, 1998), 38–65.
8. Previous efforts prior to Shafi'i have been characterized by the leading scholars in the field of *usul-ul fiqh* as not systematic. See, for example, Hallaq, *A History of Islamic Legal Theories* (Cambridge: Cambridge University Press, 1997), 1–35.
9. E. Moosa, "The Poetics and Politics of Law after Empire: Reading Women's Rights in the Contestations of Law," in *1 UCLA, J. Islamic & Near E.L.1* (2001–2002): 8 [1–28].
10. Sh. Jackson, "From Prophetic Actions to Constitutional Theory: A Novel Chapter in Medieval Muslim Jurisprudence," *International Journal of Middle Eastern Studies* (1993): 25, 71–90, 78.

11. Jackson, "Fiction and Formalism: Towards a Functional Analysis of Usul Al-Fiqh" in B. Weiss, *Studies in Islamic Legal Theory* (Leiden: E. J. Brill, 2002), 182.

12. J. Auda, *Maqasid al-Shari'ah as Philosophy of Islamic Law* (London: Internation Institute of Islamic Thought, 2008), 229.

13. M. Mumisa, "Toward an African Qur'anic Hermeneutics," *Journal of Qur'anic Studies* (2002): 1, 62–63.

14. D. Bramsen, "Divine Law and Human Understanding: Interpreting Shari'a within Institutions of Ifta'a and Qada'a in Saudi Arabia," (M.A. Thesis, Københavns Universitet, 2007), 76, 85.

15. Mansoor, "The Unpredictability of the Past—Turath and Hermeneutics" (PhD Thesis, University of California, 2000), 219–220.

16. H. N. Abu Zayd, *Politik und Islam: Kritik des Religiösen Diskurses* (Frankfurt: Dipa-Verlag, 1996), 162, author's translation.

17. A. K. Soroush, *The Expansion of Prophetic Experience—Essays on Historicity, Contingency and Plurality in Religion* (Leiden: E. J. Brill, 2009).

18. On this, see P. M. Wright, *Modern Qur'anic Hermeneutics* (PhD Study, Chapell Hill, 2008), Chapters two and three.

19. H. A. Virkler, *Hermeneutics: Principles and Processes of Biblical Interpretation* (Grand Rapids, MI: Baker Book House, 1981).

20. D. S. Ferguson, *Biblical Hermeneutics: An Introduction* (Atlanta, GA: John Knox Press, 1986).

21. Hans-Georg Gadamer, *Truth and Method*, 2nd rev. ed., trans. Joel Weinsheimer and Donald G. Marshall (London: Continuum, 2004), 164.

22. El-Fadl, *Speaking in God's Name—Islamic Law, Authority and Women* (Oxford: Oneworld, 2003), 99.

23. Weiss, *Spirit of Islamic Law*, 53.

24. This is evident in the following statement of Ibn Baz: "Ahl-Sunah wal-jama'a knows Allah's intention or purpose, *muradahu*, of His speech." A. Ibn Baz, *Majmu' fatawa wa-maqalat mutanawwi'a*, Vol. 3, (Riyadh: no publisher), 55. For a more detailed discussion on this issue, see the next section of the chapter below.

25. Bramsen, Divine Law, 75–86.

26. Ibid.,75.

27. M. Sharify-Funk, "From Dichotomies to Dialogues—Trends in Contemporary Islamic Hermeneutics, in ed. A. Abdul Aziz, M. Abu-Nimer, and M. Sharify-Funk, *Contemporary Islam-Dynamic not Static* (New York: Routledge, 2006), 67 [64–80].

28. El-Fadl, *Speaking in God's Name.*

29. Saeed, *Interpreting the Qur'an—Towards a Contemporary Approach* (New York: Routledge, 2006) 103.

30. Jackson, *Fiction and Formalism*, 191.

31. Which is clearly evident in its actual structure and content. See T. Izutsu, *Ethico-Religious Concepts in the Qur'an* (Montreal: McGill University Press, 2002).

32. Soroush, *The Expansion of Prophetic Experience*, 90–123.

33. Saeed, *Interpreting the Qur'an*, 117.

34. K. Ali, *Sexual Ethics and Islam* (Oxford: Oneworld, 2006).

35. Izutsu, *Ethico-Religious Concepts*.

36. S. Younis, "Islamic Legal Hermeneutics: The Context and Adequacy of Interpretation," *Journal of Islamic Studies* (2002): 41–4, 585–615, 597.

37. Ibid. Which was a result of the process of progressive, purposeful unfolding of revelation.

38. Abu Zayd, *Islam und Politik*, 95–96.

39. Ibid.

40. I have referred to these in the context of discussing *ahad hadith* in the first chapter on 34–36.

41. For example, Rippin maintains that the primary function of *asbab* reports was haggadic in nature and that those which could be used for halakhic purposes, generally speaking, were not used in such capacity A. Rippin, "The Function of Asbab al-Nuzul in Qur'anic Exegesis," *Bulletin of the School of Oriental and African Studies* 51 (1988):1–20.

42. Kamali, "Methodological Issues in Islamic Jurisprudence," *Arab Law Quarterly* 11, no. 1 (1996): 9.

43. This part of the article relies heavily on G. H. Hourani, "Ethical Pre-suppositions of the Qur'an," *Muslim World* 70 (Jan. 1980): 1–28.

44. Right or wrong have no objective meaning and their value can vary from person to person.

45. There are real qualities or relations of acts that make them right independent of opinions of people or Revelation.

46. That is, that ethical value terms mean only what is approved or disapproved, commanded, or forbidden by God. In terms of legal theory (*usul-ul-fiqh*) this would translate into a view that all ethicomoral and legal rules must ultimately be derived from prescriptions enunciated by God.

47. Reason is here defined as used in a broad sense as espoused by naturalist and instinctutionist theories of ethics. Hourani, "Ethical Pre-suppositions," 2.

48. And therefore advocate what Hourani terms *complete rationalism*; see Ibid.

49. Hourani terms this *partial rationalism*; see Ibid.

50. Hourani terms this approach *traditionalism*; see ibid.

51. Kamali, "Methodological issues," 5; A. N. Emon, *Islamic Natural Law Theories* (New York: Oxford University Press, 2010).

52. A. Zayd, *Islam und Politik*, 47

53. Weiss, *Spirit of Islamic Law*, 36. A minority of legal theorists theorized about and developed natural Islamic law theories that conferred "ontological authority" on reason, i.e., considered reason to be an authoritative source of normative teachings of Shari'ah. This would include the works of Abu Bakr al-Jassas (d. 370/981), a Hanafi jurist, titled *Usul al-Jassas :al-fusul fi al-Usul*, ed. M.Tamir (Beirut: dar ul-Kutub al-'Ilmiyya, 2000); Al-Qadi 'Abd Al-Jabbar's (d.414/415/1025), a Mu'tazila theologian, *Al-Mughni*, vols. 16, ed. Taha Husayn (Cairo: n.p., 1960:); and Abu al-Husayn al-Basri's, a Mu'tazila jurist, *Al-Mu'tamad fi usul al-Fiqh* (Beirut: Dar al-Kutub al-'Ilmiyya, n.d.).

54. Weiss, *Spirit of Islamic Law*, 37

55. Weiss, *Spirit of Islamic Law*, 53–65; a more detailed discussion on voluntarism in law and ethics will be dealt with in the subsequent parts of this chapter. Cf. Sh. Jackson, "Fiction and Formalism." Jackson uses the term "classical legal formalism" to describe this approach.

56. Weiss, *Spirit of Islamic Law*, 35.

57. I.e. human's and God's perspective.

58. Moosa, "The Poetics and Politics of Law after Empire," 8.

59. M. Al-Attar, *Islamic Ethics: Divine Command Theory in Arabo-Islamic Thought* (New York: Routledge, 2010), xi.

60. See footnote 3.

61. A. Achrati, "Arabic, Qur'anic Speech and Postmodern Language: What the Qur'an Simply Says," *Arabic* 54, no. 2 (2008): 161–203.

62. G. J. H. Gelder, *Beyond the Line: Classical Arabic Literary Critics on the Coherence and Unity of the Poem* (Leiden: E. J. Brill, 1982), 1–14.

63. Z. ibn Awad Al Alma'i, *Dirasat fi at-Tafsir al-Maudu'i li al-Qur'an al-Karim*, Riyadh,1984,18; M.B.Al-Shadr, *Al-Madrasa Al-Qur'aniyya; at-Tafsir al-maudu'I wa at-tafsir al-tajzi fi al-Qur'an al-Karim* (Beiru: Dar at-ta'arruf li al-Matba'a), 7–9.

64. E. Moosa, "Introduction" in F. Rahman, *Revival and Reform in Islam* (Oxford: Oneworld, 2000), 17

65. M. Mir, *Coherence in the Qur'an: A Study of Islahi's Concept of Nazm in Tadabbur–I-Qur'an* (Indianapolis, IN American Trust Publication, 1986).

66. Abdul-Raof, "Conceptual and Textual Chaining in Qur'anic Discourse," *Journal of Qur'anic Studies* 5, no. 2 (2003): 73.

67. Auda, *Maqasid Al-Shari'ah*, 31–33.

68. Soroush, *The Expansion of Prophetic Experience*, 63–90.

69. Abu Zayd, *Islam und Politik*, 92.

70. Kamali, "Methodological Issues," 5.

71. M. Fathi Al-Darini, *Khasa'is al-Tashri al-Islami fi'l Siyasa wa 'l Hikma*, 1987.

72. Hallaq, *A History of Islamic Legal Theories*, 1–36.

73. See Ibid., Chapters 3, 4, and 5.

74. Ibid., especially Chapter 2.

75. i.e., in the presence of any Qur'an-hadith body of evidence.

76. See A. Kamaruddin who examined the methodology of hadith criticism as espoused by one of the leading authorities of NTS thought, Nasiruddin Al-Albani; A. Kamaruddin, "Nasiruddin Al-Albani on Muslim Sahih: A Critical Study of His Method," *Islamic Law and Society* 11, no. 2 (2004).

77. Ibn Habban Al-Busti(d. 354/965), a prominent hadith scholar, considers that the entire corpus of prophetic hadith is indeed *ahad*, as is evident from his following statement: The entirety of the [prophetic] ahadith are ahad reports since there is no report based on the witnesses of two transmitters in all tiers going back to the prophet. Thus it is understood that all ahadith are ahad. Ibn Habban, *al-Ihsan fi taqrib sahih Ibn Habban*. cf. al-Kattani, M. B. J. *Nazm al-mutanathir min al-hadith al-mutawatir*. Beirut: Dar ul-kutub al-'ilmiyya, 1987. See Chapter 1, footnote 57 in this study.

78. B. M. Wheeler, *Applying the Canon in Islam—The Authorization and Maintenance of Interpretive Reasoning in Hanafi Scholarship.* (Albany: SUNY Press, 1996), 47–49.

79. *al-kitab* [Qur'an] *ya'ti bi-'l-jumal yakshifu-ha al-hadith wa-'khtisar tadulla 'alay-hi al-sunna- Ibn Qutayba, Ta'wil Mukhtalif al-Hadith,* ed. M. Z.al-Najjar (Beirut: 1393/1972), 87.

4 NTS Religiously Ideal "Believer" and "Muslim Woman" Concepts

1. Explained later in this section.

2. I.e., the *mushrikun* ("polytheists"), the *munafiqun* ("hypocrites"), and *Ahl-Kitab* ("the People of the Book"—primarily, Jews and Christians).

3. Among many 2:76, 98:1, 2:120.

4. Ambivalence and contextuality are also found in non-Qur'anic elements of the tradition as embodied in various *Hadith* corpora. On Qur'an's ambivalence in relation to the "Other," see M. Maghen, "The Interaction between Islamic Law and Non-Muslims," *Islamic Law and Society*10, no. 3 (2003): 267–275, 268.

5. These accumulated meanings are based on her chronological approach to the investigation of the development of meanings of the concept of Kufr in the Quran.See M.R. Weldmann,The Development of the Concept of Kufr in the Quran, Journal of the American Oriental Society, Vol. 88, No. 3 (Jul. – Sep., 1968), 442–455.

6. Ibid, 443.

7. The Christians had a much smaller numerical presence in Medina. Furthermore, they had much less economic influence. Thus, the Qur'an's "complaints" about Christians pertain primarily to the domain of dogma. J. McAuliffe, *Qur'anic Christians: An Analysis of Classical and Modern Exegesis* (Cambridge: Cambridge University Press, 1991).

8. A group of people in Medina who only superficially became Muslims in order to procure certain benefits but, in reality, supported the enemies of Muslims.

9. W. M. Watt., *Muhammad at Medina* (Oxford: Oxford University Press, 1956), 217.

10. For the analysis of the relevant Qur'anic verses see footnote 5.

11. J. Waardenburg, *Muslims and Others: Relations in Context* (Berlin and New York: Walter de Gruyter, 2003), 99.

12. Y. Friedmann, *Tolerance and Coercion in Islam: Interfaith Relations in the Muslim Tradition* (Cambridge: Cambridge University Press, 2003), 1.

13. K. Zebiri, *Muslims and Christians Face to Face* (Oxford: Oneworld, 1997), chapter 1; F. Donner, *Muhammad and the Believers at the Origins of Islam* (Cambridge, MA and London: Belknap Press, 2010).

14. Such as belief in Allah (One, True God), the previous prophets, the Hereafter, the Day of Judgment.

15. The latter trend being more prominent in the context of Medinan Muslim community.
16. Zebiri, *Muslims and Christians face to face*, chapter 1. Donner, *Muhammad and the Believers*.
17. F. Donner, "From Believers to Muslims: Confessional Self-Identity in the Early Islamic Community. *Al-Abhath* (2002–2003): 12, 9–53, 50–51; Maghen, "The Interaction between Islamic Law and Non-Muslims," 268–269.
18. Donner, *Muhammad and the Believers*, 71.
19. Ibid., 68–74.
20. Friedmann, *Tolerance and Coercion in Islam*, 195.
21. Such as the importance of Jerusalem and the Muslim practice of turning to it in prayer.
22. Waardenburg, *Muslims and Others*, 44. A case in point is that of the change of direction in prayer from Jerusalem to Mecca. Traditions reportedly going back to the Prophet, such as those found in *Sahih Bukhari*, stress largely the distinctiveness and uniqueness of the Islamic religious identity.
23. M. N. Miraly, *The Ethic of Pluralism in the Qur'an and the Prophet's Medina* (Montreal: McGill University Press, 2006), 33.
24. A. Shboul, "Byzantium and the Arabs: The image of the Byzantines as Mirrored in Arabic Literature," in *The Formation of the Classical Islamic World*, Vol. 8, ed. M. Bonner (Ashgate, UK: Variorum, 2004), 242 [235–260].
25. E. Beck. *Die Gestalt des Abraham am Wendepunkt der Entwicklung Muhammads: Analyse von Sure 2* (Paris: Le Muse'on), 65, 73–94, 118(124)–135(141).
26. Waardenburg, *Muslims and Others*, 87–94.
27. Ibid., 106–107.
28. In other words, Qur'anic criticisms of certain practices of Jewish and Christian communities living in seventh-century Hijaz apply to all previous and subsequent Jewish and Christian communities in an ahistorical, decontextualized manner.
29. Here we restrict ourselves with just a number of these verses for the sake of brevity. For additional verses, see M.S. Qahani, *Al-Wala' Wa'l–Bara' according to the 'Aqeedah of the Salaf*, Part 2 (London: Al-Firdous ltd. 1999).
30. In this book Yusuf Ali's translation of the Qur'an is used. Yusuf Ali, The Meaning of the Holy Qur'an, (Maryland: Amana Publications, 1977).
31. See Al-Tabari, *Jami al-bayan 'an tawil ay al-Qur'an*, vol. 4 (Beirut: Dar al-Fikr, 1995); For an example of a non-Muslim work on this, see K.Armstrong, *Muhammad: A Western Attempt to Understand Islam* (London: Victor Gollancz, 1991).
32. M. Lecker, *The 'Constitution of Medina': Muhammad's First Legal Document* (Princeton, NJ: The Darwin Press, 2004).
33. "Verily, this brotherhood of yours is a single brotherhood, and I am your Lord and Cherisher: therefore serve Me (and no other)" (Q 21:92).
34. Miraly, *The Ethic of Pluralism*, 59.
35. Armstrong, *Muhammad*, 183–184
36. Miraly, The Ethic of Pluralism, 47. There are a number of interpretations of the motivations behind the fate of Banu Qurayza and, in particular, of whether

the killings were large scale or restricted to some of the leaders. For two oppos- ing views, see W.N. Arafat, "New Light on the Story of Banu Qurayza and the Jews of Medina," *Journal of the Royal Asiatic Society of Great Britain and Ireland* (1976):100–107. M. J. Kister, "The Massacre of the Banu Quraiza: A Re-examination of a Tradition," *Jerusalem Studies in Arabic and Islam* 8 (1986): 61–96.

37. Kister, "The Massacre of the Banu Quraiza".
38. Miraly, *The Ethic of Pluralism*, 62.
39. Armstrong, *Muhammad*, 207.
40. Esack, *Qur'an, Liberation and Pluralism: An Islamic Perspective of Interreligious Solidarity Against Oppression* (Oxford: Oneworld, 1997), 163.
41. Miraly, *The Ethic of Pluralism*, 39.
42. Ibid. Abu Dawud, Sunnan, available http://www.muslimaccess.com/sunna/ hadeeth/abudawud/index.htm, hadith number 5186. cf. Muslim, *Ṣaḥīḥ*, 5389, accessed May 26, 2011.
43. M. Al-Qahtani received his Masters from the Department of the Umma Al-Qura University in Mecca. His study was titled *Al-Wala' wa'l Bara' (Loyalty and Disassociation) according to the 'Aqeedah of the Salaf* and has been widely circulated both in form of a book as well as on the Internet. It was endorsed by, among others, NTS Saudi Arabian scholars Shaikh A. Razak 'Affifi, a former head of the PCIRF and a member of the Senior Scholars of Saudi Arabia.
44. Qahtani, http://www.scribd.com/doc/17199503/Al-Wala-Wal-Bara-According- to-Salafi-Aqeedah pages here refer to this ebook version, p.88
45. Qahtani, *Al-Wala-Wal-Bara*, 93.
46. Ibn Taymiyya was an influential Muslim theologian. He was and continues to be a highly controversial figure in terms of how his views/scholarship was understood/appropriated and (re)-constructed. His scholarship was particu- larly revived/revised by the Wahhabi movement and used for their purposes. He belonged to the Hanbali school of thought. For more on him, see http:// www.livingislam.org/n/itay_e.html.
47. This claim, has however been disputed by scholars such as Kh. Abou El Fadl. See his *The Search for Beauty in Islam* (Lanham, MD: The University of America Press, 2001).
48. Qahtani, *Al Wala' wa'l Bara'*, 158.
49. 2; 109; 135; 3:72; 3:105.
50. Qahtani, *Al Wala' wa'l Bara'*, 170.
51. Ibn Hazm was a historian, jurist, and theologian who lived in Al-Andalus and belonged to the "literalist" Zahiri school of thought. In his *Kitab al-Fisal* (Detailed Critical Examination) he mounts an attack on all other schools of thought which rely on reason and reason-derived sources of knowledge when interpreting Qur'an and Sunna.
52. Ibn Qayyim was primarily a *muhaddith* and *faqih* of sunna and to a lesser extent a *mufassir*. He belonged to the Hanbali *madhhab*, was a student of Ibn Taymiyya. What was said about Ibn Tamiyya in footnote 44 to a large extent applies to Ibn Qayyim too.

53. At-Tabari was a *mufassir* and a historian. He is the most important source for the early history of Islam because his commentary of the Qur'an, *Jami al-bayan fi ta'wil al-Qur'an* and his *Tarikh al-Rusul wa al-Muluk*, with 30 volumes each, has accumulated and summarized a vast section of traditional material.

54. Qahtani, *Al Wala' wa'l Bara'*, 193–197, 208.

55. Al-Madkhalee, *The Methodology of Ahlus-Sunnah Wal-Jamaa'ah on Criticising Individuals, Books and Groups*, trans. Abu Maryam Isma'eel (Alacron: Al-Ibaanah Publishing, 2005), 30–31.

56. A Maliki scholar who specialized in *fiqh* and hadith. His most notable work of is a twenty-volume *Tafsir al Jami' li-ahkam al-Qur'an*. Some volumes have been translated into English by A. Bewley (London: Dar al Taqwa, 2003).

57. Qahtani, *Al Wala' wa'l Bara'*, 205.

58. They take their priests and their rabbis to be their lords beside Allah. And they take (as their lord) Christ, the son of Mary, yet they were command to worship Allah alone.

59. In blasphemy indeed are those that say that Allah is Christ the son of Mary. Say: "Who then hath the least power against Allah, if His will were to destroy Christ the son of Mary, his mother, and all everyone that is on the earth? For to Allah belongeth the dominion of the heavens and the earth, and all that is between. He createth what He pleaseth. For Allah hath power over all things; They do blaspheme who say: "Allah is Christ the son of Mary." But said Christ: "O Children of Israel! worship Allah, my Lord and your Lord." Whoever joins other gods with Allah, Allah will forbid him the garden, and the Fire will be his abode. There will for the wrong-doers be no one to help.

60. http://www.calgaryislam.com/pdf/current/CA01.pdf, 5–6.

61. Ar Ruhaylee, *Advice to Youth of Ahlus-Sunna*, 1.

62. http://www.calgaryislam.com/pdf/manhaj/MJ19.pdf.

63. http://www.islam-qa.com/en/cat/148/ref/islamqa/10213, accessed April 8, 2011.

64. In this part of the analysis, we have not included verses that address the *kāfirūn* rather than *ahl-al-kitāb* (such as Q 4:76, 9:5, 9:73, 47:4, 48:29). However, as we shall see in the next section, in several instances *ahl-al-kitāb* are also linked to the root *k-f-r*, and, following the methodology of NTS, these verses could be and are applied to the *ahl-al-kitāb*, including those of the present time, i.e., the Jewish and Christian communities of today.

65. N. Al-Albanee, "Responding to Salaams of the Jews and the Christians," accessed October 15, 2007, www.bakkah.net.

66. Found in Bukhari, *Sahih*, 11/38, hadith number 6254, Muslim, *Sahih*, 3/1422, hadith 1798.

67. Qahtani, *Al-Wala wal Bara'*, 281.

68. O you who have believed, do not take My enemies and your enemies as allies, extending to them affection while they have disbelieved in what came to you of the truth, having driven out the Prophet and yourselves [only] because you believe in Allah, your Lord

69. http://www.calgaryislam.com/pdf/manhaj/16.pdf,p.7, accessed January 14, 2011.

70. Most commonly translated as "unbelief." For more on the meaning of *kufr*, see main text below.

71. Weldman, *The Development of the Concept of Kufr*, 443.

72. Or more precisely, *mu'min*. However, since the religion of the Qur'an and the Prophet Muhammad is termed Islam and its adherents Muslims, the word *muslim* is used here. That this was a later development in Islamic history, see Donner, *Muhammad and the Believers*.

73. T. Izutsu, *Ethico-religious Concepts in the Qur'an* (Montreal, McGill University Press, 2002), 156–162.

74. Ibid, 178–183.

75. J. Smith, *A Historical and Semantic Study of the Term 'Islam'* (Ph.D. Thesis, University of Montana, 1975).

76. F. Rahman, *Revival and Reform in Islam* (Oxford, Oneworld Publications, 2000).

77. Izutsu, *The Concept of Belief.*

78. Ibid.,83–102

79. Ibid, 93.

80. For example, whether or not *'amāl*, or good works, were necessary for someone to be considered a "Believer."

81. Barlas, *Believing Women in Islam—Unreading Patriarchal Interpretations of the Qur'an* (Austin University of Texas Press, 2004), 129–167.

82. K. Ali, *Marriage and Islam in Early Islam*, (Cambridge, MA: Harvard University Press, 2010), 26

83. Ibid., 7.

84. Ibid., 182.

85. L. Shehadeh, *The Idea of Women in Fundamentalist Islam* (Gainsville: University of Florida Press, 2003).

86. S. Shaikh, "Knowledge, Women and Gender in the Hadith: A Feminist Interpretation", in I. Omar, *Islam and Other Religions-Pathways to Dialogue* (New York: Routledge,2006), 87–97, 88–90.

87. Mernissi, *Beyond the Veil—Male-Female Dynamics in a Modern Muslim Society* (Cambridge, MA: Schenkman Publishing Company, 1975), 13.

88. Ibid., 15.

89. For more on *fitna* and *kayd* as insatiable female sexuality causing sociopolitical disorder, see F. Malti-Douglas, *Woman's Body, Woman's Word: Gender and Discourse in Arabo-Islamic Writing*, (Princeton, NJ: Princeton University Press, 1991), Chapter 3.

90. El-Fadl, *Speaking in God's Name*, 245.

91. Mernissi, *Beyond the Veil*, 16, 138–140.

92. Ali, *Sexual Ethics and Islam: Feminist Reflections on Qur'an, Hadith, and Jurisprudence* (Oxford: Oneworld, 2006).

93. Ahmed, *Women and Gender in Islam* (New Haven, CT: Yale University Press, 1992).

94. Ali, *Marriage and Islam.*

95. Ibid., 6, 12, 29–65.

96. K. Ali, "Progressive Muslims and Islamic Jurisprudence: The Necessity for Critical Engagement with Marriage and Divorce Law," in O.Safi (ed.), *Progressive Muslims—On Justice, Gender and Pluralism* (Oxford: Oneword, 2003), 169, 172–179.

97. Ibid., 170. For one example where this opinion is advocated and defended on the basis of *ahad hadith*, see As-Sayyid bin Ahmed Abu Sayf (Abdul Ahad ed.), *The Choice of Every Woman* (Lahore: Darussalam, 2004), 115–116. For more, see main text below.

98. Fair in the eyes of men is the love of things they covet: Women and sons; Heaped-up hoards of gold and silver; horses branded (for blood and excellence); and (wealth of) cattle and well-tilled land. Such are the possessions of this world's life; but in nearness to Allah is the best of the goals (to return to).

99. The woman and the man guilty of adultery or fornication, flog each of them with a hundred stripes: Let not compassion move you in their case, in a matter prescribed by Allah, if ye believe in Allah and the Last Day: and let a party of the Believers witness their punishment.

100. O ye who believe! Truly, among your wives and your children are (some that are) enemies to yourselves: so beware of them!

101. M. A. Ibn Ismail, *The Veil-Evidence of Niqab*, trans. Abdallah Elaceri (London: Al-Firdous, 2009), 24, 25, 30.

102. El-Fadl, *Speaking in God's Name*, 236.

103. According to the NTS *manhaj*, as we discussed in detail in the second chapter, these *ahad hadith* are considered as "legally" binding.

104. El-Fadl, *Speaking in God's Name*, 221.

105. A. Ibn Baz, M. Al-Uthaymeen, and Z. Al-Madkhalee, *Three Essays on the Obligation of Veiling*, trans. Abu Maryam Isma'eel (Alacron, Al-Ibaanah, 2003), 22.

106. Ibid.

107. Ibid., 69.

108. Ibn Ismail, *The Veil Evidence of Niqab*, 25–29.

109. M. Mahmood, *How to Protect Yourself from the Fitnah of Women*, trans. Taalib ibn Tyson al Britaanee (Ammaan: Sootaree's Center, 2008). 2–21.

110. Al-Nawawi, *Sharh Sahih Muslim*, 9/10, 181, as cited by El-Fadi, *Speaking in God's Name*, 237.

111. W. A. Maymani, *Qa'idah al-Dhara'i* (Jeddah: dar al-Mujtama', 2000), 22, 32, 50.

112. M. Al-Musnad, ed., *Islamic Fatawa Regarding Women*, trans. J. Zarabozo (Darrussalam: Riyadh University Press, 1996),181–182, 209.

113. Ibid, 309–317.

114. i.e., Covering of hair without covering the face.

115. i.e., Covering of both hair and most of the face (apart from the eyes).

116. Al-Musnad, *Islamic Fatawa Regarding Women*, 295.

117. A. Ibn Baz et al., *Three Essays*, 9–11.

118. Ibid., 32, 65–74

119. Ibid., 14

120. Ibid., 21

121. Ibid., 22.

122. Ibid., 31.
123. Ibid., 38.
124. Ibid., 40.
125. Ibid., 44.
126. Ibid., 45
127. Ibid., 46.
128. Ibid., 69.
129. Al-Hashimi, *The Ideal Muslimah–The True Islamic Personality of the Muslim Woman*, (Riyadh: International Institute of Islamic Thought, 2005), 75.
130. Ibn Baz, *Three Essays*, 23.
131. Ibid., 31.
132. Ibid., 39–40.
133. Ibid., 41–44.
134. Ibid., 46.
135. Ibid., 69.
136. Ibid., 46–49.
137. Ibid., 49–52.
138. Ibid., 52–59.
139. H. Anwar, *Wilayah al-mar'ah fi al-Fiqh al-Islami* (Masters thesis, Imam Saud Islamic University, Dar Balansiyah, 1999), 107.
140. As cited in Al-Hashimi, *The Ideal Muslimah*, 82
141. Ibn Baz, *Three Essays on Veiling*, 21.
142. http://www.calgaryislam.com/articles/islaamic/current-affairs/563-women-in-masjids-and-politics.html, accessed January 14, 2011.
143. El-Fadl has reviewed the opinions of early classical scholars on the definition of *'awrah* and notices that the term was predominantly used in the context of jurists' discussions on what needs to be covered during the performance of prayers (*salat*) and not in terms of what should be covered outside of prayer, which is the common view today. El-Fadl, *Speaking in God's Name*, 255–258.
144. Ibid.
145. As argued by progressive Muslims. See Chapter 7 of this study.
146. See, for example, Umm 'Abdillah Al-Waadi'eeyah, "The Manners of the Woman Leaving the Home," accessed October 16, 2007, www.therightous-path.com; M. Ismail, *The Hijab Why?*, www.saaid.net.
147. For the sake of brevity only several will be examined in this segment of the chapter.
148. That is fasting not done during the fasting month of Ramadhan.
149. According to traditional Muslim personal law, argues Ali, "the major spousal right established by the contract is the wife's sexual availability in exchange for which she is supported by her husband." On this see K. Ali, "Money, Sex and Power: The Contractual Nature of Marriage in Islamic Jurisprudence of the Formative Period" (PhD Thesis, Duke University, 2002).
150. M. Shooman. *The Righteous Wife*, trans. Abu Talhah Dawood (Al-Hidaayah Publishing and Distribution, 1996),12; Abu Saif, *The Choice of Every Woman*, 115.
151. Shooman, *The Righteous Wife*, 12, 15, 25

152. Ibid.
153. Abu Saif, *The Choice of Every Woman*, 112.
154. M. Ash-Shahawi, *Marital Discourse: Causes and Cures*, (Houston, TX: Dar-us-salam Publishers, 2004), 37–40.
155. Al-Dhahabi was a major hadith master and authority of canonical readings of the Qur'an. See http://www.sunna.org/history/Scholars/al_dhahabi.htm, accessed January 15, 2010.
156. Shooman, *The Righteous Wife*, 27
157. As-Sa'di, *Taysirul-Karim-Rahman*, as cited in M. Shooman, *The Righteous Wife*,10.
158. Such as Surah 33:35; 30:21; 7:189; 24:26; 49:13, 4:1.These verses uphold the ontological equality of the sexes and the essential equality of the entire humanity despite their differences in terms of language, skin colour or ethnicity. Some of these will be discussed in the seventh chapter in relation to progressive Muslims' concept of a religiously ideal "Muslim Woman."
159. Shehadeh, *The Idea of Women*, 248.

5   Progressive Muslims—Conceptualizing and Engaging the Islamic Tradition

1. I have borrowed the term *progressive* from the already cited volume edited by Omid Safi.
2. Ibid, 118–120.
3. Ibid, 119.
4. H. Azam, "Sexual Violence in Maliki Legal Ideology—From Discursive Foundations to Classical Articulation" (PhD thesis, Duke University, 2007).
5. This does not however mean that these do not play an important role in the way its worldview is constructed.
6. E. Moosa, "Transitions in the 'Progress' of Civilisation," in O. Safi, ed., "Voices of Change," Vol. 5, in V. J. Cornell, ed., *Voices of Islam* (London: Praeger, 2007), 115–130, 126.
7. Moosa, "Transitions," 115-118.
8. See F. Esack, "Contemporary Democracy and Human Rights Project for Muslim Societies," in, *Contemporary Islam,* ed. Abdul Aziz Said, et al. (London and New York: Routledge, 2006), 117–129.
9. Esack, "Contemporary Democracy," 125–126
10. Ibid., 127
11. Safi, *Progressive Muslims*, 3.
12. Ibid.
13. Ibid.
14. Ibid, 120–121
15. S. Mahmood, "Secularism, Hermeneutics, Empire: The Politics of Islamic Reformation," *Public Culture*18, no. 2 (2006): 323–347.

16. Esack, "Contemporary Democracy," 125–126.
17. Safi, *Progressive Muslims*, 2.
18. O. Safi, "Challenges and Opportunities for the Progressive Muslim in North America," http://sufinews.blogspot.com/2005/10/challenges-and-opportunities-for.html, accessed May 26, 2011.
19. O. Safi, "What is Progressive Islam?" http://etext.lib.virginia.edu/journals/jsr-forum/pdfs/SafiProgressive.pdf, accessed May 26, 2011, 49.
20. Ibid.
21. Safi, *Progressive Muslims*, 8.
22. Ibid.
23. Ibid.
24. He describes progressive Muslim thought as "hermeneutic Islam" for good reasons as shall be argued in the next chapter.
25. M. Bamyeh, "Hermeneutics against Instrumental Reason: National and Post-National Islam in the 20th Century," *Third World Quarterly* 29 (2008): 3567.
26. Safi, *Progressive Muslims*, 7
27. F. Esack, *Qur'an, Liberation and Pluralism: An Islamic Perspective of Interreligious Solidarity against Oppression* (Oxford: Oneworld, 1997).
28. Bamyeh, "Hermeneutics," 571.
29. O. Safi, "What is Progressive Islam?," *International Institute for the Study of Islam in the Modern World* (December 2003): 49 [48-49].
30. http://www.drsoroush.com/English.htm.
31. http://www.othermalaysia.org/index.php?option=com_content&task=view&id=15&Itemid=6.
32. http://www.csss-isla.com/IIS/aboutus.php.
33. http://www.fin.ba/ba/index-a-z/prof.-dr.-enes-kari-/h-3.html; http://www.fin.ba/ba/index/-a-z/prof.-dr.-mustafa-ceric-/h-3.html, accessed May 26, 2011.
34. http://web.uct.ac.za/depts/religion/Staff/shaikh.php, accessed May 26, 2011; http://web.uct.ac.za/depts/religion/Staff/tayob.php, accessed May 26, 2011.
35. http://www.bu.edu/religion/faculty/bios/ali.html, accessed May 26, 2011.
36. http://www.has.vcu.edu/wld/faculty/wadud.html, accessed May 26, 2011.
37. See the list of the contributors to the Progressive *Muslims* book.
38. Safi, "Challenges and Opportunities."
39. A. Karamustafa, " Civilisational Project in Progress,"in Safi, *Progressive Muslims*, 109–110.
40. M. Arkoun, "Limits of Western Historical Boundaries," in *Contemporary Islam*, 224 [215–227].
41. A detailed discussion on this is presented in the next chapter.
42. El-Fadl, "The Ugly Modern and the Modern Ugly: Reclaiming the Beautiful in Islam," in *Progressive Muslims*, ed., O. Safi (Oxford: Oneworld, 2003), 33–78.
43. Ibid.
44. E. Moosa, "The Poetics and Politics of Law after Empire: Reading Women's Rights in the Contestations of Law," 1 UCLA, *J. Islamic & Near E.L.*1 (2001):3.
45. Safi, *Progressive Muslims*, 8.

46. Ibid.
47. Moosa, "Transitions," 126
48. See, for example, K. Ali, "Progressive Muslims and Islamic Jurisprudence: The Necessity for Critical Engagement with Marriage and Divorce Law.' in *Progressive Muslims—On Justice, Gender and Pluralism,* ed. O. Safi (Oxford: Oneword, 2003), 175–182; Moosa, "The Debts and Burdens of Critical Islam" in *Progressive Muslims,* 120–126; Safi, *Progressive Muslims,* 20–22.
49. Moosa, "The Debts and Burdens," 121.
50. Soroush, *The Expansion of Prophetic Experience—Essays on Historicity, Contingency and Plurality in Religion* (Leiden: E. J. Brill, 2009), 93–115.
51. This section relies heavily on the work of P. Wright, "Modern Qur'anic Hermeneutics," (PhD Thesis, University of North Carolina, Chapell Hill, 2008).
52. Not to be confused with the Industrial Revolution as it is broader in its scope including not only advanced industries but also societal elements such as banking, health care, police, etc. See M. Hodgson, *The Venture of Islam, 3 Volumes* (Chicago: University of Chicago Press, 1958).
53. Wright, "Modern Qur'anic Hermeneutics,"19, 38. The historical or cultural temporality differs from natural temporality in three ways. Unlike natural change, historical change as determinant of social reality is subject to variability of "acceleration" and "deceleration" and its characterized "heterogeneity" and "multilevelledness." H. White, Foreword to K. R. Koselleck, *The Practice of Conceptual History—Timing History, Spacing Concepts,* trans. T. S. Presner et al. (Stanford: Stanford University Press, 2002), xi.
54. C. Fasolt, *The Limits of History* (Chicago: The University of Chicago Press, 2004), 3–45.
55. Koselleck defines historical time as being "tied to social and political units of action, to particular acting and suffering human beings, and to their institutions and organizations." Koselleck, *The Practice of Conceptual History,* 110.
56. Ibid., 42.
57. Wright, "Modern Qur'anic Hermeneutics," 19.
58. Ibid., 41.
59. Ibid., 45.
60. R. Rorty, *Contingency, Irony, and Solidarity* (Cambridge: Cambridge University Press, 1989), 7–8.
61. Wright, "Modern Qur'anic Hermeneutics," 36
62. Ibid., 54.
63. C. West, The American Evasion of Philosophy: *A Genealogy of Pragmatism* (Madison: University of Wisconsin Press, 1989), 233.
64. Wright, "Modern Qur'anic Hermeneutics," 47.
65. Ibid., 54.
66. Ibid., 51.
67. Cited in Ibid., 50.
68. Ibid., 88.
69. Ibid., 89.

70. Ibid., 90.
71. Moosa, "The Debts and Burdens," 117–120.
72. S. Taji-Farouki, *Modern Muslim Intellectuals and the Qur'an* (Oxford: Oxford University Press), 2004, 15.
73. He refers to them simply as Muslim modernists.
74. Soroush, *The Expansion*, xv–xix.
75. Bamyeh, Hermeneutics, 565.
76. Moosa, 'The debts and Burdens," 119. Abu Zayd refers to it as "modernity without rationality." H. N. Abu Zayd, "The Nexus of Theory and Practice."
77. Al-Azmeh, "The Muslim Canon from late Antiquity to the Era of Modernism," in *Canonization and Decanonization,* ed., A.van der Kooij and K.van der Toorn (Leiden ,1998), 215.
78. See Moosa, 'The Debts and Burdens," 113–128.
79. Ibid., xix–xx; Cf. Bamyeh, "Hermeneutics," 565.
80. Phrase borrowed from Moosa, see "The debts and Burdens."
81. As defined by A. Giddens, *The Consequences of Modernity* (Stanford: Stanford University Press, 1990).
82. Here used as developed by M. Foucault in his *Order of Things: An Archaeology of the Human Science,*(1966) to mean the historical a priori that grounds knowledge and its discourses and thus represents the "condition of their possibility" within a particular epoch.
83. In sense of its emphasis on human agency and possibility of change.
84. See Moosa, "Transitions," 124–126
85. Phrase borrowed from Soroush in his *Reason.*
86. Rahman, "Islam: Challenges and Opportunities," in *Islam: Past Influence and Present Challenge,* ed., A. T. Welch and P. Cachia (Edinbrugh: Edinburgh University Press,1979).
87. A. N. Emon, "Towards a Natural Law Theory in Islamic Law: Muslim Juristic Debates on Reason as a Source of Obligation,"*JINEL*, vol.3. pt1 (2003): 3 [1–51].
88. Moosa, "Transitions," 124.
89. Soroush, *Reason.*
90. Bamyeh, "Hermeneutics," 573.
91. Sh. Jackson,*On the Boundaries of Theological Tolerance in Islam, Abu Hamid Al-Ghazali's Faysal al-Tafriqa Bayna al-Islam wa al-Zandaqa* (Oxford: Oxford University Press, 2002),Introduction.
92. Safi, *Progressive Muslims,* 7.
93. Moosa, "Transitions," 123.
94. Safi, *Progressive Muslims,* 6.
95. Moosa, "Transitions," 125.
96. Gaebel,M. *Von der Kritik des arabischen Denkens zum panarabischen Aufbruch: Das philosophische und politische Denken Muhammad Abid Gabiris,* (Berlin: Klaus Schwarz Verlag, 1995), 5–45
97. Cited in I. J.Boulatta, *Trends and Issues in Contemporary Arab Thought* (Albany: State University of New York Press, 1990), 16.

98. Mansoor, *The Unpredictability*, 59.
99. Bamyeh, "Hermeneutics," 573.
100. Ibid., 567.
101. H. Azam, "Sexual Violence in Maliki Legal Ideology-From Discursive Foundations to Classical Articulation," (PhD thesis, Duke University, 2007), 8.
102. T. Asad, *The Idea of Anthropology of Islam* (Occasional Paper Series, Georgetown University Center for Contemporary Arab Studies, March 1986); cf. Moosa, *Transitions*, 123–126.
103. Moosa, "Transitions," 123–126.
104. I.e., Approaches in whose worldview the primary sources of the Islamic Weltanschauung and the derivative body of knowledge comprising the cumulative Islamic tradition are considered of no value, have no authority or normativeness and are not used as points of reference at all.
105. Safi, *Progressive Muslims*, 7.
106. Ibid.
107. Moosa, "Transitions," 118–126.
108. Safi, *Progressive Muslims*, 7–9.
109. Safi, *Progressive Muslims*, 2, 8 ,16.
110. S. Taji-Farouki, *Modern Muslim Intellectuals and the Qur'an* (Oxford: Oxford University Press, 2004), 12–16.
111. Soroush, *The Expansion*, xv, xii.
112. A. Salvatore, "The Rational Authentication of Islamic Tradition in Contemporary Arab Thought: Muhammad Al-Jabiri and Hassan Hanafi," *The Muslim World* 85, no. 3–4 (1995): 195 [191-214].
113. Soroush, *The Expansion*, xxiii
114. Ibid., xxii.
115. Esack, "Contemporary Democracy," 127.
116. On this, see Esack, *Qur'an, Liberation and Pluralism*.
117. Moosa, "Transitions."
118. Moosa, "The Debts and Burdens."
119. Moosa, "Transitions," 117.
120. Taji-Farouki, *Modern Muslim Intellectuals*, 10.
121. Ibid, 4.
122. D. L. Johnstone, "Maqasid al-Shari'ah: Epistemology and Hermeneutics of Muslim Theologies of Human Rights," *Die Welt des Islams* 47,no. 2 (2007): 149–187.
123. S. Benhabib, *Situating the Self-Gender, Community and Post-Modernism in Contemporary Ethics* (New York: Routledge, 1992).
124. M. Kadivar, "The Principles of Compatibility of Islam and Modernity," http://www.irri-kiib.be/speechnotes/04/islam-modern-04/Kadivar-EN.htm, accessed May 26, 2011.
125. Esack, "Contemporary Democracy," 127.
126. A. Sajoo, Muslim Modernities: Expressions of the Civil Imagination (New York: Macmillan, 2008).
127. Safi, "What is Progressive Islam?," 48.

6   Progressive Muslims' Model of Interpretation (Manhaj) and Their Interpretational Implications

1. Cf. T. Winter, "Qur'anic Reasoning as an Academic Practice," *Modern Theology* 22, no. 3 (2006): 451 [450–463].
2. For more on this, see Y. Rahman, "The Hermeneutical Theory of Nasir Hamid Abu Zayd" (PhD Dissertation, McGill University, 2001).
3. Mansoor, "The Unpredictability of the Past—Turath and Hermeneutics," (PhD Thesis, University of California, 2000), 220.
4. al-Qaˉdiˉ 'Abd al-Jabbaˉr Abuˉ al-Hasan Ahmad b. al-Husayn, *al-Mughniˉ fiˉ abwaˉb al-tawhiˉd wa-l-'adl*, various editors, 16 vols. Cairo:Various publishers, 1380/1960yi389/1969, vol.8, p. 3/2 (*al-kalaˉm alladhiˉ yajuˉzu an yatanaˉwala al-muraˉda bi-l-lugha*).
5. al-Qaˉdiˉ Abuˉ Bakr Muhammad b. al-Tayyib al-Baˉqillaˉniˉ. *al-Taqriˉbwa-l-irshaˉd al-saghiˉr*, ed. 'Abd al-Hamiˉd b. 'Aliˉ Abuˉ Zunayd, 3 vols.[Beirut]: Mu'assasat al-Risaˉla, 1413/1993yi418/1998, vol. 1,429-431.
6. Mansoor, "The Unpredictability of the Past," 219–220.
7. H. Hanafi, *Islam in the Modern World*, Vol.II, (Cairo: Dar ul-Kebaa, 2000), 211.
8. H. N. Abu Zayd, *Politik und Islam: Kritik des Religiösen Diskurses*, trans. Cherifa Magdi, (Frankfurt: Dipa-Verlag, 1996), 161.
9. A. Neuwirth, "Some Reflections on Qur'anic History and the History in the Qur'an," *Journal of Qur'anic Studies* 5 (2003): 2 [1-18].
10. A. K. Soroush, *The Expansion of Prophetic Experience—Essays on Historicity, Contingency and Plurality in Religion* (Leiden: E. J. Brill, 2009); Neuwirth, 'Qur'an and History'.
11. Adonis (pseudo-name)-'Ali Ahmad Sa'id Isbir, "Reflections on the Manifestations of Intellectual Backwardness in Arab Society," in I. Mansoor, "The Unpredictability of the Past," 28.
12. Abu Zayd, *Politik und Islam*, 160
13. Ibid.
14. H. N. Abu Zayd, *Reformation of Islamic Thought—A Historical Analysis* (Amersterdam: Amsterdam University Press, 2007), 99.
15. Soroush, *The Expansion of Prophetic Experience*; Sukidi, "**Nasr Hāmid Abū Zayd and the Quest for a Humanistic Hermeneutics of the Qur'ān**," *Die Welt Des Islams* 49, no. 2 (2009): 181–211.
16. Ibid. Some examples of this will be given in the subsequent part of the chapter on the *maqasid*-based approach to Qur'anic interpretation.
17. Sukidi, *Nasr Hamid Abu Zayd.*
18. K. Amirpour, *Die Entpolitisierung des Islam: Abdolkarim Sorushs Denken und Wirkung in der Islamischen Republik Iran* (Eron Verlag, 1999), 20.
19. Rather than that of the reader or of the nature of the text.
20. F. Esack, "Qur'anic Hermeneutics: Prospects and Problems," *The Muslim World* 83, no. 2 (1993): 138 [118–141].
21. Rahman, "The Hermeneutical Theory of Nasir Hamid Abu Zayd," 40

22. Ibid., 33. In this context, it is worth noting that Bauer, in her analysis of pre-modern Qur'anic exegesis, found that two major factors that had the greatest effect on the exegetical process where the personal opinions and the mores of the society in which the exegetes lived. K. Bauer, "Room for Interpretation: Qur'anic Exegesis and Gender" (PhD thesis, Princeton University, 2008).

23. Sh. Jackson, "Fiction and Formalism," 195; see also194–200.

24. Mansoor, "The Unpredictability of the Past," 269

25. Abu Zayd, *Politik und Islam,* 157 (author's translation).

26. Mohamad Ashraf, Islam and Gender Justice (New Delhi,Kalpaz Publications,2005), 25.

27. Wahyudi, "The Slogan," 253.

28. Abu Zayd, *Politik und Islam,* 85.

29. Amirpour, *Die Entpolitisierung des Islam,* 23.

30. Mabrook, "A New Historical Discussion in Islam," 280–281.

31. S. Fish, *Is There a Text in This Class?: The Authority of Interpretive Communities* (Cambridge, MA: Harvard University Press, 1980), 14, 16, 317; In Qur'anic studies, see Jane Dammen McAuliffe, "Text and Textuality," 68–69.

32. See El-Fadl, *Speaking in God's Name,* 132–141

33. P. Ricouer, *Hermeneutics and the Human Sciences: Essays on Language, Action and Interpretation,* ed. and trans. J. B. Thomson (Cambridge: Cambridge University Press, 1981).

34. U. Echo in D. A. Carson, *The Gagging of God: Christianity Confronts Pluralism* (Grand Rapids, MI: Zondervan Publishing House, 1996), 76–77.

35. N. Wolterstorff, *Divine Discourses: Philosophical Reflections on the Claim that God Speaks* (Cambridge: Cambridge University Press, 1995), 202.

36. El-Fadl, *Speaking in God's Name,* 132–141.

37. Barlas, *Believing Women in Islam,* 6, 34.

38. Amirpour, *Die Entpolitisierung des Islam,* 20.

39. Rahman, "The Hermeneutical Theory," 43.

40. Wahyudi, "The Slogan," 255.

41. A. Saeed, *Interpreting the Qur'an—Towards a Contemporary Approach* (New YorkL Routledge, 2006), 102–109.

42. Moosa, "The Poetics and Politics of Law after Empire: Reading Women's Rights in the Contestations of Law," in 1 UCLA, *J. Islamic & Near E.L.*: 2 [1-28].

43. F. Esack, "Islam and Gender Justice: Beyond Apologia" in eds. J. Raines and D. Maguire, *The Justice Men Owe To Women: Positive Resources from World Religions* (Albany: SUNY Press, 2000), 187–210, 205.

44. Saeed, *Interpreting the Qur'an,* 117

45. Abu Zayd, *Politik und Islam,* 95

46. Soroush, *The Expansion of Prophetic Experience,* 63–90.

47. "It goes without saying that the culture, history and reality in which the sources were grounded differ radically from the contemporary Muslim experience." Moosa, "The Poetics," 2.

48. S. Younis, "Islamic Legal Hermeneutics : The Context and Adequacy of Interpretation," *Journal of Islamic Studies* 41, no. 4 (2002): 585–615.

49. Rahman, "The Hermeneutical Theory," 55n55

50. Barlas, *Believing Women*, 22–23.

51. Rahman, "The Hermeneutical Theory," 56n56.

52. Wadud, *Qur'an and Woman*, 1–15.

53. E. Moosa, "The Debts and Burdens of Critical Islam," in *Progressive Muslims—On Gender, Justice and Pluralism*, ed. O. Safi (Oxford: Oneworld, 2003).

54. A. Achrati, "Arabic, Qur'anic Speech and Postmodern Language: What the Qur'an Simply Says," *Arabica* 54(2) (2008): 161–203.

55. N. Abu Zayd, "The Qur'an: God and Man in Communication," unpublished paper available: http://www.stichtingsocrates.nl/teksten/The%20Qu%27ran%20God%20and%20man%20in%20communication%20-%20Oratie%20Rijksuniversiteit%20Leiden.pdf, accessed May 26, 2011.

56. Soroush, *The Expansion of Prophetic Experience*, 3–13, 63–90.

57. Saeed, *Interpreting the Qur'an*, chapter seven.

58. These will be the subject of our discussion below.

59. Kamali, "Methodological Issues in Islamic Jurisprudence," *Arab Law Quarterly* 11, 1 (1996): 14 [3–33]. (emphasis mine).

60. For one such attempt, see Saeed, *Interpreting the Qur'an*, chapter 11.

61. F. Rahman, *Major Themes of the Qur'an* (Minneapolis, MN: Bibliotheca Islamica, 1994), xi; Y. Auda, *Maqasid Al-Sharia'h as Philosophy of Islamic Law* (London: International Institute of Islamic Thought, 2008), 199.

62. Auda, for example, provides some evidence of rudimentary holistic—like approaches to Islamic Law such as Juwayni's notion of *qiyas kulli* (holistic analogy) or Al-Shatibi's *kulliyat al-shari'ah* (single and partial rulings are there to support holistic fundamentals). However, he argues that the implication of these views on the jurists' and theologians' methodology did not materialize. Auda, *Maqasid al-Shariah*, 199.

63. See chapter three p. XX

64. Auda, *Maqasid Al-Shari'ah;* Abdul-Raof, "Conceptual and Textual Chaining, in Qur'anic Discourse," *Journal of Qur'anic Studies* 5, no. 2: (2003).

65. Al-Shadr, *Al-Madrasa Al-Qur'aniyya: at-Tafsir al-maudu'I wa at-tafsir al-tajzi fi al-Qur'an al-Karim* (Beirut: Dar at-ta'arruf li al-matba'a, n.d.).

66. Achrati, "Arabic, Qur'anic Speech," 187.

67. Ibid.

68. For the purposes of Islamic law derivation, these "indicants" do not necessarily need to be restricted to the Qur'an only. Here I refer to Prof. Jackson's principles of "juristic induction" defined as the aggregate of a number of texts, *literally* interpreted, that point to a meaning that transcends each text individually but implicitly inheres in the group, the whole equaling more than the sum of its parts. Sh. Jackson, "Literalism, Empiricism, and Induction: Apprehending and Concretizing Islamic Law's Maqâsid al-Sharî," *Mitch. St.L.Rev.* (2006):1471.

69. S. Al-Awa, *Textual Relations in the Qur'an: Relevance, Coherence and Structure* (London: Routledge, 2006).

70. Mabrook, "A New Historical Discussion in Islam,"280.

71. Esack, "Qur'anic Hermeneutics," 138.
72. B. Weiss, "Exotericism and Objectivity in Islamic Jurisprudence," in *Islamic Law and Jurisprudence*, ed. N. Heer (Seattle: University of Washington Press, 1990), 33–53, 63.
73. Jackson, "Literalism, Empiricism, and Induction," 1477.
74. Barlas, *Believing Women*, 18
75. H.Al-Turabi, *Al-Tafsir al-Tawhidi*, Vol. I, (London: Dar Al-Saqi, 2004), 20.
76. See also 6: 91; in Y. Ali, *The Holy Qur'an: Text, Translation and Commentary* (New York: Tahrike Tarsile Qur'an, 1988), 314.
77. Barlas, *Believing Women*, 16.
78. A. Sachedina, "Scriptural Reasoning in Islam," *Journal of Scriptural Reasoning* 5, no. 1 (April 2005).
79. Auda, *Maqasid Al-Shari'ah*, 26–56.
80. Rahman, "Islam: Challenges and Opportunities," in *Islam: Past Influence and Present Challenge*, ed., A. T. Welch and P. Cachia (Edinbrugh: Edinburgh University Press, 1979), 256–257.
81. Auda, *Maqasid Al-Shariah*, 177–179.
82. T. Al-Ashur, *Alaysa al-Subh bi Qarib*? (Tunis: Al-Shakirah al-Tunisiyyah li-funun al-rasm, 1988), 237.
83. Y. Rahman, "The Hermeneutical Theory," 58. This approach would however go beyond the premodern jurists' abstractions of the *maqâsid al-sharî'ah* to what Jackson terms *practical concretions* that are responsive to the realities of the modern world. Jackson, "Literalism, Empiricism, and Induction," 1470
84. Abu Zayd, *Politik und Islam*, 50.
85. See Abu Zayd, *Politik und Islam*, 57–58.
86. M. Mumisa, "Toward an African Qur'anic Hermeneutics," *Journal of Qur'anic Studies* 4, no. 1 (2002): 62.
87. The scope of *maslaha* in legal theory in premodern Islamic literature was much more "constrained" and had to function within and was hermeneutically subservient to other four sources of law (Qur'an, Sunna, *ijma'a* and *qiyas*). Auda, *Maqasid Al-Shariah*.
88. K. El-Fadl, "The Place of Ethical Obligations in Islamic Law," 4 *UCLA , J. Islamic and Near E.L.*1 (2005):31–32.
89. Ibid., 10.
90. Esack, *Islam and Gender Justice*, 205.
91. M.Ashrof, *Islam and Gender Justice-Questions at the Interface*, Kalpaz Publications,Delhi, 2005,24.
92. Souaiaia, "On the Sources," 134–135; Auda, *Maqasid Al-Shariah*, 9–13.
93. Souaiaia, *Contesting Justice—Women, Islam, Law , and Society* (Albany: State University of New York Press, 2008), 71.
94. Younis, "Islamic Legal Hermeneutics," 596.
95. Auda, *Maqasid Al-Shariah*.
96. Abd-Al-Salam Al-Sulaymani, *Al-Ijtihad fi al-fiqh al-Islami* (Rabat: Wuzarat al-Awqaf, 1996), 132–3.
97. Souaiaia, "On the Sources," 134–135.

98. Muḥammad ibn al-Ḥasan al-Ḥijwī, al-Fikr al-Sāmī fī Tārīkh al-Fiqh al-Islāmī (Beirut: Dār al-Kutub al-'Ilmiyya, 1995), 385.

99. A. Al-Raysuni, *Nazariyyat al-Maqasid 'ind al-imam al-Shatibi* (Herndon: International Institute of Islamic Thought, 1992).

100. See M. K. Imam, *al-dalil al-irshadi Ila maqasid Al-Shari'ah al-islamiyyah* (London: Maqasid Research Centre, 2006).

101. Ed. Mohammad Sadiq Bghar al-ulum, *'Ilal al-Shara'i,* (Najaf: Dar al Balaghah, 1966).

102. Ed. Ahmed Ghurab, *al-I'lam bi-Manaqib al-Islam* (Cairo: Dar al Kitab al-'Arabi,1967).

103. Ed. Abdul Al Azim al-dccb, *Al-Burhan fi usul al-Fiqh* (Mansurah: Al-Wafa, 1998).

104. *Al-Mustasfa* (Cairo: Makba'at dar al-kutub al-misriyya, 1997).

105. Beirut, Dar al-nashr, n.d.

106. Ed. Khalil Mansour, *al-Furuq* (Beirut: dar al-kutub al-'ilmiyyah, 1998).

107. Ed. Taha Abdul rauf Saad, Beirut, Dar alJil, 1973.

108. Matba'at al maktabah al-tujariyah, 1920.

109. Cairo, Mu'asasah 'izz al-din,n.d.

110. Ed. El-tahir el-Mesnawi, Kuala Lumpur, Al-fajr, 1999.

111. 1st ed.,Cairo, Dar al-Shoruq, 1999.

112. 1st ed. Beirut and Dar al-Hadi, 2001.

113. Auda, *Maqasid Al-Shari'ah,* 17

114. Moosa, "The Poetics," 5

115. Moosa, "The Poetics," 10.

116. Auda, *Maqasid Al-Shari'ah,* 19.

117. Ibid.

118. i.e., Qur'an , Sunna, *ijma'* and *qiyas.*

119. Moosa, "The Poetics," 11. Al-Tufi uses words that *maslaha* is *"qutb maqsud ash-shar"*—the aim and the very pillar of religion.

120. Moosa, "The Poetics," 11.

121. Auda, *Maqasid Al-Shari'ah,* 20.

122. Ibid., 20–21.

123. Ibid., 21.

124. Ibid., xxv

125. Wahyudi, "The Slogan," 285, 266.

126. Ibn Ashur, *Maqasid al-shari'ah al-islamiyyah.*

127. Auda, *Maqasid Al-Shari'ah,* xxviii.

128. Ibid., 186.

129. God's will, however, is always subject to the interpretation of those who engage in deducing meaning of the text; El-Fadl, *Speaking in God's Name,* 115–132.

130. There was a degree or variation on these issues between different as well as within schools of thought. For an exhaustive discussion on this issue, see K. Reinhart, *Before Revelation—The Boundaries of Muslim Moral Thought* (Albany: State University of New York Press), 11–37.

131. Hourani, "Ethical Pre-Suppositions," 2–3.

132. K. Reinhart, *Before Revelation*, 178.

133. Ibid, 183.

134. For example, M. Al-Attar, *Islamic Ethics*.

135. Hourani, "Ethical Pre-Suppositions," 25.

136. Ibid, 23.

137. Ibid.

138. Reinhart, *Before Revelation*, 23

139. M. A. Draz, *The Moral World of the Qur'an* (London: I. B. Taurus, 2008).

140. M. Guraya, "The Concept of Sunna in the Muwatta of Malik b. Anas," (unpublished PhD thesis McGill University, 1969), Introduction.

141. Ibid, 15; Hallaq, *The Origins*, 53.

142. Z. I. Ansari, "An Early Discussion on Islamic Jurisprudence: Some Notes on al-Radd 'al-Siyar al-Awza'i," in *Islamic Perspectives: Studies in Honour of Sayyid Abul A'la Mawdudi* (Leicester: 1979), 153.

143. Schacht, *Introduction to Islamic Law* (Oxford: Clarendon Press,1964), 35.

144. Hallaq, *The Origins*, 52–53.

145. Ibid.

146. F. Rahman maintains, for example, that Shaibani (d. 189 A. H.) "has often recourse to istihsan (juristic preference) in opposition to earlier precedents and [that he] exercises absolute reasoning." Fazrul Rahman, "The Living Sunnah and al-Sunnah wa'l Jama'ah" in *Hadith and Sunnah—Ideals and Realities-Selected Essays,* ed. P. K Koya (Kuala Lumpur, Islamic Book Trust, 1996).140.

147. Reinhart, *Before Revelation*, 178.

148. G. H. A. Juynboll, *Muslim Tradition—Studies in Chronology, Provenance and Authorship of Early Hadith* (Cambridge: Cambridge University Press, 1983), 36–37.

149. Z. I. Ansari, "Islamic Juristic Terminology before Shafi'i: A Semantical Analysis with Special Reference to Kufa," *Arabica* xix (1972): 289 [255-300]; *Ra'y* seems to have dominated jurist thought until the middle of the second century—Hallaq, *The Origins*, 75–76.

150. Ibid.

151. A. N. Emon, "Towards a Natural Law Theory in Islamic Law: Muslim Juristic Debates on Reason as a Source of Obligation," *JINEL* 3, no. 1, 2003.

152. Sachedina, "The Nature of Scriptural Reasoning in Islam," *Journal of Scriptural Reasoning* 5, no 1 (April 2005).

153. Kh.El-Fadl, "The Place of Ethical Obligations in Islamic Law," 2

154. Kh.El-Fadl, *The Place of Tolerance in Islam* (Boston: Beacon Press, 2002), 15.

155. i.e., aim /objective /purpose of the Revelation. M. Gaebel, *Von der Kritik des arabischen Denkens zum panarabischen Aufbruch: Das philosophische und politische Denken Muhammad Abid Gabiris* (Verlag: Klaus Schwarz, 1995), 32.

156. Al-Attar, *Islamic Ethics*, 12–16.

157. Moosa, "The Poetics," 7.

158. Al-Attar, *Islamic Ethics*.

159. El-Fadl, *The Great Theft—Wrestling Islam from the Extremists* (New York: Harper Collins, 2005), 262–274.
160. Saeed, *Interpreting the Qur'an*, 122–123.
161. For one such model, see Ibid., 149–152.
162. Barlas, *Believing Women*, 13–15; cf. G. Adnan, Women and the Glorious Qur'an: An Analytical Study of Women Related Verses (Goettingen: Sura Al-Nisa'a, 2004), 1–12.
163. Saeed, Interpreting the Qur'an, 149–152
164. Duderija, "The Evolution in the Canonical Sunni Hadith Body of Literature and the Concept of an Authentic Hadith during the Formative Period of Islamic Thought as Based on Recent Western Scholarship," *Arab Law Quarterly* 23, no. 4 (2009): 1–27.
165. A. Hasan, *Early Development of Islamic Jurisprudence* (Islamabad, 1970), 87.
166. F. Rahman, "The Living Sunna and al-Sunna wa'l Jama'ah'"; Ansari, "Islamic Juristic Terminology before Shafi'i"; I. Ahmed, *The Significance of Sunna and Hadith and Their Early Documentation*, (PhD Thesis, Edinbrough University, 1974);.Y. Dutton, *The Origins of Islamic Law, The Qur'an, the Muwatta and Madinian 'Amal*. (New York: Routledge, Curzon, 2002); El-Fadl, *Speaking in God's Name;* M. S. Mathnee, "Critical Reading of Fazrul Rahman's Islamic Methodology in History," (M. A. Thesis, University of Cape Town, 2005); Duderija, "Toward a Methodology"; A. Kamaruddin, *The Reliability of Hadith-Transmission: A Re-examination of Hadith-Critical Methods* (PhD thesis, Friedrich-Wilhelms Universitaet, Bonn, 2005); Abd Allah, "Malik's Concept of 'Amal"; Guraya, "The Concept of Sunna."
167. Dutton, *The Origins of Islamic Law*, 168.
168. www.understanding-islam.org/sourcesofislam.
169. We use the expression practical/'*amal*-based Sunna as per Malik, see Abd Allah, "Malik's Concept of 'Amal."
170. This opinion is shared by Dutton who quotes a number of instances in Malik's Muwatta that validate this assertion. e.g., Abu Yusuf said (to Malik) "you do the adhan with tarji, but you have no Hadith from the prophet about this. Malik turned to him and said, Subhana allah! I have never seen anything more amazing than this! The call to the prayer has been done [here] every day five times a day in front of witnesses, and sons have inherited it from their fathers since the time of Messenger of Allah, may Allah bless him and grant him peace. Does this need "so-and-so from so-ands-so? This is more accurate in our opinion than Hadith." Dutton, *The Origins of Islamic Law*, 43; also 41–52.
171. F. Rahman, Islamic Methodology in History, (Lahore: Central Institute for Islamic Research, 1965) 1–84.
172. John C. Wilkins, *Ibadism: Origins and Early Developments in Oman* (Oxford: Oxford University Press, 2010), 234.
173. Kamaruddin, *The Reliability of Hadith-Transmission*; Kamali, *Hadith Methodology*.
174. See footnote 140.

175. For a brief summary of (non)-Muslim, Western scholars of hadith criticism, see H. Motzki, "Dating Muslim Traditions—A Survey" *Arabica* 52, no. 2 (2005): 206–253. Also, Kamaruddin, *The Reliability of Hadith-Transmission.*
176. Such as the "conscientious pause" and "authorial enterprise," hermeneutical methods found in El-Fadl's *Speaking in God's Name.* These two will be discussed in the sixth chapter.
177. A. Duderija, Evolution in the Canonical Sunni Hadith Body of Literature. Shukurow presents a number of *ahad hadith* that were not acted upon by the Muslim community at large and therefore left out by the founders of the four Sunni *madhahaib.* A. Shukurow, *Towards Understanding Hadith,* ebook.
178. In his *Islamic Methodology in History,* Fazrul Rahman employs almost all of these principles but does not directly apply them to the subject matter at hand so I do not discuss his ideas here specifically. Two examples here suffice: "it must be emphatically pointed out that a reevaluation of different elements in Hadith and their thoughrough interpretation under the changed moral and social conditions of today must be carried out.Thus can be done only by a historical study of the Hadith-by reducing it to living Sunnah and by clearly distingushing from situational background the real value embodied in it"(p.78)."On the very same principle of situational interpretation, by resurrecting the real moral value from the situational background ,must be handeled the problem of legal hadith.We must view the legal hadith as a problem to be re-treated and not as a ready made law to be directly applied" (p.79).
179. Abd ul Halim Abu Shuqqa, Vol 1., (Kuwait: Dar al-Qalam) ,275
180. Found in Abu Shuqqa's, Tahrir' Al-ma'ra, 53.
181. Ibid., 100.
182. F. A. Qadir, *Hadith and Gender Justice—Understanding the Prophetic Traditions* (Fahmina Institute, 2007).
183. Ibid., xx-xxi
184. Ibid., xxi.
185. Ibid., 23
186. El-Fadl, *Speaking in God's Name,* 89.
187. Ibid., 93.
188. Ibid.
189. Auda, *Maqasid Al-Shari'ah,* 233, 257.
190. Ibid., 213–226.
191. http://papers.ssrn.com/sol3/papers.cfm?abstract_id=1712968.
192. See footnote 184.
193. Qadir, *Hadith and Gender Justice,* 2.

7 PROGRESSIVE MUSLIMS' RELIGIOUSLY IDEAL "BELIEVER" AND "MUSLIM WOMAN" CONCEPTS

1. Esack, *Qur'an, Liberation and Pluralism: An Islamic Perspective of Interreligious Solidarity against Oppression,* Oxford: Oneworld, 1997),146.

2. Ibid., 159.

3. Those who have been expelled from their homes without a just cause except that they say: Our Lord is Allah. And had there not been Allah's repelling some people by others, certainly there would have been pulled *down cloisters and churches and synagogues and mosques in which Allah's name is much remembered;* and surely Allah will help him who helps His cause; most surely Allah is Strong, Mighty.

4. Ibid., 173.

5. Ibid., 174.

6. Ibid., 158.

7. Ibid., 15.

8. This is shown in relation to the work of Esack in detail in the following section of the chapter.

9. See, for example, R. Shah-Kazemin, *The Other in the Light of the One: The Universality of the Qur'an and Interfaith Dialogue* (Cambridge: The Islamic Texts Society, 2006); A. S. Asani, "On Pluralism, Intolerance,and the Qur'an," *The American Scholar* 72,no. 1 (Winter 2002).

10. T. Ramadan, *The Western Muslims and the Future of Islam* (Oxford: Oxford University Press, 2004), 203–204; El-Fadl, *Great Theft–Wrestling Islam from the Extremists* (New York: Harper Collins, 2005), 203–219.

11. Cf. Saeed, *Interpreting the Qur'an—Towards a Contemporary Approach* (New York: Routledge, 2006), 149–154.

12. Esack, *Qur'an, Liberation and Pluralism*, 115.

13. Ibid., 114–179, chapters four and five.

14. Ibid., 115.

15. Ibid., 125–128.

16. Esack uses a capital 'I' in "Islam" to indicate the reified concept form and noncapital 'islam' for a nonreified form. Hence, it is replicated here.

17. Ibid.,132

18. Ibid., 120–125.

19. In this context Esack points out the Qur'an itself, at times, describes reprehensible acts committed by those who belong to the Muslim or the believing community at the time of the Prophet with *kufr* or *shirk*. He gives an example of surah Az-Zumar, 39:7, which states: If you are ungrateful (*takfuru*), then surely Allah is Self-sufficient above all need of you; and He does not like ungratefulness (*el-kufr*) in His servants.

20. Ibid., 134, 139

21. Usually translated as friendship or guardianship.

22. Ibid., 203.

23. Ibid., 152.

24. Abu Zayd, *Re-thinking the Qur'an–Towards a Humanistic Hemeneutic* (Utrecht: Humanities University Press, 2004).

25. M. Shahrur, *The Qur'an, Morality and Critical Reason: The Essential Muhammad Shahrur, trans.* A. Christman (Leiden: E. J. Brill, 2009), 21–71.

26. Cf. Miraly, *The Ethic of Pluralism in the Qur'an and the Prophet's Medina* (Montreal: McGill University Press, 2006).

27. M. Al-Habash, *Ihtikar al-khalas, Tishrın al-Usbu'i* no. 97, January 31, 2000; and in Nahwa ta'sıl ıdiyulujı̄ li al-hiwar bayn al-adyan, *Tishrı̄n*, May 27, 2001.

28. Introduction written by al-Habash to the Arabic translation of W. W. Baker, *More in Common than You Think (Al-mushtarak akthar mimmā ta_taqid,)* trans. M. Abū al-Sharaf (Damascus, 2002), 7–34.

29. In our terminology progressive Muslims. For a definition of moderates, see El Fadl, *Great Theft*, 16–25.

30. As per Qur'an 5:48, see above, also 5:2, "Help ye one another in righteousness and piety but help ye not one another in sin and rancor: fear Allah: for Allah is strict in punishment"—Y.Ali; El-Fadl, *The Great Theft*, 207–208.

31. Esack, *Qur'an, Liberation and Pluralism*, 174

32. Cf. Miraly, *The Ethic of Pluralism*, 37.

33. Z. Mir-Hosseini, "The Construction of Gender in Islamic Legal Thought and Strategies for Reform," *Hawwa* 1,no. 1 (2003): 1–29.

34. Adnan, *Women and the glorious Qur'an: An Analytical Study of Women Related Verses* (Goettingen: Sura Al-Nisa'a, 2004), vi.

35. Ashrof, Islam and Gender Justice, 25.

36. Barlas, *Believing Women*, 143

37. Ibid, 159–160; Emphasis hers.

38. Ibid., 166; cf. Adnan, *Women and the glorious Qur'an*, vi.

39. See below.

40. Barlas, *Believing Women*, 56; cf. Sayed,. "Shifting Fortunes: Women and Hadith Transmission in Islamic History," PhD thesis, Princeton University, 2005, 103–121.

41. Ibid., 55.

42. El-Fadl, *Conference of the Books—The Search for Beauty in Islam* (Lanham, MD: University of America Press, 2001), 293; cf. Shahrur, *The Qur'an*, 303–304.

43. El Fadl, *Conference of the Books*, 294–296.

44. Shahrur, *The Qur'an*, 304–328.

45. Ibid., 298–299

46. For a full analysis of the context behind this verse, see F. Mernissi, *The Veil and the Male Elite–A Feminist Interpretation of Women's Rights in Islam* (Cambridge, MA: Perseus Books, 1991), 85–102.

47. El-Fadl, *Speaking in God's Name—Islamic Law, Authority and Women* (Oxford: Oneworld, 2003), 242; Shahrur, *The Qur'an*, 304–328.

48. For more on 'amal-based Sunna that is independent of hadith, see, Dutton, *The Origins of Islamic Law–The Qur'an, the Muwatta and Madinian 'Amal* (New York: Routledge, 2002); 'Abd Allah, *Malik's Concept of 'Amal* in the Light of Maliki Legal Theory (PhD Thesis, University of Chicago, 1978); Guraya, "The Concept of Sunna in the Muwatta of Malik b. Anas" (unpublished PhD thesis, McGill University, 1969).

49. Mernissi, *The Veil and the Male Elite*, chapters 8 and 10.

50. Mir-Hosseini, "The Construction of Gender in Islamic Legal Thought and Strategies for Reform," *Hawwa* 1, no. 1 (2003): 1–29, 3–4.

51. Ali, "Money, Sex and Power: The Contractual Nature of Marriage in Islamic Jurisprudence of the Formative Period" (PhD Thesis, Duke University, 2002).
52. Ibid.
53. Adnan, *Women and the glorious Qur'an*, 1–12.
54. A. El-Fadl, *The Great Theft*, 262
55. There are many alternative meanings for the word *qawwama* including guardians, supporters, masters or servants, Ibid., 267.
56. Shahrur's analysis of this verse is unique based upon his reinterpretation of keywords such as *ar-rijal, an-nisa',* and *nushuz.* He argues that *qiwama* is not gender specific concept but based upon certain qualities that both gender can embody. Shahrur, *The Qur'an*, 272–292.
57. See Wadud, *Qur'an and Woman—Rereading the Sacred Text from a Woman's Perspective*, 2nd ed. (Oxford: Oxford University Press, 1999), 66–74; Barlas, *Believing Women*, 184–189.
58. In this context, it is important to mention that Abu Zayd makes a hermeneutically important distinction of a *Qur'anic* value or practice being only that which is *initiated* by the Qur'an rather then being reflective of its revelatory milieu. In other words, only those values or practices *initiated* by the Qur'an can be considered as Qur'anic and those that were assumed to be operative by its contemporary addressees in the seventh century Hijaz are seen as merely contingent and not absolute or normative. See Abu Zayd, "The Nexus of Theory and Practice," in *The New Vioces of Islam–Rethinking Politics and Modernity, A Reader*, ed., M. Kamvara (Berkley and Los Angeles: University of California Press, 2006).
59. And others not quoted here of the same genre and having the same effect.
60. El-Fadl, *Speaking in God's Name.* See chapter seven in his book in particular.
61. Ibid., 246-247.
62. Duderija, "A Paradigm Shift."
63. See for example, Ashrof, Islam and Gender Justice, 58.
64. Found in Ibn Al-Athir, *Jami' al Usul* 4, no.1977 (1969): 414.
65. Barlas, *Believing Women,* 184
66. Qodir, *Hadith and Gender Justice*, 49–51.
67. Ibid., 51, 54
68. A. Al-Hilbri, *Windows of Faith. Muslim Women Scholar-Activists in North America: An Introduction to Muslim Women's Rights,* ed., Gisela Webb, (Syracuse, NY: Syracuse University Press, 2002), 51–72, 53.
69. Ashrof, Islam and Gender Justice, 22.
70. Kodir, *Hadith and Gender Justice*, 29–47.

CONCLUSION

1. Ahmed, *Women and Gender in Islam* (New Haven, CT: Yale University Press, 1992); Mernisi, *The Veil and the Male Elite, A Feminist Interpretation of Women's Rights in Islam* (Cambridge, MA: Perseus Books, 1991).

2. A. Afsaruddin, *First Muslims—History and Memory* (Oxford: Oneworld, 2007), 199.
3. El-Fadl, The Great Theft—Wrestling Islam from the Extremists (New York: Harper Collins, 2005), 1–25.

Selected Bibliography

Abbott, N. *Studies in Arabic Literary Papyri, Quranic Commentary and Tradition,* *Vol. 2.*, Chicago: University of Chicago, 1967.

Abd-Allah, U. F. "Malik's Concept of 'Amal in the Light of Maliki Legal Theory," PhD Thesis, University of Chicago, 1978.

Abd Al Wahhab, M. *Kitab Al-Tawhid.* http://islamicweb.com/beliefs/creed/abdulwahab.

Abdul Aziz, A., Abu-Nimer, M., and Sharify-Funk, M. *Contemporary Islam—Dynamic Not Static.* New York: Routledge, 2006.

'Abd Al-Jabbar, Al-Qadi. *Al-Mughni.* Vol 16. Edited by Taha Husayn. Cairo.

Abdul-Raof, H.' "Conceptual and Textual Chaining in Qur'anic Discourse." *Journal of Qur'anic Studies* 5, no. 2 (2003): 72–94.

Abrahamov, C. *Islamic Theology: Traditionalism and Rationalism.* Edinburgh: Edinburgh University Press, 1998.

Abu Dawud, S. *Sunnan,* http://www.muslimaccess.com/sunnah/hadeeth/abudawud/index.htm.

Abu Rabi', I. *The Blackwell Companion to Contemporary Islamic Thought.* Hoboken, NJ: Blackwell Publishing, 2006.

———. *Intellectual Origins of Islamic Resurgence in the Arab World.* Albany, NY: SUNY, 1996.

Abu Sayf, A. *The Choice of Every Woman.* Edited by Abdul Ahad. Lahore: Darussalam, 2004.

Abu Zahra, M. *Ibn Hanbal.* Cairo: Dar al-Fiker al-'Arabi, 1965.

———. *Tarikh al-Mathahib al-Islamiyyah.* Cairo: Dar al Fiker al-'Arabi, n.d.

Abu Zayd, H. N. *Re-thinking the Qur'an—Towards a Humanistic Hermeneutic.* Utrecht: Humanities University Press, 2004.

———. *Politik und Islam: Kritik des Religiösen Diskurses.* Translated by Cherifa Magdi. Frankfurt: Dipa-Verlag, 1996.

———. "The Nexus of Theory and Practice," in *The New Voices of Islam—Rethinking Politics and Modernity, A Reader.* Edited by M. Kamvara. Berkley and Los Angeles: University of California Press, 2006.

———. *Reformation of Islamic Thought—A Historical Analysis.* Amsterdam: Amsterdam University Press, 2007.

———. *Mafhūm al-Nass: Dirāsah fī 'Ulūm al-Qur'ān.* 5th ed. Beirut and Cairo: Dirasat Adabiyah, 1998.

Achrati, A. "Arabic, Qur'anic Speech and Postmodern Language: What the Qur'an Simply Says." *Arabica* 54, no. 2 (2008): 161-203.

Adnan, G. *Women and the Glorious Qur'an: An Analytical Study of Women Related Verses.* Goettingen: Sura Al-Nisa'a, 2004.

A. Afsaruddin, *First Muslims—History and Memory.* Oxford: Oneworld, 2007.

Ali Ahmad Sa'id Isbir, A., "Reflections on the Manifestations of Intellectual Backwardness in Arab Society." In "The Unpredictability of the Past—Turath and Hermeneutics." Edited by I. Mansoor. PhD Thesis, University of California, 2000.

Al-'Ali, I. M. *Muhammad Nasir Al-Din al-Albani: Muhaddith al'asr wa nasir al-sunna.* Damascus: dar al Qal'a, 2001.

Ahmad, A. "The Structural Interrelations of Theory and Practice in Islamic Law: A Study of Takhrij al-Furu ala al-Usul Literature." PhD Thesis, Harvard University, 2005.

Ahmed, I. "The Significance of Sunnah and Hadith and Their Early Documentation," PhD Thesis, Edinburgh University, 1974.

Ahmed, L. *Women and Gender in Islam,* New Haven, CT: Yale University Press, 1992.

Ahmed, R. "Qur'anic Exegesis and the Classical Tafsir." In E. Karic, *Kur'an u Savremenon Dobu, (Qur'an in Contemporary Times).* El-Kalem: Bosanski Kulturni Centar, 1997.

Al-Albanee, N. *The Principals of Salafee Methodology: An Islamic Manual For Reform.* Toronto: T.R.O.I.D., 2003.

———. "Responding to Salaams of the Jews and the Christians," www.bakkah. net.

———. *The Hadith Is Proof Itself in Belief & Laws.* Calgary: A Daar of Islamic Heritage, 1995.

Al-Alma'i, I. A. *Dirasat fi at-Tafsir al-Maudu' i li al-Qur'an al-Karim.* Riyadh, 1984.

Al-'Asqalani,I. H. *Huda al-Sari, Muqaddimat fath al-bari.* Vol 13. Cairo: Al-Matba'a al-Bahiya al-Misriya, 1928.

———. *Al Isaba fi Mayiz Al-Sahaba.* Vol. 8. Cairo: Maktaba al-Dirasa Al-Islamiya, Dar al-Nahda, n.d.

Al-Atharee, F. *Clarification that the Ahlul-Hadeeth are the Saved Sect and Victorius Group.* Toronto: T.R.O.I.D., 2003.

Al-Attar, M. *Islamic Ethics: Divine Command Theory in Arabo-Islamic Thought.* New York: Routledge, 2010.

Al-Azami, M. *On Schacht's Origins of Muhammadan Jurisprudence.* Riyadh: King Saud University, 1985.

———. *Studies in Hadith Methodology and Literature.* Selangor: Islamic Book Trust, 2002.

———. *Studies in Early Hadith Literature.* Beirut: Al-Maktab al-Islami, 1968.

Al-Azmeh, A. *Islams and Modernities.* London: Verso, 1993.

———. "The Muslim Canon from late Antiquity to the Era of Modernism." In *Canonization and Decanonization.* Edited by A. van der Kooij and K. van der Toorn. Leiden: E. J. Brill, 1998.

———. *Arabic Thought and Islamic Societies*. London: Croom Helm, 1986.

———. "Orthodoxy and Hanbalite Fideism." *Arabica* 35, no. 3 (1988): 253–267.

Allievi, S., and Nielsen, J., eds. *Muslim Networks and Transnational Communities in and across Europe*. Leiden: E. J. Brill, 2003.

Al-Basri's, A. *Al-Mu'tamad fi usul al-Fiqh*. Beirut: Dar al-Kutub al-'Ilmiyya, n.d.

Al-Bukhari, M. *Sahih al-Bukhari*. Vol. 9. Translated by M. M. Khan. Lahore: Kazi Publications, 1979.

Al-Darimi, M. *Khasa'is al-Tashri al-Islami fi'l Siyasa wa 'l Hikma*. Damascus, 1989.

Al-Dawish, A., ed. *Fatawa al-lajna al-da'ima lil-buhuth al 'ilmiyya wal ifta', Maktabat al-Ma'arif*. Vol. 20. Riyadh: American Trust Publications, 2002.

Al-Faruqi, L. *Women, Muslim Society and Islam*. Indianapolis, IN: American Trust Publications, 1991.

Algar, H. *Wahhabism: A Critical Essay*. New York: Islamic Publications International, 2002.

Al-Ghazalli, M. *Al-Sunnah al-nabawiyya bayna ahl al-fiqh wa ahl-hadith*. 13th edition. Cairo: Dar al-Shuruq, 2005.

Al-Ghumari,'A. *Tawjih al-'inaya li-ta'rif'ilm al-hadith riwaya wa diraya*. Edited by Safwat Jawdah Ahmad. Cairo: Maktabat al-Qahira, 2002.

Al-Ghumari, A. *Dar 'al-da'f 'an hadith man 'ashiqa fa-'aff*. Edited by 'Iyad al-Ghawj. Cairo: Dar al-Imam al-Tirmidhi, 1996.

Al-Haddaadee, A. Y. *The Book of Forthy Hadith Regarding the Madhhab of the Salaf*. Translated by Abu Khadeejah Abdul-Waheed. Birmingham: Minhaj As-Sunnah Publications, 2005.

Al-Habash, A. "Ihtikar al-khalas," *Tishrın al-Usbu'i*. no. 97, January 31, 2000.

———. Nahwa ta'sıl ıdiyulujı˜ li al-hiwar bayn al-adyan, *Tishrı˜n*, May 27, 2001.

Al-Hajjaj, I. M. *Sahih*. http://www.muslimaccess.com/sunnah/hadeeth/muslim/index.htm.

Al-Ḥasan, K. B. *Al-Ijtihād bi-l-Ra'y fi Madrasat al-Ḥijāz al-Fiqhiyya*. Cairo: Maktabat al-Zahrā', 1997.

Al-Hashimi, M. A. *The Ideal Muslimah: The True Islamic Personality of the Muslim Woman as Defined in the Qur'an and the Sunna*. Translated by N. Al-Khattab. Riyadh: International Islamic Publishing House, 2005.

A.Al-Hibri,'An Introduction to Muslim Women's Rights Gisela Webb, ed., *Windows of Faith. Muslim Women Scholar-Activists in North America*. Syracuse: Syracuse University Press, 2002, 51-72, 53.

Al-Ḥijwī, M. *Al-Fikr al-Sāmī fi Tārīkh al-Fiqh al-Islāmī*. Beirut: Dār al-Kutub al-'Ilmiyya, 1995.

Ali, K. "Progressive Muslims and Islamic Jurisprudence: The Necessity for Critical Engagement with Marriage and Divorce Law." *Progressive Muslims—On Justice, Gender and Pluralism*. Edited by O. Safi. Oxford: Oneword, 2003.

———. "Money, Sex and Power: The Contractual Nature of Marriage in Islamic Jurisprudence of the Formative Period," PhD Thesis, Duke University, 2002.

———. *Sexual Ethics and Islam: Feminist Reflections on Qur'an, Hadith, and Jurisprudence*. Oxford: Oneworld, 2006.

Ali, K. *Marriage and Islam in Early Islam.* Cambridge, MA: Harvard University Press, 2010.

Ali, Y. *The Holy Qur'an: Text, Translation and Commentary.* 2nd ed. New York: Tahrike Tarsile Qur'an, 1988.

Al-Jassas, A. B. *Ahkam al-Qur'an.* Vol. 1. Edited by 'Abd Al-Rahman Muhammad. Cairo: al-Matba'a al-Bahija, 1928.

———. *Usul al-Jassas :al-fusul fi al-Usul.* Edited by M. Tamir. Beirut: Dar ul-Kutub al-'Ilmiyya, 2000.

Al-Jaza'iri', T. *Tawjih al-nazar ila usul al-athar.* Edited by 'Abd al-Fattah Abu Ghudda. Aleppo: Maktabat al-Matbu'at al-Islamiyya, 1995.

al-Kattani, M. B. J. *Nazm al-mutanathir min al-hadith al-mutawatir.* Beirut: Dar ul-kutub al-'ilmiyya, 1987.

Al-Madanee, A., *A History of the Ahlul-Hadeeth—A Study of the Saved Sect and that It Is The People of Hadeeth.* Translated by Aboo 'Ubaidah ibn Basheer. Birmingham: Salafi Publications, 2005.

Al-Madkhalee, R. *The Methodology of Ahlus-Sunnah Wal-Jamaa'ah on Criticising Individuals, Books and Groups.* Translated by Abu Maryam Isma'eel. Alacron: Al-Ibaanah Publishing, 2005.

———. *The Status of the People of Hadeeth (the Ahlul-*Hadeeth): *Their Feats and Praiseworthy Effects in the Religion.* Translated by Abu Hakeem Bilal Davis. UK: Salafi Publications, 2003.

Al-Majdub, M.*'Ulama' wa mufakkirun 'araftuhum: al-juz al-awwal.* Cairo: Dar al I'tisam, 1980.

Al-Qasimi, J. *Qawa'id al-tahdith min funun mustalah al-hadith.* Damascus, 1935.

Al-Raysuni, A. *Nazariyyat al-Maqasid 'ind al-imam al-Shatibi.* Herndon: International Institute of Islamic Thought, 1992.

Al-Shadr, M. *Al-Madrasa Al-Qur'aniyya: at-Tafsir al-maudu'I wa at-tafsir al-tajzi fi al-Qur'an al-Karim.* Beirut: Dar at-ta'arruf li al-matba'a.

Al-Suhaymee, S. *The Methodology of the Salaf in Aqidah and Its Influence on Muslim Unity.* Translated by Aboo Aaliyah Dwight. Salafi Publications, 2001.

Al-Sulaymani, Abd-Al-Salam. *Al-Ijtihad fi al-fiqh al-Islami.* Rabat: Wuzarat al-Awqaf, 1996.

Al-Turabi, H. *Al-Tafsir al-Tawhidi.* 1st ed. Vol. I. London: Dar Al-Saqi, 2004

Al-Uthaimeen, M. S. *A Reply to the Doubts of the Qutubiyah concerning Ascription to Sunnah and Salafiyyah,* www.salafibuplications.com.

———. *Bida'ah and their evil effects—The Unique Nature of the Perfection Found in the Sharee'ah and the Danger of Innovating into It.* Translated by Aboo 'Abd-illaah as-Sayalaanee. Salafi Publications, 1999.

Al-Waadi'eeyah, U. "The Manners of the Woman Leaving the Home." Accessed October 16, 2007. www.therightouspath.com.

Amirpour, K. *Die Entpolitisierung des Islam: Abdolkarim Sorushs Denken und Wirkung in der Islamischen Republik Iran.* Würzburg: Eron Verlag, 1999.

Ansari, Z. I. "Islamic Juristic Terminology before Shafi'i: A Semantic Analysis with Special Reference to Kufa." *Arabica* xix (1972).

Ansari, Z. I., and Ahmad, K. "An Early Discussion on Islamic Jurisprudence: Some Notes on al-Radd 'al-Siyar al-Awza'i." In *Islamic Perspectives: Studies in Honour of Sayyid Abul A'la Mawdudi.* Leicester: The Islamic Foundation, 1979.

Anwar, H. *Wilayah al-mar'ah fi al-Fiqh al-Islami*. Masters thesis, Imam Saud Islamic University, Dar Balansiyah, 1999.

Arafat, W. N. "New light on the story of Banu Qurayza and the Jews of Medina." *Journal of the Royal Asiatic Society of Great Britain and Ireland* (1976).

Arkoun, M. *Rethinking Islam—Common Questions, Uncommon Answers*. Translated by R. D. Lee. Boulder: CO. Westview Press, 1994.

———. "Introduction: An Assessment of and Perspectives on the Study of the Qur'an." In *Formation of the Classical Islamic World*. Vol. 24. Edited by I. Conrad. Ashgate, 2001.

"Rethinking Islam Today." In *Liberal Islam—A Sourcebook*. Edited by C. Kurzman. Oxford: Oxford University Press, 1998.

———. *The Unthought in Contemporary Islamic Thought*. London: The Institute of Ismaili Studies, 2002.

Armstrong, K. *Muhammad: A Western Attempt to Understand Islam*. London: Victor Gollancz, 1991.

Asad, T. *The Idea of Anthropology of Islam*. Occasional Paper Series, Georgetown University Center for Contemporary Arab Studies, March 1986.

Asani, A. "On Pluralism, Intolerance and the Qur'an." *The American Scholar* 72, no. 1 (Winter 2002).

Ash-Shahawi, M. *Marital Discourse: Causes and Cures*. Houston, TX: Dar-us-salaam Publishers, 2004.

Ashraf, Mohamad, Islam and Gender Justice (New Delhi: Kalpaz Publications, 2005).

Al-Ashur, A. *Alaysa al-Subh bi Qarib*? Al-Shakirah al-Tunisiyyah li-funun al-rasm. Tunis, 1988.

At-Tabari, I. J. *Tarikh al-Rusul wa al-Muluk*. Edited by. M. J. de Goeje et al. Leiden: Brill Press, 1879–1901.

———. *Jami al-bayan 'an tawil ay al-Qur'an*. Vol. 4. Beirut: Dar al-Fikr, 1995.

Attia, G. E. *Towards Realization of the Higher Intents of Islamic Law*. 2nd ed. London: International Institute of Islamic Thought, 2007.

Auda, Y. *Maqasid Al-Shari'ah as Philosophy of Islamic Law*. London: IIT, 2008.

Al-Awa, S. *Textual Relations in the Qur'an: Relevance, Coherence and Structure*. New York: Routledge, 2006.

Azam, H. "Sexual Violence in Maliki Legal Ideology—From Discursive Foundations to Classical Articulation." PhD thesis, Duke University, 2007.

Baker, W. W. *More in Common Than You Think (Al-mushtarak akthar mimma ta_taqid)*. Translated by M. Abu al-Sharaf. Damascus: Defenders Publications, 2002.

Bamyeh, M. "Hermeneutics against Instrumental Reason: National and Post-National Islam in the 20th Century." *Third World Quarterly* 29, no. 3 (2008): 555–574.

Barlas, A. *Believing Women in Islam—Unreading Patriarchal Interpretations of the Qur'an*. Austin: University of Texas Press, 2004.

Al-Bassam, A. *'Ulama Najd khilal themaniyat qurun*. Vol. 2. Riyadh: Dar al-Asima, n.d.

Baz, B. *A Statement and Clarification of Al-Salafiyyah: Concepts and Principals*. Translated by M. Mohar Ali. Ipswich: Jam'iat Ihyaa Minhaaj Al-Sunna, 2000.

Beck, E. *Die Gestalt des Abraham am Wendepunkt der Entwicklung Muhammads: Analyse von Sure 2.* Paris: Le Museon, 1952.

Benhabib, Sh. *Situating the Self-Gender, Community and Post-Modernism in Contemporary Ethics.* New York: Routledge, 1992.

H. Berg, ed. *Method and Theory in the Study of Islamic Origins.* Leiden: E. J. Brill, 2003.

Bramsen, D. "Divine Law and Human Understanding: Interpreting Shari'a within Institutions of Ifta'a and Qada'a in Saudi Arabia." MA Thesis, Københavns Universitet, 2007.

Brown, D. *Rethinking Tradition in Modern Islamic Thought.* Cambridge: Cambridge University Press, 1996.

Boulatta, I. *Trends and Issues in Contemporary Arab Thought.* Albany: State University of New York Press, 1990.

Carson, D. A. *The Gagging of God: Christianity Confronts Pluralism.* Grand Rapids, MI: Zondervan Publishing House, 1996.

Chaumont, "E.'al-Salaf wa'l-Khalaf'." In *Encyclopedia of Islam.* Leiden: E. J. Brill, 1954–2003.

Conrad, I., ed. *Formation of the Classical Islamic World.* Vol. 24. Aldershot: Ashgate/Variorum, 2004.

Cooke, M. "Deploying the 'Muslimwoman.'" *Journal of Feminist Studies in Religion* 24, no. 1 (2008): 91–119.

Dahlen, A. *Islamic Law, Epistemology and Modernity—Legal Philosophy in Contemporary Iran.* New York: Routledge, 2003.

Dickinson, E. *The Development of Early Sunnite Hadith Criticism: The Taqdima of Ibn Abi Hatim Al-Razi.* Leiden: E. J. Brill, 2001.

Donner, F.M. "From Believers to Muslims: Confessional Self-Identity in the Early Islamic Community." *al-Abhath* 50–51 (2002–2003): 9–53.

———. *Muhammad and the Believers at the Origins of Islam.* Cambridge, MA and London: Belknap Press, 2010.

Draz, M. *The Moral World of the Qur'an.* London: I. B. Taurus, 2008.

Duderija, A. "Toward a Methodology of the Nature and the Scope of the Concept of Sunnah." *Arab Law Quarterly* 21, no. 3 (2007): 269–280.

———. "Identifying Factors Determining Religious Identity Constructions among Western Born Muslims: Towards a Theoretical Framework." *Journal of Muslim Minority Affairs* 28, no. 3 (2008): 371–400.

———. "The Evolution in the Canonical Sunni Hadith Body of Literature and the Concept of an Authentic Hadith during the Formative Period of Islamic Thought as Based on Recent Western Scholarship." *Arab Law Quarterly* 23, no. 4 (2009): 1–27.

———. "The Evolution in the Concept of Sunnah during the First Four Generations of Muslims in Relation to the Development of the Concept of an Authentic Hadith as Based on Recent Western Scholarship." Peer-reviewed conference paper, unpublished.

Dutton, Yasin. *The Origins of Islamic Law—The Qur'an, the Muwatta and Madinian 'Amal.* New York: Routledge, Curzon, 2002.

———. *The Role of the Reader: Explorations in the Semiotics of Texts.* Bloomington: University of Indiana Press, 1979.

Eickelman, F., and J. Piscatory, *Muslim Politics*. Princeton, NJ: Princeton University Press, 1996.

El-Fadl, K. *Speaking in God's Name—Islamic Law, Authority and Women*. Oxford: Oneworld, 2003.

———. *The Place of Tolerance in Islam*. Boston: Beacon Press, 2002.

———. *Conference of the Books—The Search for Beauty in Islam*. Lanham, MD: University of America Press, 2001.

———. *The Great Theft—Wrestling Islam from the Extremists*. New York: Harper Collins, 2005.

———. "The Ugly Modern and the Modern Ugly: Reclaiming the Beautiful in Islam." In *Progressive Muslims*. Edited by O. Safi. Oxford: Oneworld, 2003.

———. "The Place of Ethical Obligations in Islamic Law."4 *UCLA J. Islamic and Near E.L.*1 (2005): 1–40.

Emon, A. N. "Towards a Natural Law Theory in Islamic Law: Muslim Juristic Debates on Reason as a Source of Obligation." *JINEL* 3, no. 1 (2003): 1–51.

———. *Islamic Natural Law Theories*. Oxford: Oxford University Press, 2010.

Esack, F. *Qur'an, Liberation and Pluralism: An Islamic Perspective of Interreligious Solidarity against Oppression*. Oxford: Oneworld, 1997.

———. "Contemporary Democracy and Human Rights Project for Muslim Societies." In *Contemporary Islam—Dynamic not Static*. Edited by Abdul Aziz Said, M. Abu Nimer, and M. Sharify-Fumk. London and New York: Routledge, 2006.

———. "Qur'anic Hermeneutics: Prospects and Problems." *The Muslim World* 83, no. 2 (1993): 118–141.

———. "Islam and Gender Justice: Beyond Apologia." In *The Justice Men Owe To Women: Positive Resources from World Religions*. Edited by J. Raines and D. Maguire. New York: Suny Press, 2000.

Esposito, J., and D. Mogahed. *Who Speaks for Islam? What a Billion Muslims Really Think*. Gallup Press, 2008.

Encyclopedia of Islam. Leiden: E. J. Brill, 1954–2003.

Fasolt, C. *The Limits of History*. Chicago: The University of Chicago Press, 2004.

Ferguson, D. S. *Biblical Hermeneutics: An Introduction*. Atlanta, GA: John Knox Press, 1986.

Fish, S. *Is There a Text in This Class?: The Authority of Interpretive Communities*. Cambridge, MA: Harvard University Press, 1980.

Friedmann, Y. *Tolerance and Coercion in Islam: Interfaith Relations in the Muslim Tradition*. Cambridge: Cambridge University Press, 2003.

Fletcher, M. "How Can We Understand Islamic Law Today?" *Journal of Islam and Islamo-Christian Relations* 17, no. 2 (April 2006): 159–172.

Gadamer, H. *Truth and Method*. 2nd rev. ed. Translated by Joel Weinsheimer and Donald G. Marshall. London: Continuum, 2004.

Giddens, A. *The Consequences of Modernity*. Stanford, CA: Stanford University Press, 1990.

Gaebel, M. *Von der Kritik des arabischen Denkens zum panarabischen Aufbruch: Das philosophische und politische Denken Muhammad Abid Gabiris*. Berlin: Klaus Schwarz Verlag, 1995.

Gelder, G. *Beyond the Line: Classical Arabic literary Critics on the Coherence and Unity of the Poem.* Leiden: E. J. Brill, 1982.

Goldziher, I. *Die Zahiriten—Ihr Lehrsystem und ihre Geschichte.* Leipzig: Schultze, 1884.

———. *Introduction to Islamic Theology and Law.* Translated by A. and R. Hamori. Princeton NJ: Princeton University Press, 1981.

———. *Muslim Studies.* Vol. II. Translated by Barber and Stern George. London: Allen & Unwin ltd., 1971.

———. *Die Richtungen der islamischen Koranauslegung.* Leiden: Neudruck, 1952.

Graham, W. A. *Divine Word and Prophetic Word in Early Islam-A Reconsideration of the Sources, with Special References to the Divine Saying or Hadith Qudsi.* Mouton: Hague, 1977.

Guenther, S. "Assessing the Sources of Classical Arabic Compilations: The Issues of Categories and Methodologies." *Br. J. Middle Eastern Studies* 32, no. 1 (2005): 75-98.

Guraya, M. 'The Concept of Sunnah in the Muwatta of Malik b. Anas', McGill University, unpublished PhD thesis, 1969.

Haddad, G. F. *Albani and his Friends—A Concise Guide to the Salafi Movement.* Aqsa Publications, 2004.

———. http://www.abc.se/~m9783/n/sdb_e.html.

Hakim, A. "Conflicting Images of Lawgivers: The Caliph and the prophet Sunnat 'Umar and Sunnat Muhammad." In *Method and Theory in the Study of Islamic Origins.* Edited by H. Berg. Leiden: E. J.Brill, 2003.

Hallaq, W. *A History of Islamic Legal Theories.* Cambridge: Cambridge University Press, 1997.

———. *Authority, Continuity and Change in Islamic Law.* Cambridge: Cambridge University Press, 2001.

———. *The Origins and Evolution of Islamic Law.* Cambridge: Cambridge University Press, 2005.

———. "The Authenticity of Prophetic Hadith:a Pseudo Problem." *Studia Islamica* (1999): 75–90.

Hanafi, H. *Islam in the Modern World.* Vol I and II. Cairo: Dar ul-Kebaa, 2000.

Hasan, A. *Early Development of Islamic Jurisprudence.* Islamabad, 1970.

Haykel, B. "On the Nature of Salafi Thought and Action." In *Global Salafism : Islam's New Religious Movement.* Edited by R. New York: Meijer Columbia University Press, 2009.

Haywood, J. "Al-Suyuti." In *Encyclopedia of Islam.* Leiden: E. J. Brill, 1954–2003

Hodgson, M. *The Venture of Islam, 3 Volumes.* Chicago: University of Chicago Press, 1958.

Hourani, G. "Ethical Presuppositions of the Qur'an." *Muslim World* 70 (Jan. 1980).

Hoyland, R., ed. *Muslims and Others in Early Islamic Society.* Ashgate: Variorum, 2004.

Hussein, F., ed. *Muslim Women.* London: St. Martin Press, 1984.

———."The Ideal and Contextual Realities of Muslim Women." In *Muslim Women.* Edited by F. Hussein. London: St. Martin Press, 1984.

Ibn 'Abd al-Salâm. *al-Qawâ`id al-Kubrà.* Beirut: Dar al-Ma'rifa, n.d.

Ibn Bahadur al-Zarkashi. *Al-Ijaba li-irad ma istadrakathu ,'A' isha 'ala al-sahaba.* Cairo, 1960.

Ibn Al-Athir. *Jami' al Usul.* Cairo, 1969.

Ibn Baz. A. *Statement and Clarification of Al-Salafiyyah: Concept and Principles.* Translated by M. M. Ali and J. Ihyaa. Riyadh: 'Minhaj Al-Sunnah, 1996.

———. *The Obligation of Acting Upon the Sunnah of the Messenger And The Unbelief of Those Who Reject It.* Translated by Abu Talhah Dawood. Birmingham: Minhaj As-Sunnah Publications. 2004.

Ibn Baz, A., M. Al-Uthaymeen, and M. Al-Madkhalee. *Three Essays on the Obligation of Veiling.* Translated by Abu Maryam Ismaeel Alarcon. Toronto: Al-Ibaanah Book Publishing, 2003.

Ibn Faris, M. *Mu'jam Maqayis al-Luga* (1368 A.H.). Vol 6. Edited by Abd al-Salam Muhammad Harun. Cairo.

Ibn Habban, B. *Al-Ihsan fi taqrib sahih Ibn Habban.* Vol. 1. Edited by Sh. Arna'ut. Beirut: Mu'assaset al-Risalah, 1998.

Ibn, Qayyim al-Jawi. *Ahkam al-Nisa'a.* Edited by 'Ad al-Majid tu'ma. Beirut, 1997.

Ibn, Qutayba. *Ta'wil Mukhtalif al-Hadith.* Edited by M. Z. al-Najjar. Beirut, 1393/1972.

Imam, M. K. *al-dalil al-irshadi Ila maqasid Al-Shari'ah al-islamiyyah.* London: Maqasid Research Centre, 2006.

Iqbal, M. The Reconstruction of Religious Thought in Islam. Lahore: Kazi Publications, 1999.

Islahi, A. *Juristic Differences and How to Resolve Them in an Islamic State.* Translated by S. A. Rauf. Lahore: Islamic Publications, 1986.

Ismail, M. *The Hijab Why?* www.saaid.net. accessed May 25, 2009.

Ismail Ibn, M. A. *The Veil-Evidence of Niqab.* Translated by Abdallah Elaceri. London: Al-Firdous, 2009.

Izutsu, T. *The Concept of Belief in Islamic Theology.* Montreal: McGill University Press, 1965.

———. *God and Man in the Qur'an: A Semantical Analysis of Qur'anic Weltanschauung.* Montreal: Mc Gill University Press, 1964.

———. *Ethico-Religious Concepts in the Qur'an.* Montreal: Mc Gill University Press, 2002.

Jackson, Sh. "Fiction and Formalism: Towards a Functional Analysis of Usul Al-Fiqh." in B. Weiss, *Studies in Islamic Legal Theory.* Leiden: Brill, 2002.

———. *On the Boundaries of Theological Tolerance in Islam (Abu Hamid Al-Ghazali's Faysal al-Tafriqa Bayna al-Islam wa al-Zandaqa).* Oxford: Oxford University Press, 2002.

———. *Islamic Law and the State—The Constitutional Jurisprudence of Shihab al-Din al-Qarafi.* Leiden: E. J. Brill, 1996.

———. "Taqlid, Legal Scaffolding and the Scope of legal injunctions in the post-formative theory: Mutlaq and 'Amm in the Jurisprudence of Shihab al-Din al-Qarafi." *Islamic Law and Society* 3, no. 2 (1996): 165–192.

———. "From Prophetic Actions to Constitutional Theory: A Novel Chapter in Medieval Muslim Jurisprudence." *International Journal of Middle Eastern Studies* 25 (1993): 71–90.

Jackson, Sh. Literalism, Empiricism, and Induction: Apprehending and Concretizing Islamic Law's Maqâsid al-Sharî. *2006 Mitch.St.L.Rev*: 1469–1486.

Johnstone, D. L. "Maqasid al-Shari'ah: Epistemology and Hermeneutics of Muslim Theologies of Human Rights." *Die Welt des Islams* 47, no. 2 (2007): 149–187.

Juynboll, G. H. A. *Muslim Tradition—Studies in Chronology, Provenance and Authorship of Early Hadith*. Cambridge: Cambridge University Press, 1983.

Kadivar, M. "The Principles of Compatibility of Islam and Modernity." http://www.irri-kiib.be/speechnotes/04/islam-modern-04/Kadivar-EN.htm.

Kamali, H. M. *Hadith Methodology—Authenticity, Compilation, Classification and Criticism of Hadith*. Malaysia: Ilmiah Publishers, 2002.

———. *The Principles of Islamic Jurisprudence*. Cambridge: Cambridge University Press, 1991.

———. "Methodological Issues in Islamic Jurisprudence." *Arab Law Quarterly* 11, no. 1 (1996): 3-33.

———. "Istihan and the Renewal of Islamic Law." http://www.google.com.au/search?hl=en&rlz=1T4IRFA_enAU319AU321&q=madhahib+istihsan&aq=f&aqi=&aql=&oq=.

Kamaruddin, A. "Nasiruddin Al-Albani on Muslim Sahih: A Critical Study of His Method." *Islamic Law and Society* 11, no. 2 (2004).

———. *The Reliability of Hadith-Transmission: A Re-examination of Hadith—Critical Methods*. PhD thesis. Friedrich-Wilhelms Universitaet, Bonn, 2005.

Kamvara, M., ed. *The New Voices of Islam—Rethinking Politics and Modernity: A Reader*. Berkley and Los Angeles: University of California Press, 2006.

Karamustafa, A. "A Civilisational Project in Progress." In *Progressive Muslims—On Justice, Gender and Pluralism*. Edited by O.Safi. Oxford: One World, 2003.

Kassis, H. E. *A Concordance of the Qur'an*. Berkley: University of California Press, 1983.

Shah-Kazemin, R. *The Other in the Light of the One: The Universality of the Qur'an and Interfaith Dialogue*. Cambridge: The Islamic Texts Society, 2006.

Keller, Nuh Ha Mim, http://www.masud.co.uk/ISLAM/nuh/bida.htm. accessed October 10, 2010.

Kister, M. J. "The Massacre of the Banu Quraiza: A Re-examination of a Tradition." *Jerusalem Studies in Arabic and Islam* 8 (1968): 61–96.

Koselleck,K. *The Practice of Conceptual History-Timing History, Spacing Concepts*. Translated by T. S. Presner et al. Stanford, CA: Stanford University Press, 2002.

Kurzman, C., ed. *Liberal Islam—A Sourcebook*. Oxford: Oxford University Press, 1998.

———.*Modernist Islam, 1840–1940: A Source-Book*. Edited by Charles Kurzman. Oxford: Oxford University Press, 2002.

Lauziere, H. The Construction of Salafiyya: Considering Salafism from the Perspective of Conceptual History. *Int. J. Middle East Stud.* 42 (2010): 369–389.

Lecker, M. *The 'Constitution of Medina': Muhammad's First Legal Document*. Princeton, NJ: The Darwin Press, 2004.

Mabrook, A. "A New Historical Discussion in Islam." In *The Blackwell Companion to Contemporary Islamic Thought*. Edited by I. M. Abu Rabi'. Hoboken, NJ: Blackwell Publishing, 2006.

Madelung, W. *The Succession to Muhammad*. Cambridge: Cambridge University Press, 1997.

Maghen, Z. "The Interaction between Islamic Law and Non-Muslims." *Islamic Law and Society* 10, no. 2 (2003): 267–275.

Mahmood, M. *How to Protect Yourself from the Fitnah of Women*. Translated by Taalib ibn Tyson al Britaanee, 2009.

Mahmood, S. "Secularism, Hermeneutics, Empire: The Politics of Islamic Reformation." *Public Culture* 18, no. 2 (2006): 323–347.

Malti-Douglas, F. *Woman's Body, Woman's Word: Gender and Discourse in Arabo-Islamic Writing*. Princeton, NJ: Princeton University Press, 1991.

Mamdani, M. *Good Muslim, Bad Muslim: America, the Cold War, and the Roots of Terror*. New York: Pantheon Book, 2004.

Mansoor, I. "The Unpredictability of the Past-Turath and Hermeneutics." PhD Thesis, University of California, 2000.

Masud, M. Kh. "Islamic Modernism." In *Islam and Modernity—Key Issues and Debates*. Edited by M. Kh. Masud, A. Salvatore, and M. Bruinessen. Edinburgh: Edinburgh University Press, 2009.

Mathnee, M. "Critical Reading of Fazrul Rahman's Islamic Methodology in History." M. A. Thesis, University of Cape Town, 2005.

Maymani, W. A. *Qa'idah al-Dhara'i*. Jeddah: Dar al-Mujtama', 2000.

McAuliffe, J. *Qur'anic Christians: An Analysis of Classical and Modern Exegesis*. Cambridge: Cambridge University Press, 1991.

———. "Text and Textuality: Q.3:7 as a Point of Intersection." In *Literary Structures of Religious Meaning in the Qur'an*. Edited by I. Boullata. London: Curzon Press, 2000.

Melchert, C. *The Formation of the Sunni Schools of Law in the 9th-10th Centuries*. Leiden: E. J. Brill, 1997.

———. "Ibn Mujahid and the Establishment of Seven Qur'anic Readings." *Studia Islamica* No.91 (2000): 5–22.

Mernissi, F. The *Veil and the Male Elite—A Feminist Interpretation of Women's Rights in Islam*. Cambridge, MA: Perseus Books, 1991.

———. *Beyond the Veil—Male-Female Dynamics in a Modern Muslim Society*. Cambridge, MA: Schenkman Publishing Company, 1975.

Mir, M. *Coherence in the Qur'an: A Study of Islahi's Concept of Nazm in Tadabbur—I-Qur'an*. Plainfield, IN: American Trust Publication, 1986.

Miraly, M. N. *The Ethic of Pluralism in the Qur'an and the Prophet's Medina*. M.A. Thesis, McGill University, 2006.

Mir-Hosseini, Z. "The Construction of Gender in Islamic Legal Thought and Strategies for Reform." *Hawwa* 1, no. 1 (2003): 1–29.

Moosa, E. "The Poetics and Politics of Law After Empire: reading Women's Rights in the Contestations of Law" *1 UCLA, J. Islamic & Near E.L.* 1 (2001–2002): 1–28.

———. "Ghazali and the Poetics of Imagination." Berkeley: University of California Press, 2005.

———. Introduction to F. Rahman's *Revival and Reform in Islam*. Oxford: Oneworld Publications, 2000.

Moosa, E. "Transitions in the 'Progress' of Civilisation." In *Voices of Islam*. Edited by O.Safi. London: Praeger, 2007.

———. "The Debts and Burdens of Critical Islam." In *Progressive Muslims—On Gender, Justice and Pluralism*. Edited by O. Safi. Oxford: Oneworld, 2003.

Motzki, H. *Die Anfaenge der islamischen Jurisprudenz* (Deutsche Morgenlaendische Gesellschaft). Berlin:Franz Steiner Verlag ,1991).

Mourad, S. A, *Early Islam between Myth and History*. Leiden: E. J. Brill, 2006.

Mumisa, M. "Toward an African Qur'anic Hermeneutics." *Journal of Qur'anic Studies* 4, no. 1 (2002): 61–77.

Neuwirth, A. "Some Reflections on Qur'anic History and the History in the Qur'an." *Journal of Qur'anic Studies* 5 (2003).

Noor, F. A. "What is the Victory of Islam ?Towards a different understanding of the ummah and the political success in the contemporary world." In *Progressive Muslims—On Justice, Gender and Pluralism*. Edited by O. Safi. Oxford: Oneworld, 2003.

Noth, A. "Problems of Differentiation between Muslim and Non-Muslims: Re-reading the 'Ordinaces of Umar' (Al-Shurut Al'Umariyya)." In *Muslims and Others in Early Islamic Society*. Edited by R. Hoyland. Ashgate:Variorum, 2004.

Osman, A. The History and the Doctrine of the Zahiri madhhab. PhD thesis, Princeton, 2010.

Peter, F., and E. Arigita. "The Muslim World." *Authorizing Islam in Europe* 96, no. 4, 2006.

Qodir, F. *Hadith and Gender Justice—Understanding the Prophetic Traditions*. Fahmina Institute, 2007.

Qaradawi, Y. *Halal and Haram in Islam*. Kuala Lumpur: Islamic Book Trust, 1995.

———. *Approaching the Sunnah: Comprehension & Controversy*. International Institute of Islamic Thought, 2007.

Qahhani, M. S. *Al-Wala' Wa'l—Bara' according to the 'Aqeedah of the Salaf*. Part 2. London: Al-Firdous ltd. 1999.

Rahman, F. *Revival and Reform in Islam: A Study of Islamic Fundamentalism*. Edited by E.Moosa. Oxford: Oneworld, 2000.

———. "Islam: Challenges and Opportunities." in *Islam : Past Influence and Present Challenge*. Edited by A.T. Welch and P. Cachia. Edinburgh: Edinburgh University Press, 1979.

———. *Islam*. 2nd. ed. Chicago: Chicago University Press, 1979.

———. *Islam and Modernity: Transformation of an Intellectual Tradition*. Chicago: University of Chicago Press, 1982.

Rahman, Y. *The Hermeneutical Theory of Nasir Hamid Abu Zayd*. PhD Dissertation, McGill University, 2001.

Raines, J., and D. Maguire, eds. *The Justice Men Owe To Women: Positive Resources from World Religions*. Albany: SUNY Press, 2000.

Ramadan, T. *The Western Muslims and the Future of Islam*. Oxford: Oxford University Press, 2004.

Reinhart, K. *Before Revelation—The Boundaries of Muslim Moral Thought*. Albany: State University of New York Press, 1995.

Ricouer, P. *Hermeneutics and the Human Sciences: Essays on Language, Action and Interpretation,* Edited and translated by J. B. Thomson. Cambridge: Cambridge University Press,1981.

Rippin, A. "The Function of Asbab al-Nuzul in Qur'anic Exegesis." *Bulletin of the School of Oriental and African Studies* 51, 1988.

Robson, J. "Tradition: Investigation and Classification." *Muslim World* 41 (1951): 98–112.

Rorty, R. *Contingency, Irony, and Solidarity* (Cambridge: Cambridge University Press, 1989).

Roy, O. *Globalized Islam—The Search for the New Ummah.* New York: Columbia University Press, 2004.

Rudolphs, P. "Idjtihad and Taqlid in 18th and 19th Century Islam."*Die Welt des Islams* 20 (1980): 131–145.

Sabbah, F. A. *Woman in the Muslim Unconscious.* Translated by M. J.Lakeland. New York: Pergamon Press, 1984.

Sachedina,A. "The nature of Scriptural Reasoning in Islam." *Journal of Scriptural Reasoning* 5, no. 1 (April 2005).

Saeed, A. *Interpreting the Qur'an—Towards a Contemporary Approach.* New York: Routledge, 2006.

———. Trends in Contemporary Islam: A Preliminary Attempt at a Classification. *The Muslim World* 97, no. 3 (2007): 395–404.

Safi, O., ed. *Progressive Muslims—On Justice, Gender and Pluralism.* Oxford: Oneworld, 2003.

———. "Challenges and Opportunities for the Progressive Muslim in North America." http://sufinews.blogspot.com/2005/10/challenges-and-opportunities-for.html. accessed April 13, 2009.

Sajoo, A. *Muslim Modernities: Expressions of the Civil Imagination.* New York: Macmillan, 2008.

Salvatore, A. "The Rational Authentication of Turath in Contemporary Arab Thought: Muhammad Al-Jabiri and Hassan Hanafi." *The Muslim World* 85, no. 3–4 (1995): 191–214.

Sayed, A. *Shifting Fortunes Women and Hadith Transmission in Islamic History.* PhD Thesis, Princeton University, 2005.

Schacht, J. *Introduction to Islamic Law.* Oxford: Clarendon Press, 1964.

———.*Origins of Muhammedan Jurisprudence.* Oxford: Claredon Press, 1950.

Schacht, J. "Ahl-Hadith." In *The Encyclopaedia of Islam.* Vol. 1. Leiden: E. J. Brill, 1960.

Shahrur, M. *The Qur'an, Morality and Critical Reason: The Essential Muhammad Shahrur.* Translated by A. Christman. Leiden: E. J. Brill, 2009.

Shafi', M. I. *Al-Risala.* Edited by M.S. Killani. Cairo: Mustafa Babi al-Halabi, 1969.

Sharify-Funk, M. *Encountering the Transnational, Women, Islam and the Politics of Interpretation.* Ashgate: Aldershot, 2008.

———. "From Dichotomies to Dialogues—Trends in Contemporary Islamic Hermeneutics." In *Contemporary Islam-Dynamic not Static.* Edited by

A. Abdul Aziz, M. Abu-Nimer, and M. Sharify-Funk. New York: Routledge, 2006.

Shehadeh, L. R. *The Idea of Women in Fundamentalist Islam*. Gainsville: University of Florida Press, 2003.

Shaikh, S. "Knowledge,Women and Gender in the Hadith: A Feminist Interpretation." In I. Omar. *Islam and Other Religions—Pathways to Dialogue*. New York: Routledge, 2006.

Shooman, M. *The Righteous Wife*. Translated by Abu Talhah Dawood. Al-Hidaayah Publishing and Distribution, 1996.

Shboul, A. "Byzantium and the Arabs: The Image of the Byzantines as Mirrored in Arabic Literature." In *The Formation of the Classical Islamic World* Vol. 8. Edited by M. Bonner. Ashgate: Varlorum, 2004.

Shukurov, A. *Towards Understanding Hadith*. 2010. ebook.

Soroush, A. K. *Reason, Freedom and Democracy in Islam*. Oxford: Oxford University Press, 2000.

———. *The Expansion of Prophetic Experience—Essays on Historicity, Contingency and Plurality in Religion*. Leiden: E. J. Brill, 2009.

Smith, J. I. "An Historical Study of the Term 'Islam' As Seen As a Sequence of Qur'an Commentators." PhD Thesis, University of Montana, 1975.

Souaiaia, A. "On the Sources of Islamic Law and Practices." *Journal of Law and Religion* 20 (2005): 125–149.

———. *Contesting Justice—Women, Islam, Law, and Society*. Albany: State University of New York Press, 2008.

———. *The Function of Orality in Islamic Law and Practices: Verbalizing Meaning*. Lewiston, NY: Edwin Meller Press, 2006.

Stowasser, B. "The Status of Women in Early Islam." In *Muslim Women*. Edited by F.Hussein. London, 1984.

Sukidi, 'Nasr Hāmid Abū Zayd and the Quest for a Humanistic Hermeneutics of the Qur'ān." *Die Welt Des Islams* 49, no. 2 (2009): 181–211.

Taji-Farouki, S. *Modern Muslim Intellectuals and the Qur'an*. Oxford: Oxford University Press, 2004.

Tibbi, B. *The Challenge of Fundamentalism—Political Islam and the New World Disorder*. Berkeley: University of California Press, 2002.

Van Ess, J. *Zwischen Hadith und Theologie*. Berlin: Walter de Gruyter, 1975.

Virkler, A. Hermeneutics*: Principles and Processes of Biblical Interpretation*. Grand Rapids, MI: Baker Book House, 1981.

John C.Wilkins, *Ibadism: Origins and Early Developments in Oman*,(Oxford University Press,2010).

Waardenburg, *Muslims and Others—Relations in Context*. Berlin: Walter de Gruyter, 2003.

Wadud, A. *Qur'an and Woman—Rereading the Sacred Text from a Woman's Perspective*. 2nd ed. Oxford: Oxford University Press, 1999.

Wahyudi, Y. "The Slogan "Back to the Qur'an and Sunnah"—A Comperative Study of the Responses of Hasan Hanafi, Muhammad Abid Al-Jabiri and Nurcholish Madjid." PhD Thesis, McGill University, 2002.

Watt, M. W. *Muhammad at Medina*. Oxford: Oxford University Press, 1956.

G. Webb, ed., Windows of Faith. Muslim Women Scholar-Activists in North America. Syracuse: Syra- cuse University Press, 2002.

Weiss, B. "Exotericism and Objectivity in Islamic Jurisprudence." In *Islamic Law and Jurisprudence*. Edited by N. Heer. Seattle: University of Washington Press, 1990.

Weiss, B. G., ed. *The Spirit of Islamic Law*. Atlanta: University of Georgia Press, 1998.

Wheeler, B. M. *Applying the Canon in Islam—The Authorization and Maintenance of Interpretive Reasoning in Hanafi Scholarship*. Albany: SUNY Press, 1996.

Welch, A. T., and Cachia, P., ed. *Islam: Past Influence and Present Challenge*. Edinburgh: Edinburgh University Press, 1979.

West, C. *The American Evasion of Philosophy: A Genealogy of Pragmatism*. Madison: University of Wisconsin Press, 1989.

Winter, T.'Qur'anic Reasoning as an Academic Practice." *Modern Theology* 22, no. 3 (2006): 450–463.

Wolterstorff, N. *Divine Discourses: Philosophycal Reflections on the Claim that God Speaks*. Cambridge: Cambridge University Press, 1995.

Wright, P. M. *Modern Qur'anic Hermeneutics*. PhD Thesis, Chapell Hill, 2008.

Younis, S. Islamic Legal Hermeneutics: The Context and Adequacy of Interpretation. *Journal of Islamic Studies* 41, no. 4, 585–615.

Zarabozo, J. *Life, Teachings, and Influence of Muhammad Ibn Abdul Wahhab*. Riyadh: Ministry of Islamic Affairs, Endowments, Dawah, and Guidance, 2005.

Zaynoo, M. *The Methodology of the Saved Sect*. London: Invitation to Islam, 1999.

Zebiri, K. *Muslims and Christians Face to Face*. Oxford: Oneworld, 1997.

Zysow, A. "The Economy of Certainty: An Introduction to the Typology of Islamic Legal Theory." PhD Dissertation, Harvard University, 1984.

Index